Business and Human Rights

Dilemmas and Solutions

Edited by Rory Sullivan

Business and Human Rights

DILEMMAS AND SOLUTIONS

EDITED BY RORY SULLIVAN

Greenleaf
PUBLISHING
2 0 0 3

© 2003 Greenleaf Publishing Limited

Published by Greenleaf Publishing Limited
Aizlewood's Mill
Nursery Street
Sheffield S3 8GG
UK

Printed and bound in Great Britain by
MPG Books Group, Bodmin, Cornwall.

FSC
Mixed Sources
Product group from well-managed
forests and other controlled sources
Cert no. SGS-COC-2953
www.fsc.org
© 1996 Forest Stewardship Council

Cover by LaliAbril.com/Utter.

British Library Cataloguing in Publication Data:
  Business and human rights : dilemmas and solutions
    1. Business ethics   2. Human rights   3. Social responsibility of
    business   4. International business enterprises - Moral and
    ethical aspects   5. Globalization - Social aspects
    I. Sullivan, Rory
    174.4

  Hardback: ISBN 1874719705
  Paperback: ISBN 1874719810

Contents

Acknowledgements

As this is an edited collection, the primary acknowledgements and thanks must be given to the contributing authors, who endured unreasonable delivery dates and pedantic editing with unfailing patience.

As usual, my parents (John and Carmel Sullivan), my brother John, and my sisters Jean, Irene (Connell), Maeve, Olive and Mary provided support and a certain 'grounding' on those few occasions when my ambitions ran ahead of the reality.

Finally, Melinda (Sweeting) has endured and supported yet another project. As always, I am extremely grateful.

Foreword

Mary Robinson

Executive Director, Ethical Globalisation Initiative, USA
Former United Nations High Commissioner for Human Rights

Fundamental questions are being asked around the world about the responsibilities of businesses for the protection and promotion of human rights. These
questions have arisen, both as a consequence of the broad concerns about the
impacts of globalisation on the poor, as well as a series of high-profile incidents
(e.g. Shell in Nigeria, BP in Colombia, Nike in Vietnam) involving leading multinational companies. My sense is that there has been a clear shift in business's
responses to these questions. While the 1990s could be characterised as a period of
business reluctance to become actively involved in the human rights debate,
recent years have seen a growing willingness, at least among the leading companies, to seize the opportunities and responsibilities that global citizenship brings.
The language of 'corporate social responsibility', which clearly locates companies
as actors within society, with associated rights and responsibilities, is indicative of
how far corporate attitudes to human rights have shifted. This is further illustrated
by the fact that some 40 multinational companies have explicit policy commitments to the protection and promotion of human rights.

Despite these changes, companies' approaches to corporate social responsibility
are not universal or objective but are culturally relative, largely philanthropic and
subjective by nature. Of course there is nothing wrong with community-focused
approaches or philanthropy; in fact, they are essential parts of the business
contribution to the protection and promotion of human rights. But it remains the
case that virtually all of the corporate social responsibility debates around the
world make no reference to international human rights standards. Consequently,
it is difficult to draw meaningful comparisons between different companies, differ-

ent countries or communities and the impacts that companies can have on the many different thematic issues that comprise the 'social dimension' of human existence.

This is compounded by the common misconception among the public and many politicians, especially in the West, that human rights is just about civil and political rights—the areas in which high-profile groups such as Amnesty International and Human Rights Watch have traditionally focused. Yet, reading the 1948 Universal Declaration of Human Rights, we see that issues such as health, housing and education have equal prominence. Those businesses that have looked at their activities across the full spectrum of civil, political, economic, social and cultural rights have seen that they are already doing much that should be informed by human rights. As just one example, companies' human resources policies intersect with human rights as a result of an increasing interest in issues of diversity, the need to guard against any forms of discrimination, as well as the more traditional discussions around labour rights and health and safety at work.

Perhaps the other major change in recent years has been the emergence of clear drivers for companies to see human rights as an integral part of their overall operations. There are many 'carrots' for a business that is sincere in looking for opportunities of being a global-class employer, provider and partner to its stakeholders. There are also some clear 'sticks' emerging that will concentrate attention of business in the years to come. It is interesting to note that it is sometimes in countries with relatively new constitutions based on international human rights law, South Africa being a good example, that the greatest progress towards understanding business responsibility for the 'right to health' or the 'right to housing' has been made. The recent ruling of the African Court of People's and Human Rights on the activities of the Nigerian government in the mid-1990s, and by association the oil companies involved, is clear about how the economic, social and cultural rights of the local population were abused. In the USA, there has been a growth of claims against transnational companies under the long-dormant Alien Tort Claims Act of 1789. A recent series of high-profile lawsuits has shown that international businesses can be brought to a US court when they are seen to be complicit in the abuses by foreign governments relating to genocide, war crimes, slavery, torture, executions, crimes against humanity or unlawful detention.

The growing international interest in the 'ethics' of business means that it is becoming more difficult for business to deny the need for a 'level playing field', an ethical baseline below which no business can go. When such a standard emerges, it is highly likely that it will be based on international human rights norms. The UN Human Rights Sub-Commission's 'Draft Norms of Responsibilities of Transnational Corporations and Other Business Enterprises with Regard to Human Rights' gives an indication of what might eventually become the basis for international law. There is a significant opportunity for progressive companies to play a leading role in shaping the architecture for the regulation of corporate governance, not just in the self-interest of each business but in the interests of all stakeholders and humankind in general.

Despite the growing consensus that companies do have responsibilities for the protection and promotion of human rights, and despite the business and moral arguments for companies to take these responsibilities seriously, there are many questions around the direction that we need to take. I find that many business leaders are unsure about where their responsibilities for human rights begin and end. They are concerned that, by expressing their commitment to international standards such as the Universal Declaration of Human Rights, they might be going beyond their proper role into the realm of government responsibility for the promotion and protection of human rights. Despite initiatives such as the United Nations Global Compact, which has made some progress in engaging companies from around the world to address their contribution to human rights, labour and environmental standards, there is still the feeling that asking companies to take responsibility for human rights is asking them to take on the responsibility of governments. Furthermore, these discussions are complicated by the many uncertainties that remain around corporate responsibility for human rights, such as:

- How far should companies be expected to go in defining and promoting global standards in areas such as corporate governance, financial accounting and reporting, ethics, environmental impacts, consumer rights, labour conditions and human rights?

- Is legal compliance sufficient in countries where governments are administratively weak or deemed to be corrupt or illegitimate by their citizens?

- Does business have any business in poverty alleviation? If so, how does it tackle this challenge in an innovative and profitable manner?

- How do companies avoid 'letting governments off the hook' or substituting the company for government in terms of meeting people's needs and aspirations?

While there has been much talk of what companies should do, there has been less analysis of what companies have done in practice. It is here that this book makes such a valuable contribution, through its analysis of the actual experiences of companies in responding to specific human rights issues in the context of their own operations, in their supply chains and in specific countries. I am particularly pleased that the chapters in this book cover such a wide range of case studies from so many countries dealing with the full complexity of human rights issues and different actors. The inspiration of this book is to offer insight into what factors have been critical in the stories of those businesses that have made progress in this area, both in terms of their strategic management and operational impact. I am particularly encouraged that some of the examples here show that business can effectively contribute to human rights issues beyond their areas of direct operations. However, many of the case studies also remind us that most businesses have yet to engage with human rights at all and prefer more philanthropic approaches to social problems. These companies resist any added regulation or what they perceive as additional responsibilities that should belong to government. Yet, with increasing attention given to the very nature of corporate governance, the interface between the state and private actors is recognised as one that can benefit from a shared agenda of upholding human rights.

It is my view that the manner in which companies address human rights is a litmus test for the fairness of the globalisation process. Companies are one of the key actors in the realisation of human rights and their contribution is essential. This book takes stock of progress made in translating aspirations into reality, through showing how companies can play their role in ensuring that globalisation works to the benefit of all.

Mary Robinson
New York, July 2003

1
Introduction

Rory Sullivan
Insight Investment, UK

1.1 Globalisation, business and human rights

The globalisation of the world economy offers both unprecedented opportunities and unprecedented threats for companies. Companies have, increasingly, found themselves, their partners or their contractors mired in countries where human rights violations are occurring. For example, media investigations into the conditions in Nike factories in Vietnam revealed beatings, sexual harassment and workers being forced to kneel for extended periods with their arms held in the air. More generally, millions of child workers are enslaved through forms of debt bondage in countries such as India; forced labour is widely used in countries such as Burma (Myanmar) and China; trade unionists receive death threats in Colombia, are banned outright in Burma and are routinely pressured into resigning in Guatemala. Furthermore, it has often been the case that the presence of multinational enterprises in a country has been interpreted as providing support for government policies and actions. The silence of Shell in Nigeria, when Ken Saro-Wiwa and eight other Ogonis were executed after unfair trials, was interpreted by the Nigerian government as tacit support for the actions taken. Similar criticisms have been made of many other multinational oil/energy companies, such as Total in Burma and BP in Colombia. These concerns have been exacerbated by the absence of effective legal mechanisms to ensure the human rights performance of companies. Privatisation, free trade agreements and economic integration have limited governments' ability to regulate transnational corporations. Furthermore, the demand for foreign direct investment has meant that governments are less willing to contemplate regulating companies.

1.2 So where does this book fit in?

The intersection between human rights and business is chaotic and contested. On the one hand are those who see companies as 'the source of all evil'. On the other are those who have a touching faith in the ability of companies, economic growth and 'the market' to resolve all of these human rights problems. Yet the truth, if there is such a thing, is far more complex and indeterminate than either of these extreme perspectives allows. Despite the increasing use of human rights language in public policy discourses, the expectations of companies remain unclear. That is, what are the ethical imperatives? What are the legal expectations? How far does responsibility extend? What can companies actually do in practice? The debate is further complicated by the range of actors (companies, governments, international institutions, local communities, non-governmental organisations [NGOs], trade unions, consumers) involved; by debates around free trade versus fair trade; by the discussion of the specific role of governments; by broader concerns about globalisation and narrower concerns about community development; and by questions about regulation versus self-regulation.

This book provides an assessment of the relationship between companies and human rights in the context of globalisation. The analysis is in two parts. The first maps the reasons (financial, ethical, regulatory) why human rights have become a business issue. But it is not enough simply to say that companies should protect and promote human rights, and then sit back and wait for it to happen. It is also necessary to understand the manner in which companies can and have responded to these pressures. For example, certain human rights issues may be outside the control of companies, others may be too large for companies to address on their own and, in other situations, the pressures on companies to address specific issues may be outweighed by countervailing pressures. Therefore, the second part of the book considers specific examples and case studies of how companies have behaved in situations where human rights violations have occurred or where companies have a role or influence in protecting or promoting human rights.

The focus of this book is on transnational corporations (TNCs).[1] This focus is not intended to suggest that the legal obligations or moral responsibilities of TNCs differ from those of other companies. Nevertheless, TNCs deserve specific attention because, through foreign direct investment, they can make an important contribution to the promotion of economic and social welfare, the improvement of living standards, the creation of employment opportunities and the realisation and enjoyment of basic human rights. However, it has also been argued that TNCs are the cutting edge of a development strategy that destroys local cultures, exploits workers, bankrupts the local poor and widens the gap between the rich and often politically repressive elite and the rest of society. Furthermore, TNCs are key players in the process of globalisation. They are the primary drivers of cross-border involvement and the conveyor belts of international trade. Increasingly, they

---

1 Other terms are commonly used in the literature such as 'multinational corporation' (MNC), 'multinational enterprise' (MNE), 'global corporation' and 'multinational' (see, generally, Voon 1999: 220).

operate through complex, integrated global production networks, and many SMEs and family businesses are connected to TNCs through extended supply chains.

1.3 What are human rights?

Human rights are fundamental principles allowing individuals the freedom to lead a dignified life, free from fear or want, and free to express independent beliefs. Since the end of the Second World War, human rights have been increasingly described in terms of the international human rights legal framework. This framework provides the basis for much of the dialogue around corporate responsibility for the protection and promotion of human rights. While the international human rights architecture, for the purposes of this book, is taken as broadly defining the scope of corporate responsibility for the protection and promotion of human rights, there is one important caveat: namely, that moral rights exist independently of international law. That is, there are moral human rights that may not yet be captured in legislation. Furthermore, the fact that governments legislate against specific human rights (e.g. restrictions on the right to privacy as a consequence of fears of terrorism) does not mean that those rights do not or should not exist.[2]

The 1948 Universal Declaration of Human Rights (UDHR) is the most widely accepted codification of universal human rights in existence. The UDHR encompasses the right to life, the right to recognition before the law, freedom of thought, conscience and religion, freedom from torture, freedom from slavery and freedom from imprisonment for debt or from retroactive penal legislation. The preamble to the UDHR calls on 'every individual and every organ of society' to respect and promote the rights set out in the UDHR. It is widely argued that these requirements to respect and promote human rights apply to companies as 'an organ of society' (see, for example, Amnesty International 1998; Frankental and House 2000: 22-24; International Council on Human Rights Policy 2002: 58-64; Addo 1999: 27-32). It has been suggested that companies have responsibilities in two main areas. The first is that companies must protect human rights within all of their areas of operation. This includes not only direct employees but also contractors, suppliers, family members, local communities and other parties affected by the company's activities. The second is that companies have a responsibility to support human rights protection more generally through activities such as public statements supporting the protection of human rights, government lobbying, and the integration of human rights considerations into all decision-making processes.

The provisions of the UDHR have inspired or have been cited as the justification for many of the conventions and protocols adopted by the United Nations, defining in greater detail the scope and content of international human rights standards. Because the UDHR is a declaration that has been adopted in the form of a

---

2 For a more detailed discussion of the nexus between legal and moral conceptions of human rights, see Pogge 2002: 52-70.

resolution of the United Nations (UN) General Assembly, it is, as such, not legally binding. However, the various human rights treaties and conventions that have been produced by the UN are legally binding obligations on the states that are party to them. The two key human rights covenants are the International Covenant on Civil and Political Rights 1966 (which includes the rights to life, freedom from torture or cruel and degrading treatment, freedom from arbitrary arrest and detention, the right of peaceful assembly and freedom of association, and ethnic minority rights) and the International Covenant on Economic, Social and Cultural Rights 1966 (which includes the rights to fair wages, freedom from child labour and forced labour, the right to work, the right to education, the right to join trade unions and bargain collectively, and the right to health and safety in the workplace). These covenants, together with the core conventions of the International Labour Organisation,[3] represent the most widely accepted codification of human rights standards in international law.

Companies are not the explicit subjects of international human rights law. That is, international law is addressed to national governments (as the signatories to the various instruments) and nation-states are the primary, if not the exclusive, holders of duties to implement international human rights law. Yet it is also the case that, in many developing countries, governments do not have the capacity or resources to meet these obligations. This raises the question of what companies could or should do, and how far their responsibility extends in such situations. Furthermore, because national governments are the subjects of international law, the specific implications of international human rights law for companies are by no means self-explanatory. The UN Sub-Commission on Human Rights recently issued its Draft Norms on the responsibilities of companies with regard to human rights (UN Sub-Commission on Human Rights 2002b; see Chapter 3 by Peter Muchlinski for a more detailed analysis). The Sub-Commission recognised that, even though states have the primary responsibility to protect and promote human rights, companies, as organs of society, are also responsible for promoting and securing the human rights set forth in the UDHR. A summary of the Sub-Commission's recommendations is presented in Box 1.1.

While there is a growing consensus on what the specific human rights responsibilities of companies should be, it is also necessary to recognise that the degree of responsibility is restricted by the ability to exert influence. A company is, of course, fully responsible for its own actions. It also has a degree of responsibility for situations that it does not control but can influence, although determining that degree will frequently be difficult. In broad terms, there are three levels of influence (Amnesty International [The Netherlands] and Pax Christi 2000: 45-54):

---

3   The eight core ILO conventions are: Conventions 29 (forced labour), 87 (freedom of association and protection of the right to organise), 98 (right to organise and collective bargaining), 100 (equal remuneration), 105 (abolition of forced labour), 111 (on discrimination), 138 (minimum age of workers) and 156 (equal opportunities and equal treatment for men and women workers; workers with family responsibilities). In addition, ILO Conventions 182, 190 (child labour) and 169 (the rights of indigenous and tribal peoples) are increasingly seen, at least by NGOs, as part of the core set of labour standards.

Companies must respect and promote the following rights:

- Right to equal opportunity and non-discriminatory treatment
- Right to security of person
- Rights of workers (companies shall not use forced or compulsory labour, shall respect the rights of children, shall provide a safe and healthy workforce, shall provide workers with remuneration that allows for an adequate standard of living for them and their families, shall ensure the freedom of association and the right to collective bargaining)
- Respect for national sovereignty and human rights (including not paying bribes, ensuring that the company's goods and services are not used to abuse human rights, respecting civil, cultural, economic, political and social rights in particular, the rights to development, adequate food and drinking water, highest attainable standard of physical and mental health, adequate housing, education, freedom of thought, conscience and religion, freedom of opinion)
- Consumer protection
- Environmental protection

These obligations apply to the company itself and also to contractors, subcontractors, suppliers and licensees.

Box 1.1 Recommendations of the UN Human Rights Sub-Commission on Companies and Human Rights

I. A company has direct control (i.e. its own operations and activities) and can be held responsible for the realisation of human rights. This responsibility relates to issues such as labour standards, expectations that the company will not use, procure or offer goods that have been produced using forced or bonded labour or the worst forms of child labour, the treatment of indigenous peoples, and security arrangements.

2. A company can exert influence over a situation and thus can contribute to the realisation of human rights by or in conjunction with others. In the context of TNCs, these responsibilities relate particularly to supply chains and relationships between the company and its suppliers, subcontractors and business partners. In these situations, TNCs can usually require these parties to meet certain standards (including human rights standards). Another dimension to these responsibilities is that companies should consider the manner in which their products or services may be used to violate human rights. The obvious example is military equipment but another example could be the provision of aviation fuel to a repressive regime.

3. A TNC can contribute to the creation of an enabling environment for the realisation of human rights. Even in situations where a TNC has no direct control over a situation, it still has a responsibility to contribute to the creation of an enabling environment for the realisation of human rights

by all. While the main contribution of TNCs tends to be through the provision of economic benefits (i.e. overcoming economic barriers to the realisation of human rights), the responsibility does not end there. TNCs can also contribute to the protection and promotion of human rights through their public commitment to the UDHR, by making public statements of support or concern regarding human rights violations, and by contributing to or supporting development activities.

1.4 Structure of the book

The book is divided into two main sections. The first section is a discussion of the reasons why human rights are important to companies. Geoffrey Chandler starts by locating the business and human rights debate in the context of NGO campaigns, of corporate mistakes and misdeeds and of changes in the international geopolitical situation, in particular since the collapse of communism. Peter Muchlinski, David Kinley and Adam McBeth then look at the legal context within which TNCs operate. Muchlinski looks at efforts to directly regulate or otherwise ensure the performance of companies. In contrast, Kinley and McBeth look at the specific issue of trade law ('the rules of the game') and argue that, if the conduct of 'the players' cannot be guaranteed directly, the rules by which they play could instead be amended. Both of the chapters confirm the feasibility of directly regulating TNCs and provide examples of how this has been done. Yet both conclude that there is limited political appetite for directly regulating TNCs.

The weakness of the regulatory threat raises the question of why companies should be concerned about human rights. Denis Arnold considers the ethical (or moral) reasons why companies must protect and promote human rights, and highlights the benefits that can accrue from such an approach. Companies often argue that, despite the ethical reasons, they do not have a mandate to engage with governments on human rights. Frans-Paul van der Putten, Gemma Crijns and Harry Hummels challenge these arguments, proposing that it is in companies' interest to protect and promote human rights. Furthermore, they argue that shareholders (as the owners of companies) must accept their moral responsibility for the protection and promotion of human rights. This theme is developed by David Coles, who examines the role and responsibility of shareholders in some detail. Finally, Rory Sullivan and Nina Seppala look at the business costs and benefits of protecting and promoting human rights. Taken together, the chapters in the first section provide a model of 'regulation', where the pressures that are brought to bear on companies are not just traditional legal approaches but include reputational, financial and ethical pressures. While each of the pressures on its own is relatively weak, the combined effect is synergistic and reinforcing. It is increasingly clear that not only do companies have a responsibility for the protection and promotion of human rights but there are also ever-stronger pressures on companies to discharge these responsibilities.

The chapter by Sullivan and Seppala, which considers how companies organise themselves (through management systems and processes) to respond to these pressures, provides a bridge between the first section of the book and the second, which looks at the experiences of companies in responding to human rights pressures. The section is divided into three parts: operations, supply chains, and community and government. While this division is somewhat arbitrary (and, indeed, many of the case studies could belong to more than one of these categories), it reflects the manner in which many TNCs organise themselves (i.e. supply chain management tends to be a separate function from operations and from community and government issues, which are frequently covered under 'external relations').

Four case studies are presented that relate to companies' direct area of operations. Charles Woolfson and Matthias Beck look at the question of 'corporate killing' and the responsibility of companies to protect the well-being of their employees, using the example of the offshore oil industry and the tragedy of Piper Alpha. They use this example to raise broader questions about the manner in which public policy can be captured or influenced by business interests. Simon Handelsman covers a similar theme in his chapter, looking at case studies from mining operations in Indonesia and Bolivia. In both countries, the companies inadvertently caused, or contributed to, situations where people were killed. Handelsman compares the corporate responses—one company learned from its experience and has subsequently implemented a range of development, capacity-building and conflict-reduction measures, whereas the other appears to continue in a 'state of denial'—and draws important conclusions about the manner in which companies can prevent conflict.

Norbert Goldfield looks at the potential for a company's products to contribute to human rights violations (in this case, the manner in which transplant rejection medicine has contributed to the problem of the harvesting of body organs from executed prisoners in China). Goldfield uses this example to discuss the role of professionals (in this case, medical specialists) within the corporation and examines what these individuals should do in situations where professional and personal ethics conflict with corporate norms. Finally, Christopher McDowell deals with an emerging issue that, in many ways, is typical of the debates around globalisation. The displacement of indigenous populations (with associated problems such as lack of prior informed consent, forced or violent displacement, inadequate consideration of indigenous peoples' rights, inadequate compensation) has been a consequence of many large-scale infrastructure projects such as dams. Historically, governments have managed the displacement process (albeit extremely badly in many cases). There is a growing trend for the private companies building or managing large projects (not just traditional infrastructure such as roads and dams but also large industrial developments) to have the primary responsibility for managing the relocation of local populations. McDowell describes the issues that are likely to be faced by companies and analyses more generally the implications of the private sector supplanting government in these situations.

The discussion of supply chains comprises four distinct case studies: Steven Lim and Michael Cameron's chapter on the potential for rural development (in particular, the location of TNCs' manufacturing facilities in rural areas) to contribute to reducing the incidence of HIV/AIDS; Bahar Ali Kazmi and Magnus Macfarlane's chapter on the efforts to eliminate child labour in the football stitching industry in Pakistan; Deborah Leipziger and Eileen Kaufman's chapter on the potential for standards and certification processes to contribute to improved labour conditions in supply chain factories; and Luis Reygadas's chapter on the maquiladoras in Mexico. The chapters all identify the potential for TNCs, through their supply chains, to contribute positively to the protection and promotion of human rights, through the provision of economic benefits such as wages and salaries to employees, the provision of safe workplaces, and other initiatives such as employee training and community development or philanthropy. However, the case studies also emphasise the importance of a socially and culturally sensitive approach to supply chain management. While the motivations of companies may be positive (e.g. to eliminate child labour), the consequences of inappropriate approaches can be to transfer problems elsewhere, to exacerbate the problem that it was originally intended to address or even to have no impact at all on the issue in question.

Finally, the discussion of community and government (e.g. business–government relationships, business–NGO relationships, business and community development) comprises five case studies, looking at different aspects of this question. Jessica Banfield, Gary MacDonald and Timothy McLaughlin, and Bennett Freeman and Genoveva Hernández Uriz provide different perspectives on the role of companies in conflict situations and the potential for companies to contribute to peace-building and/or to exacerbate conflict. Banfield's chapter provides the overall framework for understanding the contribution of companies to conflict or, more positively, to peace-building. MacDonald and McLaughlin discuss the reasons why mining companies so often find themselves in conflict situations. They argue that it is not simply 'because of the nature of their activity' but it is more to do with the way companies see the world as a mechanical system where problems can be 'fixed' (e.g. through the provision of more money for community development). The consequence is that companies tend to reward the wrong behaviours (e.g. communities protest and get 'rewarded' with community development benefits). Freeman and Hernández Uriz then look at the contribution that TNCs can make to conflict prevention at the global level, using the example of the Voluntary Principles on Security and Human Rights. While their chapter also shows how governments can use their influence to encourage responsible corporate behaviour, the question of whether this form of global self-regulation will prove effective remains unanswered.

Corruption remains one of the critical barriers to the realisation of human rights. David Hess and Thomas Dunfee look at the measures that can be adopted by companies to combat bribery and the business arguments for companies to take a strong position on this issue. Finally, Heike Fabig and Richard Boele look at the potential for companies and NGOs to work together to promote human rights and the potential challenges faced by companies and NGOs seeking to 'sleep with the enemy'.

Part 1
Why are human rights a business issue?

The evolution of the business and human rights debate

Geoffrey Chandler
UK

2.1 A new world for companies

The corporate world has an inescapable impact on human rights and therefore a responsibility for them. Workplace and supply chain issues such as labour conditions, the health and safety of employees and the right to organise are all human rights issues for which companies have direct responsibility. The impact of company operations on the environment, often adversely affecting local communities, came into prominence in the 1970s. However, it was the physical environment, rather than the impact on human rights, which was the main focus of critical attention. Civil and political rights, the chief concern of the human rights movement, were seen to lie in the domain of governments rather than non-state actors such as commercial companies. Events were soon to show that so narrow a perception was misguided. This chapter deals with the context in which companies came face to face with human rights, the incentives to recognise their responsibilities and the response of the main actors involved.

The fall of the Berlin wall, the end of the Cold War and the virtual disappearance of communism brought radical change to the world scene. Economic 'globalisation'—the accelerated internationalisation of the world economy—was not new in principle. What was new was the speed with which privatisation and foreign investment were embraced by countries that had previously believed in state control of the economy. Countries of the North and South now competed for the skills, technology, investment, management and access to markets that foreign companies could bring. Companies seized the opportunities offered. The supply chains of the supermarkets and the consumer goods industries spread ever more widely and deeply into the developing countries of Asia, Africa and South America. Investment by the major transnational corporations (TNCs), in particular in the oil and mining industries, was accepted in areas previously denied them by political or ideological barriers.[1]

With the opportunities of this new world came risks. No company, whatever its activities, was free from these risks. Companies had seized opportunity with little if any understanding of the dangers inherent in the situations into which they now moved. Many countries, with governments lacking any democratic legitimacy, provided a context of corruption, injustice, internal conflict and human rights violations. Supermarket supply chains could involve exploitative child labour, sweatshops and discrimination. Investors faced similar problems, but in addition confronted new challenges of physical security for personnel and plant and of working under governments that blatantly violated human rights. An increasingly alert and critical world, aided by the Internet, acted as watchdog, leaving companies no hiding place. Without appropriate policies, companies were in danger of contributing to these ills and being condemned for complicity in them. However, few companies had such policies. With the economic benefits that globalisation could bring came significant collateral damage to human rights for which companies were responsible. With their growing spread, scope and influence, companies now had greater unfulfilled potential for improving the context in which they worked than any other constituency, including government. It became increasingly clear that the principled treatment of all stakeholders—those on whom a company depends for its success or who are affected by its operations— could have a significant impact on human rights.

Unlike the environment movement, the human rights movement came late in seeking positive engagement with business, regarding governments as its traditional target. Human rights organisations sporadically exposed and condemned direct corporate involvement in human rights violations. But they were slow to attempt to recruit the influence of the corporate world for the protection of such rights, though there was an obvious logic in harnessing the influence of entities that were increasingly part of the bloodstream of the international economy. It was clear that, for far too long, non-governmental organisations (NGOs) and business had regarded each other with mutual ignorance, prejudice and hostility and that this divide needed to be crossed if each was to fulfil its objectives. Companies needed the knowledge of NGOs in areas in which they had little or no capability themselves—development, child labour, the environment and human rights— and NGOs would not attain their own ends without the positive involvement of the corporate world.

The United Kingdom Section of Amnesty International (AIUK) had set up a Business Group in 1991 with the objective of encouraging companies to use their legitimate influence in defence of the civil and political rights that were Amnesty International's main focus. However, the attempts in the early 1990s of the Business Group to engage on the issue with senior members of the chief UK-based TNCs met with no encouragement. In some companies there was a failure even to recognise the reality of the violations that went on around them; in all of them,

---

1 Nowhere is the juxtaposition of opportunity and risk more visible than in the oil-rich Caspian Sea Basin, now divided between Azerbaijan, Kazakhstan and Turkmenistan and open to private oil companies.

human rights were seen as the business of government, not of companies, and human rights violations were regarded as an internal political issue with which companies should on principle not interfere. Human Rights Watch, which had also begun to target the impact of corporate action on human rights, first contacted Shell over its role in Nigeria in January 1995. Belatedly, in September 1995, Amnesty International (AI) adopted a resolution for the international movement as a whole 'to carefully develop outreach to members of the business community . . . in order to motivate constructive action by them against the violations within AI's' mandate'. But this was no more than a tentative toe in the water, which had no effective international follow-up in practice.

2.2 The beginnings of change

The catalyst for change was not NGO action or company forethought, but company disaster. The arbitrary execution of Ken Saro-Wiwa and eight other Ogonis by the Nigerian dictatorship of General Abacha in November 1995 is a story that does not need re-telling (see, generally, HRW 1999b; Eide *et al.* 2000). The insistence of Shell, the largest foreign investor in Nigeria and the operator, though minority shareholder, of its partnership with the Nigerian government, that it was improper for the company to play any role in trying to deflect the course of events led to international condemnation. While some of the accusations against Shell should more properly have been directed at the Nigerian government, and even though the potential influence of the company was certainly exaggerated, its silence until the last moment could find no justification. The accusations of condoning human rights violations in the interest of profit and of complicity with an oppressive regime which the company's activities helped to sustain proved overwhelming to the reputation of one of the most sophisticated and respected companies in the world. The issue was further aggravated by accusations about environmental damage from associated gas flares in the Niger Delta and by growing evidence that the security arrangements for the protection of Shell employees and plant had, through the calling-in of government forces, led to the death of innocent civilians at an earlier date. This episode, following on the heels of the international outcry that had greeted Shell's plans to jettison the Brent Spar oil platform in the deep ocean, proved a watershed both for the company and for the human rights movement.

There were few NGOs that had not protested to Shell over its inaction in Nigeria. But it was now primarily individual representatives from the Dutch and British Sections of AI and from Pax Christi in the Netherlands who negotiated with the company its development of human rights policies (for a more detailed description of these dialogue processes, see Pax Christi 1998; Lawrence 2002). A series of discussions during 1996 led to the commitment by Shell to revise its Statement of General Business Principles to include respect for the human rights of employees and 'support for fundamental human rights in line with the legitimate role of business' (Royal Dutch/Shell 1997). This was a significant breakthrough. Shell's courageous public acknowledgement that it had failed to keep pace with the views of society had opened the door for a wide consultation process initiated by the company and for the discussions noted above. BP, faced in 1996 with accusations about its handling of security problems in Colombia, again the result of inadequate policies and lack of management foresight, followed suit. Two of the world's largest TNCs now acknowledged that the defence of human rights was part of their direct legitimate responsibilities. The United Nations Universal Declaration of Human Rights (UDHR), of whose existence few, if any, companies had knowledge, with its call for 'every individual and every organ of society' to support the rights delineated there, had proved an important lever in bringing about this change. And for the first time both companies were made aware of and adopted into their policies the UN Code of Conduct for Law Enforcement Officials and the UN Basic Principles on the Use of Force and Firearms.

For NGOs, the most important lesson from these developments was that, while protest could raise issues, engagement was needed to win the argument. For the companies, the chief lesson was that it was not enough to avoid harm, but it was also their responsibility to support human rights positively, as called for by the UDHR, if they were to avoid the accusation of complicity with oppressive regimes. It was also clear that, if this breakthrough were to be exploited, it was necessary to maintain dialogue to ensure that words were translated into deeds. Appropriate materials to assist companies to respond constructively were also needed. In November 1997 the AIUK Business Group produced its *Human Rights Guidelines for Companies* to help companies understand their human rights responsibilities and to assist in the development of corporate human rights policies (Amnesty International 1998). This was followed in April 2000 by a more substantial document, *Human Rights: Is It Any of Your Business?*, produced jointly with the Prince of Wales International Business Leaders Forum (Frankental and House 2000). This second publication had the advantage of being able to include case studies from companies that had embraced human rights, corporate example frequently being a more potent influence on other companies than NGO preaching. To stimulate corporate awareness of the human rights risks in many countries, a further publication, *Business and Human Rights: A Geography of Corporate Risk,* was produced in 2002 (Amnesty International and International Business Leaders Forum 2002). This publication illustrated the risk exposure to human rights violations of companies in six major industrial sectors.

Few companies, however, adopted the Shell and BP examples of their own volition. A small number of TNCs in the UK and the Nordic countries followed suit as a result of approaches from the AIUK Business Group and the relevant AI national sections. These companies included a responsibility for human rights in their corporate principles, but, while the written commitment was an essential point of departure, the test would be the extent to which they were applied in practice. For the majority of companies there was no such acceptance of their responsibility. The most frequent arguments for inaction remained (and remain) an expressed belief in the need for 'political neutrality' and the assertion that the development of a resource will lead inevitably to an improvement of life for the totality of the community involved. The latter has to be seen against the background of a world of increasing international inequality and is demonstrably untrue in a number of countries where there has been no attempt to ensure equity in the distribution of wealth. Political neutrality, other than in the sense of abstaining from interference with government or party politics, is not within a company's capability. The company's very presence is a factor in the situation. As a corporate citizen, silence and inactivity in the context of oppression and human rights violations will be taken as complicity with a regime that is economically supported by its activities. The UDHR provides legitimacy for a company to speak out and defines in principle a corporate responsibility.

2.3 Human rights on the agenda

A climate of awareness about corporate responsibility grew rapidly in the late 1990s. The Internet provided an immediate means of communicating corporate involvement in human rights violations or practices in conflict with company codes. New initiatives and codes of conduct set out both to define the breadth of company responsibilities and to encourage companies to implement them. Human rights now featured prominently and explicitly in all.[2] Of these, the United Nations Global Compact was to prove the most significant: the authority of the UN Secretary-General, its initiator, stimulated the participation of companies that would otherwise have remained aloof. The Compact, proposed by Kofi Annan at the 1999 World Economic Forum, requires companies to address human rights, labour standards and environmental protection. While this and other initiatives have proved helpful in raising the profile of the issues involved, their proliferation has also had the perverse effect of allowing companies to 'subscribe' to one or other, disguising the fact that their core principles and practices may be left unchanged. Lip service is more prevalent than practical application of the principles laid down.

Moreover, none of these initiatives covers the whole spectrum of company responsibilities set out in Box 2.1. The boundaries of direct responsibility are defined by a company's stakeholders and by the extent of its 'footprint' in the societies in which it operates. While most stakeholders might find some recognition in existing company codes, the interpretation of codes into practice is increasingly seen to be inadequate: disclosure, reporting and monitoring demonstrably falls short of requirements. Of the dilemmas listed in the box, the legitimacy of trying to diminish governmental human rights violations, if only through private discussion, has been accepted by those companies that acknowledge the UDHR. The rest represent genuine dilemmas in that the responsibility for them lies primarily with government, but they would not have arisen either in principle or in the same degree without the presence of company operations. Under oppressive regimes or in the context of corrupt or ineffective government, companies face challenges of

---

2   There is a plethora of conventions and codes relating to TNCs, produced by a wide variety of organisations. Even the most apparently authoritative of these, however, the OECD Guidelines for Multinational Enterprises, offers little real incentive for companies to act.

In the country of investment

Direct responsibilities

- The profitable conduct of the business
- Employment conditions consonant with international standards in the company and in its supply chains
- Safety of processes and products
- Care of the environment in accordance with international standards
- Avoidance of bribery and corruption
- Security arrangements that do not risk human rights violations by company employees or other agencies
- Avoidance of adverse impact on the community and society in which the company operates
- Defence of human rights
- Transparency of operations and policies
- Monitoring and auditing of the economic, social and environmental impacts of the company

Dilemmas—or indirect responsibilities

- Human rights violations committed by government
- Misuse of revenues accruing to government
- Inequitable division of revenues between districts
- Official corruption
- Distorted development of the country
- Economic inequality between people

Responsibilities within home-country and international forums

- Engagement in discussions on trade and investment
- Support for global standards
- Support for international social and environmental targets

Box 2.1 The responsibilities of companies

particular difficulty. Government misuse of revenues, their inequitable distribution, their employment for the purchase of armaments in the context of civil war, are matters for government. Companies must not usurp or take on the role of governments, whatever the nature of the regime. But, with increasing scrutiny of the impact of company operations, particularly those of the oil and mining industries, not just on a country's revenues but on its social, cultural and economic fabric and its political stability, it must be questionable whether companies can stand wholly aside from issues in whose origins their own economic success has played a fundamental role.

Until companies accept those direct responsibilities that are inherent in their operations, they are unlikely to have the foresight to consider the indirect challenges that may follow. But a more critical world is now a constant with which companies have to live. As a minimum it will become necessary for companies in their own defence to make public—however unpopular this may be—details of what happens to the revenues they generate for a country. This issue was brought into sharp focus in 1999 with the payment to the Angolan government of large signature bonuses for offshore blocks (BP Amoco, Exxon and the former Elf Aquitaine were the main contributors) which were used to finance arms purchases—a wholly legal transaction on the part of the companies, but one that could only contribute to a continuing civil war. Growing awareness of the problem, strengthened by the investigative work of Global Witness, led to two initiatives in 2002: a call from the UK Prime Minister at the Johannesburg Summit for an Extractive Industry Transparency Initiative; and the formation of the Publish What You Pay coalition (now comprising over 60 NGOs and supported by George Soros) calling for transparency over resource revenues to governments. If companies that publish such information are not to be discriminated against, it is essential that transparency should be mandatory, not voluntary.

By the late 1990s, 'corporate social responsibility' (CSR), long part of the vocabulary of debate about the role of business in society, now also headed the agenda, sustaining an academic industry, fostering innumerable conferences, spawning consultancies and engaging the attention of companies, NGOs and governments. At its best, CSR is defined as the responsibility of a company for the totality of its impact, with a need to embed society's values into its core operations as well as its treatment of its social and physical environment. But such clear-cut definitions are rare. More commonly, the discussion embraces a confused range of definitions which now appear to be crystallising around the concept of community development, a valuable but essentially voluntary activity in which the inventiveness of individual companies may give them competitive advantage. This has allowed companies to insist that CSR is voluntary, an 'add-on' requiring company initiative rather than government regulation. But the observance of human rights cannot be a voluntary activity or a matter of competitive advantage; nor is there necessarily a 'business case' that can demonstrate financial reward for such observance. As with the Global Compact, CSR has helped to raise the profile of the issues while also providing a smokescreen for inaction at the heart of most companies' operations.

2.4 Voluntarism or regulation?

The main incentives for companies to change and accept their wider responsibilities for the protection and promotion of human rights have so far been reputational damage and external pressure from NGOs and public opinion. The arguments for companies to avoid or forestall such damage should now be abundantly clear, whether as a matter of principle or self-interest. But, if companies fall short of their responsibilities, it will be necessary to examine the possibility of a role for the governments of their 'parent' countries or for the international community. Companies have no inhibitions about arguing with their home governments and with international organisations for an investment and trading regime that will protect their commercial position. They would be wise to encourage a regime that also assists in alleviating some of the main social and environmental problems they confront and to which they contribute. The Multilateral Agreement on Investment (MAI), proposed by the Organisation for Economic Co-operation and Development (OECD) with the support of major companies, signally failed to do this, offering only protection for investment without requiring reciprocal responsibilities in relation to the social and environmental impacts of such investments. There would be value in a framework that provided greater security for investment together with social and environmental obligations. The law is likely to be no more than a minimum for good companies, but its existence would bring up the standards of poor companies and prevent them undercutting the good. It might also help to improve the performance of governments.

It is here that the debate is currently focused: between the need for regulation and mandatory disclosure on the one hand and voluntary action by companies on the other. Historically voluntarism has never worked. The interests of all stakeholders other than shareholders have had to be fought for and imposed by external pressure or government legislation. A few business leaders are beginning to talk of the need for a 'regulatory framework' (e.g. see Holliday *et al.* 2002), but in practice their companies oppose it at both national and international levels. Eventually some international regulatory framework will be necessary to make companies operating transnationally accountable. The internationally accepted instruments of the United Nations UDHR, the Convention on the Rights of the Child and the core International Labour Organisation conventions provide the basis for such a framework which would be in the interest both of the public and of good companies which would then have a more level playing field on which to compete. But such a framework, requiring international treaties, is a long way off and requires the political will from governments which is currently lacking. The introduction in 2000 by the US and UK governments of the Voluntary Principles on Security and Human Rights for oil and mining companies was an important move (see Chapter 19 in which Bennett Freeman and Genoveva Hernández Uriz discuss these principles in some detail). However, the reality is that the principles are voluntary and, therefore, significant companies can simply choose to ignore them.

The development by the United Nations Sub-Commission on the Promotion and Protection of Human Rights of draft 'Norms on the Responsibilities of Transnational Corporations and other Business Enterprises in Regard to Human Rights' points a way ahead. This document, pulling together a large number of internationally recognised standards, and the product of consultation with companies, NGOs and governments, covers the spectrum of corporate responsibilities more comprehensively than any other of the many initiatives in the field. Norms set by a United Nations body, based on the UDHR and its subsequent conventions and the International Labour Organisation conventions, would have an influence greater than any of the current initiatives and provide a template for company codes and a model for national legislation. At the start of 2003 it had still to work its way through the UN mechanism, but it would be in the interest of governments, NGOs and good companies to replace the current plethora of external codes and initiatives with a single set of norms whose acceptance would help market forces to judge more than the financial results of companies.

2.5 Companies and NGOs

International law or regulation may go some way towards setting a framework and the search for this is likely to continue. So far such efforts have made little impact. National aims are often in conflict and company operations in a fiercely competitive world are too fast-moving and complex for the law to deal with. At the end of the day it will require a new paradigm—corporate practice stemming from a central moral imperative which recognises responsibility towards all its stakeholders—if a company is to fulfil its responsibilities. Indeed, companies could themselves make additional legislation unnecessary by taking a proactive role in meeting their responsibilities to all their stakeholders. But management tunnel vision, reinforced by the vitiating fallacy that the purpose of a company is to maximise value for only one stakeholder, the shareholder, makes this unlikely. With governments also reluctant to take adequate action, jointly or individually, it will be left to the active citizen, raising a voice as consumer, pensioner or shareholder, and to NGOs to continue to fight for corporate behaviour consistent with international values.

NGOs today have a profile and influence which make them a major constituent in the debate. Yet, while ad hoc coalitions for particular causes are beginning to emerge, NGOs, with rare exceptions, lack the will to co-operate with each other on a long-term basis and lack also the international co-ordination within their own organisations that could make them a more effective force. Most are unable to deal effectively with companies because of a lack of sufficient understanding of the corporate world. Even where NGO interests are complementary, there is no common goal or philosophy under which each can pursue its individual objectives. The corporate world, highly competitive in its relationships, nonetheless has instruments such as the International Chamber of Commerce at the international level and business associations at the national level to fight its collective cause. These all, however, tend to be reactionary in their attitudes and represent the average rather than the best performance of their memberships. It is unlikely that the NGO world can or should replicate such organisations, but agreement on an overall philosophy, such as is implicit in the UN 'Norms', would give their effort a cohesion and impact that would strengthen the attainment of their individual objectives and frustrate the defensive mechanism of divide and rule which companies are all too ready to deploy.

2.6 Where are we now?

At the beginning of 2003, some 38 companies had been identified as explicitly supporting human rights, the majority of them expressing support for the UDHR.[3] Most of these companies are based in Europe; most of the biggest United States companies are significant absentees from the list. As a proportion of the whole this appears to be a negligible number, but it contains some of the biggest and most international of TNCs and provides an example for others. Moreover, a bridgehead of principle has been won from which no retreat will now be possible even under adverse economic circumstances. The test will now be the application of principle in practice and the extent to which it permeates the totality of a company's operations.

The chief drivers for change have so far been reputational damage and NGO protest and subsequent engagement. This is not an attractive recipe. Companies have the choice of initiating change themselves or conducting a rearguard operation against a world that now firmly regards defence of human rights as a corporate responsibility. For NGOs the challenge is to maintain their scrutiny of company operations and traditional methods of protest, but to add to these a sophisticated approach which touches companies where they are most sensitive. Shareholder resolutions, for example, bring issues into the public eye, their effectiveness reflected in the effort that companies put in to prevent them. But there is no substitute for direct engagement in dialogue with companies and their shareholders. This is a labour-intensive exercise requiring understanding of the scope and limits of corporate responsibility (something still scarce in the NGO movement) and a preparedness to assist as well as challenge.

There are limits to what can be done. It is unrealistic to ask companies to abstain from commercial opportunity even in situations of political volatility. The test today, and the criterion by which the exercise of responsibility will be judged, is the extent to which that purpose is carried out without harm to others and to which corporate influence is used for positive good. There can be no compromise over human rights or over companies' obligations towards them. But compromises are inevitably necessary on other issues: between national requirements and local needs; between the economic interests of a country as a whole and protection of a local environment. Companies should not be allowed to—or expected to—dictate the terms of such compromises: these are decisions for a country, its people and government. In a democracy there should be acceptable mechanisms for resolving differences and conflict. Where a government dictates policy without regard for or consultation with the national or local interests that may be affected, conflict can be generated in which the company becomes a target for those who feel discriminated against. In these circumstances, helping local voices to be heard, strengthening civil society that can hold government to account, and outspoken criticism will all be necessary and legitimate roles for a company, its responsibility as a corporate citizen outweighing any inhibitions that may be felt on account of its foreign origins. It will require in managers a sensitivity, understanding and

---

3 This data is obtained from the Business and Human Rights Resource Centre website, www.business-humanrights.org, the most comprehensive and valuable of databases in this field.

willingness to participate beyond the technical requirements of their jobs and a corporate framework of principle that both allows and encourages the exercise of these capabilities.

The question nonetheless remains whether or not companies should embark on a new venture in an area where there is conflict or gross violation of human rights. To do so without appropriate policies is clearly irresponsible. To do so if a company cannot follow the policies it has laid down for itself would be unprincipled. To do so without a prior human rights assessment, relating both to the inception and potential success of the venture, is to invite legitimate censure and the accusation of complicity. But, given appropriate principles and policies that confront the totality of the situations that will be encountered, and given a willingness to proclaim and practise them, it is arguable that companies can provide an enlightened example in an area of darkness.

It is for the international community to define and proscribe the evils committed by governments and to impose sanctions or boycotts. It is for the international community to decide pragmatically—which a company cannot do without being merely self-serving—whether it prefers a principled company to the less scrupulous company which will inevitably fill any vacuum. The globalisation of the world economy requires a globalised investment framework. Without this, companies have to make their own decisions. There is a danger, at a time of weaker government and inadequate international statesmanship, of looking to companies to fill the gaps that governments leave. This would be wholly wrong. But companies meeting their responsibilities to the full can be part of the solution to an unjust and unequal world: they are otherwise simply part of the problem.

Finally, companies will have no defence if their activities are not transparent. Mistakes will be made, but if they are openly acknowledged, if they are made in the context of policies and practices that reflect the breadth of a company's responsibilities, they will be accepted as mistakes, not condemned as crimes. Companies complain that if they proclaim their good intentions they will be more closely scrutinised than those that don't. That is the nature of life in any activity. But NGOs need to learn to praise as well as blame and to move on to widen the circle of committed companies, as well as ensuring that those expressing commitment are genuine in their intent. The eventual aim must be a system of corporate reporting in which the social and environmental impact of a company is measured and audited as rigorously as is the economic impact.[4] With this in place, market forces—the most potent force for change—can operate on measures other than money and help to see the values of society reflected in companies' operations.

The democratic deficit that exists today cannot be filled by NGOs alone. Governments need to act individually and collectively to ensure that companies carry out their full responsibilities if they wish to ensure the survival of the market economy, a mechanism that has proved its economic effectiveness in generating wealth for its beneficiaries, but has yet to meet the moral expectations and requirements of the 21st century.

---

4 The concept of 'the triple bottom line'—reporting on the economic, environmental and social impact of a company—was first developed by John Elkington of SustainAbility (see, further, Elkington 1997).

3

The development of human rights responsibilities for multinational enterprises

Peter Muchlinski
University of Kent at Canterbury, UK

The issue of whether, and how far, multinational enterprises (MNEs), or trans-national corporations (TNCs) in UN parlance,[1] should be required to observe fundamental human rights standards and, possibly, to be liable for their violation, has been the subject of much discussion in recent times. This may be attributed to a number of factors including increased unease at the seemingly unaccountable operations of private capital in a globalising economy, the perception that the ability of the nation-state to act in the public interest has been weakened by the effects of economic globalisation, and the greater ease of communicating cases of corporate misconduct through the media, wherever this may occur. In addition, the increased vigilance of non-governmental organisations (NGOs) that are concerned with such misconduct has led to greater awareness of this issue (see further Muchlinski 2001a: 33-35; UN Sub-Commission on Human Rights 2002a: 2-4; International Council on Human Rights Policy 2002: 1-2). Whether corpora-tions are, in fact, behaving worse now than before is not the real question. The fact that they are perceived as having to conform to certain standards of public conduct, hitherto exclusively required of the state and its public agencies, is.

This chapter discusses the developing legal consequences of this increased awareness, specifically the evolution of the debate concerning the extent to which MNEs and other business enterprises should observe, and be bound by, human rights standards. The chapter is divided into three main parts. The first is a discus-sion of the wider context of the debate on corporate social responsibility (CSR) and,

1   The terms 'transnational corporation' and 'multinational enterprise' are essentially interchangeable and are so used in this chapter (see further Muchlinski 1999: 12-15; 2002: 169-70).

in particular, the extension of human rights responsibilities to corporate actors. This provides an essential conceptual and policy background to the current debate. The second part discusses the major substantive principles that may be said to form the foundations of MNE human rights responsibilities, and offers a guide to the most important international instruments in this field. In addition it refers to the continuing debates within the UN Sub-Commission on Human Rights concerning the drafting of a new UN instrument in this field, the most recent draft text of which is now referred to as the 'Draft Norms of Responsibilities of Transnational Corporations and Other Business Enterprises with Regard to Human Rights' (hereafter referred to as the Draft Norms). This continues to be discussed by the Working Group of the Sub-Commission set up for this purpose (UN Sub-Commission on Human Rights 2002b; see Weissbrodt 2000 for a discussion of the background to the development of the Draft Norms). The third part examines the practical issues of monitoring and implementation of corporate human rights performance, including both the major practical legal issues that arise in the context of national litigation and the possible role of intergovernmental organisations (IGOs) in the supervision of MNE adherence with human rights norms.

3.1 The context: the debate on corporate social responsibility and the extension of human rights standards to corporate actors

There are at least three principal sets of issues that need to be considered in this connection: first, how should the 'social dimension' and 'social responsibility' be defined for the purposes of developing new international standards; second, following from this general issue, on what basis should human rights responsibilities extend to corporations; and, third, what are the sources of substantive standards from which a new international code of corporate social responsibility can be drawn?

3.1.1 Defining the 'social dimension' and 'social responsibility'

The phrase 'corporate social responsibility' can mean many different things and the obligations of firms in this matter can be drawn rather widely. For example, the Draft UN Code of Conduct for Transnational Corporations contained obligations ranging from respect for the sovereignty and political system of the host state, respect for human rights, abstention from corrupt practices, full disclosure or observance of tax and competition laws, to obligations on TNCs not to abuse their economic power in a manner damaging to the economic well-being of the countries in which they operate (UNCTAD 2001a: 5). Equally, the revised OECD Guidelines for Multinational Enterprises contain an extensive range of social obligations for MNEs including, *inter alia*, duties to contribute to the sustainable development of the countries in which they operate, to respect human rights, to encourage local capacity-building, and to refrain from seeking or accepting exemptions to local regulatory frameworks in the areas of environment, health and safety, labour, taxation, financial incentives or other issues (OECD 2000). In contrast, the UN Global Compact[2] focuses on just three issue areas on which world business should act by upholding the major international instruments in each field:

1. Respect for human rights as defined in the Universal Declaration of Human Rights

2. The International Labour Organisation (ILO)'s Declaration on Fundamental Principles and Rights at Work, which requires respect for freedom of association, recognition of collective bargaining, elimination of all forms of forced and compulsory labour, the effective abolition of child labour and elimination of discrimination in respect of employment and occupation

3. The Rio Declaration of the UN Conference on Environment and Development, which requires support for a precautionary approach to environmental challenges, the undertaking of initiatives to promote greater environmental responsibility and the encouragement of the development and diffusion of environmentally friendly technologies

The question of what the list of social responsibility standards should contain is, of course, a question of choice bounded by ideological considerations (Muchlinski 2000a: 373-74). However, it is clear that the list can cover potentially all aspects of corporate conduct, and that the matter may assume economic, social, political and ethical dimensions (UNCTAD 2001a: 11). It is equally clear that certain basic standards of ethical behaviour can no longer be seen as outside the responsibilities of corporate actors, even if, traditionally, such standards were, in the first instance, applicable to public bodies alone. This is particularly so when the reasons for extending human rights responsibilities to private non-state actors are considered.

3.1.2 The basis of human rights obligations for non-state actors

The use of human rights standards to assess the conduct of corporations is replete with conceptual difficulties. Indeed, there are a number of strong arguments against the extension of human rights responsibilities to TNCs.[3] First, TNCs and other business enterprises are in business. Their only social responsibility is to make profits for their shareholders. It is not for them to act as moral arbiters in relation to the wider issues arising in the communities in which they operate. Indeed to do so may be seen as unwarranted interference in the internal affairs of

---

2 www.unglobalcompact.org (last accessed 17 March 2003)
3 This section of the chapter draws on Muchlinski 2001a: 35-44.

those communities, something that TNCs have, in the past, been urged not to do.[4] Second, private non-state actors do not have any positive duty to observe human rights. Their only duty is to obey the law. Thus it is for the state to regulate on matters of social importance and for such actors to observe the law. It follows also that TNCs and other business enterprises, as private actors, can only be beneficiaries of human rights protection and not human rights protectors themselves. Third, which human rights are TNCs and other business enterprises to observe? They may have some influence over social and economic matters—for example, by ensuring the proper treatment of their workers—but they can do nothing to protect civil and political rights. Only states have the power and the ability to do that. Fourth, the extension of human rights obligations to corporate actors will create a 'free-rider' problem (Vernon 1999: 49). It is predictable that not all states and not all firms will take the same care to observe fundamental human rights. Thus the more conscientious corporations that invest time and money into observing human rights and making themselves accountable for their record in this field, will be at a competitive disadvantage in relation to more unscrupulous corporations that do not undertake such responsibilities. They may also lose business opportunities in countries with poor human rights records, as the host government may prefer not to do business with ethically driven corporations. Fifth, unfairness may be exacerbated by the selective and politically driven activities of NGOs, whose principal concern may be to maintain a high profile for their particular campaigns rather than to ensure that all corporations are held equally to account.

Such arguments can, however, be answered. First, as regards the extension of social responsibility standards to corporations, it should be noted that TNCs have been expected to observe socially responsible standards of behaviour for a long time (UNCTAD 1999a, 1999b: ch. XII). This expectation has been expressed in national and regional laws and in numerous codes of conduct drawn up by intergovernmental organisations, as will be discussed more fully below. Indeed, TNCs themselves appear to be rejecting a purely non-social role for themselves through the adoption of corporate and industry-based codes of conduct (for examples, see UNCTAD 1994: ch. VIII; 1999a: 31-42). Second, observance of human rights is increasingly being seen by TNCs as 'good for business'. It is argued that business cannot flourish in an environment where fundamental human rights are not respected—what firm would be happy with the disappearance or imprisonment without trial of employees for their political opinions? In addition, businesses themselves may justify the adoption of human rights policies by reference to good reputation (see, for example, Williams 1999; Harvard Law School Human Rights Program 1999: 19-22). The benefit to be reaped from espousing a pro human rights stance is seen as outweighing any free-rider problem, which, in any case, may be exaggerated (Muchlinski 2001a: 38-39).

Third, the private legal status of TNCs and other business enterprises may be seen as irrelevant to the extension of human rights responsibilities to such entities. As Andrew Clapham has forcefully argued, changes in the nature and location of

---

4 See, for example, the UN Draft Code of Conduct for Transnational Corporations paragraphs 15-16 (reprinted in UNCTAD 1996: 165).

power in the contemporary international system, including an increase in the power of private non-state actors such as TNCs (which may allow them to bypass traditional state-centred systems of governance) have forced a reconsideration of the boundaries between the private and the public spheres. This, in turn, has brought into question the traditional notion of the corporation as a private entity with no social or public obligations, with the consequence that such actors, including TNCs, may in principle be subjected to human rights obligations (Clapham 1993: 137-38). This position coincides with the fear that these powerful entities may disregard human rights and, thereby, violate human dignity. It follows that corporations, including, in particular, TNCs, should be subjected to human rights responsibilities, notwithstanding their status as creatures of private law, because human dignity must be protected in every circumstance (Clapham 1993: 147). Fourth, in response to the view that TNCs cannot be subjected to human rights responsibilities because they are incapable of observing human rights designed to direct state action, it may be said that, to the contrary, TNCs can affect the economic welfare of the communities in which they operate. Given the indivisibility of human rights, this means that they have a direct impact on the extent that economic and social rights, especially labour rights in the workplace, can be enjoyed.

Although it is true that TNCs may not have direct control over matters arising outside the workplace, they may nonetheless exercise important influence in this regard. Thus, TNCs may seek to defend the human rights of their employees outside the workplace, set standards for their subcontractors and refuse to accept the benefits of governmental measures that seek to improve the business climate at the expense of fundamental human rights. Equally, where firms operate in unstable environments they should ensure that their security arrangements comply with fundamental human rights standards (see further Chapter 19). Moreover, where companies have no direct means of influence they should avoid, at the very least, making statements or engaging in actions that appear to condone human rights violations. This may include silence in the face of such violations. Furthermore, all firms should develop an internal human rights policy that ensures that such concerns are taken into account in management decision-making, and which may find expression in a corporate code of conduct. Fifth, the argument that MNEs may be subjected to arbitrary and selective targeting by NGOs should not be overstated. While it is true that such behaviour can arise out of what Upendra Baxi (1998) has termed 'the market for human rights', in which NGOs strive for support from a consuming public in a manner not dissimilar to that of a service industry, TNCs and other major business enterprises are big enough to take care of themselves.

Despite the convincing arguments for extending responsibility for human rights violations to TNCs, the legal responsibility of TNCs for such violations remains uncertain. Thus, much of the literature on this issue suggests ways to reform and develop the law towards full legal responsibility, rather than documenting actual juridical findings of human rights violations by TNCs, or, indeed, other non-state actors (see, for example Kamminga 1999; Joseph 2000; Amnesty International [The Netherlands] and Pax Christi 2000; Muchlinski 2001a). We are yet to see such an event in the courts of the world, although it should be remembered that findings of human rights violations concerning slave labour practices have been made against individual German industrialists at the end of the Second World War (Clapham 2000: 166-71). Against this background, the activities of the Sub-Commission and its Working Group may be seen, first, as an acceptance of the *principle* that TNCs and other business enterprises can be responsible for the observance of human rights standards and, second, as a move towards the *clarification of the rules and norms* by which TNCs and other business entities should be made subject to human rights responsibilities. In relation to the latter, the next important issue concerns the sources of such responsibilities.

3.1.3 The sources of substantive provisions

At the outset, it must be stressed that, traditionally, international agreements regulating international business have not covered social issues, or at least not directly or expressly. In the area of foreign direct investment (FDI) the main category of treaty, the bilateral investment treaty (BIT), usually covers: non-discrimination, based on most-favoured-nation and national treatment standards; investment guarantees against expropriation or civil unrest and in support of free transfer of funds; and dispute settlement (UNCTAD 1998). Indeed, even the failed Multilateral Agreement on Investment (MAI), as originally conceived, contained no references to labour or environmental standards, only provisions, echoing BITs, for the promotion and protection of investors and their investments coupled with new standards guaranteeing entry and establishment of investors and their investments, based on US and Canadian BIT practice, and on NAFTA (for further analysis see Picciotto 1998; Henderson 1999; Muchlinski 2000b).

The vast bulk of social responsibility standards for the conduct of international business can be found in instruments outside the field of international business regulation, even, indeed, outside the sphere of work covered by IGOs. These sources are, for the most part, non-binding voluntary codes or declarations. They are 'soft law' instruments, offering little more than moral force, in that the major method of enforcement is through the shame of non-adherence. They include: codes of conduct developed by individual companies or industry sectors (see, further, UNCTAD 2001a);[5] NGO codes (see, for example, Amnesty International [UK] 1998; UNCTAD 2000a); and codes drawn up by governments[6] or IGOs of which the codes of conduct developed by the International Labour Organisation (ILO) are of special importance.[7] On the other hand, some sources are legally binding as they take the form of binding conventions on specific issues. The 1997 OECD Convention on Combating Bribery of Foreign Officials in International Business Transactions is

---

5 See esp. 37-40. See also UNCTAD 2000b; Muchlinski 2000a: 386-88 n. 14 and sources cited therein. For a full inventory of corporate codes of conduct, see OECD 1999.

6 For example the UK Ethical Trading Initiative: www.ethicaltrade.org (last accessed 17 March 2003).

7 See, for an overview, UNCTAD 2000b: n. 33 and the ILO website at www.ilo.org (last accessed 17 March 2003).

the most prominent example[8]—similarly, the numerous ILO Conventions on labour standards. Such international standard-setting conventions acquire the force of binding international treaties among the membership of the sponsoring IGO, or among the signatory states, if membership of the convention is permitted to any country including non-members of the sponsoring IGO.

3.2 The major substantive human rights obligations of MNEs

3.2.1 The basis of obligation

Given that, historically, the observance of human rights standards has been an obligation of the state alone, the first element in the evolution of substantive standards is the assertion of a direct link between the obligations of states and of non-state actors to promote universal respect for, and observance of, human rights and fundamental freedoms. An express reference to such a link can be found in the Universal Declaration of Human Rights. This instrument is addressed both to governments and to 'other organs of society'. Following this provision, the Preamble to the UN Draft Norms recognises that:

> even though States have the primary responsibility to promote and protect human rights, transnational corporations and other business enterprises, *as organs of society*, are also responsible for promoting and securing the human rights set forth in the Universal Declaration of Human Rights [emphasis added].

This is a clear acceptance of the view that corporate entities do have human rights responsibilities on the basis of their social existence. Although the first concern of the Draft Norms is to address the obligations of TNCs and other business enterprises in respect of human rights, this instrument continues to address the obligations of governments as well. Thus, the Draft Norms also contain the following general statement:

> States have the primary responsibility to respect, ensure respect for, prevent abuses of, and promote human rights recognised in international as well as national law, including assuring that transnational corporations and other business enterprises respect human rights. Within their respective spheres of activity and influence, transnational corporations and other business enterprises have the obligation to respect, ensure respect for, prevent abuses of, and promote human rights recognised in international as well as national law.

8   This Convention entered into force on 15 February 1999. See OECD Doc DAFFE/IME/ BR(97)20, 8 April 1998, or see www.imf.org/external/np/gov/2001/eng/091801.htm.

This provision places states over TNCs and other business enterprises as the principal regulators of human rights observance. In addition, it recognises that states and businesses operate in different fields and so each has a specific set of responsibilities in its particular field of operations, thereby obviating the possibility that business enterprises could supplant the state in its obligations to uphold and observe human rights.

3.2.2 The kinds of enterprises covered by human rights obligations

The discussions over the Draft Norms in the UN Sub-Commission reflect a desire to see human rights obligations being applied to all business entities and not merely to TNCs. This avoids an otherwise unjustifiable distinction between TNCs and national firms as regards responsibilities to observe fundamental human rights standards. The focus of the debate on international CSR has tended to be towards TNCs, given the transnational character of their operations. However, the underlying issues of principle would apply *mutatis mutandis* to national firms as the applicability of human rights standards to private corporate actors does not depend on the mere fact that their business operations cross borders. Such a geographically based justification for applying human rights standards to one class of corporations, rather than another, would be unprincipled.

The focus on TNCs can perhaps be explained as a pragmatic choice, evolving out of their visibility in certain widely publicised cases of mass violations of human rights and from the perception that TNCs, unlike purely national firms, can take advantage of more lax legal regimes in foreign host countries. These regimes pay scant regard to social welfare concerns, allowing unscrupulous firms to turn this to their commercial advantage (UN Sub-Commission on Human Rights 2002a: paragraphs 22-26). On the other hand, it should be noted that TNCs are more likely than local firms, in countries where social welfare issues are either un- or de-regulated, to observe good practices in this arena. Thus, the real problem may be a lack of proper regulation in the host country of local businesses and institutions for which TNCs may not be responsible. Therefore, any programme of responsibility must take into account the relationship between local and transnational practices and the influence of TNCs thereon. In addition the reference to both TNCs and other business enterprises avoids the risk that an inadequate definition could allow companies to use financial and other structures to conceal their transnational nature and to appear as a domestic company thereby avoiding responsibility under the Draft Norms.

3.2.3 The principal substantive obligations

The discussions concerning the Draft Norms have given rise to a re-examination of the range of sources from which human rights responsibilities for TNCs and other business enterprises can be drawn, making these discussions a useful stocktaking exercise concerning the current state of possible substantive obligations in this field. From the existing instruments dealing with corporate social responsibility and human rights, as synthesised into the substantive contents of the Draft Norms, at least five different types of provisions can be identified.

First, there are those that cover 'traditional' civil and political human rights issues, namely:

- The right to equal treatment (see also OECD 2000)

- The right of security of persons as concerns business engagement in, or benefit from, 'war crimes, crimes against humanity, genocide, torture, forced disappearance, forced or compulsory labour, hostage-taking, other violations of humanitarian law and other international crimes against the human person as defined by international law'

- Rights of workers dealing, in particular, with those rights listed in Article 2 of the ILO Declaration on Fundamental Principles and Rights at Work 1998, namely: the prohibition on forced or compulsory labour, the rights of children to be protected against economic exploitation,[9] and freedom of association

- Respect for other civil and political rights, such as freedom of movement, freedom of thought, conscience and religion, and freedom of opinion and expression

Second, following the contents, in the main, of the ILO Tripartite Declaration of Principles Concerning Multinational Enterprises and Social Policy,[10] the UN Draft Norms contain provisions reflecting the main economic social and cultural rights, including:

- The provision of a safe and healthy working environment

- Compensation of workers with remuneration that ensures 'an adequate standard of living for them and their families'

- Protection of collective bargaining

- Respect for the social, economic and cultural policies of the countries in which companies operate[11]

9 'Draft Norms', paragraph 6. This formulation in the text, introduced by the 'Draft Principles', replaces an earlier formulation of the 'Draft Norms' which stated that 'Companies shall not use child labour and shall contribute to its abolition.' Thus the prohibition in the earlier draft has been modified so that child labour conducted in a non-exploitative manner can be used. This reflects concern that, in some developing countries, the denial of access to labour for children might actually worsen their economic situation and that of their families. In such cases the issue is to make child labour non-abusive. To that end the 'Draft Principles' laid down a basic framework for the control of abuses of child labour. Equally, business enterprises that use child labour must create and implement a plan to eliminate this ('Draft Commentary' at page 8). By comparison, the 1998 ILO Declaration requires 'the effective abolition of child labour' without qualification.

10 ILO Tripartite Declaration on Multinational Enterprises and Social Policy 1977 as amended at the 279th Session of the ILO, Geneva, 17 November 2000: 41 ILM 186 (2002).

11 These include transparency, accountability and prohibition of corruption.

- Respect for the rights to health, adequate food and adequate housing and other economic social and cultural rights such as rights to 'adequate food and drinking water; the highest attainable standard of physical and mental health; adequate housing; education . . . and refrain from actions which obstruct the realisation of those rights'

No distinction is made in the Draft Norms between the importance of these so-called 'first'- and 'second'-generation human rights. Indeed, as the Preamble explains, the Draft Norms are based on the 'universality, indivisibility, interdependence and interrelatedness of human rights including the right to development'. This approach also covers the so-called 'third-generation' rights of collective solidarity, as expressed through the inclusion, in the Draft Norms, of the right of development and other community-based rights such as respect for the rights of local communities and of indigenous peoples.

A fourth group of provisions can be said to deal with the special problems created by the operations of MNEs for the realisation of the types of rights listed above. Thus, the Draft Norms deal with a specific issue that has arisen in a number of cases: namely, the operation of security arrangements for companies. Such arrangements must 'observe international human rights norms as well as the laws and professional standards of the country or countries in which they operate'. This general principle is further elaborated in the attached Commentary, which requires companies to observe the emerging best practices evolving in this field through various codes of conduct, particularly the UN Principles on the Use of Force and Firearms and the UN Code of Conduct for Law Enforcement Officers; and the UN Convention against Torture and the Rome Statute on the International Criminal Court. Business enterprises and TNCs are further urged not to supplant the state military and law enforcement services but only provide for their own preventative or defensive services and not to hire individuals known to have been responsible for human rights or humanitarian law violations. Other provisions that can be added to this category are: the duty to recognise and respect applicable norms of international law, national laws, regulations, administrative practices and the rule of law,[12] and the final saving provision which makes clear that

> nothing in these Human Rights Responsibilities shall be construed as diminishing, restricting, or adversely affecting the human rights obligations of States under national or international law. Nor shall they be construed as diminishing, or adversely affecting more protective human rights norms.

Not only does this provision offer a rule of interpretation favourable to the effective protection of human rights but it also emphasises that the operations of business enterprises can observe higher standards than the minimum standards required by the Draft Norms.

A fifth, and final, group of substantive provisions go beyond a conventional human rights-based agenda and belong more to a general corporate social responsibility code. This reflects the fact that many of the sources, referred to as contributing to the Draft Norms, constitute more general codes of business ethics,

---

12   This principle is echoed in the OECD Guidelines and the ILO Tripartite Declaration.

which, by their nature, deal with social issues not usually described as human rights issues. Thus, for example, the Draft Norms require that TNCs and other business enterprises shall act

> in accordance with fair business, marketing and advertising practices and shall take all necessary steps to ensure the safety and quality of the goods and services they provide. Nor shall they produce, distribute, market or advertise potentially harmful or harmful products for use by consumers.

This introduces general consumer protection standards into the instrument. Other such social responsibility provisions include a prohibition against bribery and obligations with regard to environmental protection. Whether these are truly 'human rights' issues is open to debate. On the other hand, as the Preamble to the Draft Norms notes,

> new human rights issues and concerns are continually emerging and that transnational corporations and other business enterprises often are related to these issues and concerns, such that further standard-setting and implementation are required at this time and in the future.

It may well be that consumer and environmental protection are emergent human rights issues. It has been argued, for example, that a right to a clean and healthy environment is a human right, though this has been disputed (see, generally, Fitzmaurice 1996: 909-14). Whether consumer protection is a human right seems rather more tenuous, as it is hard to see how elevating such issues to the status of quasi-constitutional rights makes such protection more effective. In any case, other established human rights could be sufficient. For example, death or serious injury caused by unsafe products or processes could come within the right to life and the right to personal security under Article 3 of the Universal Declaration on Human Rights (UDHR) and Articles 6 and 9 of the International Covenant on Civil and Political Rights. Loss of livelihood due to disability could be covered by Article 25 of the UDHR. As for bribery, who are the victims? What do they suffer? Surely, this is an area in which the wider social undesirability of such practices is in issue, rather than any significant adverse effects on any one individual.

3.3 Monitoring and enforcement

The third part of this paper deals with the question of how to ensure that the substantive human rights obligations of MNEs and other business enterprises are actually upheld. This involves a mix of national and international legal approaches. At the national level both standard setting, through new laws and regulations, and public interest litigation, taken against firms alleged to have broken their human rights obligations, may be used. At the international level there arises the possibility that IGOs could have a monitoring role that would supplement such national initiatives. In particular, they could require states to comply with certain obligations to ensure that their domestic regulatory structures adequately reflect the emergent norms in this area, and they could provide adequate and effective remedies for those who allege to have been harmed by the failure of firms to observe fundamental international human rights standards.

At the national level, there has, to date, been relatively little progress on standard setting through new laws or regulations embodying human rights standards. The most significant examples in this regard may be the US and EU initiatives to link labour rights protection to the extension of trade preferences (see, further, Trebilcock and Howse 1999: 458-60), or the UK Ethical Trading Initiative. However, specialised legislation on MNEs and human rights is virtually non-existent. One example of what might be possible arose in Australia where the draft Corporate Code of Conduct Bill contained a provision that subjected the overseas subsidiaries of Australian companies to a general obligation to observe human rights and the principle of non-discrimination.[13] That Bill was never adopted.

On the other hand there are early signs at the level of US national law that a degree of direct responsibility for human rights violations on the part of MNEs is being recognised. Thus in the United States District Court case of *Doe v. Unocal*[14] it was held, for the first time, that MNEs could, in principle, be directly liable for violations of human rights under the Alien Tort Claims Act (ATCA).[15] However, on 31 August 2000, the US District Court awarded a summary judgment to Unocal on the grounds that, although there was evidence that Unocal knew about, and benefited from, forced labour on the pipeline project in Burma (Myanmar) in which it was a joint venture partner, it was not directly involved in the alleged abuses. These were the responsibility of the Burma authorities alone. Giving the Court's judgment, Judge Ronald Lew followed a series of decisions by US Military Tribunals after the Second World War, involving the prosecution of German industrialists for their participation in the Third Reich's slave labour policies.[16] These established that, in order to be liable, the defendant industrialists had to take active steps in co-operating or participating in the forced labour practices. Mere knowledge that someone else would commit abuses was insufficient. By analogy with these cases, Unocal could not be held liable as a matter of international law and so the claim under the Alien Tort Statute failed.[17] However, the principle that

---

13 *Corporate Code of Conduct Bill 2000*, The Parliament of the Commonwealth of Australia draft of 28 August 2000, clause 10.

14 As noted in *American Journal of International Law* 92 (1998): 309. See also *Wiwa v. Royal Dutch Petroleum Company* 226 Federal Supplement 2nd series 88 (US Court of Appeal Second Circuit 2000).

15 28 United States Code s.1350.

16 *US v. Flick* (Trials of War Criminals Before the Nuremberg Military Tribunals under Control Council Law No. 10 [1952]); *US v. Carl Krauch, ibid.* Vol. 8; *US v. Alfred Krupp, ibid.* Vol. 9; *Flick v. Johnson* 174 Federal Reporter 2nd Series 983 (Court of Appeals for District of Columbia 1949).

17 *DOE v. Unocal*, US District Court for the Central District of California, 31 August 2000, 2000 US District Court Report on LEXIS at 13327. See also Branigin 2000.

a private non-state actor can be sued before the US courts for alleged violations of human rights was not questioned.[18]

The summary judgment was overturned in part on appeal to the United States Court of Appeal (USCA) for the Ninth Circuit.[19] The USCA held that there were genuine issues of material fact to be determined as regards the possible liability of Unocal for the alleged acts of forced labour, for aiding and abetting the Burma military in subjecting the plaintiffs to forced labour and for aiding and abetting the Burma military in subjecting the plaintiffs to murder and rape occurring in furtherance of forced labour. On the other hand, there were insufficient facts to justify an examination of the allegations of liability on the part of Unocal for torture. Of particular importance in this judgment is the reaffirmation of the principle that, under ATCA, private actors may be directly liable for alleged violations of fundamental human rights norms that constitute *jus cogens* and to which individual liability applies. In this context, forced labour was seen by the USCA as a modern variant of slavery, one of the crimes to which international law attributes individual liability. The incidents of rape and murder that occurred in relation to the forced labour practices of the Burma military were also of this type as they arose directly out of the furtherance of forced labour.

A second notable element in the judgment is the affirmation of the applicability of the law relating to aiding and abetting an offence to crimes or torts involving alleged violations of fundamental human rights under ATCA.[20] This allows for a finding that a corporation may be liable even if it has not directly taken part in the alleged violations, but has given practical assistance and encouragement to the commission of the crime or tort in question (the *actus reus* of aiding and abetting) and has actual or constructive knowledge that its actions will assist the perpetrator in the commission of the crime or tort (the *mens rea* of aiding and abetting). Thus the District Judge was wrong to give the weight that he had done to the 'active participation' standard used in the Nuremberg Military Tribunal cases that he had relied on. In those cases this standard had been used in response to the defendant's 'necessity defence'. No such defence was invoked, nor could be invoked, by Unocal in the present case.

Furthermore, in the case of *Wiwa v. Royal Dutch Petroleum Company and Shell Transport and Trading Company plc*[21] the US Court of Appeal held that the US interest in pursuing claims for torture under the ATCA and the more recent Torture Victim Prevention Act[22] was a significant factor to be taken into account when

---

18　See too in this regard *Kadic v. Karadzic* 70 Federal Reporter 3rd Series 232 (US Court of Appeal 2nd Circuit 1995) where it was held that the Alien Tort Statute reaches the conduct of private parties provided that their conduct is undertaken under the colour of state authority or violates a norm of international law that is recognised as extending to the conduct of private parties.

19　*DOE v. Unocal Corp.* Judgment of 18 September 2002 (2002) *International Legal Materials* 41: 1,367 (2002).

20　For this purpose the USCA held that the distinction between the aiding and abetting of a crime and a tort was not significant, in that similar principles applied in each situation.

21　US Court of Appeal 2nd Circuit, 14 September 2000: 2000 US Appeal Court Report on LEXIS at 23274.

22　28 United States Code s.1350 (1991).

determining whether an action brought on such grounds before a US court against a foreign MNE should be removed to a foreign jurisdiction on the basis that it was a more suitable forum for the litigation. On the facts, the USCA held that an action brought against the defendant corporation, for allegedly supporting the Nigerian state in its repression of the Ogoni people through *inter alia* the supply of money, weapons and logistical support to the Nigerian military which carried out the alleged abuses, could be heard in the United States. Thus the US courts have set themselves up as a forum in which allegations of complicity in torture made against private corporations can be heard.

However, this case was brought by US resident plaintiffs. It is not certain that US jurisdiction will be so readily accepted where the plaintiffs are from outside the US. Indeed, in *Aguinda et al. v. Texaco* the USCA Second Circuit upheld the decision and the reasoning of the District Court for the Southern District of New York that rejected US jurisdiction over a claim under ATCA, brought by Ecuadorian and Peruvian citizens against Texaco, alleging that the company had polluted rainforests and rivers in those two countries causing environmental damage and personal injuries.[23] The District Court had reviewed the *Wiwa* decision and concluded that it did not introduce a different test of jurisdiction under ATCA from that generally applicable to cases where the issue of whether the US, or a foreign forum, was more appropriate as the place in which the claim should be heard (the *forum non conveniens* doctrine). Given that the balance of the private- and public-interest factors used to determine the appropriate forum pointed overwhelmingly to Ecuador, the District Court held that this claim should be heard there. In any case, the corporate links between the US parent and the Ecuadorian operating affiliate were of a kind of which it could not be said that any wrong had been committed by the parent in the US such as would justify a claim under ATCA. Thus it may be difficult for a foreign claimant to assert the jurisdiction of the US courts over US-based MNEs for alleged violations of human rights where there exists an appropriate alternative forum in the host country and where there is little evidence of direct involvement by the parent in the acts leading to the alleged harm. The only possible exception may be where the plaintiff is claiming to be a victim of torture, though, even in such cases, the choice of US forum will not be decisive under the *forum non conveniens* doctrine.

Although a finding of direct responsibility for human rights violations is, as yet, unprecedented, there is some support for establishing the indirect responsibility of MNEs for human rights violations. Here the state may be held liable for the conduct of non-state actors that amounts to a violation of the human rights of a third person. Such a responsibility could be established by international convention (Kamminga 1999: 559, 569). No such responsibility has ever been expressly provided for. Instead there is some evidence from the case-law under the European Convention on Human Rights (ECHR) that the state may be under an obligation to 'secure' the rights of third persons against interference by a non-state actor. Failure

---

23 945 Federal Supplement 625 (2001) upheld on appeal 303 Federal Reporter 3rd Series. 470 (US Court of Appeal 2nd Circuit, 16 August 2002).

to do so may result in a violation of the Convention.[24] However, this case-law is uncertain in its scope and too much cannot be read into it. At most, it is clear that the state cannot absolve itself of its direct human rights responsibilities by hiving them off to a privatised entity.[25]

Turning to the role of IGOs in monitoring and enforcement, two sets of issues arise. First, what should the legal status of any standard-setting instruments be and, second, what kinds of procedure for monitoring and enforcement could be put in place? The discussions over the UN Draft Norms are instructive as these very questions have had to be faced by the Working Group. It was mentioned above that the legal status of the Draft Norms is yet to be settled. Much here depends on the goodwill of states. There are arguments in favour of, and against, a binding code. The main advantage of a voluntary instrument is that it could be used in conjunction with existing voluntary corporate codes of conduct to develop a more comprehensive system of internal values to be observed by the company. This would need to be supplemented by an effective system of accountability within the company.[26]

While the discussions on the Draft Norms have tended to favour a binding instrument, the Working Group has recognised that, given the uncertainties around the precise legal status of companies and other non-state actors, some form of 'soft law' exercise is a necessary starting point. This has been the normal pattern of operation in relation to the adoption of other binding human rights instruments. Hence, in the absence of state opinion to the contrary (perhaps an unlikely eventuality), some transition from 'soft' to 'hard' law is more likely to occur, with the Draft Norms as the first step in this process. On the other hand, as David Weissbrodt pointed out at the 54th Session of the Sub-Commission, the Draft Norms are binding to the extent that they apply human rights law under ratified conventions to activities of TNCs and other business enterprises. Moreover, the language of the document emphasises binding responsibilities through the use of the term 'shall' rather than 'should' and through the inclusion, in more recent drafts, of more comprehensive implementation measures (UN Sub-Commission on Human Rights 2002a: 6).

Connected with this issue is the question of how to give the Draft Norms 'teeth' through effective implementation and monitoring procedures. In this regard the Draft Norms require TNCs and other business enterprises to adopt, disseminate and implement internal rules of operation in compliance with the Norms. In addition, they must incorporate the principles contained in the Draft Norms in their contracts or other arrangements and dealings with contractors, subcontractors, suppliers and licensees in order to ensure their implementation and

---

24 See e.g. *Young James and Webster v. UK* (1981) European Court of Human Rights Ct.HR Series A, Vol. 44; *X and Y v. The Netherlands* (1985) European Court of Human Rights Ct.HR Series A, Vol. 91; *Arzte fur das Leben* (1988) European Court of Human Rights E.Ct.HR Series A, Vol. 139; Drzemczewski 1983: ch. 8; Clapham 1993: ch. 7.

25 *Costello-Roberts v. UK* (1993) European Court of Human Rights E.Ct.HR (1993) Series A, Vol. 247.

26 Indeed, a business representative at the 54th Session stressed the need for a voluntary approach and that businesses themselves should develop the draft (UN Sub-Commission on Human Rights 2002a: 12).

respect. This represents a significant advance on the earlier drafts, which did not contain express provisions on the use of such legal measures to give force to their contents, though such measures were recommended in commentaries on those earlier drafts. The Draft Norms also require that TNCs and other business enterprises shall monitor and verify their compliance in an independent and transparent manner, which includes input from relevant stakeholders. This monitoring and verification may be done by national, international, governmental and/or non-governmental mechanisms in addition to internal review procedures.

The original text of the Principles/Guidelines focused on corporate implementation. However, the current Draft Norms suggest that their contents could be used by other actors to assess business practice and performance in the area of human rights responsibilities. For example:

● They could form the basis of industry-wide codes.

● Unions could use them as a benchmark for their expectations of company conduct.

● IGOs outside the UN could apply them to develop their own standard-setting instruments.

● Governments could use the Draft Norms as a model for legislation or administrative rules as part of the internal regulatory structure applicable to companies with a statutory seat in the country, or to help interpret legal standards.

● The UN's human rights treaty bodies could apply the Draft Norms to create additional reporting requirements about corporate compliance.

The Draft Norms include a provision requiring TNCs and other business enterprises to 'provide prompt, effective and adequate reparation to those persons, entities, and communities who have been adversely affected by failures to comply with these Responsibilities through, inter alia, reparations, restitution, compensation and rehabilitation for any damage done or property taken'. The Draft Norms state further (in paragraph 17) that: 'In connection with determining damages and in all other respects, these Responsibilities shall be enforced by national courts.' By taking this approach, the Draft Norms envisage a binding enforcement mechanism, centred on national courts, which offers directly effective rights of reparation for the individuals or groups affected as a consequence of a violation of the instrument. This presupposes a legally binding document that is effective within the national laws of the UN Member States that adopt it. Such an effect could not be presumed from a non-binding declaration or recommendation of the UN, neither of which normally has the force of positive international law nor are they sources of directly effective individual rights that can be invoked before national tribunals.

Arguably, the Draft Norms, as an instrument that contains many binding norms of international human rights law, may be enforceable by that fact alone. However, as argued above, not all the norms contained in its provisions are uncontroversial in this respect. Some of the rights that are included may not have such a legal status. Therefore, if the reparation mechanism is to be real and effective, it requires the adoption of an instrument that has the force of law within the legal orders of the signatory states, and recognises the legal effectiveness of all the norms that it contains. This would need to be something akin to an international convention, which contains an obligation to implement its contents and enforcement mechanisms into the municipal law of the signatory state. This is a far cry from a 'soft law' instrument of the kind, as discussed above, usually adopted in this field. Equally, it is unlikely that a UN framework could enforce binding rules and norms relating to the activities of TNCs (see, for example, the views of Mr Alfonso Martinez [a member of the Working Group] in UN Sub-Commission on Human Rights 2002a: 7). In the light of these matters, there is a significant need for further clarification of what legal form this enforcement mechanism will take and how it is expected to work.[27]

A further issue that requires some comment and clarification is the identification of the precise forum before which any claim for reparations under paragraph 17 can be brought. As it stands paragraph 17 is silent on this matter. It could, therefore, be presumed that the question of forum remains to be determined by the national laws of the jurisdiction or jurisdictions in which a claim is brought. If so, then claims brought under the Draft Norms may be embroiled in lengthy and unhelpful disputes over jurisdiction, particularly in common law jurisdictions where the doctrine of *forum non conveniens* continues to apply. In such jurisdictions it may be possible for the respondent corporation—particularly if it is a TNC and the *locus* of the alleged violation of the UN Norms is in another jurisdiction— to challenge the appropriateness of the forum chosen by the claimants and, thereby, to gain a procedural advantage either by vacating the case to another forum more sympathetic to the corporation's defence, or simply by causing delay while this issue is litigated (Muchlinski 2001b; Anderson 2002; Blumberg 2002). In that process the claimants may suffer significant delay in access to justice, not to mention financial loss that might undermine their ability to continue with their claim. Some legal systems are becoming sensitive to such issues[28] but others are not (see, for example, Blumberg 2002). Thus, the Draft Norms may need to establish certain basic rules of jurisdiction so that such legal techniques are not allowed to undermine legitimate claims.

One solution would be to make available the jurisdiction of any state that adheres to the UN Norms on the basis of either the *locus* of the alleged violation, or the domicile of the corporation alleged to be responsible, with the claimant having the choice of forum. Equally, it might be necessary to ensure that the corporate (or contractual) separation between affiliates in a TNC group (or net-

---

27 In this connection a number of possible approaches were canvassed by the Working Group. These at the 54th Session include: a follow-up mechanism, composed of a group of experts, that would be incorporated into the draft; annual reporting on the activities of TNCs; the UN could ensure that respect for the Draft Norms was included in the contracts it concluded with private-sector entities for the procurement of services; the appointment of a special rapporteur on TNCs (UN Sub-Commission on Human Rights 2002a: 9-10 at paras 28-29).

28 See e.g. the UK House of Lords decision in *Lubbe et al. v. Cape plc* (2000) 2 *Lloyds Reports* 2: 383; (2000) 4 *All England Reports* 4: P 268.

work)[29] is not allowed to act as a barrier to jurisdiction against related (or co-operating) entities located outside the jurisdiction where the harm is alleged to have been suffered, but which are seen as complicit in a violation of the Draft Norms on the basis of their relationship with the affiliate (or network partner) located in that jurisdiction. This may prove to be rather controversial as it challenges long-accepted notions of separate corporate personality (and, in the case of transnational networks or alliances, freedom of contract) as the basis for attributing liability to legal persons. However, in the absence of some clarification of this matter, national laws may well come to be used to insulate discrete entities, involved in a TNC or in a transnational network enterprise, production or retailing chain that leads to a violation of human rights, from full responsibility.

3.4 Conclusions

The preceding discussion illustrates the challenges ahead for any IGO that wishes to develop a new social responsibility agenda for TNCs and other business entities. The first point to note is that the process is a slow one and is probably more likely to create 'soft law' obligations. That does not imply that the Draft Norms, or any other international corporate social responsibility instrument, are doomed to complete legal ineffectiveness if they are not legally binding. At the international level 'soft law' can 'harden' into positive law, where it is seen as evidence of emergent new standards of international law. For these purposes the origin of the legal principle in a 'soft law' instrument, such as a voluntary code of conduct or a non-binding resolution of an international organisation, is of little consequence if a consensus develops that the principle in question should be viewed as an obligatory standard by reason of subsequent practice (see, for example, Elias and Lim 1998: 230-32). Given that many of the most important international expressions of welfare values tend to be in such form (Elias and Lim 1998), the 'hardening process' may be of especial importance here. Indeed, as the debate over the social content of the MAI shows, the demand for 'hard law' in this field might be difficult to resist. On the other hand, it should not be forgotten that, even in 'hard law' agreements, provisions concerning controversial social issues have been put into very general, and probably meaningless, hortatory language, simply to show that something has been done, where there is little intention to see these provisions having any real legal effect (see, for example, Waelde 1998, 1999). It is to be hoped that such a fate will not befall the contents of the Draft Norms should it become a legally binding document.

29 It is necessary to make a distinction between equity-based linkages between affiliates in a corporate group and contractual linkages between co-operating enterprises in a network enterprise or alliance for the purposes of liability. In the former case the issue of group liability involves the lifting of the corporate veil between the affiliates, whereas in the latter it involves disregarding any contractual warranties or exclusion clauses that seek to limit the liability of some or all of the participating enterprises (see, further, Muchlinski 1999: chs. 5, 9).

A second significant issue concerns the effect of international instruments at the level of national law. It is arguable that, even if the Draft Norms were to be adopted as a non-binding voluntary instrument, without direct effect on individual rights under national law, they could conceivably acquire legal force in private law. Private law suits can be brought against any firm or organisation that holds itself out as adopting a voluntary code such as, for example, the UN Norms, by other firms or organisations, consumers or other members of the community. Such claims may allege that a failure to comply with the Draft Norms, or other international corporate social responsibility instruments adopted by a company, is evidence that the firm or organisation in question is not meeting standards of conduct that may represent accepted general principles and is, therefore, not exercising reasonable care or due diligence. Moreover, failure to follow the terms of such instruments could be evidence of a breach of contract, where adherence is an express or implied term of the agreement, or of an actionable misrepresentation, where a firm alleges that its adherence to the instrument in question entitles it to be regarded as qualifying for a governmental standard-setting mark of approval, but where in fact it fails to meet these standards. In such cases, consumers can bring an action if they claim to have been attracted to purchasing the firms' products or services in the light of such assertions of good conduct. Also the relevant government agency might bring an action for abuse of its certification scheme (Government of Canada 1998: 27; Webb 1999).

Therefore, to dismiss voluntary sources of international or national corporate social responsibility standards as irrelevant seems to fail to appreciate how formal rules and principles of law emerge. The very fact that an increasing number of non-binding codes is being drafted and adopted in this area suggests a growing interest among important groups and organisations—corporations, industry associations, NGOs, governments and IGOs—and is leading to the establishment of a rich set of sources from which new binding standards can emerge. Indeed, it is noteworthy that the Draft Norms make use of already existing standards produced by other IGOs. A kind of 'collective law of IGOs' seems to be developing, in which various organisations working in the field of corporate social responsibility cross-fertilise one another's initiatives by reference to one another's instruments.

No doubt this process can be, and is being, criticised as one in which corporate interests are trying to capture the agenda through code making and lobbying before international forums and organisations. It is fair to say that non-business NGOs are attempting the same with their codes. The real issue is when and how will all this 'codification' turn into detailed legal standards that can act as fully binding benchmarks for the control of unacceptable lapses in corporate conduct at the international and national levels. That is, of course, an issue of ideological contest, but one that seems to be veering slowly towards an acceptance of some kind of articulated set of minimum international standards for corporate social responsibility, as a trade-off for greater corporate freedom in the market. The Draft Norms represent a very important contribution to this process—one that may possibly turn out to be legally binding.

Human rights, trade and multinational corporations

David Kinley and Adam McBeth

Castan Centre for Human Rights Law, Monash University, Australia

This book is concerned with the impact—both positive and negative—of business on human rights, and proffers recommendations on how human rights can be better protected and realised in the course of commerce. In doing so, particularly given the globalised nature of modern business, it is essential to consider the legal framework relating to internationally recognised human rights on the one hand and the global economy on the other. These 'rules of engagement' have a profound effect on what corporations and governments can and cannot do, including the kinds of measures they may take to improve human rights. In the preceding chapter, Peter Muchlinski discussed the general evolution of international business and human rights law. This chapter focuses explicitly on the subject of international trade law and its effect on human rights.

The opening section of this chapter examines the position of multinational corporations in international trade law as it relates to human rights. We then address two of the common assertions about the relationship between human rights and trade law, namely (a) that 'free trade is good for the poor', and (b) that 'human rights has no part in trade law'. The second section considers a selection of existing trade law provisions that address human rights and assesses the potential for them to be applied and extended to enforce internationally recognised human rights standards on those engaged in international trade, including corporations. The third section then looks to the current round of World Trade Organisation (WTO) trade negotiations as an avenue for strengthening human rights as they are affected in the course of international trade. We conclude that a degree of trade law reform is necessary to enable more effective protection and promotion of human rights in the course of commerce, while noting that such reform will not be a panacea for human rights and that a concerted effort by all economic players, including corporations, governments and international organisations, is needed to ensure that business enhances rather than inhibits human rights.

4.1 An irresistible force and an immovable object? The interaction of human rights and trade

4.1.1 The role of multinational corporations in international trade and human rights

The relationship between international trade law and multinational corporations is defined from the outset by an anomaly: while corporations are the drivers of trade and the participants in the trading system, only states are recognised as actors under international trade law. Corporations must rely on states to negotiate and enforce favourable trade rules on their behalf, and in the event of a dispute they must rely on the surrogacy of their home state to bring a complaint.

Similarly, states are the bearers of responsibility under international human rights law. Although human rights obligations are generally expressed as being owed 'by all', including corporate actors, it is the state that is responsible for the implementation of policies and practices for human rights protection, as well as for violations under international law. However, corporations clearly have potential to breach human rights standards in the course of their commercial operations, particularly the rights of their employees, local communities at the location of particular projects and people who oppose certain operations. Furthermore, where an entity operates beyond the jurisdiction of any one state, as is the case with multinational corporations, the state's ability to regulate and enforce human rights standards is clearly curtailed. So, while the rules of international trade law regulate the conduct of states for the direct benefit of multinational corporations engaged in trade (and arguably for the indirect benefit of everybody, an argument discussed below), the conduct of entities actually engaged in international trade (principally multinational corporations) is not regulated.

International trade law, as a legal system that governs the transnational operations of corporations and creates great benefits for them, could appropriately incorporate obligations concerning how a corporation conducts itself in the course of international trade, including an obligation to respect internationally recognised human rights norms. Such an approach could both harness the positive contributions made by some corporations towards the realisation of human rights (particularly in relation to economic and social rights) and restrain the grievous conduct of others. This chapter aims to demonstrate that the foundations of such an approach are already in place, and to identify some elements of international trade law that are ripe for reform. There are, further, a number of sound arguments against using trade law as a vehicle for improved human rights accountability of corporations. Some of these arguments are discussed and evaluated in the conclusion to this chapter.

4.1.2 'Free trade is good for the poor'

The mantra of free trade advocates is that free trade is good for the poor; the most effective way for developing countries to prosper is to open their borders to foreign investment and to exploit export opportunities in foreign markets. The theory is that greater openness will promote international trade, which will in turn accelerate economic growth, leading to increased prosperity for all. Indeed, some in this camp are so bold as to suggest that 'the WTO is here to help the world's poor' (as argued, for example, by Alan Oxley, the former Australian Ambassador to and Chairman of GATT [Oxley 2002]).

It may well be true that increased trade, foreign direct investment and associated economic growth will result in a larger international economic pie, and it may also be true that the slice of that pie allocated to developing countries is larger in absolute, if not relative, terms.[1] Certainly an increase in economic activity creates, in most cases, new opportunities for employment, thus contributing to the realisation of the right to work. Furthermore, the resultant increase in wealth contributes to the right to a decent standard of living and provides resources for the realisation of other rights, such as the rights to food, education and health.[2] However, there is no guarantee from economic growth alone that these new jobs would adhere to fundamental human rights standards (e.g. freedom from discrimination in the workplace, freedom of association and the right to bargain collectively, and the prohibition on forced labour and child labour), let alone rights to health, education and housing under the International Covenant on Economic, Social and Cultural Rights (ICESCR). Furthermore, an increase in economic activity may bring side-effects invisible in economic statistics, such as the forced eviction of local inhabitants to make way for commercial projects (see, for example, Chapter 12 in this volume), the pollution of land, air and water, deforestation, and the violent treatment of individuals opposed to a particular development. These side-effects have negative ramifications for the rights to life, health, food, property and security of the person, among others.

The rule-based multilateral trading system embodied in the WTO could potentially be a tool to ensure that poor countries receive fair access to international markets for their goods. This is in contrast to the current regime where the key export sectors for many developing countries—particularly textiles and agriculture—must face high tariffs or competition from highly subsidised products in industrialised countries, while developing countries are frequently accused of dumping and slapped with anti-dumping duties if, despite all, they do manage to produce exports at a competitive price (Annan 2001: 22). However, even with the benefits of such a modified system, there will be human beings who appear as outliers on the otherwise neat graph of supply and demand, and others who constitute collateral damage in the campaign for economic development. Unfettered market forces will not protect these people. Human rights principles applied to the trade liberalisation process could ensure that vital services are delivered to

1 Figures in the United Nations Development Programme's *Human Development Report 2002* indicate that income has increased in absolute terms in the past 25 years in most regions of the world, with the notable exceptions of Central and Eastern Europe and Sub-Saharan Africa. However, the income gap between OECD countries and other countries has widened considerably in this period, indicating a reduction in the income share of non-OECD countries relative to OECD countries (UNDP 2002: 19).

2 All of these rights are identified in the International Covenant on Economic, Social and Cultural Rights 1966.

all, thereby potentially ensuring that economic development is not achieved over the bodies of forced labourers or tortured opponents, nor over poisoned rivers and contaminated food supplies.

Free trade is definitely good for some. Whether or not it is also good for the poor will, ultimately, largely depend on the degree to which the rules of trade incorporate the protections of international human rights law.

4.1.3 'Human rights has no part in trade law'

The WTO's predecessor institution, known as GATT,[3] was designed to facilitate rules for a consistent approach to international trade. The intended social and economic benefits of this new rule-based system are open to debate and historical interpretation, but the intended method was clearly the formulation of legal principles relating solely to the manner in which a state treated the exports and imports of other states. Some commentators view this as a deliberate separation of functions from parallel international institutions focusing on social issues, such as the International Labour Organisation (ILO) and the United Nations (see, for example, Petersmann 2002: 622).

When the WTO came into existence on 1 January 1995, its proclaimed aim was to facilitate international trade and economic relations (Marrakech Agreement Establishing the World Trade Organisation 1994: Preamble):

> with a view to raising standards of living, ensuring full employment and a large and steadily growing volume of real income and effective demand, and expanding the production of and trade in goods and services, while allowing for the optimal use of the world's resources in accordance with the objective of sustainable development, seeking both to protect and preserve the environment and to enhance the means for doing so in a manner consistent with their respective needs and concerns at different levels of economic development.

This formulation of the institution's goals effectively acknowledges the impact of trade on the environment and development, while the potential impact of trade on human rights, particularly labour rights, is self-evident. Despite the fact that human rights are often severely affected in the pursuit of international trade, it is often argued that trade law, as the legal system regulating that pursuit, must not be utilised as a tool to prevent such abuses on the grounds that to do so 'could too easily destroy the fundamental attributes of the trading system' and 'would take the WTO another step towards becoming an enforcer of universal norms by the powerful on the weak' (Wolf 2001: 201).

3 The General Agreement on Tariffs and Trade (hereafter 'GATT') was a 1947 treaty intended to form the cornerstone of a new international trading system known as the International Trade Organisation or ITO. When political disputes prevented the ITO's constituent document, known as the Havana Charter, from being implemented, the contracting parties to the GATT and the secretariat administering that treaty formed a de facto institution, also generally referred to as GATT. The establishment of the WTO on 1 January 1995 displaced the GATT institution as the international organisation administering the GATT treaty, which became one of many multilateral treaties making up the WTO system.

However, these Knights of the Level Playing Field have several very deep chinks in their armour. The existing provisions of a number of international trade agreements already include, variously, overt human rights protection, principles borrowed from human rights discourse and mechanisms that could be used to protect and promote human rights. Some of these provisions are examined in the following section.

4.2 Existing human rights elements of international trade law

4.2.1 Intellectual property rights

George Soros has been quoted as saying, 'The WTO opened up a Pandora's box when it became involved in intellectual property rights. If intellectual property rights are a fit subject for the WTO, why not labor rights, or human rights?' (quoted in Alston 2002: 818). Indeed, intellectual property rights can be characterised as human rights, considering that Article 15(1)(c) of the ICESCR explicitly recognises the right 'to benefit from the protection of the moral and material interests resulting from any scientific, literary or artistic production of which he is the author'. In contrast to the rest of the WTO regime, which deals exclusively with states, the Agreement on Trade-Related Aspects of Intellectual Property Rights (TRIPs Agreement) recognises and protects the rights of persons (including corporations). In so doing, the WTO departs somewhat from its position as a purely intergovernmental organisation, begging the question of where the line should be drawn concerning the types of individual rights that should be protected by an international trade organisation. What is more, the objectives of the provisions protecting intellectual property under the WTO are the very antithesis of the trade-barrier-removal objectives of the WTO itself. The TRIPs is therefore, in essence, one mighty exception to market liberalisation.

The inclusion of the TRIPs Agreement within the suite of WTO agreements is even more fascinating when one considers that it created little in the way of new rights and obligations. Instead, it attempted to bring together the existing international norms of intellectual property from instruments such as the Berne Convention for the Protection of Literary and Artistic Works 1886 (revised 1971) and the Paris Convention for the Protection of Industrial Property 1883 (revised 1967) under the authoritative umbrella of the WTO, together with the enforcement mechanisms of its dispute settlement system (Weissman 1996).

Let us consider the arguments of those who decry a human rights approach within the WTO against the backdrop of the inclusion of the TRIPs Agreement. First, the intergovernmental character of the organisation has been argued to preclude the recognition of individual rights (see, for example, Lim 2001), but the TRIPs Agreement has evaded that problem. Second, it is argued that the existence of strong international human rights treaties means that duplication within a trade organ is unnecessary and would unjustifiably complicate the WTO system.

Third, as it is an international organisation, the WTO's members are states, which are aware of their international legal obligations outside the WTO system and do not need them to be reinforced (Lim 2001). However, both of the latter arguments could apply to the international intellectual property regime that existed outside the international trade system for over a century before the formation of the WTO. The fourth and perhaps most commonly asserted argument is that the WTO is a specialist trade body that lacks the expertise for the effective protection and realisation of human rights, which task is better left to the International Labour Organisation in the case of labour rights and the specialist United Nations organs in the case of other human rights (Sampson 2001: 15). However, intellectual property is an area of law at least as specialised as human rights and which is administered at the international level by a specialist body, the World Intellectual Property Organisation (WIPO). The pre-existence of WIPO, however, did not dissuade the WTO from incorporating intellectual property rights into its own international trade system.

The protection of intellectual property rights in the course of trade predominantly benefits corporations as the holders of intellectual property in the most research-intensive sectors (and therefore the sectors where intellectual property is most valuable) such as chemicals and pharmaceuticals, electronics and information technology. Thus, free trade and the actions of states and entities engaged in trade are restrained by the requirement to protect the special interests of a particular class of non-state actors, namely the holders of intellectual property, using a rights framework. That there are sound economic and social reasons for protecting intellectual property in the course of international trade, particularly to provide an incentive for ongoing research and development, is not disputed. The point is that none of the arguments that are frequently deployed against proposals to incorporate human rights into trade law has prevented the restriction of free trade to protect one narrow class of rights that are profoundly affected by trade. The continued application of those arguments to prevent the incorporation of rules to protect other rights that are similarly profoundly affected by trade, such as labour rights, thus assumes an element of farce in the absence of a strong argument for why the different classes of rights (or indeed the classes of rights-holders) should be distinguished. In extension of Soros's enquiry, it might be asked why the protection of civil and political, economic, social and cultural rights is not also made an exception to the effects of free trade rules in the same way as intellectual property rights.

4.2.2 Non-discrimination

The underlying principle of trade law, like that of international human rights law, is the principle of non-discrimination: that is, to ensure that the protection and benefits bestowed by the particular legal system are universally available to the subjects of that system. The beneficiary of non-discrimination differs between the two fields: non-discrimination in trade law relates to the equal treatment of other states and their imports and exports, while in human rights law it operates to ensure the equal treatment of individuals or groups of individuals.

The major difference in the principle of non-discrimination as it is applied in the two legal systems is the focus on form on the one hand and effect on the other. Non-discrimination under human rights law 'does not envisage according equal treatment to everyone in all cases, but rather supports affirmative action in the interests of promoting the human rights of the poor and vulnerable' (UN High Commissioner for Human Rights 2002: paragraph 59). It is therefore possible that the selective use of economic affirmative action by governments, for example by granting subsidies to social service providers in economically disadvantaged regions to ensure levels of access comparable to wealthier regions, might violate 'trade non-discrimination' despite being designed to facilitate 'human rights non-discrimination' through affirmative action (UN High Commissioner for Human Rights 2002: paragraphs 60-61).

International trade law provides numerous exceptions to the general obligation of non-discrimination, many of which are consistent with human rights goals, such as exceptions for measures to protect human life or health. Furthermore, trade law contains its own version of affirmative action for developing countries, known as 'special and differential treatment', including longer time-frames for implementing WTO obligations, the ability to be granted preferential treatment by developed countries, and the provision of technical assistance.[4] Stronger concessions are granted to the countries designated 'least developed countries',[5] and all special and differential treatment provisions are currently being reviewed with a view to making them stronger and more effective (WTO 2001a: paragraph 44).

This raft of permissible exceptions to the general principle of non-discrimination in trade law suggests that the introduction of established international human rights norms into the trade law system would not be as destructive of, or inconsistent with, the present trade law structure as it might appear. The choice of non-discrimination as the base paradigm for international trade law indicates some degree of commonality between its conceptualisation and that of international human rights law.

4.2.3 General exceptions to trade agreements

Most of the multilateral trade agreements composing the international trade system contain numerous exceptions to the general principles contained therein. The principal multilateral trade agreement, GATT, provides a number of general exceptions to the rules set out in the agreement in Article XX. That article permits states to take measures that might otherwise breach GATT for one of ten enumerated purposes, provided that such measures 'are not applied in a manner which would constitute a means of arbitrary or unjustifiable discrimination between countries where the same conditions prevail, or a disguised restriction on

4   See, for example, Article 66 of the TRIPs Agreement, Part IV of GATT, and Article 67 of the TRIPs Agreement, respectively.
5   The list of least developed countries (LDCs) is reviewed every three years by the United Nations Conference on Trade and Development (UNCTAD). Countries can therefore move in and out of the LDC category as their circumstances change. Following the 2000 review there were 49 LDCs, all in Africa, Asia and the Pacific, except for one (Haiti) in the Caribbean. Of those, 30 are currently WTO members (UNCTAD 2001b).

international trade'. Several of those purposes are relevant to the protection of human rights, but perhaps most relevant is the allowance of measures 'necessary to protect human, animal or plant life or health' (Article XX[b]). As far as it relates to humans, this exception for the protection of life and health is clearly capable of application to protect human rights. It is an exception that is repeated throughout the multilateral trade agreements, appearing in the Agreement on Technical Barriers to Trade (Articles 2.2 and 5.4), the General Agreement on Trade in Services, 'GATS' (Article XIV[b]), and the TRIPs Agreement (Article 27[2]), while the Agreement on the Application of Sanitary and Phytosanitary Standards owes its existence to the importance of protecting human health in the course of trade.

The right to life under international human rights law is broader than mere abstention from killing, as it also imposes obligations to take positive measures to improve life expectancy (UN Human Rights Committee 1982: paragraph 5). Similarly, the right to health includes positive obligations relating to the provision of healthcare and other conditions crucial to human health, 'such as access to safe and potable water and adequate sanitation, an adequate supply of safe food, nutrition and housing, [and] healthy occupational and environmental conditions' (UN Committee on Economic, Social and Cultural Rights, 'CESCR', 2000: paragraph 11). Thus measures to improve health and life expectancy, including placing obligations on corporations for the way they conduct their business, could conceivably be taken under the life and health exception to the relevant trade agreement.

Furthermore, the CESCR has noted that the right to health requires, *inter alia*, accessibility and affordability of health services to all, 'especially the most vulnerable or marginalized sections of the population' (UN CESCR 2000: paragraph 12). Given these expansive definitions of the rights to life and health, many different restrictions or forms of intervention might be justifiable, possibly including measures to make medicines more accessible for the poor or cross-subsidisation of water, health or housing costs in poor or isolated areas.

At the 2001 WTO Ministerial Conference in Doha, the WTO member states reiterated the legitimacy of 'life and health' exceptions, but also stressed the subjugation of those exceptions to the spirit of free trade (WTO 2001a: paragraph 6):

> We recognize that under WTO rules no country should be prevented from taking measures for the protection of human, animal or plant life or health, or of the environment at the levels it considers appropriate, subject to the requirement that they are not applied in a manner which would constitute a means of arbitrary or unjustifiable discrimination between countries where the same conditions prevail, or a disguised restriction on international trade, and are otherwise in accordance with the provisions of the WTO Agreements.

It is this hierarchy that is at the heart of the dilemma over the proper relationship between human rights and the regulation of international trade. The starting point is a collection of trade rules, with protection of life and health, among other purposes, constituting permissible exceptions to those rules, provided that the exceptions are consistent with other general trade law principles. The result is that free trade doctrine is both the alpha and the omega for the protection of human life and health in the course of trade. This is perhaps the main reason that health and life exceptions have been less effective at protecting human rights in trade than one might expect, prompting the UN High Commissioner for Human Rights to make the following observation in the context of GATS (UN High Commissioner for Human Rights 2002: paragraph 63):

> While a human rights approach would place the promotion of human rights at the centre of the objectives of GATS rather than as permitted exceptions, these links nonetheless provide an entry point for a human rights approach to [trade] liberalization and a means of ensuring that the essentially commercial objectives of GATS can be implemented with respect for human rights.

In short, we must deal with the position at present: namely, that human rights concerns, while not ignored, are mediated only through certain limited exceptions to the overriding free trade objectives of the WTO. Still, the very existence of the vast array of other non-human rights exceptions to general trade rules, including exceptions for the protection of public morals, for the conservation of exhaustible natural resources and for national security,[6] illustrates the potential flexibility of the free trade predisposition of international trade law. On that basis, there is little reason to suppose that explicit recognition of established international human rights norms,[7] as binding principles of international law, could not be incorporated into multilateral trade agreements in the future.

4.3 Human rights protection through reform of international trade law

4.3.1 Current round of negotiations

The WTO launched a new round of trade negotiations in Doha in November 2001, to be concluded by 1 January 2005. At the top of the agenda for these negotiations are the issues of agriculture, services, intellectual property and the relationship between trade and the environment (WTO 2001a). Each of these areas affects human rights to a significant extent. The new round of trade negotiations is therefore an opportunity to strengthen human rights protection within the respective regulatory spheres, but also poses a threat to human rights if practices affecting

---

6 See, *inter alia*: Articles XX(a), XX(g) and XXI of GATT; Article XIV of GATS; and Article 2.2 of the Agreement on Technical Barriers to Trade.
7 Precisely which human rights norms constitute 'established international human rights norms' for the purposes of incorporation into trade law is beyond the scope of this chapter. A reasonable interpretation is that, as a minimum, these are those human rights norms that constitute customary international law (and are therefore binding on all states), together with the core labour rights of non-discrimination at work, freedom from forced labour, freedom from oppressive child labour, freedom of association and the right to bargain collectively.

human rights are further entrenched without adequate protective measures. This section examines some of the issues in two of the most controversial aspects of the current round: the expansion of GATS and the availability of patented essential medicines to the poor under the TRIPs Agreement.

4.3.2 The General Agreement on Trade in Services

The delivery of social services by the state has historically been a major means for states to meet their obligations for the realisation of human rights. Health services, education, housing, welfare services and water utilities are just some of the services traditionally operated by governments that directly contribute towards the realisation of human rights. However, the global trend in recent times has been the privatisation of services such as these, leading to a dilemma for human rights responsibility: if water utilities are run by a private company, for example, who is responsible for ensuring that everyone has access to clean water?

The answer to that question should be that responsibility is plural, such that the corporation owes a duty to protect human rights, at least within its sphere of influence, which in this example might include an obligation not to make water inaccessible to a particular sector of the community. This, however, does not alter the fact that the state retains the ultimate duty under international human rights law to ensure that the manner of private service provision does not lead to a violation or deterioration of human rights (*Human Rights Quarterly* 1998). One of the most important parts of that duty is to maintain accessibility based on need, rather than market forces, as noted by the UN High Commissioner for Human Rights (2002: paragraph 45):

> Human rights law does not place obligations on States to be the sole provider of essential services. However, States must guarantee the availability, accessibility and adaptability/quality of essential services, including their supply, especially to the poor, vulnerable and marginalized, and to do so requires constant monitoring of policies and targeted action on behalf of independent regulators.

Where the provision of a social service to a geographically isolated or economically depressed region is not profitable for a private service provider, the state may need to intervene by imposing contractual conditions on the private operator or by providing subsidies or financial incentives to ensure accessibility.

GATS sets out a legal framework for international trade in services, part of which applies to all services (except those supplied exclusively by government on a non-commercial basis), and part of which applies only to sectors nominated by individual states. Contrary to some contemporary claims, GATS itself will not force governments to privatise any particular service (although pressure to do so could conceivably be applied by other countries, perhaps through cross-trading of positions on other agreements). However, once a service has been privatised and opened up to international competition through the nomination of that service under GATS, the trade rules of non-discrimination will apply, which could pose a threat to the ability of states to provide selective subsidies, determined by need, in order to maintain accessibility and discharge their human rights obligations.

In the ongoing negotiations on an extended GATS, WTO members should bear in mind the essential role of subsidies and other selective regulations in relation to services that affect human rights. The effective caveat on these would violate the human rights obligations of WTO member states (UN High Commissioner for Human Rights 2002: paragraphs 69-70).

4.3.3 Access to essential medicines under the TRIPs Agreement

The standardised patent protection afforded by the TRIPs Agreement, described above, provides useful protection to new inventions, purportedly providing an incentive for ongoing research and development, by granting an effective monopoly to the patent holder for 20 years in all jurisdictions where the patent is registered (TRIPs Agreement: Articles 28 and 33). In the case of medicines for chronic diseases, especially HIV/AIDS and tuberculosis, the effective monopoly for patented drugs could mean that sufferers in poor countries cannot access essential life-saving treatments because of patent-inflated prices, clearly contradicting the importance of access to treatment under the right to health, discussed above. This has caused the issue of access to patented essential medicines under the TRIPs Agreement to become an issue of major concern and engagement by developing countries and NGOs.

In November 2001, the WTO ministerial conference reaffirmed the legitimacy of certain exceptions to blanket patent protection under the TRIPs Agreement (WTO 2001b), the most important of which, for the case of essential medicines, is the permissibility of compulsory licensing. This would permit a generic manufacturer to produce the relevant drug under a state-issued licence without the consent of the patent holder. This generally results in much cheaper medicines, since the cost of research and development does not need to be recovered by the licensee and the lack of monopoly protection prevents artificial inflation. However, Article 31(f) of the TRIPs Agreement only allows compulsory licensing 'predominantly for the supply of the domestic market', which necessarily precludes all but a few developing countries and all 'least developed countries', as they lack pharmaceutical manufacturing capacity and would need to rely on imports of generic drugs. Although WTO members failed to meet the 2002 deadline for resolving this problem, a plan to allow the import of generic drugs with the consent of both the importing and exporting states was agreed among 25 WTO members at an informal meeting in Sydney in November 2002 (Kerin *et al.* 2002). However, this plan has attracted criticism from some NGOs, as the requirement that both the importing and exporting countries agree to override the relevant drug patent could easily be frustrated by pressure from industrialised countries, particularly the United States and the European Union (Oxfam and Médecins Sans Frontières 2002).

While the entirety of the issue of access to medicines under the TRIPs Agreement is yet to be fully developed, this snapshot serves to illustrate that it is possible to incorporate measures for the realisation of human rights into trade agreements—even an agreement that is itself an exception to the principle of free trade—and that the international community is prepared to demand such action. A human rights approach to international trade law, while not explicitly embraced, was certainly encouraged by the WTO Ministerial Council when it declared on this issue (WTO 2001b: paragraph 4): 'We affirm that the Agreement can and should be interpreted and implemented in a manner supportive of all WTO members' right to protect public health and, in particular, to promote access to medicines for all.'[8]

4.3.4 Other aspects of the current round of negotiations

A number of other areas under negotiation in the current round could potentially have a profound effect on human rights. Chief among these is agriculture, in which attempts to phase out agricultural subsidies, particularly by the United States and the European Union, could improve the economic well-being of farming communities in developing countries by increasing commodity prices and improving market access, but could also have the effect of increasing food costs in developing countries. Negotiations on agricultural trade therefore pose challenges to the realisation of the right to a decent standard of living and the right to food, among others. Other areas of the current round of negotiations of particular relevance to human rights include the relationship between trade and environmental agreements and the examination of the principle of sustainable development (WTO 2001a).

4.3.5 The dispute settlement process

The WTO dispute settlement system, which is capable of enforcing binding decisions backed by economic sanctions,[9] is central to the perception of the WTO as a powerful institution compared with other international treaty-monitoring bodies, none of which has effective powers of enforcement. It is also one of the main reasons why advocates of 'non-trade issues', such as human rights and environmental protection, are so keen to have international legal principles from their respective fields recognised within the WTO system.

Disputes can arise where one WTO member state alleges that the action taken by another member state violates provisions of a WTO agreement, thereby depriving the complainant state of the 'benefits' it could expect under the agreement (Jackson 2000: 173). The primary method of dispute resolution is 'consultations' between the disputing states facilitated by the WTO, followed by mediation (Dispute Settlement Understanding [DSU]: Articles 4 and 5). When a dispute

8 Note, however, that the right referred to is expressed as a right of *members* (i.e. states) to protect public health, rather than a right of people in general to the highest attainable standard of health, as expressed in international human rights law.

9 The Understanding on Rules and Procedures Governing the Settlement of Disputes, Annex 2 to the Marrakech Agreement (hereafter the 'Dispute Settlement Understanding'), Article 3(7), provides that the hierarchy of outcomes of the dispute settlement process in a case where a violation is established is, in order of preference, the withdrawal of the offending measures or regulations, or if that is not immediately feasible, the payment of voluntarily negotiated compensation to the 'injured' state, or as a last resort, the 'suspension of concessions' in relation to the other party (in other words, retaliatory trade discrimination against the other state).

remains unresolved, it can be referred to a dispute settlement panel, which assesses the case in a quasi-judicial manner and makes recommendations to the Dispute Settlement Body, made up of all the member states of the WTO (DSU: Articles 6 and 12 and Annex 3). The panel's report will automatically be adopted and therefore become binding on the disputing states unless the Dispute Settlement Body decides by consensus not to adopt it, or if one of the parties gives notice of its intention to appeal to the Appellate Body (DSU: Article 16[4]).

In the dispute settlement system, as with all elements of the WTO, only states are recognised actors. This means that private actors—individuals and corporations alike—cannot bring a complaint or be required to defend a complaint. In reality, it is these private actors, whether as individual entities or as a group such as an industry sector, who are most likely to be injured, or otherwise affected, by conduct that violates WTO rules. As such, the underlying reality of WTO disputes is often a complainant state bringing a complaint on behalf of a corporation or a group of corporations based in that state whose economic interests have been adversely affected by the policies or regulations of the respondent state, which were usually taken to protect competing corporations in its own country. WTO disputes in such cases could therefore be characterised as a dispute between private trading enterprises, each represented by its own state. The importance of a particular corporation or industry sector to a government, in political and/or economic terms, is therefore of great significance in determining whether a grievance ends up within the WTO dispute settlement system. To be sure, there are generally legitimate reasons for the state's involvement, such as the consequences for employees of the relevant company or sector, or the fear of setting an unfavourable precedent of acquiescence over violations of trade rules. However, the centrality of corporations to the dispute settlement process should not be overlooked.

It is important to recognise that many of the elements of trade law that effectively curtail the ability to protect human rights arise not from the texts of the relevant multilateral treaties, but from their interpretation during the dispute settlement process. Among these is the zealously restricted reading of the terms 'like products' and 'necessary', which, respectively, limit the ability of states to differentiate between products on the basis of the way in which they are made (such as the observance of minimum labour standards),[10] or to go beyond minimalist measures to achieve an objective such as protecting life or health.[11]

10 See, for example, *United States—Restrictions on Imports of Tuna* (1994) 33 International Legal Materials 936, commonly known as the 'second Tuna/Dolphin case', where the GATT panel condemned United States legislation that differentiated between tuna products originating in different countries, depending on whether the relevant country used dolphin-friendly harvesting methods. The principle that 'like products' cannot be distinguished merely on the basis of 'process and production methods' would clearly prevent a country from banning the import of products manufactured with poor labour standards, such as the use of child labour or slave labour, although a trade dispute on those facts has never been brought before the WTO or the GATT panel.

11 See, for example, *Thailand—Restrictions on Importation of and Internal Taxes on Cigarettes* (1991) 30 International Legal Materials 1122, where the GATT panel held that a measure 'necessary to protect human life or health' meant the least trade-restrictive measure available that would achieve that result, thus holding that a ban on the importation of cigarettes was not 'necessary', as less trade-restrictive health measures could have been

Such blinkered interpretations are exacerbated—or perhaps facilitated—by the make-up of dispute settlement panels exclusively by trade experts (DSU: Article 8[1]). Panels are entitled to seek information from any relevant source and to consult experts in specialised fields (DSU: Article 13), but this provision is generally only used in the case of scientific or technical aspects of a dispute. It has never been used to consult an expert body such as the World Health Organisation or the ILO, for example, on the effectiveness or appropriateness of disputed trade-affecting measures relating to health or labour standards or the relative merits of alternative options. However, the Appellate Body in the 'Shrimp/Turtle' case held that this authority allowed dispute panels to accept and consider unsolicited material at its discretion, including so-called '*amicus curiae* briefs' from non-governmental organisations.[12] This development may help to broaden what has hitherto been a fairly insular trade focus in the WTO dispute settlement system.

This brief exploration of some aspects of the dispute settlement system immediately suggests a number of reforms that could be adopted to take better account of human rights, none of which requires amendment of any treaty, but merely a change in approach or, at most, an authoritative interpretation by the WTO.[13] These include a broader interpretation of key terms to include non-trade considerations and more effective use of the authority to seek advice from human rights and other non-trade experts. Perhaps the most valuable reform for the protection of human rights affected by trade and commerce would be to interpret the trade agreements in a manner consistent with states' co-existing obligations under international law, including human rights law. The European Union's embracing of the jurisprudence of the European Court of Human Rights into its own essentially trade-based legal system is testimony to how this object can be achieved. Indeed, the dispute settlement process is intended to interpret the trade agreements 'in accordance with customary rules of interpretation of public international law' (DSU: Article 3[2]), which some commentators argue includes consideration of fundamental human rights at least as a contextual interpretative tool (Petersmann 2002: 645). Such a holistic approach is undermined by the narrow trade focus of the usual terms of reference for a WTO dispute and by prevailing WTO practice.

All WTO members have at least some obligations under international human rights treaties and all are bound by customary international human rights law. The consideration of provisions of trade law and trade-related actions in isolation from their human rights consequences and the corresponding obligations under inter-

used. This contrasts with *European Communities—Measures Affecting Asbestos and Asbestos-Containing Products*, Report of the Appellate Body 12 March 2001, WTO document no. WT/DS135/AB/R, where the Appellate Body held that a French ban on the import of asbestos products was necessary to protect public health and that 'controlled use' of asbestos would not achieve the same objective.

12   *United States—Import Prohibition of Certain Shrimp and Shrimp Products* ('Shrimp/Turtle' case), Report of the Appellate Body, 12 October 1998, WTO document no. WT/DS58/AB/R, paragraph 108.

13   The Marrakech Agreement, Article IX(2), empowers the Ministerial Conference or the General Council of the WTO—both of which comprise a representative from all member states—to adopt an interpretation of any of the WTO multilateral agreements by a three-quarters majority.

national human rights law risks violating those human rights obligations. Such an approach potentially violates the legal obligations of all WTO member states to guarantee human rights and to protect people within their jurisdiction from human rights abuses, including abuses carried out in the course of international trade as well as abuses resulting from the acts or omissions of corporations.

4.3.6 The road ahead: some stumbling blocks

It might be argued that it is not only in the context of the dispute resolution process that trade law should pay heed to the co-existing obligations under international human rights law. The UN High Commissioner for Human Rights (2002: paragraph 5) notes that: 'whatever the human rights treaty obligations undertaken by particular States, WTO members have concurrent human rights obligations under international law and should therefore promote and protect human rights during the negotiation and implementation of international rules on trade liberalization'.

In other words, ongoing negotiations of multilateral trade agreements ought to be conducted with an awareness of international human rights norms and agreements formulated in a manner that does not conflict with them, but makes a positive contribution towards the realisation of human rights. There is no doubt that the promotion of economic activity, especially in developing countries, can improve the realisation of human rights, although such positive outcomes are not automatic and require great care in terms of instituting safeguards and of monitoring the situation. This is the challenge for the so-called 'Development Round' of WTO negotiations currently under way.

There are two traditional bogeymen threatening an enlightened human rights approach to international trade law: namely, 'disguised protectionism' and 'comparative advantage'. The former is a fear that industrialised countries will manipulate any newly broadened ability to block human rights-violating trade in order to protect their own industries from competition. Unfortunately, the history of selective enthusiasm of industrialised countries for links between trade and the environment suggests that there is some basis for this fear (Figueres Olsen *et al.* 2001), including and especially in respect of the broad protection of that most commercialised of individual human rights—intellectual property—under the elaborate TRIPs Agreement.

The second threat is related, but is perhaps more relevant to multinational corporations. Briefly, the theory of comparative advantage dictates that economic activity of a particular kind will be attracted to the location where that activity is most efficient. In the case of industries that can move from place to place (as opposed to extractive industries, for example), efficiency can include the relative cost of labour or the costs of compliance with environmental, industrial or other regulations. It is therefore possible that a country that fails to implement its human rights obligations, including maintaining minimum labour standards, would have a comparative advantage over a country whose human rights observance imposed costs on corporations. Comparative advantage is vigorously guarded by developing countries, particularly in the case of labour costs, as they see it as their only chance to compete successfully with wealthier countries, thereby increasing the prosperity of their country and possibly improving the potential realisation of human rights of the general population (Mehta and Singh 2001).

This is a difficult debate which is beyond the scope of this chapter. For present purposes, it should be noted that the issue of comparative advantage has long been an obstacle to the inclusion of social and environmental concerns in international trade, as illustrated by this declaration by the First Ministerial Conference of the WTO in 1996 (WTO 1996: paragraph 4):

> We renew our commitment to the observance of internationally recognized core labour standards . . . We reject the use of labour standards for protectionist purposes, and agree that the comparative advantage of countries, particularly low-wage developing countries, must in no way be put into question.

In our view, comparative advantage, like all economic principles, must be subject to the universal obligation to protect and promote human rights. An advantage derived from a violation of fundamental human rights cannot be a legitimate competitive advantage (Joseph 1999: 171). The question of precisely where the line of legitimacy for a comparative advantage ought to be drawn, however, remains to be answered.

4.4 Conclusion

Our foregoing argument, contemplating an international solution to the global issue of human rights violations by corporations, is premised on the primacy of human rights law as grounded in the United Nations Charter[14] and reaffirmed in countless international instruments and resolutions. In considering other legal systems that might be deployed in support of human rights in the course of international commercial operations, the logical starting point is international trade law: the system governing the sphere in which multinational corporations operate and the source of many of their benefits.

Central to the options that we have canvassed in this chapter for human rights protection in trade law are questions of the feasibility of alterations to international trade law. These include how to interpret trade law provisions subject to the human rights obligations of states and corporations alike, and how to incorporate substantive amendments such as a new general exception to allow 'measures necessary to ensure compliance with recognised human rights standards' (or wording to a similar effect).

We recognise that reform of international trade law is but one option and we do not deny the importance of other means of ensuring human rights protection in

---

14 The United Nations Charter nominates two purposes: namely, the maintenance of peace and the protection and promotion of human rights (Article 1 paragraphs [1] and [2]-[3], respectively), which ends are to be served by all facets of international relations and international law.

the global commercial realm. Such other options might include: direct corporate liability under international human rights law; the extension of indirect state liability for direct actions by corporations; expanded home-state jurisdiction (through both extraterritorial legislation and curial acceptance of jurisdiction) to litigate or prosecute human rights violations occurring in host states; and stronger complaints and enforcement mechanisms for existing initiatives regarding human rights and multinational corporations (see, for example, Ward 2001; Kinley 2002). Another important step might be the development of alternative dispute resolution for victims of human rights abuses and accused corporations, although this is perhaps more likely to develop out of business practice than from formal legal reform.

While these alternative options are subjects for future analyses, this chapter has sought to demonstrate that incorporating human rights into international trade law as a method for ensuring corporate responsibility is not only possible, but is far more straightforward than is generally thought, since human rights concepts are already selectively applied in trade law for different purposes. Whether political will can take advantage of this legal opportunity is another question altogether.

Treaties and international instruments

Agreement on the Application of Sanitary and Phytosanitary Measures 1994, Annex 1A to the Marrakech Agreement, (1996) *British Treaty Series* 54.

Agreement on Technical Barriers to Trade 1994, Annex 1A to the Marrakech Agreement, (1996) *British Treaty Series* 11.

Agreement on Trade-Related Aspects of Intellectual Property Rights 1994 ('TRIPs Agreement'), Annex 1C to the Marrakech Agreement, (1994) *International Legal Materials* 33: 1,197.

Berne Convention for the Protection of Literary and Artistic Works 1886 (revised 1971), (1980) *United Nations Treaty Series* 1,161: 31.

General Agreement on Tariffs and Trade 1947 (GATT 47), (1950) *United Nations Treaty Series* 55: 194.

General Agreement on Tariffs and Trade 1994 (GATT 94), Annex 1A to the Marrakech Agreement, (1994) *International Legal Materials* 33: 1,154.

General Agreement on Trade in Services 1994 (GATS), Annex 1B to the Marrakech Agreement, (1994) *International Legal Materials* 33: 1,167.

International Covenant on Economic, Social and Cultural Rights 1966 ('ICESCR'), (1976) *United Nations Treaty Series* 993: 3.

Marrakech Agreement Establishing the World Trade Organization 1994, (1994) *International Legal Materials* 33: 1,144.

Paris Convention for the Protection of Industrial Property 1883 (revised 1967), (1972) *United Nations Treaty Series* 828: 305.

The Understanding on Rules and Procedures Governing the Settlement of Disputes 1994 ('Dispute Settlement Understanding'), Annex 2 to the Marrakech Agreement, (1994) *International Legal Materials* 33: 1,226.

5

Human rights and business
An ethical analysis

Denis G. Arnold
University of Tennessee, USA

Ethical concerns are at the core of the dispute concerning global labour practices. Critics charge multinational enterprises (MNEs) with the inhumane and unjust treatment of workers in developing nations. Economists retort that satisfying the demands of these critics will result in fewer jobs in developing nations, thereby reducing social welfare. In order to evaluate these and other claims properly, it is first necessary to provide an analysis of the ethical obligations of MNEs regarding global labour practices.

One set of ethical norms that is a prominent feature of contemporary public discourse, especially as it pertains to international affairs, is that of human rights. The promulgation of the United Nations Universal Declaration of Human Rights, together with the advocacy of organisations such as Amnesty International and Human Rights Watch, has led to the widespread acceptance of human rights as a basic tool of moral evaluation by individuals of widely divergent political and religious beliefs. Increasingly, the language of human rights is a prominent feature of debates regarding globalisation and global labour practices. This chapter explains how an understanding of basic human rights can help MNE managers to produce morally innovative solutions to global labour challenges. The chapter provides both a justification of the rights to freedom and well-being, and an application of those rights to the circumstances of MNE workers. Other important human rights issues confronting MNEs, such as the morally appropriate stance to take towards regimes that engage in systematic human rights violations, are necessarily beyond the scope of this essay.

The chapter is divided into four main sections. The first section introduces the challenge that many MNE managers confront regarding global labour practices via a hypothetical example. The second section provides a justification of the human rights to freedom and well-being, while the third explains what it means to respect the freedom and well-being of workers. The final section summarises the positive impact that MNEs can have on the welfare of workers in developing nations.

5.1 Global labour practices

Suppose that an MNE sourcing manager must choose between two offshore factories that wish to serve as suppliers. Both suppliers operate factories in a developing nation with an emerging democracy that has completed two rounds of free and fair elections. Workers in this nation have recently become entitled to freedom of association, collective bargaining, and a national healthcare pro-gramme funded by social security payroll deductions. However, the ability of government officials to enforce these laws is minimal, as the enforcement agencies are underfunded and understaffed, while residual corruption undermines the enforcement of labour laws. Furthermore, there is a well-grounded concern on the part of government officials that the enforcement of existing labour laws will result in higher costs for MNEs, and that because of this MNEs will place fewer orders in its domestic manufacturing sector.

The two suppliers submit bids, together with product samples. Both sets of samples meet minimum quality standards. However, the bid of Supplier A is 20% more than the bid of Supplier B. The bid differential is attributable to the fact that Supplier A has substantially higher employee costs than Supplier B. Supplier A provides workers with legally required overtime pay; deducts and pays to the government social security payroll taxes; provides bonuses for meeting specified quality standards; provides annual pay rises; provides opportunities to workers for promotion; and has invested in health and safety measures in order to prevent basic risks to the lives and health of employees while at work. Employees of Supplier A who work 50–60 hours per week are able to avoid conditions of overall poverty as defined by the United Nations (see Table 5.1).

Types of poverty	Deficiencies	Measures
• Extreme poverty (also known as absolute poverty)	• Lack of income necessary to satisfy basic food needs	• Minimum caloric intake and a food basket that meets that requirement
• Overall poverty (also known as relative poverty)	• Lack of income necessary to satisfy basic non-food needs	• Ability to secure shelter, energy, transportation, and basic healthcare
• Human poverty	• Lack of basic human capabilities	• Access to goods, services, and infrastructure

Table 5.1 Definitions of poverty

Source: UNDP 2000b

Supplier B, on the other hand, does not pay workers as required for overtime; deducts but does not turn over social security payroll taxes to the government; provides no bonuses or regular pay rises; provides no opportunities for promotion (instead making exclusive use of foreign nationals as supervisors); and has taken no special measures to prevent basic risks to the lives and health of employees. Employees of Supplier B who work 50–60 hours per week typically live in conditions of extreme poverty.

It is platitudinous, but necessary, to observe that different individuals may agree that the correct choice is obvious, yet disagree about *which* choice is correct. Various interested parties—factory workers, economists, MNE shareholders, customers and so on—will have their own distinct perspectives. For example, some labour or human rights activists might reason as follows: 'The very existence of Supplier A is unusual, as most factories in developing countries better fit the description of Supplier B. The opportunity to work with supplier A should be embraced by the MNE, since doing so will promote human and labour rights. The additional costs are minimal for an MNE.' Some MNE sourcing managers, or individuals sympathetic to the arguments put forth by such managers, might reason as follows: 'Supplier B is the norm in nearly all developing countries. It is the responsibility of national governments to enforce existing labour laws uniformly. When governments do not enforce such laws uniformly, an MNE cannot be expected to bear the costs of adhering to local labour laws, let alone the costs of providing the comfortable working conditions and high wages present in supplier A. To do so would place the MNE at a competitive disadvantage.'

What more can be said in defence of the view that the MNE manager should choose Supplier A? In order to answer this question properly, it is necessary to provide a justification and explanation of basic human rights. It is to this task that we now turn.

5.2 The justification of human rights

In order to think about human rights in a meaningful way, it is necessary to answer certain philosophical questions about their nature. Three of the most basic questions are the following: How can human rights be justified? What specific human rights exist? How do human rights differ from other rights, such as legal rights? Let us consider each question in turn.

Human rights are rights enjoyed by humans not because we are members of the species *Homo sapiens*, but because fully functional members of our species are persons. Personhood is a metaphysical category that may or may not be unique to *Homo sapiens*. To be a person one must be capable of reflecting on one's desires at a second-order level, and one must be capable of acting in a manner consistent with one's considered preferences (Dworkin 1988; Frankfurt 1988). First-order desires are the assortment of desires that occupy one's conscious mind and compete for one's attention. Second-order desires are desires about those first-order desires. When one embraces a particular first-order desire at a second-order level, it becomes a preference. A mundane example will help to illustrate this concept. Each of us is likely to have found ourselves staring at a bedside clock after having turned off an early morning alarm. Lying comfortably in bed, one might reflect on one's immediate desires: to get up and go for a run; to get up and prepare for an early morning meeting; or to roll over and return to sleep. The process of reflecting on these competing desires takes place at a second-order level of consciousness. It is the capacity to reflect on one's competing desires and to act in a manner consistent with our second-order preferences that distinguishes persons from mere animals. This is not to say that one cannot sometimes fail to act in a manner consistent with one's better judgment and still be regarded as a person. Indeed, most of us are intimately familiar with such weakness of the will. The point is that we enjoy this capacity, and we are capable of acting in a manner consistent with this capacity. Furthermore, if a human were constitutionally incapable of acting in a manner consistent with his or her second-order preferences, he or she would not be properly described as a person. It is in this sense that the idea of personhood is properly understood as metaphysical rather than biological (Melden 1977).

The derivation of human rights from the concept of personhood is one of the most important accomplishments of 20th-century philosophy. Much of the most important foundational research on this subject has been produced by the philosopher Alan Gewirth. In his book *Reason and Morality* (1978), Gewirth provides a rigorous and detailed justification of human rights. As with any major philosophical theory, Gewirth's defence of human rights has been criticised on various grounds. However, Deryck Beyleveld has provided a masterful and persuasive defence of Gewirth's arguments concerning the justification of human rights in his own important work on the subject (Beyleveld 1991). It is sometimes argued that human rights cannot be justified without appealing to specific religious or legal traditions. To see that this is not the case, it will be helpful to provide a summary of Gewirth's philosophical defence of human rights.

Gewirth begins with the idea that every person regards his or her purposes as good according to his or her own criteria. By rising each morning and pursuing their own individual goals, individuals demonstrate in a practical way those things that they value.[1] Such actions are possible only in so far as the necessary conditions of one's acting to achieve one's purposes are satisfied. In other words, via the act of pursuing their individual aims, individuals demonstrate that they value the necessary conditions of action. The necessary conditions of action are freedom and well-being. Without freedom and well-being, one cannot pursue those things that one values. Freedom is here understood as controlling one's behaviour by one's unforced choice while having knowledge of relevant circumstances. Possessing well-being entails having the general abilities and conditions required for a person to be able to act in a manner consistent with his or her considered, or second-order, preferences. Anyone who pursues a particular good must, on pain of

---

1 One might object to this view on the grounds that some people pursue ends that they themselves do not regard as valuable. Such an objection fails to undermine Gewirth's point since, on his account, one demonstrates that one regards some ends as valuable in so far as one pursues that end. Here Gewirth's position may be regarded as consistent with those social scientists who are interested in studying not what people say they value, but what they demonstrate they value through their actions.

contradiction, claim that they have a right to freedom and well-being. As such, all persons must accept that others have rights to freedom and well-being. Gewirth puts the matter this way (Gewirth 1978: 63):

> Since the agent [or person] regards as necessary goods the freedom and well-being that constitute the generic features of his successful action, he logically must hold that he has rights to these generic features, and he implicitly makes a corresponding rights claim.

Gewirth is not arguing, as some might think, that because persons require freedom and well-being in order to function, they are thereby entitled to freedom and well-being (MacIntyre 1984). Such an argument, one grounded in *empirical necessity*, would not be convincing because it does not follow from the fact that one requires something that one has a right to that thing. While Gewirth's argument does have an empirical component, it is properly understood as a transcendental argument in the Kantian tradition. A transcendental argument is one that establishes the truth of a proposition by appealing to necessary conditions of human experience. Gewirth's argument is that, as a matter of *rational consistency*, a person must acknowledge that she is a purposive being, and that the pursuit of her ends requires freedom and well-being. Hence she must claim a right to freedom and well-being. To do otherwise would be irrational. Because all other persons share these qualities, she must—again, as a matter of rational consistency—ascribe these rights to all other beings. To deny that persons have the right to freedom and well-being is to deny that one is a purposive being. Since the denial is a purposive act, it contradicts the proposition being asserted. In this way, Gewirth provides a deep and satisfying justification for human rights. Because the justification is grounded in rational reflection on the human condition, it can be embraced by individuals of diverse religious faiths and different cultural identities.

At this point in our discussion, it is worthwhile to consider an objection to the foregoing argument concerning human rights. This criticism stems from the observation that the idea of human rights emerged from the Western philosophical tradition, but is taken to be universal in its applicability. The claim is then made that human rights are of less importance in the value systems of other cultures. For example, it is argued that 'Asian values' emphasise order, discipline and social harmony, as opposed to individual rights. In this view, the freedom and well-being of individuals should not be allowed to interfere with the harmony of the community, as might be the case, for example, when workers engage in disruptive collective action in an effort to secure their rights. This view might also be used to defend the claim that the moral norms that govern Asian factory operations should emphasise order and discipline, not freedom and well-being.

Several points may be made in reply to this objection. First, Asia is a large region with a vast and heterogeneous population. As Amartya Sen and others have argued, to claim that all, or even most, Asians share a uniform set of values is to impose a level of uniformity that does not exist at present and has not existed in the past (Donnely 1999; Sen 1999a, 2000; Tatsuo 1999). Second, in secular, democratic Asian societies such as India, respect for individual rights has a long tradition. Indeed, there are significant antecedents in the history of the civilisations of the Indian subcontinent that emphasise individual freedom and well-being. For example, in the 3rd century BCE, the Emperor Ashoka granted his citizens the freedom to embrace whatever religious or philosophical system they might choose, while at the same time he emphasised the importance of tolerance and respect for philosophical and religious beliefs different from one's own (Sen 1999a). Third, even if it was the case that Asian cultures shared a uniform set of values that de-emphasised human rights, this would not by itself provide good reasons for denying or disrespecting the rights to freedom and well-being. This is because the justification of human rights provided above is grounded in rational arguments that are valid across cultures. Jack Donnely makes a similar point in his recent defence of universal human rights (Donnely 1999: 87):

> One of the things that makes us human is our capacity to create and change our culture. Cultural diversity has in recent years increasingly come to be valued in itself. Westerners have in recent centuries been especially insensitive in their approach to such differences. Nonetheless, the essential insight of human rights is that the worlds we make for ourselves, intentionally and unintentionally, must conform to relatively universal requirements that rest on our common humanity and seek to guarantee equal concern and respect from the state for every person.

The critic is likely to retort that such a view reflects Western prejudices grounded in Enlightenment ideals. This response is unpersuasive. Diverse intellectual traditions have emphasised the importance of values derived from reason, rather than mythology, traditionalism, mere sentiment, or some other source. For example, in the 16th century the Moghul Emperor Akbar wrote (Sen 2000: 37): 'The pursuit of reason and rejection of traditionalism are so brilliantly patent as to be above the need for argument. If traditionalism were proper, the prophets would merely have followed their own elders (and not come with new messages).'

Akbar arranged to have philosophers representing diverse religious and philosophical beliefs engage in rational discussions regarding the merits of their competing views, and sought to identify the most persuasive features of each view. In so doing, Akbar was able to emphasise the power and force of rational analysis. Given that a similar emphasis on rational analysis concerning values may be found in the histories of other non-Western cultures, the claim that such analysis is uniquely Western is unpersuasive.

Human rights are moral rights that apply to all persons in all nations, regardless of whether the nation in which a person resides acknowledges and protects those rights. It is in this sense that human rights are said to be *inalienable*. Human rights differ from legal rights in that, unlike legal rights, the existence of human rights is not contingent on any institution. Many nations grant their citizens certain constitutional or legal rights via foundational documents or legal precedent. However, the rights that are protected vary among nations. Some nations ensure that the rights of citizens are protected by effective policing and an independent judiciary. Frequently, however, poor citizens and disfavoured groups are not provided with the same level of protection for their legal rights as the economic and political elite. Persons who are deprived of their rights do not thereby cease to have those rights. As A.I. Melden has argued (Melden 1977: 167-68):

the complaint that persons are deprived of their human rights when, for example, they are subjected to forced indenture by their employers, is a complaint that their rights have been violated and implies, clearly, that they have rights they are unjustly prevented from exercising. If one were deprived of one's rights in the sense in which one would be deprived of things in one's physical possession by having them taken away, one would no longer have the rights, and there would be no grounds for the complaint. So it is with the denial of a person's right—this does not consist in denying that he has the right but, rather, in denying him, by withholding from him, that to which he has the right or the means or opportunity for its exercise.

Employers may deny employees their inalienable right to freedom and well-being, whether or not local governments are complicit, but in doing so they in no way diminish the legitimacy of the claims of their employees to those rights. However, by virtue of their failure to operate from the moral point of view, such employers succeed in diminishing their own standing in the community of rights holders.

5.3 Human rights and labour practices

We have seen how a right to freedom and a right to well-being can be justified. If persons have a right to freedom and well-being, then at a minimum other persons have an obligation to refrain from interfering with those rights. It is in this sense that rights entail corresponding duties on the part of other persons. What are the specific obligations or duties of MNE managers with respect to the freedom and well-being of employees and how are these obligations to be balanced against the obligations of managers to their employers?

Because freedom and well-being are basic rights, the obligation to respect those rights is equally basic. As such, no labour practices may be undertaken that will violate a worker's right to freedom and well-being. MNEs are in a unique position to ensure that basic rights are respected in the workplace by virtue of their power and the vast resources under their command. In the words of the United Nations:

> Society no longer accepts the view that the conduct of global corporations is bound only by the laws of the country they operate in. By virtue of their global influence and power, they must accept responsibility and be accountable for upholding high human rights standards (UNDP 2000b: 80).

MNEs typically have well-defined internal decision structures that provide an internal mechanism for enforcing human rights standards. The internal decision structure of an organisation comprises its offices and levels of responsibility, together with the rules that allow managers to differentiate between enterprise, level decisions and the decisions of individual employees (French 1979, 1995). For this reason, morally innovative managers are well positioned to play a constructive role in ensuring that the rights of workers in developing nations are respected.

MNE managers should regard respect for their employees' rights to freedom and well-being as constraints on the activities they undertake on behalf of their employers. However, the rights to freedom and well-being are very general. Greater specificity regarding the content of these rights must be provided. Let us begin with freedom. Previously we characterised freedom as controlling one's behaviour via one's unforced choice, while having knowledge of relevant circumstances. Gewirth provides a helpful summary of the content of the right to freedom (Gewirth 1982: 56-57):

> This consists in a person's controlling his actions and his partici-pation in transactions by his own unforced choice or consent and with knowledge of relevant circumstances, so that his behaviour is neither compelled nor prevented by the actions of other persons. Hence, a person's right to freedom is violated if he is subjected to violence, coercion, deception, or any other procedures that attack or remove his informed control of his behavior by his own unforced choice. This right includes having a sphere of personal autonomy and privacy whereby one is let alone by others unless and until he unforcedly consents to undergo their action.

Possessing freedom entails having the general abilities and conditions required for a person to be able to act in a manner consistent with his or her second-order preferences. A right to freedom, then, involves the right to pursue one's own goals and preferences without interference from others. Specifically, it includes control over one's own physical integrity, freedom of belief and expression, and freedom of association. Traditionally, the right to freedom is thought to be as extensive as is compatible with a like right to freedom for all. Such freedom is not, however, unlimited. It may be rightfully curtailed if a person's actions illegitimately infringe on the freedom or well-being of others.

The rights one enjoys as a human being are not unlimited in the sense that one is free to exercise all of them under any circumstances. Legitimate restrictions may be placed on the exercise of one's rights by both the state and private enterprise. It is, for example, not an illegitimate infringement of one's right to freedom of belief and expression if an employer prohibits proselytising on behalf of one's religious convictions while at work. Such activity is typically disruptive and as such incom-patible with the purposes for which employees are hired. Furthermore, employees are free to engage in such activity when they are not working. Restricting employee activity in this manner does not infringe on an employee's dignity as a person. There are, however, certain restrictions on employee freedom that always violate human dignity because they treat the employee as a tool rather than as a person. Control over one's physical integrity is one such example. This freedom could, for example, be violated by a rule that permitted only one bathroom break each day.

Several international covenants and conventions are available to MNEs inter-ested in specific guidance with respect to their global labour practices. For exam-ple, the Articles of the United Nations Universal Declaration of Human Rights (UDHR) (1948) provide specific examples of what it means to respect an employee's right to freedom at work (see Box 5.1). Articles 3, 4 and 5 provide a basis for the prohibition of all forced labour, indentured servitude, corporal punishment of employees by supervisors and seriously unsafe working conditions. Article 23,

- Article 3: Everyone has the right to life, liberty and security of person.
- Article 4: No one shall be held in slavery or servitude; slavery and the slave trade shall be prohibited in all their forms.
- Article 5: No one shall be subjected to torture or to cruel, inhuman or degrading treatment or punishment.
- Article 23, Section 4: Everyone has the right to form and to join trade unions for the protection of his interests.

Box 5.1 Articles of the UDHR concerning the right to freedom with special relevance to the obligations of MNEs to workers

Section 4 provides a basis for the prohibition of the termination of employees for organising or joining a trade union.

Now let us turn to well-being. As we have seen, well-being entails having the general abilities and conditions required for a person to be able to act autonomously. The most important component of well-being, and the one that we shall focus on here, is basic goods. Basic goods are the general physical and psychological capabilities necessary for human functioning. In recent years, the relationship between well-being and human functioning has received a great deal of attention from economists and philosophers. Some of the most important work on this topic has been produced by Amartya Sen (1985, 1987, 1999b) and Martha Nussbaum (2001). Their distinctive variety of quality of life assessment, known as the capabilities approach, has become increasingly influential. This is partly due to the fact that it has been adapted by the UNDP and has been incorporated into the UNDP *Human Development Reports* since 1993. The relationship between human functioning and well-being is usefully articulated by Sen (1985: 197-98):

> The primary feature of well-being can be seen in terms of how a person can 'function,' taking that term in a very broad sense. I shall refer to various doings and beings that come into this assessment as functionings. These could be activities (like eating or reading or seeing), or states of existence or being, e.g., being well nourished, being free from malaria, not being ashamed by the poverty of one's clothing or shoes (to go back to a question that Adam Smith discussed in his *Wealth of Nations*).

It is important to note that not all persons will have the same capacity to function well with the same goods. Variations in the transformation of goods into constituent elements of well-being will vary significantly among persons. For example, as noted by Sen (1985: 198-99):

> Take, for example, the consumption of food, on the one hand, and the functioning of being well nourished, on the other. The relationship between them varies with (1) metabolic rates, (2) body size, (3) age, (4) sex (and if a woman, whether pregnant or lactating), (5) activity levels, (6) medical services, (7) nutritional knowledge, and other influences.

Access to the basic goods necessary for human functioning does not mean that a person who enjoys the basic goods necessary to function well will do so. Two individuals may have access to the same goods necessary for each of them to achieve the same level of well-being, yet fail to do so because one of them made choices that reduced his or her ability to function well. For this reason, it is necessary to emphasise an individual's *capability* to function. What are these capabilities? Nussbaum (2001) identifies ten capabilities as necessary for humans to enjoy well-being (see Box 5.2). The list is itself the product of years of cross-cultural study and discussion and represents a sort of overlapping consensus on the part of individuals with widely disparate views of human life. Nussbaum is careful to point out both that the list is open-ended and that items on the list may be interpreted somewhat differently in different societies. However, each item on the list is of central importance and as such it must be regarded as a significant loss when a person falls below any one of the central areas.

The Articles of the UDHR provide a valuable resource for determining what it means for an employer to respect an employee's right to well-being (see Box 5.3). Article 23, Section 2 provides a basis for the prohibition of discrimination based on arbitrary characteristics such as race or sex. Article 23, Section 2 and Article 25, Section 1 provide a basis for paying employees wages that are consistent with living with dignity. They also provide a basis for thinking that it is the responsibility of MNEs to ensure that social security and other taxes are paid to appropriate governmental authorities. Article 24 provides a basis for the view that employees are entitled to wages adequate for a dignified standard of living without working extensive overtime hours.

Some individuals who are concerned with the welfare of workers in developing nations will disagree with the conclusion that MNE labour practices must not violate a worker's right to freedom and well-being. The claim is frequently made, with varying degrees of sophistication, that respecting employee rights will result in greater harm than good. For example, in a recent book, David Henderson argues that the expenditure by MNEs of corporate resources in the interest of human rights will result in workers being made worse off (Henderson 2001). Henderson's conclusion is shared by Ian Maitland who claims that 'attempts to improve on market outcomes may have unforeseen tragic consequences' for workers in developing nations (Maitland 2001: 603). The core argument of both Henderson and Maitland, as it pertains to formal sector workers in developing nations, is that the imposition of wages or labour standards greater than those demanded by the market will increase costs, and that this will inevitably lead to lay-offs and higher unemployment. How persuasive is this argument?

To see that voluntarily improving employee wages and working conditions will not inevitably lead to the 'tragic consequences' that Henderson and Maitland predict, consider the following points.[2] First, with regard to the lowest-paid formal-sector wage earners in developing countries, the assumption that productivity is independent of wage levels is mistaken. Put simply, workers whose minimum daily dietary requirements are met, and who have basic non-food needs met, will have more energy and better attitudes at work, will be less likely to come to work ill, and

---

2 For a more thorough reply to this objection, see Arnold and Bowie 2003.

1. **Life.** Being able to live to the end of a human life of normal length; not dying prematurely, or before one's life is so reduced as to not be worth living.

2. **Bodily health.** Being able to have good health, including reproductive health; to be adequately nourished; to have adequate shelter.

3. **Bodily integrity.** Being able to move freely from place to place; having one's bodily boundaries treated as sovereign, i.e. being able to be secure against assault, including sexual assault, child sexual abuse, and domestic violence; having opportunities for sexual satisfaction and for choice in matters of reproduction.

4. **Senses, imagination and thought.** Being able to use the senses, to imagine, think, and reason—and to do these things in a 'truly human' way, a way informed and cultivated by an adequate education, including, but by no means limited to, literacy and basic mathematical and scientific training. Being able to use imagination and thought in connection with experiencing and producing self-expressive works and events of one's own choice, religious, literary, musical and so forth. Being able to use one's mind in ways protected by guarantees of freedom of expression with respect to both political and artistic speech, and freedom of religious exercise. Being able to search for the ultimate meaning of life in one's own way. Being able to have pleasurable experiences, and to avoid non-necessary pain.

5. **Emotion.** Being able to have attachments to things and people outside of ourselves; to love those who love and care for us, to grieve at their absence; in general, to love, to grieve, to experience longing, gratitude and justified anger. Not having one's emotional development blighted by overwhelming fear and anxiety, or by traumatic events of abuse or neglect. (Supporting this capability means supporting forms of human association that can be shown to be crucial in their development.)

6. **Practical reason.** Being able to form a conception of the good and to engage in critical reflection about the planning of one's life. (This entails protection for the liberty of conscience.)

7. **Affiliation.**

   A Being able to live with and towards others, to recognise and show concern for other human beings, to engage in various forms of social interaction; to be able to imagine the situation of another and have compassion for that situation; to have the capability for both justice and friendship. (Protecting this capability means protecting institutions that constitute and nourish such forms of affiliation, and also protecting the freedom of assembly and political speech.)

   B Having the social bases of self-respect and non-humiliation; being able to be treated as a dignified being whose worth is equal to that of others. This entails, at a minimum, protections against discrimination on the basis of race, sex, sexual orientation, religion, caste, ethnicity or national origin. In work, being able to work as a human being, exercising practical reason and entering into meaningful relationships of mutual recognition with other workers.

8. **Other species.** Being able to live with concern for and in relation to animals, plants and the world of nature.

9. **Play.** Being able to laugh, play, to enjoy recreational activities.

10. **Control over one's environment.**

    A **Political.** Being able to participate effectively in political choices that govern one's life; having the right of political participation, protections of free speech and free association.

    B **Material.** Being able to hold property (both land and movable goods), not just formally but in terms of real opportunity; and having property rights on an equal basis with others; having the right to seek employment on an equal basis with others; having the freedom from unwarranted search and seizure.

Box 5.2 Central human functional capabilities

Source: Nussbaum 2001: 78-80

- Article 23(2): Everyone, without any discrimination, has the right to equal pay for equal work.
- Article 23(3): Everyone who works has the right to just and favourable remuneration ensuring for himself and his family an existence worthy of human dignity, and supplemented, if necessary, by other means of social protection.
- Article 24: Everyone has the right to rest and leisure, including reasonable limitation of working hours and periodic holidays with pay.
- Article 25(1): Everyone has the right to a standard of living adequate for health and well-being of himself and of his family, including food, clothing, housing and medical care and necessary social services, and the right to security in the event of unemployment, sickness, disability, widowhood, old age or other lack of livelihood in circumstances beyond his control.

Box 5.3 **Articles of the UDHR concerning the right to well-being with special relevance to the obligations of MNEs to workers**

will be absent with less frequency. Workers are thus likely to be more productive and loyal. Increased productivity resulting from better nutrition and increased employee loyalty alone may offset the cost of higher wages. The wage which, if reduced, would make the firm worse off because of a decrease in worker productivity is known as the efficiency wage. Firms that pay employees at rates higher than the efficiency wage may enjoy other economic advantages such as reduced training costs as a result of greater employee loyalty.

Second, it is economically feasible for MNEs to raise wages and improve working conditions in factories in developing economies without causing increases in unemployment. MNEs may *choose* to improve wages and working conditions while maintaining existing employment levels. Profit margins vary among products. For the manufacturers of brand-name retail goods, a significant increase in labour costs may be readily absorbed as an operating expense. Indeed, the expense may be offset by the value added to the good in so far as consumers demonstrate a preference for products produced under conditions in which the rights of workers are respected.

Third, there may be cases where increased labour costs are not offset by greater productivity, and where the increase in costs cannot be readily absorbed as an operating expense. For example, manufacturers of generic goods with low profit margins *may* find it difficult to simply absorb the cost of increased labour expenses. In such cases, the added cost of labour may instead be balanced by internal cost-cutting measures,[3] or it may be passed on to consumers via higher prices,[4] or it may

3 One set of obvious targets for expense reduction is the cost of supporting significant numbers of home-country managers in the country of the supplier. While some presence may be necessary, it will often be more cost-effective to employ host-country nationals in this capacity. Another attractive set of targets is executive perks. While such perks vary significantly among firms, it does appear morally inconsistent to argue that improving the welfare of the factory workers is cost-prohibitive while executive perks remain substantial.

4 Given the frequently fierce competition among the manufacturers of generic products

be passed on to the owners of the business enterprise via lower return on equity.[5] In such cases, the costs of respecting human rights must be regarded as a necessary condition of doing business. This point should not be problematic for anyone who recognises the existence of basic human rights. For in so far as we recognise the rights of other persons, we have an obligation to respect those rights. It is by acting in a manner that respects basic human rights that we raise ourselves above other species.

5.4 Conclusion

The vast majority of workers in most developing nations operate outside or at the periphery of formal employment relations. As formal-sector employment increases in these nations, MNEs that demonstrate respect for the rights of workers can be expected to have an influence on the local norms governing labour practices disproportionate to the number of workers that they actually employ. This is because they, together with morally innovative indigenous employers, will be setting the standard against which other employers must be measured. The result will be a substantially improved quality of life for the growing ranks of workers in the formal sector. Correspondingly, morally innovative MNEs and their suppliers can be expected to enjoy the most productive and loyal indigenous workers since they will be ranked among the most desirable employers. Furthermore, as increasing numbers of workers leave the informal sector in pursuit of better opportunities in the formal sector, less pressure will be exerted on the scarce productive resources of the informal sector. This should permit an enhanced standard of living for those remaining in the informal sector. Far from causing a decrease in overall social welfare by spurring unemployment, MNEs that demonstrate respect for worker rights are well positioned to enhance the welfare of citizens in developing nations.[6]

targeted at cost-conscious consumers, it may be difficult for one retailer to remain competitive while raising prices to cover increased labour costs, while others do not. For this reason, industry-wide standards concerning labour practices may prove valuable as a way of distributing costs equitably.

5   To keep investors informed regarding such policies it will be important to report on efforts to protect worker rights in annual reports and other appropriate communications.

6   Suggested further reading on business ethics: Bowie 1999 is a highly engaging application of Kantian moral philosophy to the conduct of business; Bowie 2002 is a collection of essays that together constitute a guide to the field of business ethics; DeGeorge 1993 is an important and subtle discussion of the ethics of international business; DesJardins 2003 is an excellent and accessible introductory text; Donaldson 1989 is an important, if somewhat technical, discussion of the ethics of international business; Frederick 1999 is a collection of essays that constitutes a comprehensive survey of the field of business ethics; and Hartman *et al.* 2004 is a collection of theoretical essays and original case studies on global labour practices.

6

The ability of corporations to protect human rights in developing countries

Frans-Paul van der Putten, Gemma Crijns and Harry Hummels*

Nyenrode University, The Netherlands

In recent decades, multinational companies have been confronted with public pressure to contribute to improved human rights conditions in various developing countries. This chapter deals with the relationship between such demands and the nature of corporate behaviour, and focuses on whether multinationals have certain fundamental limitations in their ability to actively promote better human rights conditions in such countries. While in Chapter 5 Denis Arnold commented on the question of what companies *should* do, this chapter focuses on the question of what companies *can* do.

The largest multinational enterprises (MNEs) originated in countries with highly developed economies and political systems, and subsequently acquired a more or less global presence (Jones 1996: 194-95). Many of the human rights-related demands addressed to these companies come from non-governmental organisations (NGOs) that originated in the same types of country.[1] The demands themselves are mostly aimed at MNE activities in countries with less developed economies and political systems, the so-called developing countries.

There are two extremes in the relationship between MNEs and human rights abuses in developing countries that are considered intolerable by NGOs. At one extreme is the situation where an MNE itself directly abuses human rights: for instance, working with security personnel who use violence against the local

---

* The authors are grateful to Hessel Willemsen for his support.
1   Demands are also put forward by governmental organisations and business sectors such as finance and insurance (Hummels *et al.* 2001; Sullivan and Frankental 2002: 90).

population, abusing land rights of indigenous peoples, or forcing employees to refrain from unionising. At the other extreme is the situation where a country's government engages in large-scale, serious violations of human rights, and the mere fact that the company does business with or in this country is interpreted as supportive of the government. However, in practice, the relationship between MNEs and human rights lies somewhere between these extremes. In such situations, human rights abuses take place outside the company itself, but near enough for human rights advocates to believe that they fall within the MNE's sphere of influence. Rather than pressure the company involved to withdraw from particular countries, they demand that the company modifies its operating policy in order to contribute to an improved human rights situation. Western-originated, internationally active NGOs thus approach MNEs as a tool to improve human rights conditions in developing countries where human rights are perceived to be violated.

Although protecting human rights, or preventing human rights violations, is primarily a state responsibility, the idea that companies also have a function in this respect has become increasingly common. States do not control everything that goes on in society, in particular not at the international level. Moreover, it is often the government itself that initiates and continues the suppression of human rights. Therefore, according to prominent human rights NGOs such as Amnesty International and Pax Christi, business enterprises 'have become necessary partners to national governments and international governmental organisations in the formulation and implementation of global public policies' (Amnesty International [The Netherlands] and Pax Christi 2000: 17), and have a role to play in addressing human rights issues. This idea is not new: it is reflected also in the preamble to the 1948 Universal Declaration of Human Rights: 'every individual and organ of society . . . shall strive . . . to promote respect for these rights' (Jägers 2002: 50). However, since the 1960s and especially since the 1990s, the number of demands made of MNEs regarding human rights has grown very rapidly.

Representatives from the business community generally agree that companies should not become involved in human rights violations. To a lesser extent, they may also agree that (at least in theory) there are countries in which investing is impossible without directly contributing to serious human rights violations. However, in situations where a company is operating in a country where human rights violations are occurring, business managers and investors often put up strong resistance to NGO demands that the company plays an active role in improving human rights conditions. Statements made in 1996–97 by the then top managers of two very large Dutch–British multinationals are illustrative of the point of view of business. C.A.J. Herkströter, then the top executive of Shell, stated that multinationals are not suited for the active promotion of human rights, among other social or environmental aims (Herkströter 1996, 1997). Two of his arguments seem particularly important. First, he argued that MNEs have no mandate to be autonomous actors in international relations since it is unclear to whom they would be accountable. The reason presented was that there is no mechanism to regulate MNE influence aimed at promoting a certain set of social values in developing countries, and there are questions around who would make sure that MNEs used their influence properly. That is, human rights promotion is fundamentally a political activity because it is directed at or closely related to the relationship between a government and its citizens, and, according to this argument, without a regulatory system MNEs cannot take responsibility for political action, even if this concerns a traditionally 'good' cause such as human rights or if the impulse to take action comes from major NGOs. Second, he pointed out that rich countries and developing countries do not make the same demands in respect of human rights. Developing countries tend to assign a higher priority than rich countries to economic progress and stability rather than such topics as human rights and environmental protection. This raises the question of whose views a company should listen to. At about the same time, Unilever NV Chairman, M. Tabaksblat, expressed similar views (Tabaksblat 1997). He, too, emphasised that human rights values are interpreted and accepted differently around the world, and stated that:

> companies must not be entrusted with the job of protecting general social standards and values. Companies are not equipped to determine what those standards and values ought to be. Nor are the control mechanisms within business appropriate for that purpose.

The remainder of this chapter takes a closer look at these two arguments in order to establish whether and how they obstruct the ability of MNEs to actively improve human rights conditions in developing countries outside these companies' direct operations. Rather than approach the two topics as isolated issues, they are addressed from a single perspective. The context in which Tabaksblat and Herkströter made their remarks seems to suggest that, by their nature, MNEs are not 'equipped' to engage in human rights promotion in developing countries. Therefore the central question for this chapter is whether the two arguments are related to the very nature of MNE behaviour.

6.1 The nature of MNE behaviour

In order to understand the basic abilities and limitations of MNEs we must look at the nature of MNE behaviour. A primary problem that demands attention is the definition of MNE. A compact definition that is widely used in studies of international business is provided by John Dunning: MNEs (also called transnational corporations) are enterprises that own or control value-added activities in two or more countries (Dunning 1993: 1). Obviously there are still enormous differences between the various firms that fit this description. Companies that are directly approached by NGOs with demands regarding human rights make up only a small portion of all MNEs. The following analysis therefore applies specifically to MNEs that have the following characteristics:

● The company originated in a developed economy, where its head office is still located. From this head office it controls assets or operations in a developing country where human rights abuses take place.

- The company is large in terms of turnover and employees, making it a comparatively large participant in the economy of the developing country.

- The company may be active in any field: resource extraction, manufacturing or services. Whatever field or combination of fields it is active in, it is among the largest market participants in at least one of these fields.

- The company is listed on a stock exchange. It is owned by a small number of majority shareholders, a large number of minority shareholders or a combination of these two types of shareholder.

- The company is directed, from the top to the work floor, by professional managers (i.e. people who are hired by the company for this job and who receive a salary for this work). Management is organised hierarchically, with sub-hierarchies based on activity types or geographical focus. At the strategic level the sub-hierarchies do not operate independently from the corporate centre.

MNEs with these characteristics bridge the gap between rich and developing economies and have a certain degree of economic influence—especially in developing countries—due to their size, market position, and access to technology and capital. They include not just the 'usual suspects' in human rights literature such as oil and mining firms, but the whole range of manufacturing, extractive and services companies. Their ownership and management structure is a result of being large and present in multiple locations (Chandler 1977: 491-92).

Having established the main features of multinationals that are relevant in the context of this chapter, we now turn to the nature of their behaviour, in particular the inability of companies to do certain things (the business arguments against promoting human rights are focused on things that companies are unable to do). Obviously, there are certain physical, financial or legal obstacles to companies undertaking certain actions. However, what Tabaksblat and Herkströter seemingly pointed at are obstacles inherent in the nature of MNEs.

The influential psychologist B.F. Skinner noted that behaviour is to a large extent related to the perceived desirability of its outcome (Hjelle and Ziegler 1981: 189-235). Perceived undesirable situations are avoided while perceived desirable situations are sought. Skinner pointed out that this is not a matter of so-called free will, but a basic rule that applies to most observable behaviour of organisms. It is not uncommon in the business literature to use an organic approach to explain the behaviour of companies (e.g. De Geus 1997). Applying Skinner's approach to the objections raised by business, we might hypothesise that there is something in the nature of MNEs that makes it undesirable for them to assign a high priority to promoting human rights.

The mechanism that defines how desirable or undesirable an expected outcome of behaviour is, can be described in terms of a conflict for power (Minzberg *et al.* 1999: 213-41), which results in a balance of power system. The persons who have actual or potential influence on, or an interest in, a company's behaviour are commonly referred to as stakeholders (Van der Putten 2003). In the balance-of-power system, only the stakeholders with influence play an active role (or have the ability to influence the manner in which a company operates). For the types of MNE that are the subject of this chapter, these influential stakeholders are primarily the company's 'technostructure',[2] capital suppliers, and dominant customers and suppliers. In the categories of technostructure and capital suppliers there are important sub-groups, such as management (Chandler 1977: 492-93) and shareholders (Frentrop 2002). Within management, the relationship between top and middle management is particularly important as it reflects the shared interests of the managerial hierarchy in a firm. Top management cannot implement strategies that are opposed by major sections of middle management, while sub-hierarchies in middle management can be played off against one another by top management (Chandler 1977: 381-414). On the capital suppliers side, shareholders tend to have a strong influence, both through the formal decision-making rights attached to individual or collective majority shareholdings and through their influence on prices at the stock exchange (see also Chapter 7 by Coles in this volume). Because of the size and multinational nature of MNEs, the direct influence of non-business stakeholders such as governments, trade unions, local inhabitants or NGOs is often limited to specific issues rather than overall behaviour.

The various groups and individuals that participate in the balance-of-power system have their own interests. Their mutual relationships are characterised by a conflict for influence on the company. The interests of the strongest stakeholders prevail—often in the shape of a compromise—and become the company's overall interests (Minzberg *et al.* 1999: 221). It is this overall corporate interest that defines which situations are desirable and which are not. In other words, if the overall corporate interest of an MNE is negatively affected by active human rights promotion, then it is against the nature of the company to embark on an active human rights policy. A multinational enterprise with an intact managerial hierarchy will not act against its corporate main interests.

While the nature of MNE behaviour as outlined above in itself does not explain why multinationals might be unable to actively improve human rights conditions in developing countries, it does provide a framework within which the two issues raised by Herkströter and Tabaksblat can be addressed.

6.2 The lack of a regulatory mechanism for political MNE behaviour

The first of these issues is the lack of a regulatory mechanism. It is commonly considered acceptable when companies do what they were created for: namely,

2 Introduced in the 1960s by J.K. Galbraith (1967: 70-71), the term 'technostructure' applies to all members of an organisation who can influence its behaviour: such as management, which has formal decision-making capacities, and technical specialists, who can exercise influence to the extent that the organisation depends on their specific knowledge or capabilities.

perform economic functions. However, as soon as a company interferes in political affairs, the matter becomes controversial. While it is seen as undemocratic if large companies influence political processes, human rights NGOs demand that MNEs promote human rights standards wherever they operate. In countries where the government is considered undemocratic or performing inadequately with regard to the protection of human rights, MNEs are particularly urged to take action. This topic may be approached from political or legal perspectives, but the main interest in this chapter is in behavioural limitations inherent in MNEs.

Given the nature of MNE behaviour, as has been indicated above, these companies can perform human rights tasks only if this corresponds to their interests. This means that the controlling stakeholders must have a shared interest in such a situation. If there was a governmental or intergovernmental system with the power to enforce a legal obligation on MNEs to take human rights related action, then it would be in the interest of the controlling shareholders for the company to comply with these legal rules. However, such a system does not currently exist (see, further, Muchlinski 1999). Alternatively, the controlling shareholders themselves might have an interest in using their company for political action. In such a case, the political actions of the stakeholders themselves should—if we follow the reasoning of Tabaksblat and Herkströter—be subject to a control mechanism. The stakeholders who use their influence on an MNE should be accountable to a system that represents the interests of all persons affected by corporate political activity.

The arguments raised by the business executives make certain sense. To begin with, if stakeholders use their influence in the company for political aims in foreign countries, then the stakeholders cannot be held accountable for this. There is no supervisory system that represents the interests of all persons who are affected by corporate political actions, and which has the power to systematically compel controlling stakeholders of companies to account for these actions. This scenario would thus involve major problems. However, this does not mean that the nature of MNE behaviour makes it impossible for companies to become tools for human rights promotion in developing countries.

What is directly related to the fundamental abilities of MNEs is the fact that, in current practice, controlling stakeholders have little interest in using their influence for non-economic aims. Managers, shareholders, suppliers and customers primarily enter into a relationship with a company with economic motives. For this reason it seems unlikely that a new type of controlling stakeholder will emerge in the near future who has economic and human rights motives for engaging in a relationship with an MNE. Theoretically, human rights NGOs could play this role by becoming majority shareholders in MNEs, but, given the practical (primarily financial) obstacles involved, it seems unlikely also that this will happen on a large scale in the near future. However, the foregoing analysis does not block all routes that are currently feasible.

Most controlling stakeholders in most large MNEs have economic interests, and—regardless of their personal views on human rights—tend to play a purely economic role in relation to these companies. However, if they perceive non-economic issues to be of relevance to the performance of the company, these issues may affect the way the stakeholders influence the company's behaviour. Thus human rights considerations are likely to play a role in MNE behaviour if these considerations affect the company's interests. The perception of non-economic risks can have a major impact on MNE behaviour (van der Putten 2001). Therefore it is not so much a positive stimulus (i.e. stakeholders having a direct interest in human rights promotion) as a negative one (i.e. the perceived risks of not addressing human rights issues may lead MNEs to change their behaviour). In this context, the main risk that multinationals currently face is that of reputation damage, in particular those with branded consumer goods.

In the past decade there have been various instances in which NGOs organised consumer boycotts which threatened to damage corporate brands (Frankental and House 2000: 74). There have also been various cases in which these boycotts, or threats of such boycotts, induced MNEs to adopt a more concerned attitude towards human rights abuses in developing countries. Whether and how multinational enterprises respond to such pressure depends on how these pressures relate to their overall interests. On the one hand there is a risk caused by ignoring NGO pressure, which grows as the NGOs involved are more able to reach sensitive areas in the company's interest profile. On the other hand, there may be possible disadvantages but also advantages to complying with NGO pressure. The relationship between the pressure and the company's overall interests is, therefore, central to the effectiveness of NGO activities.

NGO action targeting consumer brands mainly takes place in the large, highly developed economies. Herkströter and Tabaksblat rightly pointed at the problem of accountability in the absence of regulation: who decides whether the NGOs and the consumers who take action against MNEs make the right choice? However, there is no reason to assume that MNEs are, by nature, unfit to act as tools for international political pressure. External pressure on companies to actively promote human rights can be effective for the NGOs involved, as long as it alters the controlling stakeholders' perception of the balance between risks and opportunities in such a way that it is in the company's interest to embark on human rights promotion.

6.3 The gap between views on human rights of rich and developing countries

The second issue raised by Herkströter and Tabaksblat is that the urgency of human rights improvement is conceived differently in highly developed, rich economies and developing economies. Large MNEs tend to be well integrated into both types of economies. There is a broad consensus that human rights and economic progress and stability are closely related and that all are important. However, opinions differ on their relative urgency. The dominant view in highly developed economies is that there is a set of human rights norms that should be seen as an absolute precondition for any possible government policy. This view is shared by the United Nations (UN), the world's most prominent intergovernmental organisation, which has resulted in various UN treaties, declarations and resolutions.

However, in some developing countries the improvement of human rights is seen as bearing a strong relation to economic progress and stability, and therefore as a more relative issue. The matter is made more complicated by the fact that there are also countries that have practices or values that conflict with the basic set of human rights that originated in the developed economies and that is adopted by the UN. The difference in views applies primarily to Asia and Africa. Although most Asian and African countries are members of the UN, and although as such they formally support the Universal Declaration of Human Rights, they sometimes regard the UN as a Western-dominated institution that was established before these countries even existed as independent states. Therefore, in spite of their UN membership, their interpretation of human rights priorities may differ from that of countries in other parts of the world.

Let us assume that a situation occurs in which a large number of MNEs are pressured by NGO activity to adopt an active attitude towards the improvement of human rights in developing countries. In those instances where MNEs, individually but especially in co-operation, have a strong economic influence, they may pressure governments to better protect the human rights of their citizens. While the potential impact of MNE action varies by company and by country, there is no reason why, in this sense, they cannot act as energetic and forceful promoters of human rights. However, there is a reason why major MNEs would perceive this to be in their interest only under the most extreme pressure. Many of them, such as Shell and Unilever, not only have widespread activities in developing countries but also long histories and a deep familiarity with these countries.

To understand the relationship between developing countries and MNEs we must take into consideration a long-term, historical perspective. In this perspective, most developing countries have long been subject to formal or informal political influence from many of the currently rich countries. This influence has been used to serve the interests of the latter countries, often contrary to the interests of the developing countries themselves. It was under and largely due to colonialism that MNEs first became active in developing countries. Even though these countries have now gained formal independence, a general sense of suspicion continues to exist towards the former colonialist or imperialist countries in large parts of the developing world, especially in Asia and Africa. Political independence has often been acquired through violence or massive popular action, and recent terrorist actions against Western targets in various parts of the world indicate that the potential for these powerful movements still exists. In many countries, such as those with large Muslim populations but also China, nationalism and an aversion to Western dominance are genuine popular sentiments that underlie the government's attitude in international relations. The fact that many countries do not have democratically elected governments, which themselves may be engaging in human rights violations, does not justify the frequently made assumption that their populations would unconditionally welcome foreign human rights interventions.

At present a certain measure of economic dependence—in particular, in the shape of direct investment by MNEs—is tolerated because most developing countries see no alternative. Therefore the 'licence to operate' for MNEs in developing countries is that they bring economic benefits such as technology and capital.

However, should they emerge as tools of foreign political influence, then the ability of MNEs to stay in many countries would be undermined. While most human rights-related action is already political by nature, certain human rights activities might easily be interpreted as mere excuses for political domination. In international politics a clear line between human rights and purely political concerns does not exist in the eyes of many inhabitants of developing countries.

Against this background, it is understandable that companies such as Unilever and Shell, which depend on developing countries for their raw materials and for their future market growth, perceive active human rights promotion as a major threat. It is a basic interest of these companies to be able to stay in the developing world, and, consequently, their controlling stakeholders perceive NGO demands in relation to human rights as undesirable. Again, this is not a matter of choice, as has been indicated earlier. The nature of the behaviour of these companies (with a large number of stakeholders participating in a company's balance of power system) is that they can engage in active human rights promotion only if external pressure to do so is extreme. Such pressure might, in the longer run, cause serious damage to MNEs as their ability to operate in many developing countries would be undermined.

Yet the inability of MNEs to promote human rights is not always as extreme as indicated here. First, some of the MNEs relevant here may not perceive that there are many risks involved. Either they have only short-term interests in developing countries, as a result of which there is less at stake for them, or they may not perceive the threat of anti-foreign nationalism because of their lack of experience of operating in such countries. Second, MNEs might engage in types of human rights promotion that are acceptable to their host societies. On the one hand, it is possible that countries in Asia and Africa will gradually adopt a more neutral view of international human rights standards, as their impact on international decision-making grows. For example, the emergence of NGOs with strong local roots that play a prominent role internationally may well be of great importance in this respect. The main precondition for this scenario is that populations in developing countries feel that international human rights standards are no less theirs than anyone else's, and that the agenda for international political action is not dominated by the richest and strongest states. On the other hand, MNEs might use the fact that they often have long-term relationships with local societies, and that these societies accept foreign influence as long as they believe that it is beneficial, to engage in low-key and subtle forms of human rights promotion.

Like the issue of regulatory mechanisms and accountability, the difference in views on human rights is rightly identified by Tabaksblat and Herkströter as an obstacle to MNEs engaging in active human rights promotion in developing countries. However, there is no inherent reason why MNEs cannot take such actions. Multinationals can embark on an active policy of human rights promotion if they have only short-term interests in or little experience with developing countries. More constructively, they can do so if the risk of losing acceptance for their presence from the local society remains small because the MNEs choose their human rights aims and methods with great consideration for local circumstances.

6.4 Conclusion

In 1996–97 the leading executives of Shell and Unilever claimed that MNEs are not suited to act as a tool to promote—among other social or environmental aims—human rights in developing countries. They identified two major obstacles: namely, the lack of a regulatory mechanism to protect and/or hold to account those MNEs that interfere in political issues in developing countries, and the difference in views between rich and developing countries on human rights priorities and promotion. This chapter has approached these two topics from a single perspective, in order to establish whether there are structural limitations that prevent MNEs adopting an active policy towards human rights promotion in the countries where they operate. Seen from the perspective of the nature of MNE behaviour, it becomes clear that there is no reason why MNEs are inherently unfit to act as active promoters of human rights. External pressure on companies to actively promote human rights can be effective, if it alters the stakeholders' perception of the balance between opportunities and risks in such a way that it is in the company's interest to embark on human rights promotion. Multinational enterprises are therefore potential political actors and the controlling stakeholders are collectively responsible for any aspect of MNE behaviour, irrespective of whether or not they can be held accountable. Furthermore, in many developing countries major multinationals with long-term interests have the ability to engage in an active policy of human rights promotion only if the perceived risk of losing acceptance for their presence from the local society remains limited. This requires that MNEs choose their human rights aims and methods with great care for local political and cultural views.

While there is no obstacle to active human rights promotion inherent in the way MNEs behave, the analysis of the issues raised by Herkströter and Tabaksblat highlights that NGO pressure is a delicate matter, with the potential for both positive and highly problematic outcomes. Two problems that require particular attention are the accountability for political MNE action and the perception of developing countries that the process of international human rights promotion is unevenly dominated by former colonisers and imperialist powers.

What is the attitude of investment markets to corporate performance on human rights?

David Coles

Just Pensions, UK

> A Corporation is a joint enterprise between its providers of capital and those boards who manage the business. It cannot be right that investors in companies have neglected to behave like owners and instead appear more like spectators observing events without any sense of being able to help determine outcomes (Hermes Pensions Management Ltd 2002: 19).

This chapter deals with the role of shareholders in influencing company performance, encompassing all aspects of the company's social, environmental and economic performance including its performance on human rights. It is possible for these aspects to conflict, but in practice this is rarely the case other than in the short term. A holistic view of performance, balancing all of the aspects, is likely to optimise shareholder value in the long term. This is particularly true if 'value' is defined widely enough to take into account the consequences of unethical behaviour on social infrastructure.

The following issues are dealt with in this chapter:

- The context of investment (i.e. the legal and policy framework)

- The legitimate role of investors and the issue of 'fiduciary duty'

- The scope of responsibility (i.e. the 'business case' and 'moral case' debates)

- The manner in which pension funds are fulfilling their duty in practice

- Future directions, including some practical suggestions on how to make the shareholder dimension effective in improving company performance on human rights

The chapter is written from a UK perspective and makes reference to UK company law and trust law. While other jurisdictions have other laws which do make a difference—in particular varying the extent of the duty owed by company directors to stakeholders other than shareholders—the generic points on how and why shareholders should influence companies' performance remain valid across jurisdictions.

7.1 The context of investment

Most shareholder investment is through collective investment vehicles. Whereas under UK Company Law the shareholders own the company and it owes a duty only to them, in practice collective investment vehicles exercise all the rights and duties of ownership on behalf of individual shareholders. In the UK, these collective investment vehicles are life assurance policies and company pension funds. Most UK life assurance policies are long-term savings policies for retirement or other needs; the insurance element is only a minor component. Pension funds are trust funds established by companies to meet their pension promises to employees and former employees. These are of two broad types: (a) defined benefit schemes (where the employer promises a level of benefit dependent on salary); and (b) defined contribution schemes (where the level of benefit is dependent on contributions and investment performance). In either case, trustees are appointed who have a fiduciary duty to employees to ensure that the employer funds the pension promise properly, which includes ensuring that the funds are invested properly.

Other developed economies have developed other collective investment vehicles (e.g. mutual funds in the USA), with the following common features:

- Most shareholder investment is through these vehicles, although the extent of such collective investment does vary significantly and is particularly high in the UK and the USA.

- The investment itself is carried out by a small number of investment managers, with a preponderance of such managers on Wall Street and in the City of London.

The increasingly global nature of investment and of investee companies' businesses means that it is becoming less relevant where a company has its head office. BP, for example, was originally a UK company, but it now has extensive businesses around the world, especially in the USA, its shares are quoted on the New York Stock Exchange as well as in London, and it has many US shareholders. Despite this globalisation, shareholders, collective investment vehicles and investment managers are almost always based in a particular country. For example, the British Telecom pensioners and future pensioners, the British Telecom pension fund, and its principal investment manager, Hermes, are all based in the UK. There are good reasons not to have global investment vehicles: in particular, because beneficiaries will live in particular countries, and both the law and custom differ from country to country. Furthermore, there are also good reasons to have investment managers investing only in companies based in a particular region, as this allows them to focus effectively on regional issues. The consequence is that collective investment vehicles and investment managers are likely to be country-based for some time to come.

In the UK, there have been a series of initiatives aimed at companies, collective investment vehicles and their investment managers. Most of the emphasis has been on corporate governance (e.g. in the Turnbull Report aimed at companies) (Institute of Chartered Accountants in England & Wales 1999) and on shareholder activism (e.g. the Myners Report [2001] aimed at investment institutions). This latter report called for collective investment vehicles to improve their decision-making, to be more active shareholders, to select appropriate benchmarks to monitor their investment managers, and to use these in monitoring performance. Incidentally, the Hermes principles quoted at the beginning of this chapter are important because Hermes is a significant investment manager. Its principles state what it expects of the investee companies in which it invests (on behalf of its collective investment clients and therefore ultimately on behalf of individual beneficiaries).

In addition to the initiatives on corporate governance, there have also been some moves on social, environmental and ethical (SEE) issues. For example, a July 2000 amendment to Section 35 of the Pensions Act 1995 requires pension fund managers to state in their statement of investment principles (SIP) whether they take SEE issues into account in their investment processes. For example, the SIP for the BP pension fund states that:

> Consistent with its obligation to act in the best interest of the Fund, the Trustee supports a bias towards investments in companies with positive social, environmental and ethical policies. This is consistent with the stance taken by BP in respect of these matters and reflects the view that such companies can be reasonably expected to deliver superior financial performance over the longer term.

The non-governmental organisations (NGOs) Traidcraft and War on Want established 'Just Pensions' in 2000 to lobby pension funds to take account of development issues as one of the key SEE issues. Just Pensions was originally funded by the Community Fund and managed by Traidcraft and War on Want. The major sponsor is now the UK's Department for International Development and Just Pensions is managed by the UK Social Investment Forum. Just Pensions has met with many people from the pensions industry and has issued three major documents so far: a guide to socially responsible investment (SRI) (Just Pensions 2001), a report on whether UK pension funds invest responsibly (Coles and Green 2002) and a report on the attitudes of member nominated trustees to SEE issues (Gribben and Olsen 2003).

7.2 The legitimate role of investors: the fiduciary duty issue

As explained above, in the UK, pension funds are trust funds and therefore trust law applies. This has been codified in the Pensions Act 1995. Trust law also applies to life assurance policies. A basic tenet of trust law is that trustees have a fiduciary duty to act in the best interests of all the beneficiaries. The requirement to act in the best interests of beneficiaries seems to be eminently sensible and to require consideration of all aspects of performance (financial and non-financial) in selecting investments. Yet the mantra of 'fiduciary duty' is often used as an excuse for not taking account of social and environmental performance.

Fiduciary duty does indeed stop trustees from putting their personal values ahead of the interests of the beneficiaries. The beneficiaries may have stated their ethical wishes (as is the case with investment in retail life assurance ethical funds) but, if this is not the case, trustees should not impose their own ethical stance on the beneficiaries. Fiduciary duty does require that trustees act as prudent business people, balancing risk and return in the best interest of the beneficiaries. Since the way that companies recognise and deal with social, environmental and ethical risks affects long-term performance and returns to shareholders, trustees do need to consider the social and environmental performance of companies as an integral part of the investment process. Indeed, 'performance' goes wider than just maximising financial return. Hermes puts the wider context in this way (Hermes Pensions Management Ltd 2002: 4):

> As a long term diversified investor, we oppose companies behaving in a way which knowingly passes costs on to other companies or to the tax payer, and as such is socially or environmentally unacceptable, or unethical. It makes no sense if business success is achieved by creating other costs ('externalising costs') which the beneficial owners of companies will ultimately pay for.

This is not to say that financial returns will be adversely affected by taking account of social and environmental issues in making investment decisions. Indeed, while there is not, as yet, definitive proof that taking a socially responsible investment approach enhances long-term returns, there is no evidence that it harms them. The CIS (Co-operative Insurance Society), for example, looked at this carefully in adopting its current investment approach of active engagement on SRI issues for all its investments (see Forum for the Future 2002).

So why do trustees use fiduciary duty as an excuse? The obligations on trustees are onerous and their pay is minimal. This makes them risk-averse and innovation-averse. Their approach, in general, is to simply follow what has gone before and follow advice on what this is. The consequence is that relatively new concepts of performance measurement are not embraced and investment decisions tend to be left to investment managers.

In fact, it is not in the best interest of beneficiaries for this to happen. There is a difference of interest between long-term investors, individual investment managers and company directors (who have a fiduciary duty to act on behalf of shareholders). Long-term investors are interested in investment performance over decades, whereas individual investment managers are rewarded by performance over quarters and executive directors are rewarded by performance during their period of office. What is needed are performance measures that deal with the long-term performance of investment managers based on their investment processes, including the way in which the assessment of social, environmental and ethical risks is integrated into the assessment of company performance. This integration would better reflect the interests of the beneficiaries and therefore be in line with fiduciary duty.

7.3 The scope of responsibility: the 'business case' and 'moral case' debates

The business case for investors taking proper account of social, environmental and ethical issues in investment decisions is not opposed to the moral case. Indeed, it is best to think about the business case as overlapping with the moral case.

This contention can be illustrated by using the example of the purchase of cocoa by a chocolate company. Cocoa is, of course, an essential ingredient of chocolate. But it is only one ingredient; milk, sugar and paper (for packaging) are also ingredients. Furthermore, in cost terms, marketing and distribution are also important. So, in practice, cocoa is essential but, at the same time, represents a relatively small part of the cost of your favourite chocolate sweet. Given that it only constitutes a relatively small proportion of the total cost of a chocolate sweet, it therefore is reasonable to argue that the quality and security of cocoa supply and brand reputation should be more important issues to a chocolate company than the cost of cocoa. This is an important issue; there are allegations of exploitation of poor cocoa farmers and poor labour practices in the cocoa farms, even going as far as slavery.[1]

---

1 The arguments and examples presented here are based on the debate that has surrounded the use of forced child labour on cocoa farms. There are more than a million cocoa farms in West Africa alone. Many of these farms are small with children who live and work on them in appropriate roles as members of the family. However, there has been a series of reports regarding the use of forced child labour on cocoa farms in Côte d'Ivoire in West Africa. Major international chocolate manufacturers (through the International Cocoa Initiative) have started to work together to ensure that all cocoa is grown without abusive child labour or forced labour practices by July 2005. This has involved commissioning a number of surveys into labour conditions (conducted by international expert bodies including the International Labour Organisation) on cocoa farms in West Africa. These surveys led to the development of pilot programmes designed to strengthen cocoa farming communities and address labour issues. The aim is that, by 1 July 2005, the industry, in partnership with other stakeholders, will have developed and implemented credible voluntary industry-wide standards of public certification that cocoa beans and their derivative products have been grown and/or produced without any of the worst forms of child labour or forced labour. For further information, see the Biscuit, Cake, Chocolate and Confectionery Alliance website at www.bccca.org.uk and, for an

7.3.1 The base business case: quality and security of supply

One would expect any chocolate company to be concerned about the risk from buying all of its cocoa on commodity markets (i.e. from unnamed suppliers based in unnamed countries). To do so gives it no control over the price at which the cocoa is being bought from farmers and whether this provides the farmer and the farm workers with a living wage. If the price paid is too low, the farmers will not be able or willing to maintain cocoa quality. Those chocolate companies dependent solely on the commodity markets will, therefore, have no means to control quality and security of supply and no means to escape from dependence on the commodity markets if either the quality or security of supply is threatened. Furthermore, buying only from commodity markets similarly gives the chocolate company no information (even if the price is high enough) on whether the cocoa producers employ unacceptable labour practices or other unsustainable (e.g. leading to long-term environmental degradation) production methods. By definition, dependence on unsustainable farming methods risks quality and security of supply.

Clearly, it would take a chocolate company that bought all its cocoa on commodity markets significant time and resources to acquire the know-how to buy direct from farmers and to ensure that these farmers used sustainable methods, including labour practices. The lead-time and resources required are likely to be prohibitive for all but the largest manufacturers. Purely from a business perspective, one would therefore expect the company to mitigate the risk of deteriorating quality in the commodity markets by sourcing at least some of its cocoa direct on ethical terms. In that way, the company would have developed the know-how and could expand direct purchasing if and when required.

Similarly, one would expect a substantial long-term investor to engage with the chocolate company to ensure that it had effectively managed its risks of deteriorating quality and of security of supply. For the reasons set out above, an individual investment manager would be interested in whether the risks of deteriorating quality and of poor security were properly reflected in the company's share price and would buy or sell the shares based on this assessment. However, the long-term investor is unlikely to buy or sell particularly on only one or two factors. Therefore it is in the long-term investor's financial interest to engage with the chocolate company to reduce the risks and so protect its investment.

7.3.2 The extended business case: reputation

Buying some of the requirement of cocoa on the general commodity markets still leaves chocolate companies exposed to a risk of brand damage. In the case of the leading brands, this reputation is very valuable. It can be badly affected by allegations of complicity in slave labour practices through ignorance of how any of its cocoa is sourced. There is, therefore, a strong business case for ensuring that all of the cocoa that goes into leading brands of chocolate goods is produced in

industry perspective, see the Cadbury Schweppes website at www.cadburyschweppes. com.

compliance with minimum standards of labour rights. This can be done by sourcing direct and monitoring suppliers' labour practices, and by sourcing from countries or producer associations with credible systems of labour rights monitoring.

One would, therefore, expect a substantial long-term investor in a leading brand chocolate company to want to ensure that the company had mitigated its reputation risk properly by buying its cocoa on an ethical basis. Not to do so could potentially adversely affect the company's reputation and therefore its share price. Therefore one would expect the long-term investor to engage with the company to find out how it had mitigated this risk.

7.3.3 The moral case: fair trade

Buying cocoa on a fair trade basis goes further than the minimum required to protect reputation. There may be good business reasons to do so: for example, building a brand reputation for fairness to poor farmers and further improving quality over time by establishing long-term relationships. While these may be good business reasons, there is also a moral argument: that is, to help poor farmers to rise out of the extremes of poverty.

One could argue for a substantial long-term investor taking a moral or ethical attitude and pressing its investee companies to adopt such a basis. The investor has the rights of ownership and therefore should have the obligations of ownership, which include ensuring that investee companies do not profit from human misery. But this is essentially a moral or ethical question because it goes beyond the business case. However, it should be clear from the above that the business case is not opposed to the moral case but instead is adjacent to it and overlaps with it. The base business case (security of supply) is met by adopting the extended business case (reputation) which overlaps with the moral case (fair trade). The trade-off of profits against ethics only becomes relevant when a company goes beyond the business case, taking a moral approach even where this is not dictated by business logic.

Yet many shareholders are sceptical about the business case. So it is important that the business benefits of the company's corporate social responsibility (CSR) approach to its main business activities are explained well in its CSR report. The CSR manager is often the main author of this report and therefore has a critical role to play in ensuring that this is the case. That is, the business case arguments can be harnessed to support the moral argument (i.e. doing the right thing is good for business). The converse also applies. NGOs are increasingly using moral arguments (e.g. appealing to the principles in the Universal Declaration of Human Rights) to emphasise the importance of these issues to businesses. In doing so, they heighten the reputation risks (e.g. adverse media coverage) for those companies that do not effectively manage these issues.

7.4 Pension funds: how they are fulfilling their duty in practice

> We can only conclude that poor practice by major pension funds on socially responsible investment is the norm. Many pension funds are seriously exposed (Coles and Green 2002).

Many UK pension funds have changed their SIP to include social and environmental issues, following the requirements in the amendment to the Pensions Act 1995. However, a Just Pensions report of July 2002 (an analysis of pension fund SRI performance based on in-depth interviews with scheme administrators) showed that most pension funds have failed to translate these changes into action two years after these changes were made. This means that either their SIP does not fully reflect the reality of investment risks arising from SEE factors, or that the words in their policies are not backed up by appropriate action. The funds are therefore exposed to long-term under-performance because the fund managers, trustees and administrators are not taking proper account of SEE risks in their investment strategy and process.

The report authors contacted 14 pension funds managing around 20% (£170 billion [thousand million]) of the assets held by pension funds in the UK. They found that most of the examples of good practice come from just a handful of pension funds, principally the following five funds: British Telecom (managed by Hermes), Universities Superannuation Scheme, West Midlands, Strathclyde and BP. While these funds are not perfect, they do take some account of SEE risks in their investment process. They show other funds what can be done while still acting within existing legal and financial constraints.

The report showed that:

- Funds have made more progress on policies than action and this disparity leaves them open to criticism.

- Poor practice in relation to socially responsible investment is the norm; SRI issues are not generally considered as part of investment strategies.

- Most pension funds have failed to invest in the staff, training or research required to implement their stated SRI policies.

- Almost all funds delegating SRI decisions to external fund managers have no means of assessing or rewarding the performance of these fund managers.

- Pension funds are failing to use their websites as a means to communicate on SRI issues with beneficiaries or the wider public.

In a similar manner to the wide acceptance in the corporate sector that the poor management of social, environmental and ethical issues is a business risk, those pension funds that do not consider these issues properly are seriously exposed. The most exposed are those that ignore these issues altogether, but even the better funds are exposed because they often do not have the capacity to implement the commitments they make in their SIPs.

In practice, companies direct the investment activities of their pension funds, within the constraints to act properly set by the Pensions Act 1995. The fund is set up to meet a pension promise made by the company to its employees. The money is kept in a separate trust fund in case the company experiences financial difficulties during the period of the promise, but it remains a promise made by the company to its employees. It is appropriate therefore for the company to influence the fund's investment activities, within the legal constraints of fiduciary duty owed by the trustees to the beneficiaries. Therefore, the pension fund's investment activity should take into account the company's approach to CSR. In particular, the CSR manager should ensure that the company board has discussed the issue of coherence between its own CSR position and the stance on SRI taken by its pension fund. Indeed, the board should also discuss the business reasons for the company's own CSR approach so that the board really understands the business case.

7.5 Future directions

Investment practices are moving in the right direction. However, the move towards incorporating SRI practices into mainstream investment practice is slow—far too slow. Investors are still often acting as constraints on the CSR instincts of company directors, pushing them to produce short-term share price improvement, which is mistakenly equated to shareholder value, rather than to act in the long-term interests of the business.

So what can be done to speed up the move, which is in the interests of all the company's stakeholders including its long-term investors? The analysis presented in this chapter, together with the author's own experience with Just Pensions, points to a number of important and necessary first steps:

- The UK government should clarify the legal definition of fiduciary duty to make it crystal clear that acting in the best interests of beneficiaries should not be narrowly interpreted as just acting in their short-term financial interests. There is, in fact, nothing wrong with the current definition. However, the definition is being used as an excuse for inaction on SRI issues and, therefore, clarification would help.

- The UK government should implement the Myners Report (2001) recommendation to regulate the investment activities of long-term institutional investors (pension funds, life assurance companies and charitable foundations), to require them to actively monitor the performance of their investment managers in influencing the performance of investee companies.

- For investment consultants and investment performance measurers, the most serious gap is in relation to the area of measurement of investment performance, and consequently in appraisal and rewards. Investment managers are measured on short-term performance (i.e. has their investment portfolio beaten the relevant index over the last quarter, year or, at most, three years?). The reality, however, is that most institutional investors are in for the long term: up to 50 years for pension funds. Therefore, performance measures need to be developed that take a long-term approach, measuring the investment process, including how social, environmental and ethical risks are dealt with, rather than simply being based on share price movements. Such measures would also help to spread best practice in SRI. The investment consultants and investment performance measurers should begin to develop such measures.

● CSR managers should ensure that all CSR reports are focused on the company's main business activities, are clear on the business benefits of its CSR approach and are consistent with other communications to shareholders. Following this approach will ensure that shareholders (and other stakeholders) are clear that CSR is both central to how the company does business and good for business.

● CSR managers should ensure that the board discusses the issue of coherence between its own CSR position and the SRI position taken by its pension fund.

The implementation of any of these five suggestions will advance the day when the issues of human rights are taken seriously by investors—are understood to be key investment issues—and shareholders put positive pressure on companies for good performance. All would be good, but any will do. So get to it on any that are in your power!

8

From the inside looking out
A management perspective on human rights

Rory Sullivan
Insight Investment, UK

Nina Seppala
Warwick Business School, UK

The earlier chapters in this book look at the pressures (e.g. NGO expectations, shareholder expectations, legal requirements) on companies to address human rights issues. This chapter looks at how companies (in particular, transnational corporations [TNCs]) organise themselves to respond to these pressures. These organisational structures, systems and processes are important influences on the manner in which companies can and do respond to human rights issues.

The reality is that human rights is a relatively new area for management attention. Historically, these issues have been treated within areas such as personnel, health and safety, rather than as a distinct management issue. As a consequence, the description of human rights management systems presented in the first part of the chapter relies heavily on experience gained from the management of issues such as the environment and health and safety. The second part of the chapter then looks at the practical issues and dilemmas faced by companies when developing and implementing human rights management systems.

8.1 A framework for human rights management

8.1.1 Overview of framework

From an organisational perspective, the approach to human rights management follows a similar model to that of other issues such as health and safety, environment and production. This is generally described as the 'plan–do–check–review model', where companies define their corporate vision (generally through a policy), identify the key issues that need to be managed, set objectives and targets, implement systems to achieve these objectives, and monitor, report and review performance.

8.1.2 Initial review

The starting point for the development and implementation of a human rights management system is to identify the extent of the company's human rights responsibilities and the management processes and systems that are in place to manage these issues. The scope of this review should include:

- The scale and extent of the organisation's activities and operations. This encompasses not only direct operations but should also cover the organisation's suppliers, contractors, joint venture partners and other partners, as well as the use of the products or services of the company.

- The company's human rights issues and impacts. This requires consideration of issues relating to workers (e.g. health and safety, freedom of association, rights to collective bargaining, anti-discrimination measures, remuneration), products and services (e.g. the positive and negative impacts of goods and services, including the possibility of misuse), business partners (e.g. supply chain labour issues, bribery and corruption) and communities (e.g. community and livelihood impacts, land and indigenous rights).

- The human rights issues associated with the countries in which the company or its partners operate. This should include consideration of legal restraints and obligations (e.g. domestic legislation, international human rights conventions), political risks and opportunities (e.g. risk of conflict, risk to 'licence to operate'), and economic factors (e.g. impact on reputation, risk of sabotage or extortion, costs of security).

- Regulatory requirements. These include legislation, standards and codes of practice that apply to the company's activities or impacts, corporate policies (e.g. corporate social responsibility [CSR] commitments), external voluntary commitments (e.g. industry codes of conduct) and the expectations of stakeholders (including shareholders, NGOs, local communities, customers, suppliers) that affect or are affected by the organisation's activities, products or services.

- Current systems and management controls. The company should identify those of its existing management systems and structures (e.g. procedures, emergency response plans, monitoring and review processes, training) that can be utilised for managing human rights issues. This review should also identify those areas where gaps exist.

- The company's human rights record. This can be considered in two parts. The first relates to those aspects where performance data is already available (e.g. health and safety performance, community development expenditures, pay rates for male and female employees, degree of implementation of corporate policies on issues such as discrimination). The second relates to the external perceptions and analysis of the company's performance, gained from sources such as the media, complaints records, and discussions with stakeholders such as local communities, NGOs, trade unions and regulatory authorities. These perceptions and opinions are important indicators of areas or activities where there have been difficulties in managing human rights issues and/or in identifying where there have been failures in existing systems of management control.

8.1.3 Human rights policy

Written policies are widely used, in particular in TNCs, as public statements of the company's purpose, vision and values. An explicit human rights policy is generally seen as a necessary starting point for demonstrating corporate commitment to the protection and promotion of human rights. Amnesty International has argued that corporate human rights policies should explicitly invoke the Universal Declaration of Human Rights (UDHR) and the ILO core conventions on labour rights[1] (Amnesty International 1998). The scope of human rights policies is not limited to the company's own operations but should extend to all aspects of an organisation's operations and activities. Issuing a policy on human rights is only a starting point. Company leaders (directors, managers) should ensure that their personal commitment to human rights is clearly demonstrated: for example, in internal communications, in external statements, through the establishment of a human rights management system, through the integration of human rights in board, and other decision-making processes.

8.1.4 Objectives and targets

Based on the human rights policy and the outcomes of the initial review, companies should define the objectives and targets necessary for them to meet their policy commitments. Objectives and targets can relate to specific human rights issues (e.g. to eliminate child labour within a certain time) or to management systems as a whole (e.g. to commence public reporting on human rights performance). The scope of the objectives and targets should not be limited to the company's own activities but should also consider human rights issues as they apply to all of the company's activities and operations.

Companies should also establish a management programme defining how they will achieve their objectives and targets. The management programme should detail the resources to be allocated to achieving the objectives, the specific measures and actions to be taken, the time-frame for implementing the measures and actions, the responsible people, and the manner in which performance is to be assessed.

---

1 For the eight ILO conventions on labour rights, see footnote 3 on page 16.

8.1.5 Implementation

There are two main elements of implementation (Sullivan and Wyndham 2001: 28-32). The first relates to human resources, specifically the role and responsibilities of employees in managing human rights issues. This starts by defining responsibilities and authorities throughout the organisation (from the board level down). Training should then be provided to all employees, to ensure that all employees recognise the importance of human rights issues to the organisation, and understand the systems and processes that are in place to ensure that human rights issues are effectively managed. This knowledge must then be supplemented by providing a suitable framework within which employees can engender ownership and support of the system (i.e. through the integration of human rights requirements into job descriptions and performance appraisal processes, providing safeguards to ensure that employees are never complicit in human rights violations).

The second aspect of implementation is the development of management tools, including procedures for operations, emergency response and internal and external communications. These elements provide the formal operating framework for the management of an organisation's human rights impacts. They should include formal processes for ensuring that human rights are: (a) taken into account in risk management, project management, purchasing, product or service development, manufacturing, customer relationship management, marketing; (b) reflected in the contractual relationships the company has with its suppliers, business partners, customers; and (c) taken into consideration in the manner in which finance and infrastructure, physical infrastructure, technology, information and knowledge are managed.

8.1.6 Monitor and report on performance

System monitoring and maintenance involves tracking performance, assessing the effectiveness of management controls, ensuring that the management system is functioning as intended and implementing mechanisms to identify, record and address any deficiencies in the system. Monitoring processes should provide senior management with the information necessary for the review and evaluation of the effectiveness of the human rights management system to ensure its continuing suitability, adequacy and effectiveness. While monitoring is clearly a company-specific issue, some general principles for monitoring on-the-ground performance have been proposed (Avery 1999: 50-59):

- Monitoring must be independent of the business and the government.
- Monitoring must be ongoing, not ad hoc nor just a publicity or celebrity visit.
- The monitoring authority needs to have independent authority and sufficient resources available to do its job.
- Monitoring must involve local people who live in the country or area where human rights are being monitored.

- Monitors must be trusted by the workers and have a track record within the country.

- Monitors need to understand the work practices in question and know what is common practice and what is not.

- The monitoring work must be as open as possible and the monitor should have the right to communicate information without corporate pre-screening or control.

Reporting processes need to consider the positive and negative, likely and potential human rights implications of the organisation's activities, including impacts on democracy and sovereignty, workers' rights, human rights and broader social, economic and cultural rights (Sullivan and Frankental 2002). To ensure credibility, these assessment processes must be completely transparent and open. For example, for impact assessment processes, transparency and openness must apply at all stages including scoping, issue identification, issues assessment and development of conclusions and recommendations. In particular, there should be formal processes for the issue and review of draft impact assessment documents and all of the comments received should be explicitly considered and reflected in the final decisions made. In situations where there is the potential for human rights violations to occur, suitable safeguards must be adopted and the development should not proceed until this is done.

The discussions around monitoring and reporting are complicated by the general absence of indicators to enable companies to assess their human rights performance. For example, the human rights performance measures specified in the Global Reporting Initiative (GRI) focus primarily on the existence of policies and the degree of implementation of management systems (GRI 2002). However, human rights performance measures, with the exception of historically studied areas such as health and safety performance, are yet to be developed.

8.1.7 Management review processes

Management review is frequently the weakest area in companies' management systems, in particular for issues that are seen as 'non-core' business areas. It is common for senior managers to assume that issuing a policy is enough to demonstrate their commitment to the specific issue in question. Management review is of particular importance for human rights given the relative novelty of human rights as a management issue. The management review process should consider questions such as the ongoing relevance of the policy, objectives and targets of the organisation, the performance of the organisation against its objectives and policy commitments, and external perceptions and reports of the company's performance (e.g. in the media, from dialogue with external stakeholders).

8.2 Human rights management in practice

8.2.1 Do companies see human rights as a subject of management importance?

Companies have been slow to make human rights an explicit subject of management attention. One key indicator is the number of organisations that have explicitly adopted human rights policies (i.e. as the first step in corporate commitment to the protection and promotion of human rights). NGOs such as Amnesty International have emphasised that a human rights policy represents the key starting point for organisations that wish to address human rights issues in their operations. The Business and Human Rights Resource Centre[2] details those organisations with company policies that explicitly mention human rights issues.[3] A total of 26 companies are listed as having policies that refer explicitly to the UDHR[4] and a further 12 have policy commitments to human rights but do not explicitly refer to the UDHR.[5] The fact that such a limited number of companies have human rights policies is perhaps a sign that the message about the importance of human rights has yet to seep through to many companies.

A further analysis provides some interesting insights. Virtually all of the companies with human rights policies can be classified into to one or more of the following categories:

- The company has had at least one major issue with human rights (e.g. BP in Colombia, Shell in Nigeria).

- The company has exposure to particularly sensitive countries (e.g. Premier Oil, TotalFinaElf and Unocal in Burma, Talisman in Sudan). In this context, having a policy may be seen either as a management tool (i.e. to provide guidance on how to behave in such difficult operating environments) or as a legitimation tool (e.g. to deflect criticisms of the company for operating in such countries).

2 www.business-humanrights.org (last reviewed on 15 March 2003).
3 It is relevant to make some comments about the potential limitations of the data presented: (a) the list is biased towards the larger, Western European TNCs. It is these companies that tend to use policy statements as codifications of corporate values whereas, in other countries, published policy statements may not be the preferred way of communicating corporate commitment to human rights; (b) US TNCs tend to be less keen on expansive policy statements because of the concerns about being sued in the event of non-compliance with these policy commitments; (c) most of the companies come from countries where human rights NGOs are most active; and (d) some companies may not see the need to explicitly refer to human rights as a specific management concern (e.g. they may be confident that they already effectively manage these issues through existing management systems and processes).
4 These are: ABB, Ahold, Balfour Beatty, BG Group, Body Shop, BP, BT, CGNU, Conoco, The Co-operative Bank, Diageo, Freeport McMoran, Ikea, National Grid, Norsk Hydro, Novo Group, Premier Oil, Reebok, Rio Tinto, Shell, Skanska, Stora Enso, Storebrand, Talisman, TotalFinaElf, Unocal.
5 These are: ABN Amro, Akzo Nobel, Bonnier Group, British Airways, Cadbury Schweppes, ChevronTexaco, DLH, FLS, ICI, Nokia, SCA, Statoil.

● The company is part of the oil, gas or mining industries. The extractive industries have been particularly criticised for their role in or proximity to human rights violations.

● A human rights policy is a source or potential source of competitive advantage. Examples could be Storebrand and CGNU (which both have substantial ethical investment businesses), The Co-operative Bank (which sees its performance on social and environmental issues as a key differentiator) and ABB (which sees environmental and social issues as providing a part of its competitive advantage).

● A commitment to protecting and promoting human rights is a feature of the business climate in their home countries. Examples (albeit possibly somewhat stereotypical) could include companies from the Nordic countries (Norsk Hydro, Statoil) or the Netherlands (e.g. ABN Amro). The relatively few companies from these countries suggests that the country of origin may be a relatively minor influence.

This analysis (while, clearly, somewhat simplified) could be read as indicating that most companies do not presently see that human rights is a legitimate subject for management attention and that this only changes in response to social pressure or because of errors, scandals or accidents involving the corporation concerned (Addo 1999: 11). It may also reflect corporate confidence that human rights are already being effectively managed and that there is, as a consequence, no need to make human rights an explicit subject of management attention.

A further question is whether or not human rights policies can be relied on. While company codes and policies have an important role to play in defining minimum standards of corporate behaviour, they are non-binding and can easily be flouted by less scrupulous organisations. The experience in practice has been that many companies' policies on human rights have tended to be limited in scope, poorly defined with few concrete commitments and, in many cases, have limited impact on the actual performance of companies (Sullivan 2002; Sullivan and Frankental 2002). There has been a marked reluctance on the part of companies to open their operations and activities up to independent monitoring or verification.

8.2.2 Do companies already manage human rights issues?

Even though many companies do not have explicit policies and processes relating to human rights, many already have policies and activities that conform with their duty to respect the rights of others, even if these are not necessarily conceived of in human rights terms (Addo 1999: 28-29). For example, for extractive companies, it has been argued that the expectations of companies relate, at a minimum, to integrity, health and safety as an absolute priority, avoidance of complicity with human rights violations, commitments to gender, racial and ethnic equality, commitment to sustainable development and avoiding exploitation of the poor (Willets 1997: 221-23). Furthermore, at least in developed countries, many of the civil and political rights are already required by legislation or form a standard part of management practice. In these situations, compliance with the letter and with the spirit of the law is likely to mean that, at least in broad terms, companies discharge their core human rights responsibilities. In less developed countries, the situation is far less clear-cut, given the general absence of legislation and, even if there is legislation, the inadequacies in the implementation of this legislation.

In less developed countries, TNCs have tended to adopt one of three broad strategies (Zarsky 2002). The first is to follow local standards and to highlight their compliance with national law or custom in response to any ethical criticisms. The second is to adopt company-wide, global standards for production processes (which often include environmental, health and safety measures). The reasons for this are that it is easier to manage one set of standards rather than a patchwork of standards, and that several types of business risk (e.g. manufacturing defects) can be reduced. While global company standards are generally an improvement over following national standards (as the company will make selective commitments to best practice), the political, cultural and socioeconomic context will define how effectively the standards are implemented. The third approach is to adopt a voluntary code of conduct outlining conduct in areas of ethical concern and pledging company commitment to best practice in social and/or environmental management. Corporate ethical targets tend to be highly influenced by NGO activity (e.g. clothing companies have focused on labour issues whereas energy companies have tended to focus on community development and security issues), and the tendency is for such codes to focus only on the issues for which the company has been criticised (see, further, Chapter 2 by Geoffrey Chandler).

From a management system perspective, companies tend to use or extend the systems they have previously developed to address issues such as the environment, health and safety and community development to manage their human rights issues. In some companies, these issues, together with human rights, are folded into a single activity, covered by general terms such as corporate citizenship or corporate social responsibility, whereas in other companies 'human rights management' is treated as a separate issue. While the specific management structures differ, the underpinning management philosophies tend to be very similar. When companies decide to 'manage' a specific issue (such as human rights), the management framework tends to follow the 'plan–do–check–review' model above. Integrating human rights into existing management systems and frameworks offers the advantages of: (a) ensuring that human rights are integrated into existing systems and procedures; (b) avoiding duplication (e.g. data collected on health and safety performance are also likely to be relevant to human rights); and (c) ensuring management and employee support (as the incremental time and effort required to manage human rights is minimised). However, such integration also has one potentially major disadvantage. That is, by spreading the responsibility for the protection and promotion of human rights among different parties or subsuming human rights into various other policy areas (e.g. environmental policy, health and safety, equal opportunities, anti-corruption, community affairs) there is no specific locus for human rights (Frankental 2002). The consequence is that human rights may be seen as a lower management priority or as 'something to be done once everything else has been addressed'. Ultimately, while management processes are necessary building blocks for institutionalising human rights protection within an organisation, the ultimate measure of success is the actual performance of an organisation (Sullivan and Frankental 2002: 85). That is, has the company had human rights issues? What were they? How significant were they? What is being done to address these issues?

8.2.3 Stakeholders

The 1990s saw the emergence of an alternative to the prevalent shareholder approach to management. The stakeholder perspective challenges the view that a firm's success is primarily measured by the maximisation of returns to shareholders. Stakeholder theory argues that, when business interacts with society, a shared interest and interdependence develops between a company and other social groups and that this interaction, in turn, leads to the creation of corporate stakeholders (i.e. those groups that are affected by, or can affect, a firm's decisions, policies and operations) (Post *et al.* 1996: 8; Halal 2001). These stakeholders include consumers, investors, financiers, government, industry associations, industry members, regulators, NGOs, community groups and workers. Stakeholder theory argues that firms are expected to accept broader responsibility to balance the interests of shareholders with those of other groups that are affected by the organisation (Wartick and Wood 1998: 94-115).

In stakeholder theory (Donaldson and Preston 1995; Clarkson 1995; Post *et al.* 2002), one of the key debates is the manner in which the rights of shareholders versus the rights of stakeholders should be taken into account in business decision-making processes. A focus on stakeholders relies on the assumption that shareholders will give up their rights to a return on their investment in return for some sort of social outcomes. It has been argued that systematic management attention to stakeholder issues is critical to an organisation's success but this hypothesis has not been robustly tested in the literature.

Opinions on the social and environmental responsibilities of organisations vary from the view that profit is the sole responsibility of organisations[6] through to perspectives that business must be socially responsible. It has been argued that, in the context of a particular business sector in a particular country, the most appropriate definition of social responsibility is to comply with legislation. In this frame of reference, social responsibility can be considered as profit maximisation, where the only constraint is to comply with the law. However, given their power and responsibility, it has been argued that businesses are also subject to a social contract. In a social contract, while the primary responsibility of companies is to conduct their economic tasks (i.e. to produce goods and services profitably), they must also address the consequential effects and impacts of their activities and operations (McGee 1998: 380).

An alternative conception of social responsibility is that business has a social purpose, where this purpose is consistent with and necessary to its long-term financial interest, and that organisations must, therefore, consider the interests of all stakeholders, not just narrow shareholder needs (Nobel 1999: 1,260-63). An

---

6 Most famously articulated by Milton Friedman: that the social purpose of business is to increase its profits (Friedman 1970).

extension to this conception of corporate social responsibility is that a company should: (a) be held accountable for any of its actions that affect people, their communities or the environment; (b) acknowledge negative impacts and correct them if at all possible; and (c) forgo profit if social impacts are harmful to certain stakeholders or if these funds can be used to promote a social good (Post *et al.* 1996: 37).[7] Of course, these altruistic statements are likely to conflict with the need for organisations to make a profit and the desire for survival that drives all organisations.

While the stakeholder concept has been extensively discussed in the literature around corporate social responsibility, it is less clear that the concept has been widely accepted by companies. There has been something of a boom in stakeholder engagement ('listen to your stakeholders') but it is less clear how, if at all, this engagement is integrated into management decision-making. For example, while there is evidence that companies are increasingly starting to explicitly consider human rights issues as part of their pre-investment risk assessment processes, anecdotally, many such risk assessments are conducted after the primary decision (e.g. to go ahead with a specific project, to invest in a country with a poor human rights record) has been made. In these situations, stakeholder engagement could simply be seen as a tool for legitimising corporate actions or for building support for a company's policies and positions.

8.2.4 Is there a business case?

One of the difficulties with the business and human rights debate has been that the language of rights and responsibility has not fitted well with the manner in which business has seen or defined its own self-interest. Human rights have traditionally been seen as a cost. The debate has evolved in recent years with an increasing recognition that a proactive approach to human rights can provide commercial benefits. It is difficult to put figures on the business costs and benefits of human rights but the broad connections are clear. Companies that are perceived as being implicated in human rights violations may see their share price fall, may have difficulty in accessing resources or markets and will have difficulties in recruiting the best employees (Avery 1999: 13-14; Frankental and House 2000: 24-27; Andriof and McIntosh 2001: 13-20). Conversely, organisations with a good human rights record should be able to achieve a range of commercial (e.g. enhanced reputation and image, more secure 'licence to operate', improved employee recruitment and retention, reduced risk of boycotts or protests) and social benefits (e.g. strengthening the rule of law through the application of human rights standards, strengthening the capacity of civil society, increased trust between business and the community, decline in social unrest) (Frankental and House 2000: 25; Sullivan and Hogan 2002). In addition, given that human rights is just emerging as a management issue for companies, there are likely to be 'first-mover' advantages for companies that take a proactive approach, through

---

7   A related concept is that of the 'triple bottom line' which argues that business has three goals: namely, economic prosperity, environmental quality and social justice (Elkington 1997).

enhanced reputation and by being able to shape and influence the direction of public policy in this area.

Furthermore, a significant proportion of the equity of many companies is tied up in the value of their brands rather than in their tangible assets and, increasingly, NGOs are targeting companies with high-profile brands (see, for example, Spar 1998; Avery 1999: 16-17; Klein 2000). However, the sensitivity of firms to reputation damage (or pressure) varies and those with most to lose appear to be those in high-value, branded goods industries and those that have a high market profile due to their size or centrality in their home-country markets (Muchlinski 2001a: 38-39). There is also limited evidence that financial markets will react to reports of firms with a poor human rights record. For example, one study has indicated that, even though Shell, Nike and Monsanto were, at various times, subject to very public boycotts, there appeared to be no demonstrable effect on their share price or dividends (Zadek and Forstater 1999).

Despite the strength of the business case arguments, the reality is that many of the advantages of a good human rights record may not manifest themselves in the short term. It is frequently the case that while costs (e.g. of developing and implementing human rights management systems) are incurred in the short term, the benefits may be long-term and are, in many cases, likely to be extremely difficult to measure in financial terms. The consequence has been that many companies have yet to see the relevance of human rights to their businesses and frequently see human rights as being at odds with short-term business requirements.

8.3 Conclusions

The chapter has sketched out a framework for human rights management and canvassed some of the challenges faced by companies seeking to manage these issues effectively. Human rights is a relatively new area of management attention and the experience is limited. The case studies presented in this book further highlight the difficulties and challenges faced by companies seeking to develop and implement effective human rights management systems.

While the 'top-level' responses are clear (i.e. that companies will develop and implement policies, management processes and systems), the complexities and difficulties arise at ground level. As noted by David Rice (Director, Policy Unit, Government and Public Affairs) of BP (Rice 2002): 'It's hard to discern any rules or pattern in this. Everything is handled on a case-by case basis—very ad hoc, very intuitive.' These comments were made despite the fact that BP has a relatively well-developed human rights management system in place: including a human rights policy, transparency and reporting on policy and performance, codes of conduct for contractors and joint venture partners, new kinds of relationships with friendly governments, and speaking out on a range of human rights issues around the world.

Part 2
Corporate responses

9
Corporate social responsibility failures in the oil industry

Charles Woolfson

Glasgow University, UK

Matthias Beck

Glasgow Caledonian University, UK

The year 2003 marks the 15th anniversary of the world's worst offshore oil disaster, the explosion of the British offshore platform, Piper Alpha. The Piper Alpha disaster maintains a special place in the annals of corporate misconduct because a subsequent public inquiry under the Scottish High Court judge, Lord Cullen, clearly attributed responsibility for the disaster to the platform's owner, Occidental Petroleum (Cullen 1990).

This chapter examines the events surrounding the Piper Alpha disaster as an instance of corporate social responsibility failure. It commences with a brief overview of the regulatory regime that provided the immediate context for the disaster. It is argued that this regime was 'captured' by the industry that it was supposed to oversee and, as a consequence, provided inadequate protection for the offshore workforce. Next, the oil industry's response to the disaster is analysed. It is argued that this represented an unsuccessful attempt at corporate reputational management, which failed to forestall the groundswell of public concern over the perceived legal immunity of corporations for safety failures. Finally, the contemporary corporate social responsibility movement is critically examined and it is suggested that its protagonists have often provided little more than a containment strategy aimed at deflecting more rigorous legislative action against corporate offenders.

9.1 Piper Alpha

The Piper Alpha oil production platform, owned by Occidental Petroleum, was situated in the UK sector of the North Sea, 177 km north-east of Aberdeen. It began oil production in 1976, exporting oil to the onshore terminal at Flotta in the Orkneys and gas to the St Fergus terminal in Grampian. The platform was linked to a number of other production platforms in the North Sea, providing a key junction box for the onward export of hydrocarbons. The immediate cause of the Piper Alpha disaster appears to have been the ignition and explosion of a low-lying cloud of gas condensate, which was leaked because of the removal of a pump for maintenance purposes, and its replacement by a blank flange. When a second pump failed, the crew started what they thought was the alternative pump as the relief system, unaware that the previous shift had already removed it. In so doing, they initiated the chain of events that led to an uncontrolled gas emission, and, later on, to an initial explosion at 22:00 on the night of 6 July 1988 as the escaping gas found a source of ignition.

The initial explosion resulted in a large crude oil fire which engulfed the north end of the platform in dense black smoke. The fire was spread by oil leaking from the main oil pipeline to shore and from ruptured pipelines carrying oil and gas from the linked Claymore and Tartan platforms. Between 22:00 and 23:20, there were two further cataclysmic explosions caused by pipeline ruptures and, at this time, large sections of Piper Alpha's topsides began to disintegrate and fall into the sea. Despite the visible conflagration on Piper Alpha, the linked oil platforms continued to export oil and gas to Piper Alpha, thus feeding the inferno, because, in Lord Cullen's words, the responsible managers were 'reluctant to take responsibility for shutting down oil production' (Cullen 1990: ch. 7, paragraph 49). Summarising these events, a survivor quoted in the Cullen Report noted: 'The Piper did not burn us; it was the other rigs that burnt us' (Cullen 1990: ch. 19, paragraph 4).

From the very first moment of the disaster, all of the platform emergency systems proved to be inadequate. The initial explosion knocked out the control room and disabled power supplies and communications. Survivors spoke of an eerie silence that descended on the platform, as the familiar background noise of generators and plant abruptly ceased. The fire-water deluge system had been out of commission for several months and was inoperable. Those sprinklers that did operate did so only with the remnants of water left in the system.

Most of the persons on board the installation were in the accommodation area, many in the cinema room. Others, who were on duty, made their way to the galley area in accordance with installation emergency muster procedures. Smoke and flames quickly enveloped the accommodation area. After 10 minutes, the lighting in the galley area failed and panic began to set in. Within another 15 minutes, dense smoke began to penetrate the galley. Men were forced to crawl along the floor to escape the smoke, using wet towels to assist in breathing. Others were quickly overcome. According to one survivor, Ed Punchard, with the rupture of the gas-import riser from the Tartan at 22:20, 'the conflagration was multiplied tenfold' (Punchard 1989: 130):

> Eleven and a half miles of eighteen-inch-diameter gas pipeline started to release hydrocarbon gas at a pressure of 1800 p.s.i. The effects were devastating. A fireball shot out from below the centre of the jacket, enveloped the platform and rose to a height of some 700 feet. The roar was blood-curdling and it did not stop for the next four hours.

As the disaster unfolded, there was no systematic attempt to lead the men to safety. Eventually, some of the men decided individually, or as a group, to ignore the company advice to muster in the accommodation area and wait for evacuation by helicopter. They realised that helicopters could not land on the smoke-engulfed platform and that to remain was to face certain death. Those who survived did so because of sheer luck (some survived a jump of hundreds of metres into the freezing North Sea below). For those who made it to the water their grim struggle for survival was fierce. With the platform disintegrating above them, and the sea on fire around them, the only hope for survival was to be plucked from the water quickly. The personnel who remained in the accommodation area died, mainly of smoke inhalation. Of those who survived, many were horribly burned on their hands and feet as the platform had literally melted under them.

When dawn broke on the morning of 7 July, most of the superstructure of what had been Piper Alpha had either been incinerated or collapsed into the sea. What was left of the platform was a smouldering, tangled heap of metal and the still-burning remains of a gas flare. Of the total 167 who died that night, 30 remained missing, presumed dead.

9.2 Safety failure and corporate responsibility

In his enquiry into the Piper Alpha disaster, Lord Cullen listed a catalogue of safety failures on the part of Occidental, the platform's owner, which directly implicated the company's management in the Piper Alpha disaster. Among other things, management:

- Failed to operate an effective permit-to-work system
- Disregarded written procedures
- Provided inadequate and misleading safety induction materials
- Ignored previous concerns over the permit-to-work system
- Failed to learn the lessons from previous incidents (which had included a fatality and a near-disaster evacuation)

Lord Cullen summarised his views as follows (Cullen 1990: ch. 14, paragraph 52):

> It appears to me that there were significant flaws in the quality of Occidental's management of safety which affected the circum-stances of the event of the disaster . . . They [senior management] adopted a superficial response when issues of safety were raised by others . . . Platform personnel and management were not prepared for a major emergency as they should have been.

There were other issues that underlay this disaster, which Lord Cullen also touched on, and which remain contentious in the offshore context. At the time of the disaster, there was significant resistance to any role for organised labour and trade unions in the industry. Victimisation and intimidation, especially of the contractor workforce, which represented the majority of offshore employees, were widespread. Those who raised safety concerns, particularly those seen to be trade union activists, were often identified as 'troublemakers' and were subject to blacklisting via the notorious 'NRB' (not required back) designation. In consequence, the disempowered workforce was unable or reluctant to speak out on safety issues for fear of management retribution.

What happened on Piper Alpha could just as easily have happened on any of the platforms in the UK sector. Piper Alpha was a disaster that many had predicted and yet these warnings had not been heeded. The disaster, in this respect, had many features in common with other disasters that occurred in the mid-to-late 1980s and subsequently. Those resulting in multiple fatalities included the sinking of the *Herald of Free Enterprise*, the sinking of *The Marchioness* riverboat on the Thames, and the seemingly unending series of rail disasters, beginning with Clapham Junction through to Ladbroke Grove, Hatfield and Potters Bar in more recent times, not to mention international disasters such as Bhopal, Westray and Chernobyl. In each of these disasters, management failure was subsequently identified as a crucial factor.

In the UK, these events fatally undermined public trust in the ability of corporations to act responsibly. If we wish to identify the roots of the current calls for a reform of the law with respect to corporate killing, it is from this period that they spring. What occurred was a transformation in the perception of the public at large, in which the law was increasingly viewed as a veil behind which corporate negligence would go unpunished. On the morning after Lord Cullen's report was published the Scottish tabloid, the *Daily Record*, ran a succinct banner headline with two words: 'CHARGE THEM!'

9.3 Regulatory capture

Occidental's management failures were gross and sustained, but they would not have been possible without the implicit complicity of the governmental regulatory body charged with the responsibility of maintaining oversight of the offshore industry, namely the UK Department of Energy (DoE).

Lord Cullen eventually removed responsibility for safety matters from the DoE and transferred it to the Health and Safety Executive, the major body overseeing onshore safety. The ineptitude of the DoE may be attributed to its dual and contradictory mission: to encourage the most rapid extraction of hydrocarbons from the North Sea and to ensure the safety of operations offshore. In his pathbreaking study, *The Other Price of Britain's Oil*, W.G. Carson (1982) traced the origins of this department's failures to what he called the 'political economy of speed', i.e. the focus of government on securing tax revenues from the industry which fundamentally compromised the regulatory regime. One result of the political economy of speed was the 'capture' of the regulatory agency by the industry whose activities it was meant to supervise. Regulatory capture meant that the agency of scrutiny came to identify 'the public good' with the interests of the industry. Examples of regulatory capture are found aplenty, both in Carson's own study and in the Cullen Report, which admonishes both the laxity of inspection standards and the failure of the regulator to adopt modern approaches to safety regulation.

Evidence for regulatory capture can be found in the fact that the UK's primary safety agency, the Health and Safety Executive (HSE), was not given responsibility for offshore safety. Although parts of the onshore Health and Safety at Work Act had been extended offshore, the primary responsibility for safety remained with the DoE under an 'agency agreement'. The more modern goal-setting approach to safety regulation of the HSE was therefore not applied to the offshore industry, which remained locked in legislation dominated by an outmoded prescriptive approach (Woolfson *et al.* 1996: 249-73). In addition, key regulations from the Health and Safety at Work Act, which could have allowed for the election of safety representatives and safety committees from the workforce, were never extended offshore. Such regulations had been identified by the oil industry as a potential 'Trojan horse' for trade union influence on the platforms and the DoE had been only too willing to defend industry views (Woolfson *et al.* 1996: 270-75).

On the level of day-to-day inspection and enforcement, the DoE's practices also left a lot to be desired. Only five inspectors were responsible for policing the entire North Sea oil fields. As it happened, Piper Alpha had been visited and inspected by officials from the DoE just weeks before the disaster. The inspectors appeared satisfied that the lessons of the previous fatality, directly linked to a failure of the permit-to-work system, had been learned and that another inspection in one year's time would be appropriate. Most North Sea installations were inspected a great deal less often than this. Piper Alpha's inspection was famously described by Lord Cullen as 'superficial to the point of being of little use as a test of safety on the platform. It did not reveal any one of a number of clear-cut and readily ascertainable deficiencies' (Cullen 1990: ch. 15, paragraph 48). While Lord Cullen was reluctant to characterise the offshore regulatory regime under the DoE as having fatally compromised safety, his recommendation to transfer future responsibility for offshore safety to the HSE spoke for itself. Carson put the problem more succinctly when he described the previous regulatory regime as one of 'institutionalised tolerance of non-compliance' (Carson 1982: 231).

Occidental's response to Lord Cullen's report was a textbook case of corporate denial. While the offshore oil industry as a whole, represented by the United Kingdom Offshore Operators' Association (UKOOA), sought to salvage its own reputation by accepting Lord Cullen's recommendations, Occidental's management remained reluctant to acknowledge problems. Responsibility for Occidental's response was given to Glen Shurtz, chairman of Occidental Petroleum (Caledonia). Mr Shurtz argued that 'We have always practised the management of safety. Offshore it's our number one priority.' Shurtz had little else to say and steadfastly refused to take part in any public debate on the findings of Cullen's inquiry. In a taped interview for a television debate on the report, Shurtz observed that the report was 'bulky' and that he would need time to review it with his technical staff before making any comment. At a subsequent press conference he reiterated, 'We have just received Lord Cullen's report, and it is a little unfair for me to accept criticism which I haven't had a chance to look at.' In essence, this came to be the sum total of Occidental's acknowledgement of its part in the tragedy of Piper Alpha. Times, of course, have changed. Today, if faced with a 'crisis event' of the scale of Piper Alpha, a corporation would in all likelihood call on the public relations services of any number of 'corporate reputational management consultants', a burgeoning industry which in itself reflects growing sensitivity to wider issues of public accountability, rather than the will of companies to act responsibly.

When, in the aftermath of the disaster, Lord Cullen recommended a transfer of regulatory responsibility from the DoE to the HSE, this marked the end-point in the regulatory legitimacy of the previous 'guardians' of offshore safety. In many respects, this has been mirrored by recent events in the rail industry, where a series of disasters triggered an eventual regulatory overhaul of the industry. Piper Alpha and the rail disasters provoke an uncomfortable question: namely, does it take a substantial loss of life in multi-fatality events before any fundamental appraisal of regulatory effectiveness is conducted?

9.4 Judicial accountability

Occidental suffered no legal penalty as a result of Piper Alpha, either in terms of a corporate manslaughter prosecution (homicide under Scots Law) or in terms of a prosecution for breaches under health and safety legislation. After some deliberation, Peter Fraser, the Lord Advocate (Scotland's chief legal officer, a political appointment), took the view that the public interest would not be served by a prosecution. Neither were the financial costs to Occidental in any way proportionate to the scale of the harm that resulted. Eventually, the financial 'victims' of the Piper Alpha disaster turned out not to be the company directors or shareholders, but rather the syndicate members of Lloyd's Insurance, the so-called 'Names', whose individual £250,000 investor entrance stake now presented them with unlimited liabilities and personal ruin.

Meanwhile, Occidental was given assistance from the UK government in the form of petroleum revenue tax relief, which resulted in the construction of a new £780 million platform, Piper Bravo. Legal proceedings were initiated by Elf Caledonia (the successor company to Occidental Petroleum in the Piper field) against the offshore contracting companies that had been working on the platform at the time of the disaster. This was an attempt to recover losses inherited from Occidental as a result of the disaster, associated with compensation payments to contractors' personnel. These proceedings resulted in the longest-running court case in Scottish legal history. The result was a legal victory for the oil majors over the contractors, in which the relatives of the victims had yet again to endure the raking over of the events of the disaster. Attempts to mount a private prosecution against Occidental for corporate homicide (manslaughter) foundered due to lack of finances. Occidental Petroleum was allowed to disengage from its operations in the UK sector with scarcely a whisper of official condemnation. In the memorable words of an offshore union leader, Occidental was allowed to 'tiptoe away' from the North Sea, unmolested by the judicial authorities.[1]

With hindsight, these events indicate that safety can be compromised by political and economic expediency until it becomes politically intolerable. History provides its own jolting ironic footnotes. In the *Sunday Times* top 500 listed companies for 2001, Occidental Petroleum was ranked 422nd. It continues as a major and profitable operator in the industry. Recently, the *Financial Times* carried a one-paragraph report noting that Occidental Petroleum has now acquired and is operating assets of the failed Enron corporation.

9.5 Principles or profit? Good corporate citizenship

Nowadays, most major oil companies see (or describe) themselves as champions of good governance and of environmental and employee welfare issues. The oil multinationals are among the most aggressive players in the corporate social responsibility movement. In many respects these efforts can be traced to the special position that oil occupies in the political economy of multinational–state interactions. Oil production necessitates the temporary or permanent cession of property rights by the state to the company. For the company, in turn, oil production requires extensive sunk investments, which encourage companies to obtain the most favourable fiscal and regulatory conditions possible. Ultimately, this relationship can lead to public accusations of an exceedingly favourable treatment of these companies by the state. Throughout the 20th century, the oil industry has been well aware of the reputational dangers this situation can pose. The industry has, therefore, pioneered efforts to manipulate political sentiment. A 1954 publication by the US Oil Industry Information Committee titled *Oil's Way of Winning Friends*, published at the height of the Cold War, linked the unrestricted operation of the industry, free from regulatory interference, directly to the welfare of society (Engler 1967):

> no one part of the oil industry can prosper unless the industry as a whole is free to serve the public in its own way—free from unnecessary restraints and regulations . . . If misconceptions are allowed to persist, eventually they will threaten the very existence of the oil industry, and the jobs of oil men and women everywhere. And there is another, even greater threat hidden in these mistaken ideas. If it were possible to destroy the public's confidence in the oil and other businesses, it would be possible to destroy the public's belief in the American competitive enterprise system itself.

Today, surprisingly little has changed in the oil industry's outlook on itself, although thematic priorities may have shifted. The reality appears to be that 'Big Oil' has remained a champion of unrestrained free enterprise and a vigorous opponent of pro-regulatory forces.

---

1   Offshore Industry Liaison Committee, mass meeting, Glasgow, July 1999.

Arguably, the collapse of the 'evil empire' of communism has been accompanied by a shift in scrutiny towards the human rights and the environmental record of multinational corporations. This is not necessarily good news for oil corporations, which often find themselves operating in dubious regulatory and political environments. As a consequence, recent years have seen a renewed and growing self-absorption of large multinational oil companies with their image as corporate 'good citizens'. Virtually all of the major oil companies today claim not to put 'profits before principles' and to be genuinely concerned with human rights issues.

In the wake of the execution of Ken Saro-Wiwa in Nigeria, Shell International attempted to persuade a concerned public of the need to 'understand the dilemma in which Shell Nigeria finds itself' and that Shell 'is trying to do an honest job under difficult conditions, and . . . is a force for good in the country—probably doing more in direct help than any other single organization' (Royal Dutch/Shell 1995). After these difficulties in Nigeria and the Brent Spar debacle, Shell International embarked on a public relations offensive which saw full-page colour adverts in the UK press and the production of its first glossy 'stakeholder' annual report. The opening paragraph of the *Shell Report*, tellingly entitled 'Profits and Principles—Does There Have to Be a Choice?', begins with a 'debating expectations' section which represents a typical example of corporate agenda-setting (Royal Dutch/Shell 1998): 'Multinationals have been criticized as being overly concerned with profit and failing to take their broader responsibilities seriously: to defend human rights, to protect the environment, to be good corporate citizens.'

The brochure contained a prepaid 'Tell Shell' reply card, inviting comments to 'be taken into account and published on our web site'. The *Shell Report* outlined a corporate code of conduct and its 'Statement of General Business Principles'. Such codes are an increasingly prominent feature of contemporary 'socially responsible' corporations (Frynas 2001; Wheeler *et al.* 2002). Whatever the intentions of corporate leaders, they bear only the remotest connection with realities that are often brutal and inhumane.

9.6 Setting the agenda

Over three decades ago, the American political scientist Robert Engler (1967) argued in *The Politics of Oil* that multinationals no longer respond to criticisms and are no longer measured against established yardsticks of human and trade union rights. Equally, he suggested, they no longer seek to deflect the criticism they face from the political arena or political action groups. Rather, they centre their strategy on becoming political agenda-setters, trend-setters or policy-makers, aiming for a public credibility sufficient to paralyse unwelcome monitoring through the media and sanctioning through the legal system.

Proffering claims of self-constructed and self-regulated 'corporate citizenship' (or equivalent terms such as corporate social responsibility) provides immunity against 'misconceived' criticism, very much along the lines suggested by Engler in the 1960s; oil companies dictate terms of a corporate social responsibility debate which only rarely deviates from the party line. John Browne, the Group Chief Executive Officer of BP, has been explicit about where he sees the current position of multinationals (Browne 1997 [emphasis added]):

> Now there is a wider agenda, including the environment, employ-ment and labour standards, distribution of income, and the behavior of governments, as well as business ethics. Companies are considered to be actors on the international stage in their own right, if *not the directors of the play*. Of course there are good reasons why people should think companies have that sort of power. More than 20 companies now have the turnover greater than the GDP of Hungary or Ireland or Venezuela.

For corporate leaders such as John Browne, being candid is the order of the day (Browne 2002):

> Open markets, steady economic development and an open society are the conditions in which we can best pursue our business. This is contrary to the common belief that companies find it easier to deal with the apparent stability of repressive regimes than to manage the uncertainties of democracy.

In the harmonious meld of corporate and public goals envisaged by Browne, concerns over human rights and public welfare evolve naturally as part of a corporate, rather than a contested, political agenda. BP has embraced the United Nations Universal Declaration of Human Rights and now routinely consults with advocacy groups such as Amnesty International and Human Rights Watch, implementing a liberal democratic vision of the future. NGOs such as Amnesty International now seem prepared to concede that there has been an awakening of the corporate conscience and that there seems to be a genuine conviction that profit and principle can go together.

Local conflicts also no longer pose problems to the self-proclaimed aims of the corporation, but rather an opportunity to further develop the oil industry's corporate recipe for world salvation. Says Browne (1997):

> Geology has not restricted the distribution of hydrocarbons to areas governed as open pluralistic democracies. The cutting edge of the issue of corporate responsibility comes from the fact that circum-stances don't always make it easy for companies to operate as they would wish.

In the darker corners of the planet, collaboration between repressive regimes and oil multinationals has been documented only incompletely. These countries include Angola, Algeria, Burma, Cameroon, Chad, Colombia, Ecuador, Gabon, Iran, Iraq, Nigeria, Peru, Venezuela. This is a list with no claim to completeness, if only because it is growing day by day. As a senior oil executive of a US oil engineering group active in Algeria is alleged to have stated, '[for the oil industry] the big money is in countries whose names end with "ia" and "stan" . . . places other people don't want to go to'. In many of these countries, oil worker unions have played a key role in the wider fight for trade union and democratic rights. In Colombia, where both BP and Occidental are significant players, a particularly heavy price has been paid by oil workers: an estimated 120 union leaders have been murdered in the last ten years. From January 2003, US Special Forces began operating in Northern Colombia as advisers to the notorious 18th Brigade of the Colombian army (Wilson 2003). Their designated mission will be to train the Colombian army to protect Occidental's 500 mile pipeline from leftist guerrillas, as part of the Bush administration's congressionally approved 'global war on terrorism'. Colombia supplies only 3% of US oil but, as the US administration embarked on its Iraq intervention, in the words of the US envoy to Colombia, 'every percentage is important' (Marx 2002).

In the oil provinces of advanced capitalist nations, we would not expect to find the unfortunate excesses that have accompanied the activities of major companies in less developed parts of the world. Here repression takes more subtle forms. It includes the co-option of the debate on corporate responsibility by the oil multinationals themselves, together with the deflection of questions about safety and trade union rights through a new 'shared' agenda which views environmental issues and 'sustainability' as pre-eminent (see, for example, UKOOA 2002).

Today's oil multinationals have developed a comprehensive 'ethical toolkit' aimed at defusing threats to the industry's long-term and regional interests. Claims of social responsibility have become an integral and useful part of their business strategy. Even Occidental has its own 'social responsibility' and 'health, safety and environment' web pages claiming that health and safety has been its number one priority for the past 20 years. Occidental's website makes no mention of the Piper Alpha disaster. At the first major conference of the offshore oil industry held by the respected Society of Petroleum Engineers in Stavangar, Norway, in 2000, which devoted a special session to the issue of corporate responsibility, it was an Occidental spokesman who provided one of the key panellists.

In the UK, New Labour and the *Financial Times* annually join forces to present Business in the Community Awards to a roster of socially aware corporations. In the words of Prime Minister Tony Blair at one awards ceremony, 'business can marry competitiveness and social engagement'.[2] BP/Amoco was especially commended recently for its socially aware annual report and its corporately responsible website. Shell, too, received honourable mention in dispatches.[3]

Internationally, these activities have led to the oil companies capturing the moral high ground in international forums, such as the World Summit on Sustainable Development in Johannesburg in September 2002. Here, Tony Blair used the occasion to announce the global 'Extractive Industries Transparency Initiative', aimed at the establishment of a 'broad coalition' committed to developing a framework to promote transparency of payments from oil and mining companies to host-country governments (Department for International Development 2002). Among the high-profile oil company signatories supporting this anti-corruption initiative are BP and Shell; others (TotalFinaElf, Talisman and Statoil) are expressing interest in getting involved. In spring 2003, the UK planned to host an international conference (involving government ministers, senior officials,

2 As quoted in the *Financial Times*, 16 July 1999.
3 *Financial Times*, 19 May 2002

industry and NGO leaders) to take the initiative forward in the run-up to the G8 Summit of industrialised nations.

9.7 Conclusion

The UK passed through a period of political deregulation under the Conservative government administrations. The current New Labour government has accepted many of the business-friendly assumptions of its predecessors with respect to the need to 'free' business from what is described as 'burdensome regulation' (Beck and Woolfson 2000). This places future prospects for corporate accountability in a troubling position. If the recognition of regulatory failure with regard to safety or the environment is now dependent on sustained public reaction to disasters, such as Piper Alpha, then government has essentially ceased to play the role of a pro-active policy-maker. Vacillation in the current administration towards introducing effective legal accountability through corporate killing legislation would seem to confirm the continuing tension between the public desire for accountability and corporate resistance to external regulatory and judicial oversight. In this political vacuum, the excesses of corporate self-promotion and self-delusion flourish.

There is a series of compelling television advertisements sponsored by Shell. One shows a misty-eyed environmentalist. He is liltingly described as an 'impossible' dreamer: 'Once, he would have been an oil company's worst nightmare,' intones the Scottish actor's soft voiceover, 'today, he is their brightest hope.' The advertisement fades out as the prow of a Shell oil exploration vessel cuts through pristine blue waters, unsullied by oil pollution. This comforting cameo aptly identifies the capacity of the industry to absorb its critics, to the point of imaginative self-parody. There is another parody of corporate social responsibility. It is the famous dictum of Marx (Groucho, that is, not Karl): 'Integrity and honesty are the foundations of success . . . If you can fake those, you've got it made.'

Mining in conflict zones*

Simon Handelsman
Global Issues Advisors, USA

In order to better understand and appreciate the complexities of the impact on human rights resulting from corporate behaviour, this chapter examines the sequence of events around two incidents typical of points of conflict concerning human rights and the operations of mining companies. While the incidents are similar in that they encompass human rights abuses by state security forces in which mining companies were alleged to have been complicit, they are completely different in terms of the corporate responses.

The cases presented, in Bolivia and Indonesia, concern two different contexts for conflict, albeit both involving countries with weak, corrupt institutions (US Department of State 2002a, 2002b). Both conflicts arose in areas of poverty with indigenous peoples, although the specific dynamics of conflict differed: an under-lying internal workforce–mine management conflict in Bolivia and external separatist aspirations in West Papua. There was also a sharp contrast between how the two companies involved (a large, profitable multinational in Indonesia; a small junior company in Bolivia) reacted and engaged. The case studies illustrate the complexity and convergence of other issues when there are allegations of human rights abuses. These other issues include the rights of indigenous people and communities in the areas of mining operations; issues of conflict revolving around labour rights; and the issues of conflict between sub-jurisdictions or communities and the national jurisdiction. While not all companies will have to address security issues, the complexities and the challenges faced are similar to those faced by natural resources companies all over the world.

---

* This chapter builds on a report prepared by the author (Handelsman 2002) for the Mining Minerals and Sustainable Development Project.

10.1 Indonesia

The case of Freeport McMoRan Copper & Gold Inc. and its Indonesian affiliate, PT Freeport Indonesia, illustrates the complexities of issues that surround mining operations in areas of weak governance, corrupt administration, nationalist aspirations and strong but undisciplined security forces. It also suggests how mining companies may be able to provide for security while working to protect human rights. In Indonesia, Freeport operates the Grasberg mining and milling complex, the world's lowest-cost copper producer and one of the world's largest producers of copper and gold.

10.1.1 Background

Freeport signed a contract of work (COW) with the government of the Republic of Indonesia in 1967. That was just five years after the administration of West Papua was handed over to the Indonesian government by the United Nations Temporary Executive authority and two years before the United Nations (UN) mandated Act of Free Choice 1969 was ratified, transferring authority over the government of West Papua from the Netherlands to Indonesia. The UN Secretary-General's special representative and many educated Papuans at the time of the Act of Free Choice believed that the Act did not reflect the will of the Papua people; that belief has grown over the 34 years since West Papua's formal incorporation within Indonesia's Province of Irian Jaya (Anti-Slavery Society 1990; Saltford 2000).

The people of Irian Jaya are ethnically and culturally different from other people in Indonesia. Papuans are Melanesians, whereas most other Indonesians are subgroups of Malay and Chinese. Melanesians, like many other indigenous people, have deep physical, spiritual and emotional roots in the land. Indonesian agrarian law, according to the constitutions of 1945 and 1949, established the government as the owner of land for the benefit of 'all Indonesians'. There were no legal protections for traditional, community land rights (*hak ulayat*), although the new Special Autonomy laws for Aceh and Irian recognise community land rights and provide legal protection for those traditional land rights. Nevertheless, all surface and subsurface resources belong to the government. Mining companies in Indonesia work under a COW system with the government of Indonesia. The government owns the resource; mining companies work the deposit but do not own it. Many resource sites, including Freeport's, are designated as 'National Treasures'.

Many of these factors put the government of Indonesia and local people (Amungme and Kamoro) on a collision course. Land is life for the people; for the government, land is a resource to be exploited (Churchill 1995; Sillitoe 2000). Beyond mining activities, the government of Indonesia embarked on an extensive programme of transmigration by which Indonesians from overpopulated areas of Java and Bali move to other, less populated areas. When PT Freeport Indonesia began operations in 1972, the local population numbered fewer than 1,000 (Freeport McMoRan 2001b). By 1998, over 700,000 ha of land in Irian Jaya had been turned over to transmigrants. A large number of transmigrants are located in Freeport's mining area, which now has a population of more than 100,000.

Local people would prefer to be ruled under their system of traditional law which assumes they live in an area where they can disengage from each other. Tribal revenge attacks 'pay back' individuals or their families for a grievance (Pitts 2001). The traditional 'payback' system still works when people live far enough away from each other, so that when the system of paybacks is completed there is a way to disengage and stay disengaged (some grievances can last for several generations). However, people are moving away from remote areas into more inhabited areas, which means that disengagement is a less feasible option.

Since the Indonesians took over control of West Papua, there have been clashes between Indonesian security forces and freedom fighters from the Organisasi Papua Merdeka—Free Papua Movement (OPM). These clashes have been periodic and widely spaced geographically. The most serious recent conflicts were in Biak, the Jayapura area, Manokwari and the Sorong area. By contrast, the area where Freeport's mine operates, Mimika, has been relatively free of conflict in recent times, although an ambush in August 2002 left three civilian teachers dead. It remains unconfirmed who attacked the teachers: rebels, the army, or terrorists. People who live in local communities are not believed to have been involved.

The conflict between freedom fighters and security forces has brought accusations of human rights violations. Although the Papuans, and especially the OPM, were accused of perpetrating human rights violations, more often it has been the security forces that have faced the most serious accusations of imprisoning, torturing and killing civilians.

Alleged and proven human rights violations have occurred relatively infrequently in the area of Freeport's operations. However, those violations were widely publicised, particularly in a report published by ACFOA (Australian Council for Overseas Aid, an NGO).[1] The Robert F. Kennedy Center for Human Rights, a Washington-based NGO, and Project Underground picked up the ACFOA accusations and pressed for an independent investigation of Freeport's relationship with Indonesian security forces. A detailed discussion of the events concerning Freeport follows.

10.1.2 The 1994 events at Freeport

On 18 November 1994 a Freeport employee working on the company road was shot in the back by a high-powered rifle and killed. During that day Freeport vehicles were shot at and several employees wounded. This followed months of reports of OPM activity in the Tsinga Valley, east of Freeport's operations area. It was also reported that government security personnel had pursued the OPM in Tsinga and

---

1   The original report about events in 1994 in Freeport's operations area was published in 1995 by ACFOA. Bishop Munninghoff, the Roman Catholic Bishop of Jayapura, whose account became the basis for the ACFOA report, was more sanguine in his report. He wrote: 'Because the sources of the report are not well known, on the one hand we cannot accept it at face value, but on the other hand, what happened in these stories is challenging us to pay attention' (Munninghoff 1995).

had done as much damage to the village and its people as the OPM had done before them.[2]

At that time Freeport had an internal, unarmed security force of some 200 men and the government security forces in the area were about equal in number. Freeport's security personnel had access to ten vehicles and logistical support, whereas the armed government security personnel had a handful of vehicles and no logistical support of their own. Following the shootings, Freeport requested the government of Indonesia to provide sufficient protection to allow the mine to continue operating and for its employees to be able to live and work without fear. The government sent approximately 400 additional security forces to the area, mostly to patrol the 100 km of the road between the coast and the mine.

The government identified those who killed the employee as members of the OPM led by Kelly Kwalik, an Amungme from the area around Freeport's mine. To facilitate the capture of the OPM operatives, the government security forces took about 20 local people into custody, some of whom have never been found and are presumed dead; others, including women, were locked in shipping boxes under inhumane conditions. In spite of the government security forces' efforts, the freedom fighters escaped from the area (Munninghoff 1995: 6-9).

These activities led to increased protests by the local population against the government of Indonesia. These culminated on Christmas morning when the Papuan (Morning Star) flag was raised in Freeport's town of Tembagapura. The man who raised the flag was killed and, shortly after that, additional Papuans were arrested. During the transport of five of those who were arrested, one man was shot and killed (Munninghoff 1995: 18-24).

10.1.3 Freeport's role

There are no accusations that Freeport personnel directly participated in any of these events. The most comprehensive report was made by Bishop Munninghoff of the Catholic Diocese of Jayapura. Bishop Munninghoff's report neither exonerated nor implicated Freeport for the human rights violations reported; it simply recounted the events as attested by a large number of witnesses. The report made it clear that the direct violations were committed by government security forces.

However, other factors complicated the situation. It is claimed that the vehicle used by the security forces to transport the body of the man killed at the flag raising was a Freeport vehicle (although both Freeport and the security forces deny this). The five who were arrested were transported on a Freeport bus that was commandeered by security forces at gunpoint, and the box that was used to hold those held for questioning was a shipping box given by Freeport to the security forces 12 years earlier for storage. Four low-level government security personnel were court-martialled for human rights violation in this case and jailed for a period of time, but no officers were tried. The question arises whether these circumstances, along with the fact that Freeport requested protection from additional security forces, constituted complicity in human rights violations. Some NGOs, faith-based organisations and human rights NGOs said 'yes'; Freeport disagreed. Some local

---

2   Derived from Freeport internal communications (Munninghoff 1995: 4-5).

people and NGOs also complained that security forces either would not be in the area at all, or at least would not be there in such numbers, if Freeport were not operating in the area. That is probably true. Resource extraction brings enhanced security: 'Where indigenous people clash with developmental projects, the developers almost always win. Tensions with indigenous peoples in Irian Jaya, including in the vicinity of the Freeport-McMoRan mining concession area . . . led to a crackdown by government security forces' (US Department of State 1996).

10.1.4 The aftermath and Freeport's response

It is difficult to directly attribute events in 1995 and 1996 to the troubles that took place in Freeport's area in 1994, but, since these events were not strikingly different from what had taken place in the area prior to late 1994, there may be some discernible connection. Three events were initiated by the local people: first, in January 1996, the kidnapping of WWF (World Wide Fund for Nature) researchers from an area some 160 km east of Freeport's mine; second, in March 1996, riots in Freeport's town of Tembagapura and in the nearby town of Timika; and, third, in April 1996, a lawsuit filed in the US District Court in New Orleans on behalf of an Amungme man and, later, a similar case filed in Louisiana State court on behalf of an Amungme woman, both alleging human rights violations against the local people by the Indonesian security forces supported by Freeport.

Allegedly, the WWF kidnapping was carried out by Kelley Kwalik and his followers (i.e. the same group that was suspected of shooting the Freeport employee in November 1994). When the kidnapping first took place, the OPM claimed it was being undertaken to force the closure of Freeport's operations but that claim was never corroborated. Six of the thirteen hostages were expatriates from the UK, the Netherlands and Germany. The German hostage was released within days of the incident; the others were held by the OPM until the end of April. The International Committee of the Red Cross (ICRC) became deeply involved in negotiations with the kidnappers. The UK's New Scotland Yard antiterrorist officers joined with Indonesian security forces in attempts to free the hostages. Both the ICRC and the security forces used the airport at Timika for logistical support. Hence, although neither Freeport nor Timika was directly involved in the hostage situation, much of the news about the events carried the name of Freeport. The crisis ended with a security raid in late April 1996, after the withdrawal of the ICRC negotiators. Several Indonesian hostages were killed, reportedly by their abductors, during the freeing of the hostages. Reports indicated that security forces killed a number of the kidnappers. Equally important as what happened during the kidnapping was what reportedly happened after the kidnapping episode ended. The Irian Jaya Council of Churches alleged that security forces carried out systematic raids on villages around the kidnapping area during which local residents were tortured, raped and killed. Although these actions had no direct connection to Freeport and its operations, in the eyes of many of the local people none of this would have taken place if Freeport was not operating in the area.

The origins of the March 1996 riots, first in Tembagapura and later in Timika, remain unclear. Several different groups claim responsibility for the first riot, which took place on 12 March. No one was killed and there were only a few minor injuries. The damage, however, was substantial and the mine and mill were closed for two days. Unlike the Tembagapura riots, the riots in Timika two days later were spontaneous and uncontrolled. Three people died in Timika from accidents, two when a stolen truck ran into a tree and another when a man fell from a stolen dozer. In the aftermath of the riots the number of security forces in the area increased from approximately 400 to over 1,000, which is the current number (PT Freeport Indonesia 1996).

At the urging of national and international NGOs, the local community filed lawsuits in the United States against Freeport-McMoRan Copper & Gold Inc. The suits alleged that Freeport supported Indonesian security forces in committing human rights abuses, polluted traditional lands with mine tailings, and attempted 'cultural genocide' on the local people. Both cases were dismissed by the courts. However, the cases, together with the events outlined above, induced a number of changes in Freeport's policies and ways of relating to the local people, which are outlined below.

Freeport took five specific actions:

1. Established the Freeport Fund for Irian Jaya Development

2. Hired a high-level employee to act as a liaison with security forces

3. Built living and recreational facilities for government security forces

4. Established a corporate social, employment and human rights policy

5. Introduced human rights training for Freeport's unarmed security personnel, to which government security personnel are invited, and provided support for the government in establishing the rule of law and a legal system for all parties in the area

The first and most substantive change made by Freeport was to restructure Freeport's community development programme to give the local community a greater voice in the process. The scope of the programme was expanded from a focus on only the two most local indigenous groups (the Amungme and Kamoro) to give equal treatment to other indigenous people who had moved into Freeport's operations area from the five other contiguous tribal groups. This was the primary demand of local people following the rioting. Freeport agreed to restructure its programme by introducing the Freeport Fund for Irian Jaya Development (FFIJD), which provides 1% of PT Freeport Indonesia's net revenue for the development of the local community. The FFIJD has been attacked by some of the local people and criticised by a number of NGOs for having a divisive impact on indigenous communities, encouraging a dependency mentality, and undermining Papuan cultural norms (Diary of Online Papua Mouthpiece 2002). In response to these criticisms, the FFIJD has been restructured several times. Despite difficult beginnings, the FFIJD has provided benefits to the local people in healthcare, education and the development of village infrastructure. Over the past few years, local people have gained a stronger voice in the use of the FFIJD funds. Since 1996 the FFIJD has provided over US$74 million for the people around Freeport's mine.

The second action was to hire an experienced expatriate to co-ordinate relations with the Indonesian security forces. This has been controversial. One of the weaknesses identified by Freeport in the midst of the troubles in 1994 and 1996 was that there was little active communication with government security forces, either before or after security actions took place. Freeport claimed that it did not know that company equipment was being used in the cases where there were alleged human rights abuses until after the fact and, in some cases, until the company read reports written by human rights NGOs. The company insists that it never asked the security forces to do anything that would violate the human rights of the local people, and that the use of company facilities and equipment by security forces was intended to be on the same basis as when used by the local community or the civilian government (i.e. for the benefit of the whole community). The company viewed the security forces behaviour as unacceptable and believed that a more proactive relationship with the security forces could stop further incidents from occurring in the future. Critics, on the other hand, claim that such a liaison only enhances Freeport's relationship with government security forces to the detriment of the local population.

The third action caused even more criticism: the building of barracks and recreational facilities for the security forces that were being assigned to the area in greater numbers than before. Freeport's logic was that security personnel who were poorly housed in remote areas and who had little long-term stake in the welfare of the area would be more apt to behave poorly than those who were well housed and fed and could possibly have family members with them. Critics said that Freeport was just making life better for those who regularly abused the people. Although there is no long-term evidence for whether Freeport or its critics are right, the human rights record in the area, with the exception of a minor incident in December 1999 and the ambush in August 2002, has been far better than in other similar cities in Irian Jaya (West Papua).

The fourth action taken by the company was the approval by the Freeport-McMoRan Copper & Gold Inc.'s Board of Directors of a social, employment and human rights policy (Freeport McMoRan Copper & Gold 2001a). This policy clearly states that Freeport does not permit any employee to partake in human rights violations and that the management of Freeport will publicly condemn any rights violations of which it becomes aware. In addition, all staff employees and all security and community affairs employees are required to sign an assurance letter each year stating that they have not been part of any human rights violations and that they have not seen any, although some reports suggest that the policy is only partially implemented (Shari and Prasso 2000). All reported human rights violations are liable to company disciplinary action and such violations are reported to the Indonesian Human Rights Commission.

The fifth action supported the fourth. Freeport's security department has provided human rights training to all its personnel, using faculty from Indonesian universities and from human rights NGOs. Freeport has invited local government security to participate in these training sessions. This activity is linked with support for government efforts to establish the rule of law in the area and to set up courts to hear criminal and civil cases. Until recently there were no courts or jails in the area.

10.1.5 Conclusions

It is clear that Freeport's management did not recognise its role to protect the human rights of the local population until after the accumulation of events in 1994-96. This was despite incidents in the area in both 1977 and 1984, which were not linked to Freeport, but which were close enough that some notice should have been taken (even though there were no security forces in the area and very little communication between government and the company about security issues). There is little doubt that Freeport did not have proper human rights safeguards in place during the events that transpired in 1994 and 1996. This was a serious mistake. It is difficult to be sure that Freeport could have prevented the events of 1994 and 1996. However, if Freeport had made preparations for such eventualities, this would have better served both the local people and the company.

Since that time, Freeport has taken specific actions to address those issues. Although some of the actions described above were controversial, so far they appear to have been successful. Freeport was a company that 'went it alone' for years and remained outside the discussions on such problems as the environment and human rights. It has now become very much involved and concerned with these issues. It was one of the two mining companies that agreed to the US/UK Voluntary Principles on Human Rights and Security (see further Chapter 19 by Bennett Freeman and Genoveva Hernández Uriz) and has been involved with discussions in the United Nations Global Compact meetings. It is now also an active participant in the Fund for Peace Human Rights Roundtable.

Human rights violations continue in the area. On 31 August 2002, faculty members of the expatriate school were on their way to a picnic when they were ambushed. Three people were killed (two American teachers and an Indonesian) and 11 seriously wounded; some may never recover. Some 100–200 shots were fired from semi-automatic weapons subjecting the people from the school to 15–20 minutes of terror. Freeport has been trying to ameliorate or solve problems; they hope to discover what happened and why. Initially, the army claimed the Papuans were responsible; the Papuans claimed the army was responsible (Mapes and Dhume 2002). Investigations are under way by the Indonesian and US government and other groups. Recent reports (November 2002) in the press claim that Australia's Defence Signals Directorate (DSD), its most secretive intelligence agency (DSD monitors communications traffic, including mobile phone, radio and Internet messages, from its Canberra headquarters), passed intelligence to the US implicating Indonesia's military in the ambush (*Sydney Morning Herald* 2002). This was denied by the Indonesian army (Nakashima and Sipress 2002: A18). One of the fascinating theories emerging about the cause of the ambush is that Freeport has done too much work with the local people, making the government upset that the locals are happy. This fuels conflict against a government that then does not look so good, and encourages a desire for independence.

10.2 Bolivia[3]

The events that took place in the Bolivian mining districts of Amayapampa, Llallagua and Capasirca started as management/labour disputes, including disputes over the control of gold mining licence areas. The situation subsequently escalated into hostage taking, workers seizing the operations, and a violent confrontation with the police and military in December 1996 in which a Special Security Group Commander and nine civilians were killed, and three police officers and 32 civilians wounded.

The story of Da Capo Resources (now Vista Gold Corporation) in Bolivia contrasts sharply with the proactive engagement of Freeport. Unlike many major companies, junior mining companies face difficulties and constraints caused by lack of capital and capacity. In this case, Vista Gold management saw the problem as being the responsibility of the government and the army, and nothing to do with the company itself.

10.2.1 Background

Although the mining districts of Amayapampa, Llallagua and Capasirca in the province of Bustillos were once part of a thriving mining region, depressed metal prices (mostly tin) and inefficient, traditional mining methods led to a severe reduction in the level of mining activity, and the region became one of the most economically depressed areas of Bolivia. In the past, tin mining had funded area highways, hospitals and an airport. The miners' unions were leaders of the 1962 revolution and of the opposition to the dictatorship of the 1980s. The importance of mine production, the high concentration of workers and the difficult working conditions led to strong trade unions and a high level of labour and social unrest in the province in recent decades. Security forces intervened to repress miners resulting in massacres in 1942, 1949, 1965 and 1967.

The recent conflict dates to 1996, when Da Capo Resources, a Canadian company, bought two old gold mines from the local owners: Amayapampa (acquired 10 April 1996), which was worked in pre-Incan times, and Capasirca (acquired 15 March 1996). Da Capo Resources subsequently became part of Vista Gold Corporation, a Canadian junior mining company with a board of directors including prominent mining executives (Vista Gold 1997b, 2002).

The Amayapampa district was initially mined on a very small scale by indigenous peoples prior to the arrival of the Spanish conquistadors. Small-scale mining continued through the Spanish colonial period into modern times. The Amayapampa property had been optioned by La Compania Minera Altoro SRL. Da Capo Resources was assigned the option agreement and acquired Amayapampa for stock and cash payments to the various parties. Da Capo agreed that CEM, a miners' co-operative, could continue mining the Amayapampa mine using underground methods at current levels of production (about 220 tonnes per day) processing the ore in two mills on site until 11 August 1996. At the time, the Amayapampa mine

3   The description of the events in Bolivia is based on OAS 1997 unless otherwise indicated.

was one of the largest producing underground gold mines in Bolivia with 32 levels of underground development (Vista Gold 1997b).

Capasirca had been optioned to David O'Connor (who later became the mine manager). Da Capo Resources was assigned the option agreement for 1,000,000 shares and acquired Capasirca for stock and cash payments to its various owners. The Capasirca property was mined by underground methods at a rate of some 20 tonnes per day before its shutdown when Da Capo Resources amalgamated with Granges Inc. (another Canadian junior mining company) in 1996 to form Vista Gold Corporation.

The new owners immediately came into conflict with the mine workers, particularly at the Capasirca mine, where conflicts and debts remained from the previous owners. The new management wanted to change from traditional work practices in which the Mixed Trade Union of Mine Workers of Capasirca (especially its secretary-general) had a leading role in organising gold production and extraction. The conflict between the mine owners and the mine workers was exacerbated by ideology and regional poverty, by the background of resentment about the way COMIBOL (Corporación Minera de Bolivia, the state mining enterprise formed when the mines were nationalised in 1952) had been awarding mining concessions, and by the increasingly desperate situation faced by mining co-operatives throughout Bolivia (US Department of State 2002a).

10.2.2 April 1996 strike

The Capasirca mine workers went on strike on 10 April 1996. An inspector from the Ministry of Labour, who declared the strike illegal, said he was assaulted by miners. He had previously reported violations of health and safety regulations, including dangerous rock conditions causing unsafe workplaces, a poorly installed and dangerous electrical system, deteriorated winches and cables, inadequate pumps used by specific miners, and the need for modern drilling machines to replace obsolete equipment.

On 13 May, the company agreed to pay workers up to 75% of their wages for the days on strike, to retain the current work system but improve technology under new working conditions, and to guarantee job security. The union agreed to help the company to improve the operations. On 29 June, the union filed claims for 50% wage increases and for better conditions, and accused the company of breaching the agreement.

10.2.3 Continuing antagonism

Company representatives and union leaders met in La Paz to discuss grievances (12 August). The meeting started badly when the miners complained they had been insulted by the mine manager (David O'Connor). On the same day, the mine manager requested the government to move military troops and the national police force into the conflict area. The company withdrew its people from the area, leaving the mine in the hands of the miners and the unions. On 18 September, the miners took the mine engineer hostage (he was released on the intervention of a local priest) as pressure for the mine manager to come to the area. The company filed criminal charges against those responsible for the loss of management and the resignation of the company's staff.

At a meeting on 21 September, attended by the company and miners, the miners aired their grievances; the company said that poor productivity and financial conditions would force them to close the mine, evaluate their options and then decide what to do. At this point, the mine was still under the control of the miners who, the company complained, were producing gold and keeping it.

10.2.4 November 1996 confrontation: workers seize mine

About 130 police attempted on 14 November to detain the secretary-general of the Capasirca mining union. The local people surrounded the police, took their weapons and equipment and drove them from the area. The local prefect intervened to recover the weapons and equipment before the local troops, moving towards the area, caused a confrontation. He then initiated a meeting held on 20 November, in Potosí, in an attempt to reopen dialogue between the parties and to mediate the dispute. This meeting produced a signed statement of intent.

The Da Capo company representatives failed to attend the next scheduled meeting on 4 December 1996. The Comité Cívico of Llallagua refused to attend the rescheduled meeting (11 December) but took part in a meeting in Potosí on 17 December. While the miners were seeking the company's compliance with the agreement of 13 May, negotiations collapsed when the company learned that mine workers had illegally seized the Amayapampa mine. That morning, residents and mine workers from Amayapampa heard that two workers had been detained and accused of theft by Da Capo. The miners were upset by a company prohibition on chewing coca leaves at work. Mine workers and peasants demanded that the engineers, technical staff and 25 police guarding the mine leave. There had been agreements between management and mine workers without any major labour disputes until then. The mine was seized with minor damage (a few windows were broken). The company ended negotiations as its view was that the dialogue had broken down.

After negotiations collapsed and the Amayapampa mine had been seized, government authorities decided to employ public forces to restore order in the area, to remove the mine workers and to restore the mine to its owners. Police were moved into the area. The next day, 19 December, the peasants and miners met in Amayapampa with mine leaders and human rights representatives. A communiqué rejected any return of foreign investors to Amayapampa on the grounds that it would violate national sovereignty and the dignity of those living in the area. At the end of the meeting, dynamite explosions signalled that the national police were approaching with armed forces.

10.2.5 Lost opportunity to avert tragedy

A conflict ensued between the army and police forces and the peasants and miners who had illegally occupied the mines of Amayapampa and Capasirca. Even at the last moment, there was an opportunity for the tragedy to be avoided. The labour leaders, seeking to prevent bloodshed from the unequal forces, asked for a ceasefire and an end to hostilities. In response to a request for an hour to arrange the peaceful entry of the police and military forces, General Arriaza, Commander General of the National Police Force, offered 15 minutes, which he extended to half an hour, asserting that higher authorities had ordered the taking of the Amaya-pampa mine, regardless of anyone in the way.

The general gave the order to advance towards the mining camp before that half-hour ended, and 'the army used tear gas, rubber bullets, weapons shooting blanks, and firearms, while the peasants and the miners defended themselves with stones and dynamite fragments . . . [but] did not use firearms'. Four people were killed, including a minor (15 years old) and a peasant shot in the back. One of the dead was a mine worker leader who had tried to seek a peaceful solution with the military and police.

10.2.6 December killings

On 20 December, police and army personnel heading to evacuate the wounded and remove corpses were ambushed, a colonel was killed by a shot to his head, a civilian physician was seriously wounded (he could no longer perform surgery after being shot in his right hand and arm) and four police officers were wounded. The Braun regiment attempted to enter Llallagua where the townspeople formed a human barrier and threw stones, sticks and dynamite fragments. The military police shot tear gas, rubber bullets and, later, live ammunition, killing two people, neither of whom was involved in any conflict.

In the hills near the Amayapampa mining camp, the police and military forces opened fire on civilians wounding three plus a nursing auxiliary who was shot in the leg and later died without receiving proper medical attention.

10.2.7 Aftermath

Waldo Albarracín, president of the Permanent Human Rights Assembly of Bolivia, appealed for a speedy, independent and impartial investigation into the December 1996 killings which led to a detention order against him (Amnesty International 1997). On 25 January 1997, while travelling by public transport in La Paz, he was violently forced out of the vehicle by eight police agents who blindfolded him and took him to an unidentified location where he was subjected to beatings, ill-treatment and death threats, and was subsequently left unconscious and seriously injured at a police station in La Paz. He was detained in a cell until he was trans-ferred to a police clinic from which he was removed by relatives and hospitalised at a private clinic.

As a result of national and international pressures, the Bolivian government invited the Inter-American Commission on Human Rights (IACHR), Organisation of American States (OAS), to investigate the events at Capasirca and Amayapampa. The IACHR conducted an on-site visit, preceded by a technical mission that met with government, the military and civil society. Testimony was taken from peasants and miners living in the area and family members of the victims.

10.2.8 IACHR findings

The IACHR's mandate was to investigate the human rights situation in the events of 19–22 December 1996 to determine whether the state had an international responsibility for them. It did not have authority to determine criminal or individual liability. The IACHR concluded that the tragedy had many origins, including: an inappropriately handled labour conflict; an attempt to introduce modern mining methods conflicting with miners' expectations from their traditional work habits; and the backwardness and extreme poverty in a region that had previously been wealthy, but where the population as a whole had not benefited. It also concluded 'that the deaths of nine civilians due to direct actions of military and police agents of the state in Amayapampa, Llallagua and Capasirca between December 19–21, 1996 are imputable to the Bolivian state as a juridical person'.

The IACHR was 'not convinced that there was a strictly proportional use of force by police and military forces in all cases'. Among a host of issues, it found that mechanisms for negotiation were not used to their full potential; the security forces did not have the necessary training and discipline; there was inadequate investigation into the incidents; none of the persons responsible had been sanctioned; and adequate compensation was not paid to the victims or next of kin. Although, officially, the people died as the result of an 'armed confrontation', the Bolivian authorities did not find any evidence of arms or explosives on the corpses.

The IACHR recommended that the government should investigate the incidents and determine the individual liabilities and sanctions for the military and police, and determine the individual liabilities that may arise from the circumstances of the colonel's death. In addition, the IACHR noted that the rules regarding the use of force need to be reviewed, and that compensation should be paid to the relatives of the deceased and the wounded.

More broadly, the IACHR recommended supervising the enforcement of labour and tax legislation under which mining companies operate at Amayapampa and Capasirca. Although it did not investigate any violations, it reported that there was a perception among the workforce that the payments merited examination. It also recommended that the government guarantee the effective operation of mechanisms to resolve collective labour disputes.

It took the Bolivian Attorney General some two and a half years to complete investigations into the December 1996 events at Amayapampa and Capasirca. A US government report observed that the delays in the investigations and in the identification and punishment of those responsible for the deaths resulted in an atmosphere of impunity (US Department of State 2001). Although five military officers were found responsible, the then President Gonzalo Sánchez de Lozada and his ministers were absolved of any responsibility. Cases against the accused officers moved slowly through the military justice system; five officers were reassigned to non-operational units pending the outcome of their legal cases. There was an attempt in Congress to censure Sánchez de Lozada and his ministers.

10.2.9 **Da Capo resources/Vista Gold Corporation response**

The first question is: what happened to Da Capo Resources? It effectively disappeared, having merged on 1 November 1996 with Granges Inc., another junior mining company, to form Vista Gold Corporation. Although the merger occurred while the dispute between management and the mine workers was escalating, it was interesting to note that there were no disclosures or discussions about this evolving dispute in the Joint Management Information Circular prepared for the merger (Granges 1996).

The initial public information about the conflict presented by the company appears to have been a press release reporting that, after the breakdown of extensive negotiations between a lawless faction of miners, Vista Gold and the government, the company had been informed by the government that it had:

> sent the police into the mines at Capa Circa and Amayapampa to restore law and order after the illegal occupation of the mines was instigated by a small group of dissident miners . . . [The Bolivian] government security indicates that 13 people were injured and 3 people killed . . . The Company deeply regrets the loss of life (Vista Gold 1996a).

The company rejected assertions that there was a broader issue of indigenous peoples' rights, and said it was Bolivian officials who wanted the mines' 'rightful ownership' returned to Vista Gold to be operated legally.

Three days later, a second press release reported that the government had informed Vista Gold that 'The conflict at the Amayapampa and Capa Circa mines has been resolved' although the company was 'saddened by the violence . . . the Company appreciates the prompt action by the government' (Vista Gold 1996b). The company persisted with its explanation of events (Vista Gold 1997a). One of Vista Gold's senior officers lauded the government's 'determination to protect the assets of foreign investors and maintain law and order', saying that it was 'a clear message by the government that they want foreign investment and the benefits it can bring to improve the quality of life for all its citizens' (Vista Gold 1996b).

At that time (end of 1996), Vista Gold had expected to start construction of the Amayapampa mine in June 1997 and to start production by June 1998. Production from the Capasirca mine was expected to start about one year later. Vista Gold explained that it had closed the mining operations because they were unsafe and tailings were polluting villagers' land and water. The company continued to pay the miners for work on exploration and development activities as well as infrastructure improvements in their village (roadworks, schools, medical facilities and church) to promote goodwill and maintain social stability in the region. These payments were discontinued in 2000 and workers were laid off as a result of low gold prices.

In April 1997, Vista Gold obtained surface land rights from local indigenous people for Amayapampa and Capasirca in exchange for community programmes such as education, training and employment, and improvement and development (Vista Gold 1997c). By July 1997, a feasibility study for the Amayapampa property led Vista Gold to announce that it was proceeding to seek finance for the project, but by November it had reduced the project's size to reflect the significant drop in the price of gold and lower gold grades from additional drilling (Vista Gold 1998). As the price of gold continued to decline, the project was placed on hold pending higher prices. By March 1999, Vista Gold was considering an open-pit mine. Studies continued, but in April 2000 all the workers at Amayapampa were laid off. Vista Gold continued to provide limited community assistance during 2000 (six teachers and a nurse and restricted access to ex-miners to the old underground workings) (Vista Gold 2001).

There were reports in 1999 that miners and villagers had accepted Vista Gold's offer allowing them to mine any surface gold occurrences at Capasirca (Vista Gold 1999). In February 2000, having decided that the mine was more suitable for small-scale mining, Vista Gold sold Capasirca to a miners' co-operative for about US$300,000 in cash and a production royalty (Vista Gold 2000).

10.2.10 Conclusions

Da Capo/Vista Gold's management had some experience of working in Bolivia. The company believed it was reasonable to introduce changes that made working conditions safer and the operations more profitable. However, it did not recognise the importance of engaging in a positive way to establish a dialogue with the mine workers and local community to effect change. Within a month the new management had a strike at the Capasirca mine and soon there were problems at Amaya-pampa which had not previously experienced labour disputes. It appears that the company seriously underestimated the discontent remaining after it obtained ownership of the mines, and the resentment from the government's introduction of structural adjustments to the economy. There was an unusual alliance between mine workers and the peasant community.

The company's local manager focused on asserting management and property rights, and appears to have been operating with a command-and-control approach. More conciliatory social-political skills to manage change seem to have been required. In the end, the company changed its vision of Capasirca's potential and now (2003) the mine workers are operating the mine in their own way for their own benefits (or losses).

Vista Gold did not recognise that it had any responsibility for the actions of the police and military. It saw its property, management and economic rights threatened and did not recognise a need to engage on human rights problems. Vista Gold complained to the government and urged it to protect the rights of foreign inves-tors. In Vista Gold's view, the responsibility for the tragedy belonged to others: the lawless miners and peasants, the police and the armed forces.

As in the case of Indonesia, there is little doubt that the company did not have proper human rights safeguards in place during the events that transpired in 1996. There were serious mistakes. It is not unreasonable to expect that Da Capo/Vista Gold could have prevented the events of December 1996 if a more conciliatory approach had been taken. However, as the IACHR concluded, there were also many opportunities for others to avert tragedy. One can speculate on a different outcome if the parties had adopted an approach such as those in the US/UK Voluntary

Principles on Human Rights and Security. The IACHR specifically recommended that Bolivia address this question.

There is no evidence that Vista Gold has taken specific actions to address those issues. While the company has provided some social/community programmes, there is a significant difference between engagement in corporate responsibility and philanthropy with which many corporations are grappling.

10.3 Concluding remarks

This chapter has examined incidents in Bolivia and Indonesia involving human rights abuses by state security forces, following foreign mining companies' demands that the respective governments provide protection. The most obvious conclusion to be drawn from the case studies is that there may be unintended adverse consequences when a company believes that what it is doing is right, without considering geopolitics, local culture and history, or local issues. These unintended consequences may be exacerbated when a country has weak and corrupt institutions, and when effective investigations and punishment of those responsible for human rights abuses are delayed (if they are carried out at all).

However, as shown by the experience at Freeport, there are ways to engage positively in a manner that may help to address or overcome conflict. No doubt many will agree that international corporations operating in developing countries have responsibilities to ensure that local communities benefit from the investments these companies make. Yet it also remains the case that the state has the primary role to ensure that the rights of all stakeholders are protected. The need is for companies to accept their responsibility to join in these processes, and to do so in an effective and meaningful manner. A more detailed and nuanced analysis of the case studies enables two important conclusions to be drawn. The first is that a lack of relationship skills and insensitivity to the concerns of others can lead to problems. Because of this, mining companies need to educate their employees and engage positively to support and promote human rights in such areas as respect for human rights, conditions of work and wages, and development opportunities. A positive starting point would be to adopt appropriate codes of conduct and then to ensure that these are implemented effectively through the entire organisation and across all operations. The second conclusion is that mining companies must ensure that appropriate institutional capacity is developed in both government and state security forces.

In Bolivia, there were no signs of positive engagement in support of human rights by the corporation, nor does the company appear to have either changed its behaviour or accepted any responsibility for the tragedy. An initial reaction to the Bolivian situation is that a lack of financial capacity leaves less hope for a positive future. However, although the junior company had limited financial capacity, it possessed significant capacity in the form of prominent, capable and experienced mining executives on its board of directors, who appeared not to have provided suitable advice and guidance to avoid conflict. The company did not disclose or discuss the evolving dispute to its shareholders or in its filing to the SEC (US Securities and Exchange Commission). Its board did not endorse any positive actions or accept any responsibility after the events, but instead maintained that the problems were caused by a 'criminal element', a finding refuted by the international judicial investigation that concluded origins to the tragedy lay with the company's behaviour. The experience in Bolivia contrasts with the experience and response of Freeport in Indonesia, where a large, highly profitable, multinational company that previously did not perceive it had any obligations to protect human rights of the local population, used its resources and capacity to effectively engage positively and proactively to promote and protect human rights. It may be no coincidence that, following the August 2002 incident, unlike in the past, there were no allegations that security forces carried out systematic raids on villages around the area where the shootings took place, nor were there any complaints that local residents were tortured, raped or killed.

We saw how, in one case, a company's experiences led it to adopt a clear social, employment and human rights policy, and how these experiences fed positively into the US/UK Voluntary Principles on Human Rights and Security. These principles provide a toolbox for resource companies to use to design policies and procedures to help deal positively with human rights issues and security forces (although they cannot and do not prevent abuses). One can speculate on whether there would have been a different outcome in the Bolivia case if the parties had adopted an approach such as those in these Voluntary Principles. In order to ensure the effectiveness of such voluntary, non-binding approaches, corporations need to:

● Develop comprehensive codes of conduct

● Establish training and management practices to implement the codes

● Establish internal audit procedures

● Have independent external auditing of performance

● Publicly report on the results (see, further, Sullivan and Frankental 2002)

Auditing and the verification of performance imply the establishment of benchmarks and standards for measurement. An example that could be adopted by other companies is Freeport's requirement that staff employees and all security and community affairs employees sign a statement each year attesting they have not seen or been part of any human rights violations.

Two issues alluded to in this chapter are: first, the inherent constraints imposed by local circumstances on a mining company's ability to conduct business as it wishes; and, second, to what extent a government's conduct may be influenced. Can or should a corporation use its capacity to influence a local government's behaviour in a positive way? Clearly corporations do have opportunities to exert an influence—for good or for ill. It is argued that larger companies have more of a responsibility to use their influence to promote and protect human rights, and to encourage governments to recognise and comply with international human rights standards. Should all mining companies take an active role in encouraging governments to recognise and comply with international human rights standards?

This chapter has shown that corporations could have a positive influence when they develop, adopt and implement a human rights code of conduct.

Not surprisingly, we have also seen that there are always more questions than satisfactory answers. As a commentator on the Bolivian situation suggested (*Presencia* 1996):

> The events surrounding the conflict between the miners and the Vista Gold Corp., owner of the Capasirca and Amayapampa mines, raise a number of legal, ethical, and environmental issues, which transcend the local nature of the current conflict: to whom should the subsoil and the minerals in it belong? To the state (as in the case of Bolivia) or to the indigenous peoples? What are the responsibilities of powerful, international corporations operating in developing countries, where the local communities hardly benefit from the multi-million dollar profits these companies make? What is the role of the state in this situation? How do we define 'sustainable development' in areas where people are preoccupied, above all, with mere survival? Questions which evidently one cannot pretend to answer, but may only serve to initiate a discussion.

11

Health, business and human rights
The responsibility of health professionals within the corporation*

*Norbert Goldfield***

3M Health Information Systems, USA

The human rights literature has only begun to focus on the nexus between corporate impact on human rights and the individuals that work for the corporation. This chapter focuses on a specific professional group (physicians) within corporations and discusses the manner in which they can use their medical status to influence corporate policies and actions pertaining to human rights (with a particular focus on the right to health).

The chapter is divided into four parts. The first is a broad overview of the field of medical ethics and a discussion of the intersection between medical ethics and the principal document guiding human rights activists and professionals, namely the Universal Declaration of Human Rights. The second is a discussion of the literature dealing with health professionals and physicians working in corporations. The third is a case study to illustrate the challenges confronting health professionals, focusing on the issue of organs taken from prisoners executed in China and subsequently sold for transplantation. The fourth part then considers the specific question of how human rights NGOs can interface effectively with health professionals.

* The information presented and views expressed in this chapter are those of the author and do not necessarily represent the views of 3M Health Information Systems or 3M Company.
** The assistance of Dr Melinda Sweeting who provided substantial comments on an earlier draft of this chapter is gratefully acknowledged.

11.1 Medical ethics and the Hippocratic oath

The medical profession is confronting many challenges to its traditional role in society. The Hippocratic oath continues to serve as the broad standard by which we judge physician behaviour and obligations. All medical students (at least in the United States) swear by it on graduation from medical school. However, while the Hippocratic oath serves as a guidepost for physicians in order to assess their behaviour, the complexities of modern medicine have led to the development of entirely new theoretical disciplines within medical ethics and new organisational constructs to meet the many complex dilemmas posed by modern-day medical practice. Ethicists have proposed several distinct approaches over the past half-century, including:

- A human rights/personal autonomy approach championed by Brock (1993). In essence, Brock follows Rawls by promoting equality of access and thus countenancing limiting the individual autonomy of healthcare providers.

- A contractual approach formulated by Veatch (1981) in which medicine, for example, has contractual duties to all members of society, the limits of which are defined by society

- A case-based/clinically oriented perspective championed by Jonsen and Toulmin (1988) in which the focus is only on the case or specific situation for which there is a moral dilemma

Healthcare institutions have responded to these ethical dilemmas by developing many organisational structures (hospital ethics committees, for example) to deal with these issues as they emerge. In many ways, however, it is useful to return to the Hippocratic oath as it forms the seed for many of the intellectual responses to the ethical dilemmas that we face today. The critical aspects of the modern version of the Hippocratic oath include:[1]

- I will apply, for the benefit of the sick, all measures which are required, avoiding those twin traps of overtreatment and therapeutic nihilism.

- I will remember that I do not treat a fever chart, a cancerous growth, but a sick human being, whose illness may affect the person's family and economic stability. My responsibility includes these related problems, if I am to care adequately for the sick.

- I will prevent disease whenever I can, for prevention is preferable to cure.

- I will remember that I remain a member of society, with special obligations to all my fellow human beings, those sound of mind and body as well as the infirm.

1 Modern version of the Hippocratic oath written by Louis Lasagna as quoted in www.pbs.org/wgbh/nova/doctors/oath_modern.html.

Drawing on the Hippocratic oath, physicians have both negative and positive duties. Physicians should not do harm to their patients. The last point highlights the positive obligations of physicians to serve as good Samaritans and even actively seek out situations that can benefit humankind. However, the limits to this responsibility are not spelled out. These professional obligations mirror the positive and negative obligations imposed by the Universal Declaration of Human Rights (UDHR). For example, the UDHR imposes negative duties not to physically interfere with the life of an individual human being (e.g. Article 4 requires that no one shall be held in slavery or servitude, and that slavery and that the slave trade shall be prohibited in all their forms). These obligations are similar to the Hippocratic principle of first do no harm. The UDHR also contains principles implying a positive obligation, similar to the positive obligations implied in the Hippocratic oath. For example, Article 25 of the UDHR states that everyone has the right to a standard of living adequate for the health and well-being of himself and of his family, including food, clothing, housing and medical care and necessary social services, and the right to security in the event of unemployment, sickness, disability, widowhood, old age or other lack of livelihood in circumstances beyond his control.[2]

While it is possible to define the negative duties imposed by the Hippocratic oath and the UDHR in reasonably clear terms, the positive obligations are far more difficult to define. A contemporary example confronting physicians is the debate over the right to healthcare in the United States, a country in which 17% of the population has no health insurance and millions are underinsured (e.g. Medicare, the federal programme for citizens over 65, does not cover pharmaceuticals). Physicians mirror American society in that it is unlikely that a societal consensus will emerge on a specified set of services for the indigent population. Today's physician attempting to fulfil his or her positive obligations under the Hippocratic oath (or Brock's approach to medical ethics) stands on shaky political ground, because the historical reality is that, as American societal values have changed, so have egalitarian (but not utilitarian or libertarian) theories of justice. Thus, a 1990s egalitarian approach to healthcare would emphasise a basic package of health services for the most vulnerable Americans (a more utilitarian approach), while equal access for all services (along the lines of contract theory or John Rawls) would probably have been insisted upon during the 1960s. It is understood that today's national leadership in the US does not support a 1990s version of egalitarianism as, this year alone (2003), millions of low-income Americans will lose their government insurance for the poor. While egalitarianism represents a strong undercurrent in American popular political opinion (notwithstanding the belief in equal opportunity), high medical costs together with shifting cultural opinions have placed egalitarians in a weak position.

2 www.udhr.org/UDHR/default.htm

11.2 The corporatisation of the medical system

Even though citizens have frequently viewed physicians as among the most respected members of society, trust in physicians, in particular in the United States, has declined in recent years (Newcomer 1997). This decline has occurred for many reasons, but in large measure rests with the perception of citizens that physicians increasingly have a dual loyalty. On the one hand, physicians must have their patient's interest at the forefront of their attention. Yet cost and organisational pressures encourage physicians to consider other interests. In this context, it should be emphasised that the pressures confronting health professionals in the US and Europe are similar yet distinct. Historically, in both the US and Europe, the state has served to sponsor professionalism, in general, and healthcare professionals, in particular, by effectively providing professional trade organisations with a monopoly on continued participation in the profession and by acting as guarantor of profits (via government payment).

In the United States, the emergence of a more conservative politic has resulted in an increasingly corporatised medical system with a concomitantly diminished interest in 'protecting' the political interests of health professionals. The fact that the vast majority of physicians worked in the private sector as independent entrepreneurs facilitated the transition to a health system dominated by corporations. Historically, physicians worked in private solo fee-for-service. Not until the 1960s did the sickest Americans have access to health insurance that paid for visits to the physician (Goldfield 2001). Rapidly rising costs in all sectors of the healthcare economy, together with the appreciation that significant profits could be made from health services, resulted in corporate entry (beginning in the 1970s) into the healthcare economy. In addition, most solo fee-for-service practices have consolidated into group practices, thereby making it easier for corporations to at least attempt to dominate (and, some would argue, dictate) physician decision-making (McKinlay and Marceau 2002).

This corporatisation of American medicine has resulted in an ever-increasing number of physicians who have 'left' the profession to join other types of organisations (in particular, corporations) which, in turn, exert various levels of control on the medical profession. Similarly, a rising number of European physicians have sought employment in either corporations or government service. The rationale for leaving clinical work is manifold. It ranges from fatigue with the gruelling schedule of many physicians to the increasing belief on the part of physicians that by joining either government service or a corporation their potential impact is much greater than the one-to-one impact inherent in the doctor–patient relationship. Whether working to improve the quality within the British National Health Service or working as a corporate executive within a pharmaceutical company, an increasing number of physicians are hoping that they are able to combine their clinical background (which often now includes public health or even business training) with their executive responsibilities in order to have a positive impact on the population they are serving. While the sheer number of corporations attempting to exert control over the medical profession is far smaller in Europe, the roles of government service physicians are similar to those occurring in corporations. The roles that physicians fill within corporations include:

- Researchers within the corporation on healthcare 'products' serving the business needs of the corporation and/or tools used to 'control costs and increase quality'

- Corporate representatives to the public at large when a spokesperson with a health background is needed

- Executives within the corporation

In whichever role the physician works, corporations encourage a primary loyalty to the corporation that can challenge critical aspects of the physician's professional or ethical obligations. In this context, there are two specific aspects that have implications for human rights:

- The role of physicians as scientists within industry

- The change in the professional status of the physician as he or she assumes greater administrative/business responsibility within the corporation

Sociologists have devoted significant attention to the role of scientists in general and physicians in particular within industry. For example, Kornhauser (1962) examined the role of scientists in industry, Walsh (1987) analysed the emerging role of physicians working in either occupational medicine or corporations attempting to control healthcare costs and improve quality, while Goldfield and Nash (1989) wrote on the emerging class of physician leaders working in corporations. Kornhauser's work from almost half a century ago is still relevant today. In his study of research scientists working within industry, he identified three management preferences in working with health professionals (Kornhauser 1959: a-18):

- Management's desire for research supervisors who are oriented towards the organisation rather than the profession, versus the scientists' desire for research supervisors whose primary loyalty is to them rather than to management

- Management's desire for research supervisors who possess administrative competence, versus the scientists' desire for research supervisors who possess scientific excellence

- Management's desire for research supervisors who exercise tight control over work, versus the scientists' desire for research supervisors who are advisory rather than directive

While there initially may exist tensions between a health professional's desire for independence and de facto allegiance to a 'higher' Hippocratic oath, management's desire typically wins out and encourages the health professional to look at human rights issues through management lenses. The type of supervisory relationship between management and health professional influences the extent to which health professionals examine human rights issues from a managerial perspective. While supervisors typically demand corporate loyalty from 'their' healthcare professional, occasionally the health professional is able to work within a corporation in which management is more advisory than directive. This represents a managerial approach that appreciates the positive benefit to the corporation of a health professional who carries dual loyalty to both the corporation and the profession. Does the potential for dual allegiance inevitably lead to compromise, on the part of the healthcare professional, on the principles of the Hippocratic oath? From a theoretical perspective the answer is yes. This can occur at the expense of the patient (Goldfield 1999). The corporatisation of the medical profession has taken the potential impacts much further, potentially undermining the Hippocratic oath to a much greater degree than occurred when the physician was, for example, a solo practitioner in fee-for-service.

There are two career paths within a corporation for health professionals. On the one hand, individuals can decide that contribution to the science involving their expertise constitutes the focus of their intellectual and political energy within the corporation. In this case, the career ladder is 'limited' to those positions that focus on the research questions the health professional is pursuing. In this situation, it is more likely for management to appreciate the need for the health professional to maintain contacts and allegiances with other health professional organisations. These outside healthcare organisations can serve to influence the actions of the corporate healthcare professionals, an influence that may be pertinent for human rights issues. The second path is where health professionals (as in the interview summarised in Box 11.1) choose a career ladder within the corporation more typical of the 'standard' corporate employee. In this case, it is much more challenging for the health professional to take divergent positions from those of the corporate perspective. However, it may also be the case that these very corporate

---

The following are salient points from an interview with a physician working, as he described, in middle management with a corporation that deals with medications needed for organ transplants:

- My motivation for entering medical school (and I would say the motivation of virtually everyone entering medical school) says something about my wanting to improve healthcare for the general population.

- I left working in the hospital as it seemed that we often perform many tests that do not seem to have relevance to outcomes of care. Private practice appeared to be a similar situation but not as exciting as the hospital.

- My motivation in joining the corporate world consisted of a desire to understand the human organism. If it is out of balance I could work to help it recover. The same is true for a company. The company is a living animal. It needs to be in balance. There needs to be a balance between corporate social responsibility and need to make a profit.

- With today's globalisation we live in a somewhat Darwinian environment. We have to be aware that investors have many potential places where they can put their money. Their decisions are appropriately and significantly influenced by our financial results. While we do not live in a perfect society, those who are powerful need to meet with interest groups in an effort to contribute to benchmarks.

Box 11.1 **Understanding motivations**

health professionals are in a better position, if they are senior enough in the organisation, to influence management policies affecting human rights.

Whichever career direction health professionals pursue within a corporation, they become entangled in both the negative and the positive duties resulting from medical ethics. While, upon obtaining their medical degree, physicians commit themselves to not harm humans, a corporate physician may participate in the release of a product that may directly or indirectly harm human beings. Similarly, while committing to actively seek out means of helping as many humans as possible, a corporate physician may, intentionally or unintentionally, restrict access to a particular service or product to individuals. This harm may or may not fall within the purview of human rights organisations. For example, several organisations have sued individual physicians working as health insurance company executives asserting that the corporate physicians have restricted access to care for insured individuals. In fact, some have sued to have the physicians struck off the list of medical practitioners (*Physician's Weekly* 1998). This type of action reflects one type of ethical tension that corporate physicians may choose to work under. They may feel justified in making these types of decisions restricting access in the name of the greater good of controlling healthcare costs. This difficult balance reflects the tension within the last portion of the Hippocratic oath quoted above (i.e. the need to be benefit society at large within ill-defined constraints). While the specific topic of health insurance has not engaged the interest of human rights organisations, other issues, such as access to medications used to treat HIV in Africa, have involved human rights organisations in trying to convince pharmaceutical companies to provide anti-HIV medications either free of charge or at a significantly reduced price (Schüklenk 2001). Physicians working in these companies experienced a conflict between their perceived obligation to protect corporate profitability versus their obligations under the Hippocratic oath to provide assistance to as many individuals as possible.

Corporate health researchers may have a significant de facto human rights role in the choice of research path to pursue when developing a new product. Once a product that has healthcare implications is developed, however, decision-making on the marketing and sales process moves from the corporate researcher to other departments within the institution. At this point, it is the corporate physician executive that is likely to have the greatest ability to influence corporate decisions. The following case study illustrates the challenges and opportunities for corporate physicians working at an executive level on matters pertaining to classically understood human rights issues.

11.3 Case study: organ removals from executed prisoners in the People's Republic of China[3]

Each year, the number of executions in China exceeds by twofold the total number of executions in the rest of the world. In some instances the crimes for which

3 A useful background to the international trade in body organs is provided in Eisinger 1998.

people are put to death include those not considered capital offences in other countries, such as theft, financial crimes and discharging of a firearm. The time between arrest and execution is often days, or even hours. There is overwhelming evidence that it is common practice in China to take body parts from persons without their consent, immediately after their execution, and sell them to waiting recipients for transplant. While such a situation could not reasonably be one in which a prisoner is able to give voluntary and informed consent, in any event the evidence shows that rarely, if ever, is any manner of consent given. There are several ethical challenges to this practice:

- The execution of prisoners, in general, and specifically for often minor offences

- The inherent incentives to execute prisoners for the sole reason of harvesting the prisoner's organs thereby providing substantial monetary gain for the Chinese prison system

- The lack of legitimate informed consent

Many human rights organisations have worked to try to change this situation. Some of these organisations are trying to work collaboratively with pharmaceutical corporations (whose home offices are located in the United States, Europe and Japan) that sell transplant rejection medication in an effort to ameliorate this situation. These human rights organisations seek the immediate end to the practice of harvesting organs from the bodies of executed prisoners, replacing this source of organs, if necessary, with a truly voluntary system of live-related and cadaveric organ donation in accordance with World Health Organisation (1991) guidelines. They have also called for Chinese health professionals to refuse to participate in the retrieval of organs from executed prisoners or the use of such organs, whatever the stage of the process at which they are involved. Human rights organisations have also asked Chinese medical associations to adopt a policy against the retrieval of organs from executed prisoners or the use of such organs.

Pharmaceutical corporations are involved in the transplant issue in the following way. Many have signed the UN Global Compact, the first two principles of which are:

- Principle 1. Businesses should support and respect the protection of internationally proclaimed human rights within their sphere of influence.

- Principle 2. Businesses must make sure that they are not complicit in human rights abuses.

According to the World Health Organisation, the sale of human organs violates the UDHR (which is cited as a key document informing the Global Compact). Pharmaceutical companies manufacture medications without which transplants cannot succeed. While these medications provide benefits where appropriate transplant procedures and safeguards are met, they also create the possibility of gross human rights abuses and violation of medical and legal proclamations where such standards are not met. Trade with the Chinese of a drug that is central to the programme of the sale of body parts from executed prisoners for transplantation can be seen to involve pharmaceutical companies. Indeed, it has been stated that '[i]t was after the introduction of cyclosporine that China implemented its 1984 rule to allow for organ donation from executed prisoners' (Kram 2001).

What is the role of corporations, particularly pharmaceutical corporations, in the issue of organs removed from executed prisoners? The first point to be made is that the involvement of the pharmaceutical companies is indirect; that is, there is no claim that pharmaceutical companies have any direct involvement in the removal of organs from executed prisoners. Rather, it is the indirect role that these companies play with respect to the sale of needed medication (without which there would be no transplants from executed prisoners) that provides the rationale for involving pharmaceutical companies in the Chinese transplant issue. Given that many pharmaceutical companies have signed the UN Global Compact which states that corporations should support human rights within their sphere of influence, these companies have an ethical responsibility to raise with their Chinese customers the question of how the medications they sell are used in practice. In the light of the current difficulties facing the pharmaceutical industry in general (e.g. around intellectual property rights and the sale of HIV/AIDS retrovirals to African countries), one could argue that it is also in the industry's business interests to work with human rights groups and, independently behind the scenes, with their Chinese customers to change a practice that is clearly immoral and is recognised as such throughout the world.

Taking these ethical and business considerations into account, individually or as a group pharmaceutical companies could:

● Agree on an ethical code on transplantation, both on an individual corporate level and in conjunction with other pharmaceutical companies. This is also a collective responsibility where pharmaceutical companies can exert influence on other companies that are selling anti-transplant rejection medication. That is, pharmaceutical companies should harness peer and other pressures to ensure that all companies in the sector operate in a responsible manner.

● Work to mobilise medical opinion internationally and in China against the use of organs from executed prisoners. As part of this effort, pharmaceutical companies could place a statement in various journals (including general journals, surgical journals, specialist transplant journals, journals of pharmacology and non-medical journals) clearly expressing the industry's concern about the issues around organ collection from executed prisoners and committing the industry to work to eliminate these practices. Furthermore, medical professionals within the pharmaceutical companies should seek to establish good relationships with fellow medical professionals (both within their home country and overseas). Efforts by the pharmaceutical companies and their medical professionals to mobilise medical opinion against the use of these organs could be an important part in the process of convincing the Chinese medical profession that its involvement in this activity is hampering its full participation in the international medical community.

- Harness the influence of professional societies and associations to address the issue. For example, associations of transplant surgeons have weighed in on the issue of the removal of organs from executed prisoners. Some have tried to work with pharmaceutical companies involved in the sale to China of anti-transplant rejection medication.

- Help the move towards more donor-willingness procedures, in order to alleviate the shortfall of organs in nearly all countries. A key barrier to true informed consent is the lack of sufficient numbers of organs. Through advertising and education, pharmaceutical companies could work with Chinese organisations to increase the rates of voluntary donations of organs.

- Raise the issue of ethical transplantation procedures with the Chinese government and appeal, in a private manner, to China to end the practice of harvesting organs from the bodies of executed prisoners.

- Offer assistance to China to switch from the current system to the voluntary donation of organs upon accidental death. Many Western countries have developed extensive policies and protocols that assist in this voluntary donation of organs. These are policies that pharmaceutical companies could help the Chinese to adopt.

Even though the responsibility of pharmaceutical corporations is indirect, it is apparent that, if they had a clear corporate mandate not to assist the Chinese in the execution of prisoners for their organs, significant policy change could occur. Within corporations there are, understandably, countervailing forces that are attempting to influence corporate policies either in a positive direction on this issue or in a 'neutral' direction that emphasises maximising pharmaceutical sales irrespective of their final destination. At least in some pharmaceutical corporations, physicians have played a positive role in attempting to influence the role their employers play on the China transplant issue. In addition, there have been informal contacts between human rights activists (both generalists and physicians) and pharmaceutical companies (some of the corporate contacts are health professionals) selling anti-transplant medication to China. These contacts are ongoing but it appears that they have borne at least some fruit as the Chinese government has indicated that it is considering working on the transplant issue. Physicians working with human rights organisations and pharmaceutical companies, and the physicians working with and for the Chinese government have, informally, communicated with each other. The implicit trust between health professionals that emerged in some of these communications occurred at least in part from the shared medical experience between the participants together with a shared interest in, to the extent possible, promoting a positive resolution to the China transplant issue.

11.4 What is the role of human rights NGOs?

From the author's experience, health professionals working in the corporate sector are an obvious point of influence that NGOs could and should consider targeting. A medical degree will often confer greater acceptability when working with other medical organisations, the support of which may be critical to the achievement of the policy goal. In the China organ transplant issue, for example, corporate physicians can play a key broker role with professional societies and foundations supporting medical education in the country in question. This is a role that physicians working with human rights organisations can facilitate and maximise in terms of impact. While foundations may not always feel comfortable working directly with corporate physicians, health professionals working with NGOs can act as brokers while, at the same time, working with other NGO professionals to advance the agenda the NGO has brought to the table.

Many, but by no means all, physicians who work for corporations at least begin their career with the intent of continuing the efforts that they began when they went to medical school. That is, they hope to make an even greater difference through their corporate work than they might be able to do on an individual basis in, for example, private practice. At the same time, there is an unquestionable socialisation process that occurs through working for a corporation. By the time a physician has sufficiently climbed the corporate ladder to a point where he or she can influence corporate policy, it is perfectly possible that the physician is a physician in title only. The challenge in this situation is for the human rights professional to work, over time, with different physicians within the corporation and to identify those who are likely to either promote a human rights perspective within the corporation or influence the corporation in this regard.

Human rights organisations, naturally, pursue issues that affect the health of individuals and groups of people. This chapter has pointed out that health professionals are increasingly working in corporations on human rights issues affecting health. In order to maximise effectiveness in working with corporate healthcare professionals, human rights organisations need to consider committing resources to better understand and work collaboratively with these professionals. The meetings could range from informal gatherings to formal conferences that bring physicians together, either on an individual basis or as corporate representatives for the purposes of seeking common ground, identifying points of action and continuing education.

The human rights community has not actively pursued the health professional community within corporations, despite the fact that 'health' is so intertwined with human rights. At least in part this appears to be because NGOs do not fully recognise the potential influence of physicians working within corporations. These physicians may be interested in influencing corporate policy but may not have the political strength do so without outside backing or an external political push (e.g. from an NGO). The organ transplant issue discussed in this chapter intimately involves physicians in various ways, both inside and outside corporations. The reality is that physicians working within corporations have the potential (with sufficient support from outside) to directly influence corporate policy.

11.5 Recommendations and conclusions

Health professionals are working in increasing numbers for corporations. In addition, an increasing number of physicians are joining governmental efforts to control healthcare costs and improve the quality of the healthcare system they are serving. Both of these trends are a function of the corporatisation and bureaucratisation of healthcare delivery throughout the world but particularly in the United States. Physicians have assumed both research and executive responsibilities in corporations that involve (at least they hope) making decisions that have a positive impact on the livelihoods of large groups, even many thousands, of individuals at a time. As discussed in this chapter, many of these health professionals work on issues that either directly or indirectly affect human rights. However, these same health professionals have varying degrees of dual allegiances as they work either climbing a corporate career ladder or attempting to establish their scientific credentials within and outside the corporation.

NGOs have a key role to play as they increasingly try to influence corporate behaviour in an era of globalisation. On issues either directly or indirectly involving corporate physicians, it is in the interest of NGOs to identify and work collaboratively with corporate healthcare professionals as part of an overall strategy to influence corporate behaviour. At the same time, health professionals, such as myself, need to realise that we have assumed a significant responsibility in committing ourselves, at the start of our medical profession, to the ethical obligations implicit in the Hippocratic oath. We have ethical obligations that we cannot ignore, even in the face of pressures caused by the globalisation of the medical economy, in general, and healthcare delivery, in particular.

12

Privatising infrastructure development
'Development refugees' and the resettlement challenge

Christopher McDowell

Macquarie University, Australia

The multilateral system for international development is in a state of transition involving significant changes to the ways in which infrastructure development is financed. Flows in official development assistance (ODA) declined between 1991 and 2001, but over the same period private capital flows emerged as the 'principal external financial engine driving investment and growth' in the developing world (Mistry and Olesen 2002: 1-2).[1] In this new context of increasingly privatised and commercialised development, the discrete and co-ordinated roles of international agencies (the United Nations and multilateral development banks), donor governments, developing-country governments and the private sector are evolving but in a somewhat incoherent fashion. There are asymmetries and gaps in the process that need to be addressed by new policies, regional and global approaches, and flows of knowledge. Until they are addressed, important immediate and longer-term needs of developing countries will remain unmet, and the vulnerability of specific populations to human rights violations and the threat of continuing and new impoverishment will increase.

One major blind spot in this transition is in the domain of infrastructure development and its anti-development and anti-human rights outcomes. Specifi-

---

1 Thanks mainly to private capital, the average level of net transfers to the developing world as a whole increased from around US$15 billion (thousand million) in the 1980s to about US$80 billion between 1990 and 1994, increasing sharply to an average of US$150 billion between 1995 and 1998 before falling back to an average of US$75 billion in 1999–2000 and collapsing to an abysmally low US$19 billion in 2001 (Mistry and Olesen 2002: 5).

cally, more than ten million people each year are forcibly displaced and resettled as a consequence of the construction of dams, roads, ports and other urban and rural infrastructure projects in the developing world. This chapter considers the changing roles and responsibilities of the private sector engaged in infrastructure investments in developing countries that create involuntary population displacement and induce social, economic, cultural and political change. The aim is to contribute to the ongoing debate about the human rights and social justice implications of business activities that impact directly on people who have the misfortune to live on land that is defined as having 'development potential' and is legally, or quasi-legally, acquired by the state or private interests for economic exploitation. The chapter places this discussion in the context of new financing arrangements that contain within them the likelihood that people in the way of progress are more vulnerable now than they were in the recent past to forced displacement that is unjust, that violates human rights, increases impoverishment, and generates new divisions in society.

The details of the new financing arrangements are sketched out below, but essentially it is argued that infrastructure development and displacement arising from projects is shifting from the domain of official development assistance to the domain of the market and public–private financing strategies. Companies such as BP, operating in West Papua, are now taking direct responsibility for the uprooting and resettling of villagers who live on the preferred route of a natural gas pipeline. Rio Tinto Zinc, through its PT Kelian mining operations in East Kalimantan, has assumed responsibility for compensating villagers, miners, migrant workers and other populations affected by the ceasing of mine operations. In the past, decisions to relocate populations were regarded as issues of state responsibility. This chapter describes how the record on 'official resettlement', conducted under the auspices of the World Bank in partnership with governments, yielded few success stories; deepened impoverishment and social instability were the hallmarks of much resettlement in the second half of the 20th century.

While resettlement operations have failed to provide safeguards for affected populations, and have failed to provide the means through compensation to rebuild shattered livelihoods and communities, the chapter does suggest that recently developed guidelines and new knowledge about resettlement dynamics provide some hope for the future. However, it is also suggested that the reduced role of multilateral institutions, such as the World Bank and the Asian Development Bank, and the subcontracting of responsibility for resettlement to the private sector present new challenges which have not yet been addressed. The chapter considers one response to this new situation: namely, the tendency to draw a close association between development and conflict, and between development displacees and refugees. This conceptualising of 'development refugees' has in part led the United Nations to become more actively involved in the development process where population displacement occurs.

In its conclusion, the chapter considers what these changes might mean for companies engaged in pipeline, airport, dam, mines or road-building projects that necessitate the forced resettling of populations. It is hoped that further debate on these issues will follow.

12.1 Development-created displacement: the scale of the problem

Compared with other categories of the globally displaced, so-called 'development displacees' have a relatively low profile, despite the fact that each year more people are displaced against their will by state-planned development initiatives than by conflicts or natural disasters. The scale of development-induced displacement is bound to be upgraded over the coming decades as population growth and urbanisation significantly increase the demand for power, drinking and irrigation water, roads and airports, new urban housing and industrial zones, and ever larger and more efficient farms. As projects become more complex, witnessed, for example, in the trend towards multi-purpose hydro-schemes (for power generation, flood control, navigation and irrigation), greater areas of land and other natural resources will be required which, in turn, will affect larger populations.

In addition to dam construction and transport infrastructure, there will be an increase in the frequency and scale of involuntary displacement in other areas. Principally, considerable displacement will occur as a result of urban industrial development and regeneration which creates a ripple effect, moving people from the centre of towns to the periphery and in turn displacing populations on the city's edge with a knock-on effect in the countryside.[2] An enthusiasm for new game parks, environmental protection zones and conservation areas, and the growing trend for people to be excluded from these areas, is leading to involuntary resettlement on a huge scale in parts of southern and central Africa, and South-East Asia. Related to conservation schemes are new tourist development projects, often piecemeal and unplanned, which create a fragmented displacement removing people from coastal and riverine lands and barring their access to the sea, rivers and lakes that provide the foundations of their livelihoods. Other expanding land-hungry development sectors that create displacement include mines and other extractive industries, which are thought to have displaced 2.55 million people in India alone between 1950 and 1990 (Downing 2002: 3). Structural adjustment policies, which have led a number of less developed countries, such as Ghana, to invest heavily in mining as a source of foreign exchange, have increased the amount of land taken out of agriculture and in turn created additional displacement.

International donor commitment to infrastructure development in sectors that create involuntary displacement and resettlement continues to be significant. In the water sector, for example, the donor community invested some US$3.7 billion in 1997 (of which the World Bank contributed US$2–3 billion). However this constituted only around 12% of the US$70–80 billion spent annually on water management and the development of water infrastructure (Ministry for Foreign Affairs, Sweden 2001: ii-iii). In terms of overall displacement figures, at the time of the World Bank's last review in early 2000, 2.6 million individuals and 548,000 households were found to be 'adversely affected' in Bank projects under imple-

---

2   This was an unanticipated result of the eviction of shack dwellers in the Central Business District of Addis Ababa to make way for the new Sheraton Hotel in 1998.

mentation. While this is a significant number of people, it constitutes a relatively small proportion of the total number of people displaced by the development process.[3] There are clear indications, however, that the transition of the international development system will be marked by an increasing reluctance on the part of multilateral development banks (MDBs) and individual Western donor governments to provide direct financing for large infrastructure projects that create involuntary displacement and generate political opposition.

Official loans and grants for these types of investments, including co-financed projects, are conditional on borrower governments agreeing to conduct involuntary resettlement operations in accordance with World Bank and other lenders' involuntary resettlement policies and procedures. In so doing, governments and their partners in the private sector commit an agreed amount of the project budget to the costs of resettlement operations. With some differences between lending institutions, policies generally require that projects should avoid involuntary resettlement if possible, or minimise involuntary resettlement where population displacement is unavoidable. They further require that people who lose assets or livelihood because of a project, irrespective of tenure status, should receive assistance from the project for relocation and resettlement and be paid market or replacement value for assets acquired by the project. An objective of such policies is to ensure that affected populations receive rehabilitation assistance to achieve at least the same level of well-being with the project as without. A number of commentators have pointed out that the objective to 'rehabilitate' displaced people to the same level of well-being measured before the project is often little more than a guarantee to return people to their pre-existing state of poverty, or merely a commitment to relocate the displaced to a situation of increased vulnerability with no corresponding obligation to address additional resettlement-related impoverishment risks created by the project. Despite obvious flaws, these measures do provide some safeguards for people that find themselves 'in the way of progress'. However, as dams, roads and other large public schemes are more likely to be funded through direct private investment, or public–private partnership arrangements (such as build–own–operate–transfer contracts), rather than exclusively through the donor community, such in-built safeguards are unlikely to be an automatic feature of financing arrangements and hence not an automatic component of resettlement operations.

Under these new arrangements, resettlement will increasingly take place beyond the gaze of official international scrutiny, and beyond the reach of carefully established lender-imposed conditionalities that strive for minimum standards in resettlement alongside other reforms. In anticipation of the gap left by the withdrawal of multinational development agencies, developing-country governments have been extremely slow to adopt national resettlement legislation. The absence of effective protective legal frameworks does not augur well for the millions of

3   The numbers represent those physically or economically displaced as a result of land acquisition, or otherwise affected by minor land acquisition, and not just those who are physically relocated ('World Bank and Social Safeguards Policies', World Bank website, www.worldbank.org). Using similar definitions, the Asian Development Bank has assessed that almost 120,000 people are 'affected' annually by ADB-funded projects, of which about 40,000 require relocation and resettlement (ADB 2000).

people who will inevitably be uprooted by progress, industrialisation and policies to achieve economic growth.

From the point of view of private companies, uncertainty around the management and conduct of resettlement will be a matter of concern. The forced resettling of populations conducted in a way that violates human rights, and mismanaged resettlement that compounds those violations, leads inevitably to resistance, the breakdown of trust between affected populations and their government, and poses serious threats to company operations. These risks are potentially heightened by the reduced role of the international development community, and greater responsibilities on the part of developing-country governments and the private sector.

12.2 The changing context of involuntary resettlement

The changes in the political economy of infrastructure development leading to greater privatisation have implicit additional risks for development displacees. However, it must also be recognised that the familiar model, in which states' conduct towards their forcibly resettled citizens was shaped in part by World Bank or other lenders' conditionalities, was far from effective in addressing the needs of displaced populations or in protecting their rights. The record on resettlement conducted in the domain of multilateral or bilateral official development assistance, even with relatively stringent resettlement standards, is regrettably a long list of failed operations and missed opportunities (see WCD 2000). The overwhelming majority of resettlers, according to the World Bank's own analysis, have been plunged into deepened and spiralling impoverishment; legal protection and the basic building blocks resettlers require to re-establish their livelihoods have not been provided through compensation and other forms of assistance (World Bank 1996). The Asian Development Bank recently reported that 'ineffective implementation and limited impact of Involuntary Resettlement Policies in the overall resettlement process of the Developing Member Countries is a major concern' (ADB 2000: iii).

The economic, social and cultural, and civil and political rights of populations directly displaced, as well as those indirectly affected, including populations playing host to resettlers, have been widely violated in the displacement–resettlement process. The much more difficult and problematic risks confronting involuntary resettlers, such as loss of land, employment, education, declining health, food insecurity, psychological marginalisation (Fernandes 2000) and social disarticulation (Downing 1996), while better understood, have not been effectively addressed in any comprehensive manner (Cernea and McDowell 2000). For the most vulnerable resettlers (women, children and the landless), the livelihood and psychological risks have proved to be cumulative and long-lasting, increasing the likelihood of ill-health and even premature death (Scudder 1993).

While the traditional model is failing, it is extremely unlikely—in the short term at least—that the evolving model of infrastructure development financing and management will provide the legal protection, necessary resources, political commitment or imaginative solutions that are required to meet the complex challenge of involuntary resettlement. The new privatisation/national sovereignty model locates the key stages of the project cycle in the domain of domestic politics. By privatising resettlement, governments are, to some extent, removed from two of their core responsibilities: poverty reduction and the protection of minorities. The displaced are potentially more vulnerable to the vagaries of secretive deals between governments and private consortia, and investments that place emphasis on short-term profits for shareholders. Commercial pressures on budgets are likely to result in overall reduced resettlement expenditure and the further externalisation of environmental and resettlement costs among the most vulnerable who are adversely affected by the project and least able to cope. The welfare of 'development refugees' in the absence of international safeguards and with displacement occurring increasingly outside the domain of 'official development assistance' is less likely to attract the sympathy of the majority population or be a high political priority. Furthermore, with the IMF- and World Bank-supported processes of decentralisation, and the devolution of power to regional authorities in countries such as Indonesia, infrastructure development is accelerating. This is in the context of increased corruption and weakened legal safeguards for the environment and populations adversely affected by often haphazard development and arbitrary displacement.

The World Bank-driven initiatives on involuntary resettlement over the past decade sought to safeguard the interests of resettlers and improve resettlement outcomes, in part because the Bank agreed with critics that 'development that impoverishes' is untenable for an institution that is committed to reducing world poverty. However, the initiatives on involuntary resettlement were introduced primarily as a means to enable the Bank to continue lending large amounts of money to low-income governments for planned infrastructure projects. The Bank hoped that new resettlement policies would shape resettlement operations and that this, in turn, would break the displacement–impoverishment cycle, in so doing remove one of the major controversies and obstacles to this continuing model of economic growth-driven development. Events somewhat overtook the Bank, however, and the association between dams, environmental degradation and poverty became a powerful *leitmotif* in anti-dam campaign and academic literature. The World Bank and other donors, though still believing that economic growth through infrastructure development—in the context of structural reforms and good governance—was the key dynamic in poverty alleviation, yielded to pressure and in recent years has stepped back from funding new large-scale projects that result in population displacement. The World Bank's initiatives on involuntary resettlement had not done enough to convince opponents that the negative impacts of such projects could be ameliorated. For these reasons the leadership on resettlement from the World Bank's headquarters in Washington, DC, has probably run its course, leaving the way open for new approaches to evolve alongside what the World Bank and other regional development banks have thus far achieved.

12.3 Rethinking 'development displacees'

Any new approach to involuntary resettlement requires a detailed understanding of the human impacts of planned development processes. Over the past decade, academic researchers, NGO workers and resettlement experts in lending agencies have built up a considerable body of knowledge and improved our understanding of the negative social, cultural, economic, psychological and political impacts of forced displacement and involuntary resettlement. Knowledge about how to reverse that process, to enable the displaced to rebuild their livelihoods, is less comprehensive but gradually evolving through detailed policy and operational-relevant research.

12.3.1 'Ethnic cleansing in disguise'

Since the early 1990s, it has become common for social researchers to draw comparisons between development displacees and political or conflict refugees (Cernea 1993, 1996; Scudder 1993; Cernea and McDowell 2000). Some current thinking stresses that conflict, development processes and forced migration, rather than being discrete phenomena, are in fact major interrelated issues of global politics and critical aspects of North–South relations. There is a growing argument that forced migration, whether generated by conflict, development or economics, is a systemic element of a globalised and unequal world. There is increasing analysis of the role of Western governments and major corporations in the decision-making process that leads to the commissioning of socially and environmentally damaging development projects that yield unclear benefits. This research is producing strong evidence that development is frequently used as a disguise for discrimination and the deliberate targeting of minority and ethnic groups (Rajagopal 2001) and that, particularly in situations of instability and conflict, politically framed development decisions are manipulated by states to advance overt political objectives (Wolde-Selassie 2002). At present there is concern about 'development cleansing' in, among other places, Tibet, Colombia, Angola, southern Sudan and the Philippines (Rajagopal 2002; Pettersson 2002).

The moniker 'development refugees' is in wide circulation and suggests that populations in the third world displaced against their will by development or modernisation schemes conceived and funded in the first world are, like refugees, powerless and unable to confront the forces that result in their uprooting. The search for similarities and dissimilarities between development displacees and refugees or internally displaced people (IDPs) has served a useful advocacy function, and has revealed commonalities in the displacement–impoverishment process that can be broadened to non-displacement livelihoods and poverty research (McDowell and De Haan 1997; McDowell 2002). Examination of the displacement–impoverishment nexus led to Michael Cernea's elaboration of 'impoverishment risks'. Cernea's modelling of the resettlement effect is a major step forward in our understanding of imposed rapid social, economic and cultural change. Guided by the 'impoverishment risks and reconstruction model', research findings are generally in agreement, that both populations (refugees and development displacees) are exposed to similar risks, and are enmeshed in dynamics of power, class, gender and race that lead to comparable forced migration outcomes in terms of impoverishment and livelihoods (Cernea and McDowell 2000).

Risk and vulnerability analysis has stimulated research that suggests that forced migrants in the developing world, whatever the direct causes of their displacement, are vulnerable to uprooting and resettlement for the same or at least similar reasons. Both sets of populations are likely to be poor and marginal, often minorities, speaking a different language from the majority or national language, geographically, culturally and politically distanced from the centre of power and subsisting outside the formal economy. People vulnerable to and disadvantaged by the development process and those most severely affected by conflict, tend to be subject to intersecting human rights violations which occur because of discrimination that is related to their position in society. This is the case in India where, according to recent research by Fernandes, out of an estimated 21.3 million people displaced between 1951 and 1990 by development projects, no fewer than 40% were predominantly common property resource (CPR)-dependent tribals who form only 8.08% of the country's population. Another 40% were estimated to be from other rural poor communities (Fernandes 2000).

There is evidence that such populations' relative powerlessness makes them a target both for politically motivated conflict and for certain types of development project. For example, presented with a range of options, governments and developers may choose locations for projects where the costs in terms of compensation, ease of land acquisition and the likelihood of opposition and resistance can be minimised. Ethnic minorities or indigenous groups who lack a strong political voice, who often do not have legal title to the lands and natural resources that underpin their survival, and who constitute groups commonly excluded from the imagination of the national community, appear, when compared with more inclusive groups, to be far more vulnerable to development decisions that result in land seizing and forced resettlement.

12.3.2 Dissimilarities

Elsewhere, however, authors have pointed out the dissimilarities between the conflict refugee and development displacee experience (Scudder 1993; Turton 1996), emphasising that those differences need to be understood when framing new resettlement responses and understanding the forced migration experience.

Refugees become refugees because their government is either directly responsible for their persecution or is failing to protect them against violence and human rights violations committed by others. In seeking a place of refuge and assistance from international organisations, refugees who are victims of conflicts become stateless people or non-citizens. In the development process, however, the relationship between the state and a population displaced by a project does not necessarily irrevocably break down as it typically does in situations of conflict. In the case of development-induced displacement, it could be argued that by displacing people against their will a government is failing its duty of care, but the displaced remain citizens with exactly the same rights as any other citizen.

In some instances, as previously mentioned, states seek to justify forced displacement through the guise of development processes. However, it would be wrong to automatically assume that development is always a disguise for discrimination or ethnic cleansing. Government-led planned infrastructure initiatives provide an opportunity to set out the moral responsibilities and legal obligations of the state towards its citizens, and provide real and tangible benefits for millions of people. In the case of involuntary resettlement, displacees have rights in international law and states have corresponding obligations to respect and guarantee those rights. The development process should be an opportunity to restate a contractual agreement between a government that is committed to national development and its people. Unlike in times of war, when such obligations are suspended, these rights are morally binding, they are enforceable and judicial processes (however flawed) are normally available. Where rights are clearly violated and displacement involves the abuse of state powers, then international law as it is gathered together in the United Nations Guiding Principles on Internal Displacement provides important coverage. These points are discussed further in the concluding section of the chapter.

Development-induced displacement and conflict-generated refugees are also different in terms of time and scale. By the time people are in flight from violence and persecution, the situation is out of hand and the response to the displaced will inevitably be of an emergency and humanitarian nature. With large and sudden forced migrations, priority must be given to shelter, water and sanitation, food, healthcare, and physical protection. Such responses are, by necessity, short-term. Bridging the gap between an immediate response and longer-term assistance aimed at rehabilitation and development is extremely difficult, even with a large and well-financed international presence.

Involuntary resettlement arising out of planned development initiatives is, in contrast, forewarned and often many years elapse between the announcement of a project and actual displacement. Theoretically at least, this allows time to plan resettlement operations adequately, to inform affected populations well in advance and to initiate participative planning processes that permit the resettlers to shape their destinies. While there is no need for such displacement to resemble refugee emergency-type operations, it is frequently the case because affected populations are not forewarned and are not consulted in advance. Left to the last minute, negotiations between government agencies or private companies and those who are to be removed break down; clearances occur in an atmosphere of resistance, hostility and violence. Resettlers then find themselves in a refugee-like situation.

The humanitarian response to refugee situations tends to be formulaic following a predictable pattern in which recurrent problems are a feature. The Consolidated Inter-Agency Appeal Process (CAP), through which the international community identifies the scope and content of the humanitarian challenge in a given situation, and through which they pledge financial support, shapes responses that do not greatly differ. Each player, whether governments engaged in peace-keeping or providing aid, the UN and its agencies, international and local NGOs, or the state and non-state parties engaged in a complex emergency, is working to its own political agenda and timetable. Humanitarian operations are thus highly complex and difficult to co-ordinate. The level of commitment on the part of the major players determines the duration of a response, and their commitment—in time, money and diplomatic energy—is conditional on political calculations to do with the global importance of a particular crisis. That in turn depends on calculations around national self-interest, perceptions of geographic responsibility and, increasingly, security concerns.

Development-induced involuntary resettlement operations are less complicated. Fewer parties are involved, the amount of money required is smaller, the politics should be more conducive to compromise and agreement, and the time-frame is longer.

In some senses, then, it is useful to analyse the similarities and connections between development-created displacement and conflict refugees, but in so doing there has evolved a discourse of humanitarianism and refugeeism around development-induced displacement and resettlement that is in danger of falling into the same trap as the refugee discourse. Both appear at times too heavily based on the premise that the people involved are 'problems' that have to be solved, and are most appropriately solved through certain types of what Malkki (1995) calls 'therapeutic interventions'. In such generalisations and problematisations, development displacees are frequently cast as victims, torn from their culture, suffering their loss of identity, and dependent on external aid. Much of the literature on development displacees and, to some extent, the policies of the World Bank and bilateral donors, reflects this notion of the typical 'resettler problem', generating a uniform and technical set of solutions. Questions must be raised whether the kinds of responses such a problematisation generates are always appropriate to what are extremely varied outcomes.

There is a continuum of development-induced involuntary resettlement which ranges, at the worst extreme, from forced displacement that involves gross and deliberate violations of individual and group rights, to development projects and resettlement operations conducted with reference to international norms and with the best interests of all citizens uppermost. Most development-created displacement and involuntary resettlement operations in the developing world could be located at some point between these two extremes. The negative outcomes, impoverishment, marginalisation and unsustainability in most cases occur not because the state or private companies have deliberately set out to create these conditions but because of a lack of political commitment to resettlement, insufficient allocation of resources, poor project planning and execution of projects, and a lack of understanding of what the real impacts of resettlement are on individuals, families and communities.

The forced uprooting and resettling of populations in pursuit of growth, resulting from genuine attempts to manage expanding populations and to alleviate poverty, will become a neglected sideshow on the development stage unless there is an internationally, regionally and nationally agreed regulatory framework and set of standards for resettlement accepted by all the major governmental and non-governmental players involved in the development process. These regulations, both binding and voluntary, must constitute an overarching umbrella of commitments underpinned by shared principles and objectives which include a recognition of the rights of displacees and other affected populations. Each of the bodies involved in the process—national governments, donors and international agencies, the private sector, civil society and community-based representatives of affected populations—has roles and responsibilities that intersect; each has accumulated knowledge and well-established (formal and informal) policies and guidelines that must inform any new global resettlement strategy and framework.

It is important that the separate initiatives on resettlement are integrated into a coherent and overlapping package of legal standards and policies. The fact that companies such as Power Grid of India voluntarily adopt environmental and social policies and procedures that draw heavily on World Bank resettlement policies should not absolve the government of India from its responsibility to adopt national-level resettlement legislation. Nor should it absolve donors such as the Asian Development Bank from insisting on resettlement plans as preconditions of loans for projects that involve population displacement. Similarly, the existence of legislation at the national level, the adoption of voluntary standards by private companies, or the further strengthening of MDB resettlement policies would not obviate the need for international law that addresses the key human rights challenges.

An important and evolving reform of the international response to development-created displacement concerns an inevitably increased role for UN institutions in the oversight and regulation of involuntary resettlement. In the final section of this chapter, the implications of these reforms for the business sector are briefly considered.

12.4 Business, human rights and the international institutions

There is a strong case to reform the way in which the international community responds to the needs of the growing number of people in the developing world who are suffering the adverse impacts of development policies and projects—both directly and indirectly. There is a particularly strong demand in relation to infrastructure development because of the serious human rights challenges that are clearly involved in displacement and involuntary resettlement. The proponents of increased international official involvement in development-created displacement argue that, with privatisation and changing financing arrangements, there is an urgent need for the UN and other institutions to perform the role of ombudsman, recovering the oversight role that has been lost in recent years. The demand for more regulation and greater official intervention may over time extend to the less tangible, though nonetheless severe, impacts of governments' macro-economic policies. These trigger rapid change and include indirect but coerced uprooting of populations as a result of people's inability to remain on their lands due to loss of employment and access to essential livelihood resources. A further drive for reform has arisen because, despite donor-imposed conditionalities, there continues to be significant non-compliance on the part of governments and a reluctance to adopt national legislation to protect those adversely affected. It is argued that legal reforms should focus on displacement as a violation of human rights and develop further standards relating to the actual displacement of people. In respect of subsequent resettlement, reforms should, in particular, address the issues of land and property rights and compensation.

Two sets of reforms are currently being discussed. One proposal is for the consolidation of assistance and protection responsibilities for all forced migrants into a new organisation: the UN High Commissioner for Forced Migrants (Martin 2003). The mandate of this new body would include refugees covered under the 1951 UN Convention Relating to the Status of Refugees, as well as individuals internally and externally displaced because of repression, conflict, natural disasters, environmental degradation and, importantly, as a result of development projects. The work of the new agency on behalf of refugees would, Martin suggests, be governed by the 1951 Refugee Convention, and its work on behalf of IDPs would be governed by the United Nations Guiding Principles on Internal Displacement (UN OCHA 1992). A primary role of the new organisation would be the promotion of these international standards of assistance and protection.

Martin argues that consolidating responsibilities for all forced migrants would ensure more comprehensive and consistent approaches. The High Commissioner for Forced Migrants would be tasked with ensuring that all persons displaced by the same events are afforded comparable treatment, regardless of their location, and that the resolution of the situations causing displacement would take into account all parties that have been displaced. In respect of development displacees, the office would have the mandate to negotiate access and protection of affected populations with governments and other non-state parties. It would be responsible for developing a consolidated appeal for funding that would show donors the full range of financial needs in all countries affected by the displacement suggesting a new regional and transboundary responsibility for resettlement.

Refugee advocates would be concerned that, by equating different groups of forced migrants too closely, there is a risk of further watering down the already weakened international commitment to refugee protection and asylum. To include development processes as a cause of displacement equivalent to persecution or war would further hinder attempts at creating a comprehensive system of refugee protection that guarantees asylum for those most in need. These concerns are highlighted by the current political situation in which states, in both the North and the South, are adopting policies that undermine the principle of asylum such as accelerated involuntary repatriation and refoulement, interdiction, refugee containment, selective humanitarian intervention and detention. More restrictive policies have been adopted in a context where the general public is seemingly unable to differentiate between genuine refugees, illegal migrants and—since September 11—terrorists abusing the asylum system as another immigration route. Governments determined to elevate concerns about border security and sovereignty have been slow to correct misperceptions about global asylum-seeking, and the notion of 'dam refugees' may only add to public confusion.

The second and closely related reform proposes that the UN's Special Representative on Internal Displacement should pay closer attention to the issue of development-created displacement. This would include an unequivocal acknowledgement that development displacees are IDPs and are recognised as such by the UN's own normative framework, the Guiding Principles on Internal Displacement (Principle 6[c]). Such an acknowledgement would underscore the UN's assessment that development-created displacement involves human rights violations that are similar to the violations that occur in conflict situations. The Special Representative would then be obliged to officially raise the issue of development-created displacement with governments through UN procedures, thereby raising the problem to the level of an international political issue to which the world is forced to respond. Developments towards the end of 2002 strongly suggest that the UN has overcome its initial indifference (Pettersson 2002: 11-12) and is now prepared to take governments on and directly question what could be considered legitimate development activities in the public interest.

It would be wrong to assume, however, that the UN, through its Special Representative, will take an interest in all development projects that create displacement in both the developed and the developing world. There will be filters for establishing eligibility for UN concern and those filters will help to define a subset of displacements that are: (a) demonstrably arbitrary in nature; (b) involve human rights violations; and (c) the result of projects that are undertaken in a manner not guided by overriding public interest. The UN is likely to be concerned in the first instance with projects that are comparable to other displacements generated by human rights violations.

States will be the subject of UN involvement, because it is first and foremost the responsibility of states to provide protection and assistance to their citizens. The Special Representative will be expected to raise the issue of development-created displacement when states fail to live up to their obligations and fail to provide adequate redress to their citizens whose rights are violated in the development process. However, there is genuine concern expressed by governments that these limitations on UN intervention will be short-lived. There is already a backlash against the Guiding Principles from countries such as India and Egypt. The Group of 77 (2001) echoed concern that any broadening of the UN's mandate based on a widening of the consensus on IDPs that has not been formally ratified by developing-country governments is a further breach of sovereignty. Within the corporate sector there are concerns that a widening of the UN mandate to include the development process may have a negative impact on future investments.

Questions remain about the definition of internal displacement (which is currently paradigmatic rather than legal), what exactly constitutes arbitrariness in displacement, and how and by whom public interest is defined. While companies are increasingly willing to adopt voluntary human rights standards to guide their operations, those standards are notoriously difficult to benchmark. The so-called 'development rights' (contained in the International Covenant of Economic, Social and Cultural Rights) are generally not incorporated into the domestic laws of most governments and, therefore, the question of measuring the fulfilment of those rights in displacement and resettlement performance is extremely difficult.

It is reasonable to expect that the Guiding Principles will lead the UN to scrutinise more closely reported human rights violations by private companies, particularly where those companies have assumed greater responsibility for displacement and eviction operations. In the absence of national legislation governing displacement and resettlement, and uncertainties about the demarcation of responsibilities between governments, provincial and local bodies, and the private sector, the infrastructure development environment, with or without population displacement as an outcome of projects, will become more risk-prone. There is the danger that private companies will be held accountable for the failings of the host-country government. Many would agree that enhanced international scrutiny, through internationally accepted monitoring mechanisms, of private-sector and public– private ventures that create adverse social and environmental impacts is necessary. However, current international instruments are too blunt and vague to police this new situation adequately. Soft law in the form of World Bank and donor resettlement policies is less relevant as financing arrangements change. The UN Guiding Principles may be effective only when responding to high-profile cases of large-scale displacements that involve widespread human rights violations perpetrated by the state.

The problem of development-created displacement cannot be addressed by patching together existing refugee laws and expanding the mandates of humanitarian and emergency response agencies for which development and democracy is not the primary concern. Any new legal framework and institutional response should not begin from the assumptions that development is inevitably the same as conflict or that projects that displace populations will automatically violate human rights, create refugees and new poverty. Rather, the approach should be that there are real dangers in the development process and that these dangers have to be addressed when framing legislation that enables development to continue in a manner that strengthens the contract between the state and its citizens, generates genuine public benefits, and demonstrably improves the lives of populations whose lives, livelihoods and security are threatened by the project.

There is now a need for corporations to engage in this process by generating a dialogue about the roles and responsibilities of the private sector in displacement and resettlement. The uprooting of poor, marginalised and minority groups in the developing world is not a matter for philanthropy. Nor is it just another call on that 1–2% of an operation's budget that is traditionally expended on social investments. It is rather a momentous opportunity for the private sector to forge partnerships in the development process, to advance rights-based development, promote good governance and contribute to the alleviation of poverty.

Part 3
Supply chains

13

The contribution of multinationals to the fight against HIV/AIDS

*Steven Lim and Michael Cameron**
University of Waikato, New Zealand

The claim that multinational firms marginalise the poor and dispossessed has become a rallying point for many opponents of globalisation. Activists commonly link poverty in developing countries to the purportedly appalling working conditions and pay of multinational enterprises, and to the suppression of local businesses and alternative employment choices. This view has almost become an article of faith, based on intense suspicion of the profit motives of big business.

We offer a contrasting view, approaching the globalisation and human rights debate by linking multinational enterprises to positive employment and community health outcomes. In the developing world, particularly, multinationals have the opportunity to directly support the rights of workers and their communities to health and education. As we hope to demonstrate, such support can also make good business sense.

The chapter focuses on the triangular relationship between multinationals, poverty and HIV/AIDS prevalence in north-east Thailand. An initial discussion of poverty issues sets the scene for the remainder of the chapter. The subsequent sections outline Thai attempts to align the goals of seemingly disparate, self-interested groups, including multinationals and NGOs, and highlight the links between market forces, labour issues and social responsibility. Based on this analysis, the relationship between economic development and HIV/AIDS, in particular the question of whether development will stabilise or reduce rates of HIV/AIDS infection, is assessed.

* The authors are indebted to Anna Strutt and Krailert Taweekul for their insightful comments. The authors also acknowledge the Waikato Management School for its generous funding of this research and the Mekong Institute for its logistical support for field research.

13.1 Globalisation, human rights and HIV/AIDS

When unprofitable business decisions are punished by falling share prices and bankruptcies, there would appear to be significant hurdles in persuading big business to comply with adequate environmental, health and labour standards. However, without these standards, cycles of poverty are likely to persist, further disenfranchising the marginalised. The recent linking of HIV/AIDS to multinational activity is a natural extension of the marginalisation claim, given the contribution of poverty to cultural and sexual practices that render the poor increasingly vulnerable to health shocks (e.g. see Henry and Farmer 2001). Critics suggest that the view that globalisation may empower citizens to claim universal human rights (Vincent 1986; Clark 1999), such as the right to health, is myopic: the benefits of globalisation are not equally distributed and the providers of capital claim the greatest benefit (Evans 2002). Further, there is increasing evidence that globalisation may lead to greater levels of preventable disease. Multinational pharmaceutical companies increasingly concentrate their research and development expenditure on treatments, rather than preventions or cures, and on 'diseases of the rich', such as diabetes or obesity, rather than those that afflict the poor, such as tuberculosis or malaria. Economic conditions brought on by globalisation have contributed, at least in part, to the spread of infectious diseases such as HIV, as workers migrate in search of better economic opportunities or as part of their work (Whiteside 1998).

The theme of this chapter relates to the way in which multinationals can indirectly contribute to reducing the prevalence of HIV/AIDS, even when pursuing strictly profit-maximising goals. The underlying theme is as follows. Poverty leads to adverse social and health outcomes, including a greater supply of commercial sex and rising HIV infection. The sick become even further excluded from market opportunities, exacerbating the social disruption in which HIV/AIDS flourishes (Brundtland 2000). As adults within the household succumb to AIDS-related illnesses, the remaining able-bodied household members must consider new ways to offset the loss of income, including rural out-migration in search of jobs. But migration, especially urban migration, may involve prostitution and other high-risk behaviours, thereby resulting in further increases in HIV infection. Household vulnerability to poverty becomes significantly more acute. The key is to break the poverty–HIV/AIDS cycle with decisive interventions, particularly the creation of rural jobs in manufacturing and services, to alleviate poverty. As we seek to demonstrate, multinationals, working co-operatively with appropriate NGOs and local villagers, can have a pivotal impact on local employment, thereby reducing poverty and HIV/AIDS risk behaviour such as prostitution. This is particularly important where the potential labour force for multinational enterprises mainly comprises women, whose human rights have traditionally been repressed (Hambun and Reid 1994).

An estimated 42 million people are infected with HIV/AIDS worldwide and over 1.1% of Thailand's population is infected (UNAIDS and WHO 2001, 2002). More than 80% of those reported to be infected in Thailand are of working age. The average age at death from HIV/AIDS-related causes is 30, half the normal life expectancy. The financial burden to households of the death of a regular income earner from HIV/AIDS has been estimated at US$31,000 (Kongsin 1997). Of households that suffer an HIV/AIDS-related death, 52% reduce current household expenditure, adversely affecting the nutrition and health of household members (Pitayanon *et al.* 1997). Boochalaksi and Guest (1998) suggest that a major coping strategy of rural households in the north and north-east of Thailand involves migration to cities, especially Bangkok, by young women who can then support their family through remittances. Most frequently these migrant women are employed in the sex industry.

These effects make attempts to determine the net impact of multinationals and global capital on HIV/AIDS prevalence increasingly important for policy-makers, both in Thailand and elsewhere. Assessing the contribution of poverty alleviation to reducing HIV infection is a new research area (UNDP 2000a). Until recently, development projects and government assistance have been used as instruments in helping poor households to cope with income shocks after HIV/AIDS has struck (Kongsin 1997; Kongsin and Watts 2000; Greener 2000; Loewenson and Whiteside 2001). The approach illustrated in this chapter seeks to invert this by outlining the potential role of multinationals in community development, particularly rural job creation, which reduces the adverse economic and social conditions leading to HIV infection.

13.2 Poverty, employment and HIV/AIDS

High among the concerns of the poor is how to protect themselves from unexpected, adverse shocks, including income and HIV/AIDS shocks. Here the pivotal impact of job creation lies in its dual roles of both widening occupational choice and acting as a poverty-coping mechanism. In terms of occupational choice, job creation offers alternative employment opportunities for at-risk women, helping to swing their choice away from prostitution. Furthermore, by buffering agricultural incomes, growth in rural manufacturing employment reduces the incidence of seasonal out-migration from the village. This is especially important given the relatively high HIV infection rates among transient workers and others, such as truck drivers, whose travelling lifestyle places them in a higher risk group. The aim is to keep rural households together, thereby limiting the extent to which HIV/AIDS is brought back to the household by migrant workers.

Faced with the prospect of HIV/AIDS, households may, at least in principle, consider a range of measures to reduce their vulnerability. These include risk reduction strategies, insurance and a range of coping mechanisms. Risk reduction encompasses preventative health practices, diversification of income sources, and investing in education and physical and financial assets. Insurance mechanisms can range from maintaining buffer stocks of household goods to the support provided by extended family ties, social networks, co-operative organisations and the government. Once a shock has occurred, households might attempt to cope by increasing output or work effort, for example by working longer hours, taking children out of school, running down savings, selling assets or migrating (McCulloch *et al.* 2001).

Household insecurity and vulnerability suggest a role for rural employment creation in manufacturing. Manufacturing jobs can reduce risk by providing households with an income source that is typically uncorrelated with agricultural shocks, such as drought. In the absence of rural enterprises, labour markets may not be able to absorb large numbers of newly unemployed workers arising from a shock. However, income becomes more stable if at least one able-bodied member of an agricultural household can find work in a rural (multinational) factory. This lessens the pressure to take children out of school, a response that can reinforce inter-generational poverty. The pressures to migrate also diminish with the arrival of new factory jobs. With population movement considered to be a crucial issue in Thailand's HIV/AIDS epidemic (Singhanetra-Renard 1997), limiting the push factors behind labour migration is potentially very important.

13.3 Multinationals and NGOs working together

The creation of rural manufacturing jobs has become a critical policy issue. The activities of one NGO, Thailand's Population and Community Development Association (PDA), are particularly instructive, especially in relation to multinational enterprises.[1] A strategic programme within the PDA is the Thai Business Initiative in Rural Development (TBIRD). The objectives of the TBIRD programme are to encourage multinational and local businesses to relocate their factories to rural areas, where their presence will assist with rural employment creation, the transfer of business skills to villagers and the generation of income for the rural poor.

The PDA actively seeks out businesses that might be interested in participating in the TBIRD programme, highlighting the various incentives for the business to join. For example, by setting up factories in north-east Thailand, businesses have access to relatively cheap labour (as described below), receive tax relief for locating away from Bangkok and elsewhere in the more congested central region of Thailand, and benefit from the favourable publicity from helping out the rural poor with jobs. Within TBIRD, the PDA effectively becomes a matchmaker and mediator, identifying poorer areas in need of help and bringing villages and businesses together in a process of mutual income and profit gain.

For example, nine companies are involved with rural development projects under TBIRD-Ban Phai in Khon Kaen Province. One of the manufacturing projects produces Nike shoes while another makes medical uniforms for export to the US and Europe. Around 1,800 people from different factories work at the Ban Phai project site. With each worker currently earning at least the minimum wage of 133 baht per day, villagers are eager to work at the projects. These wages compare favourably with the minimum unskilled wage of 167 baht/day for workers in Bangkok, where living costs are considerably higher. Depending on the season,

---

1 The following description of the PDA draws heavily on Lim *et al.* 2002.

each vacancy attracts up to 9–10 applicants. Workers can earn an additional 2 baht/day if they maintain good work habits, such as arriving at work on time. A further 10–20 baht/day can be earned as a bonus, with the bonus tied to group performance. The projects provide other pecuniary and non-pecuniary benefits to their workers. Food is sold on-site at a break-even price of 10 baht per meal; a free on-site clinic provides basic health services. Pregnant women are assigned light work, and the factories guarantee to keep their jobs open if they return to work within 90 days of giving birth. Workers find that outside credit agencies make loans more readily if they know that loan applicants work at the project factories.

There is a strong gender bias in the overall TBIRD employment figures. Of the 1,400 or so workers in three of the manufacturing companies operating in TBIRD-Ban Phai, 94% are female. Employing women in their home village also provides advantages for their children. The duration of schooling for a child whose mother stays in the village tends to exceed that of migrant mothers working in Bangkok. The gender bias is important for other reasons. Empowerment of women and improvements in girls' education are important sources of change in HIV/AIDS-related behaviour and the protection of human rights (Hambun and Reid 1994; Husain and Badcock-Walters 2002). Economic empowerment is more likely to occur when new jobs become available that lie outside traditional male fields. In addition, it may well be easier for women to augment their human capital assets through access to knowledge and skills than to redistribute traditional resources to them, such as land and wealth (Keller-Herzog and Szabo 1997).

13.4 Income and other gains: the impact of multinationals

We are not claiming in this chapter that multinationals are necessarily good or even desirable. The same contribution to HIV/AIDS reduction and the protection of the right to health could (and possibly should) be made by a group of local businesses with a similar, though comparatively limited, endowment of capital, management skills and access to markets. Regardless of the previous record of foreign direct investment in Asia, welcoming globalisation appears to be important for the future. By carefully selecting suitable economic policies and promoting appropriate foreign direct investment, governments may be able to leverage the resources of multinationals to achieve social and public health goals.

The critics of globalisation often make generalised attacks on multinationals, frequently treating the multinationals and the countries in which they operate as homogeneous entities. In these attacks, the negative impact of a certain multinational in a particular country at a particular time is used to establish the general point of universal harm that globalisation brings. We suggest that a more guarded approach be adopted. Specific historical, economic and other conditions within a country influence, for better or worse, the impact of a multinational on poverty alleviation. Judging the impact requires knowledge of these specific conditions and the manner in which they shape the outcome. It may be considered inappropriate for a multinational shoe producer to set up a high-tech, capital-intensive plant if the end result is to displace labour and drive local manufacturers out of business. Yet the same multinational, by using a labour-intensive technology in a country with a labour surplus and by building a factory in a poor region where there was previously none, might be judged differently.

In the poverty–HIV/AIDS context, the actions of multinationals must relate to local factor endowments, especially the surplus of waged labour among women. Manufactured exports by multinationals using medium technology and semi-skilled labour, for example, match Thailand's rural comparative advantage in cheap labour. Thailand's rural economy is relatively poorly endowed with capital, technology and skilled management. Multinationals offer capital, marketing outlets and technology. In return they require inexpensive land, raw materials and labour. By exploiting the gains from resource complementarities, the result is more likely to meet the needs of rural development, as production transfers from agriculture to higher value-added, labour-intensive manufacturing.

The activities of the TBIRD multinationals also counter some of the specific criticisms of multinationals. Anti-globalisation activists suggest that the survival of big business requires the squeezing of workers' wages and labour rights. In this view, profit gains to the company must come at the worker's expense, a zero-sum game that is likely to worsen poverty by skewing the distribution of income. Yet in the TBIRD projects we find surprising evidence of a contrary result, that avenues for mutual gain emerge with the arrival of appropriately selected multinationals. Certainly the multinational companies involved in the TBIRD programme gain access to relatively cheaper labour in the rural areas, which more than compensates for the added transport costs of the factory products to Bangkok. Overall, wages are more than 20% lower and land rentals are about 30% lower than in Bangkok. Despite the savings in wages, the wages paid by the TBIRD multinationals exceed on average those paid by local firms in the same area. The multinationals under TBIRD have not followed a policy of squeezing wages to the lowest level as set by alternative employers.

From an economic and business perspective, TBIRD's wage and worker benefit structure is an important source of competitive advantage for the multinational firms. Higher wages and better working conditions relative to those of local non-TBIRD firms reduce moral hazard problems. Moral hazard in the workplace may arise when, having signed an employment contract, a worker's performance changes to hurt the interests of the employer. Worker absenteeism and laziness are potential problems facing any factory. However, the evidence is that by paying a wage greater than that of local competitors the TBIRD factories raise work effort. The multinationals, in effect, pay an 'efficiency wage' (see Brickley *et al.* 2000). Many workers realise that they are better off working for TBIRD multinationals, since their best alternative is to work elsewhere for much lower wages. Some other factories in Khon Kaen Province pay as little as 70–80 baht/day to their workers, a rate that is illegal under Thailand's minimum wage laws. The wage payments are sometimes made 2–3 months in arrears. On a wage of at least 133 baht/day plus bonuses, workers in the TBIRD factories have strong incentives to perform well to keep their jobs. An additional pay-off to the firms relates to lower labour turnover. Labour turnover imposes dislocations and increased training costs on a firm.

However, turnover at TBIRD factories is very low: for the first six months of 2001 the turnover rate stood at 3.3% in the garment factory and 1.3% in the factory producing Nike shoes.

In the TBIRD projects women have the opportunity to participate in training courses organised by the private companies and the PDA, such as family planning, HIV/AIDS prevention, team building, business skills development and interpersonal workplace relations. As we shall discuss later, the provision of business training programmes may be pivotal in the success of the projects in widening the long-term occupational choices facing village women. By providing better wages and education, the multinationals are ensuring that they have a healthier workforce and therefore a less interrupted supply of labour. The adverse impact on business profits of HIV infection within the workforce[2] suggests direct benefits to TBIRD firms from their in-house HIV/AIDS education programmes, both in productivity and in reduced hiring and training costs, as fewer substitute workers need to be sought. Human development is one of the key areas in which a multinational and the community can both benefit (Pieterse 1997). The community and individual workers gain through increased human capital that will continue to provide pay-offs even if the multinational withdraws.

The workplace conditions and benefits, wage levels, labour management systems and other aspects of social and environmental performance set the local standard for other factories to follow. In effect, the TBIRD project establishes competition for economic and social outcomes that benefit important stakeholders in the area. The actions of multinational firms may discipline the behaviour of their less 'socially responsible' competitors, particularly when workers from competing factories can switch to TBIRD's multinationals. While some of the other factories appear to have been bribing government officials to ignore regulations, TBIRD factories exploit the reputational benefits of complying with, and sometimes exceeding, government standards. It is clear that, regardless of their motivations for improving workplace conditions, the TBIRD multinationals create, to a degree at least, a local 'market' for ethical business behaviour, which translates into welfare gains for local villagers.

13.5 The impact on HIV/AIDS

We are reasonably confident that the multinationals in the TBIRD programme contribute positively to income generation, labour rights and poverty alleviation in the areas in which they operate. By increasing the household incomes of their workers, the TBIRD multinationals reduce the incidence of worker out-migration.

---

2 See Forsythe 2002, published by the International AIDS Economics Network (IAEN). IAEN is a network of researchers, policy-makers, programme administrators and others from development agencies, multilateral institutions, universities and NGOs, and is sponsored by the Joint United Nations Programme on HIV/AIDS (UNAIDS), the United States Agency for International Development (USAID), the World Bank, and the European Union. It is a 'virtual organisation' and may be found online at www.iaen.org.

Approximately 35% of the workers in factories at TBIRD-Ban Phai have returned from Bangkok and nearby provincial centres such as Samutprakhan and Chachoeng-sao. Sometimes the number is even higher. In April 2000, Ban Phai Union Foot-wear recruited 50 workers, of whom 35 were local people returning from Bangkok to jobs at the factory.

What is much less clear, however, is the contribution to reducing HIV infection. It is plausible that poverty alleviation reduces HIV/AIDS prevalence in developing countries. For example, some studies suggest that, over time, the availability of alternative job opportunities tends to reduce the supply of prostitution (Bond *et al.* 1997; World Bank 1997). However, actually quantifying the impact of the TBIRD multinationals on prostitution and HIV/AIDS is problematic for two reasons. The first relates to data problems and interviewee bias. Thai hospitals do not make HIV/AIDS statistics public, and people with HIV/AIDS tend to be reluctant to reveal their health status. The PDA offers scholarships to children with HIV/AIDS, for example, but few families seem willing to apply. Interviews with female factory workers are not likely to reveal a complete picture of how many would have been prepared to become prostitutes in the absence of multinational enterprises near their villages. In principle, researchers could record rates at which women from a region enter the commercial sex industry before and after the arrival of multi-nationals. In practice, obtaining reliable information is difficult, especially when women have strong incentives to conceal their occupational status in the sex industry.

The second problem is more conceptual. It is by no means certain that the availability of more rural factory jobs will decrease the supply of prostitutes. There is already a considerable gap between the TBIRD factory wages of around 150 baht/ day, which is reasonably generous by local standards, and the 800 baht/customer that a sex worker might take home in nearby Khon Kaen. Moreover, a falling supply of sex workers (should potential prostitutes opt instead to work in the factories) would put upward pressure on the wages from prostitution and attract more prostitutes in the longer term. The wage differential between prostitution and rural factory jobs may widen over time, inducing more women to leave their villages. The problem is that unskilled factory wages in Thailand are likely to increase only slowly due to competitive pressure from China and other low-wage economies. Low international agricultural prices, especially for rice, will restrain local agricultural wage growth, further dampening rural industrial wages. But rising urban incomes are likely to translate into rising demand for commercial sex, therefore increasing the returns from prostitution.

The decision by multinationals regarding their rural or urban location thus has implications for both the supply and the demand sides of commercial sex. Here, government tax and other policies will be needed to add impetus for multi-nationals to locate in rural areas. It may also be that the focus on push factors may be misplaced. The jobs created by the new factories might induce an inflow of outsiders, some of whom may already be infected with HIV (Lim 2001). The arrival of multinational enterprises is linked closely with wider issues of globalisation, including internal labour mobility and greater cross-border migration. Within the Greater Mekong Subregion (comprising Thailand, Cambodia, Laos, Burma, Viet-nam and China's Yunnan Province), most cross-border migration results from economic factors. Thailand has almost a million migrant workers in the country; the transport, manufacturing and services sectors hire many of these unskilled workers (Chantavanich 2000). TBIRD policy restricts job applications to local villagers to reduce the risk of HIV-positive outsiders seeking jobs at TBIRD factories. Nevertheless, to the extent that the TBIRD projects accept local villagers returning from big urban centres, the possibility of such villagers also being HIV/AIDS carriers cannot be discounted.

Last, the occupational choice approach needs to be supplemented with a consumer choice model. Given the widespread persistence of unsafe sexual practices among Thai men, despite their knowledge of HIV/AIDS risks (Vanlandingham and Grandjean 1997), the boosts to household income from rural industry may increase the spread of HIV/AIDS by facilitating more frequent purchases of commercial sex. More research needs to be done to determine the power relationships within households and the extent to which women's increasing income independence translates over time into greater control over household assets. Where the occupational choice model may yield bigger returns is from the reduction in male migrant labour when female factory workers augment household income. Porous borders and Thailand's recent openness to cross-border trade and tourism have provided a stimulus to many border towns and settlements. These areas have become places for thousands of migrants, transients and transport workers to mingle. Coupled with lax and often corrupt law enforcement, the areas gradually transform into hot spots of gambling, entertainment and prostitution (Chantavanich 2000). Seasonally migrant labourers, transport workers and traders in these hot spots become an at-risk group. Reducing the incentives to migrate by boosting (female) contributions to household income would be a positive step in moderating male risk behaviour.

13.6 Conclusion

The Thai Constitution of 1997 guarantees the rights to health, education, social protection and a social safety net (Teokul 1999). While business programmes might not always be undertaken with the view of promoting human rights, recent NGO initiatives in north-east Thailand demonstrate a particularly interesting development in the evolving fight against poverty and HIV infection. The Thai approach centres on exploiting the benefits of globalisation. It expands the concept of HIV/AIDS prevention, recognising that HIV/AIDS is linked to wider societal issues. These include improving income and employment opportunities, the empowering of women and reducing rural–urban migration. The vehicle for such changes is a programme of export-oriented rural industrialisation, a programme in which multinationals have an important role to play.

Recent research stresses collaboration between the private sector, the government and donor agencies in countering the HIV/AIDS epidemic (Varghese 2002). The willingness of the TBIRD multinationals to invest in job creation and worker education in north-east Thailand is an illustration of this. That, in this period of globalisation, multinationals might in fact promote the economic and health rights of individuals is contrary to the view of Evans (2002) that such rights would remain mere aspirations. However, as the Thai approach shows, some multinationals are already playing a role in promoting health rights in developing countries, and are addressing their moral obligations to workers.

In claiming that the TBIRD multinationals address their obligations, we stress that our views are conditioned by the reference points from which the normative assessments are made. In many cases the standard of judgement to which multinationals are held by activists is too high, at least in our view. The fallacy of the 'Nirvana principle' (i.e. the comparison of an actual outcome with an idealised outcome, with the rejection of the actual outcome if it fails to match the ideal) is evident in the Thai case study. Workers in the multinational factories under TBIRD receive wages of slightly more than US$4 per day. Many anti-globalisation activists would cite this as evidence of exploitation, demanding an ideal wage well in excess of this. We reject the 'Nirvana principle', preferring to compare actual outcomes with the specific alternatives that are available. A closer inspection of the wage structures would then reveal something quite different. At TBIRD there is a wedge between the lowest wage that workers would accept to work for a multinational (loosely defined by the wage offered by the best alternative employers in the region) and the maximum wage that the multinational could afford to pay before high wages and competitive pressures forced it to close down its operations and withdraw local job opportunities. The TBIRD multinationals do not push wages to their minimum, preferring to share the gains implied by the wage gap. Local workers near the TBIRD site thus have the opportunity to defect from a harsher and less rewarding employer to a better one. It is in this more modest sense that we suggest that the presence of multinationals enhances the welfare of local workers.

Similarly, while we are hard-pressed to show a definitive, quantitative link between employment creation and reductions in prostitution and HIV/AIDS prevalence, we believe that the multinational and PDA initiatives are moving in the right direction. As structural transformation progresses over the long term, Thailand's labour-intensive rural enterprises will face pressure as wage rates rise locally and foreign competition forces the relocation of some industry overseas. The pressures will worsen with the further integration of these countries into the global trading system. Over time, Thailand's comparative advantage in cheap rural labour will be eroded (Lim 2002), making upskilling and business management training imperative. The PDA and TBIRD multinationals are taking the lead in worker training programmes and the development of business skills among women, despite the increased risk of labour turnover and its associated costs to the multinational. Increasing the business skills of women will contribute to their lifetime income earning potential, narrowing the gap between their pay and the returns from prostitution. Through the mediating efforts of the PDA, the Thais are moderating the forces of globalisation to suit their own development needs, including positive steps to combat HIV/AIDS and protect the individual's right to health.

The key is to mesh the goals of big business, NGOs and local villagers, and to link market forces to social responsibility. The Thai approach presents a model of mutually reinforcing stakeholder interests in the fight against poverty and HIV/AIDS. An important outcome is that the private sector acts in the broad interests of the villagers, while still pursuing higher profits. The motivation of multinationals to relocate to poorer areas of Thailand stems from the relatively cheaper labour and land in the targeted areas, corporate tax advantages for relocation to more remote economic zones outside Bangkok, and their enhanced image when they are seen to act in the social interest. In addition to their direct impacts on widening employment opportunities, TBIRD multinationals are involved in worker training programmes and the longer-term development of business skills among women. An obvious advantage that this confers to firms relates to their reputation. In a world where price and quality are no longer the sole determinants of buying behaviour, multinationals are increasingly differentiating their products based on image, branding and reputation. Reputation affects shareholder value and is guarded jealously. It should not be surprising, then, to sometimes see multinationals providing better-than-average wages and working conditions, as is the case with the TBIRD projects. Ultimately, TBIRD stands as an exemplar of how a country can reconcile policies to attract foreign direct investment with trying to solve important social problems.

14
Elimination of child labour
Business and local communities*

Bahar Ali Kazmi and Magnus Macfarlane
Warwick Business School, UK

In the past decade, consumer groups, trade unions, media and non-governmental organisations have criticised the labour practices of global companies and conducted several campaigns against them. It has been argued that companies that sell garments, sporting goods, carpets, coffee, toys, footwear, surgical instruments and furniture items have maintained unfair wages, poor labour conditions, gender discrimination and child labour in their Southern supply chains. Significant though all these labour issues are, the issue of child labour has often been the main focus of such campaigns (e.g. the Foul Ball Campaign and the Global March Against Child Labour). As a consequence, many global companies, often in alliance with their Southern suppliers, have taken strategic steps to eliminate child labour from their supply chains.

While the problem of child labour in Southern supply chains involves the complex interplay of labour supply and demand factors (Grootaert and Patrinos 1999), corporate strategies to eliminate child labour have traditionally addressed the demand factors and have tended to rely on strategies such as the formalisation of the labour market, the restructuring of production activities and the replacement of primitive technology. Evidence has emerged to suggest that strategies that exclusively address demand factors may actually have a negative impact on working children and their families. Consequently, companies have begun to deliver social protection programmes for those working children and their families who are negatively affected by the implementation of their demand strategies. The emerging corporate social responsibility (CSR) approach to eliminate child labour therefore addresses demand factors with social disaster mitigation programmes.

* The financial support from the UK Department for International Development (DFID) and the Resource Centre for the Social Dimensions of Business Practice for the research that has informed this chapter is gratefully acknowledged.

This approach must be differentiated from the social development approach to eliminate child labour which focuses on the supply factors of child labour that include, but are not limited to, family size, access to education, the quality of schooling and levels of poverty.

The business case for the adoption of the child labour CSR approach by global companies is persuasive. It is well documented that it can enhance the loyalty of staff, improve the quality of the product, make supply chains more visible, improve customer loyalty, may provide some social benefits to working children and is also considered cost-effective (Winstanley *et al.* 2002). Although CSR appears to be a more socially sensitive approach to addressing child labour in Southern supply chains, it cannot truly be considered 'socially responsible' unless it is subject to a social assessment that indicates that it introduces positive social impacts that convincingly outweigh any negative social impacts on working children, their families and wider local community. Assessments of this kind remain woefully scarce.

Within the social development sector it is now widely accepted in theory, if not always in practice, that social interventions need to be accompanied by some form of evaluation, monitoring or audit to assess their actual, rather than their intended, socioeconomic impacts on target groups or beneficiaries of developing countries. However, CSR interventions have not been subject to the same levels of assessment, even though they can often be rightly viewed as social development interventions. If the emerging CSR interventions are to gain wider and more sustained acceptance among affected target groups in developing countries, they will have to attest to their 'social responsibility' through similar levels of social assessment.

This chapter attempts to fulfil this assessment void by exploring the socioeconomic impact of the CSR approach to eliminating child labour from supply chains in developing countries. The chapter draws on the authors' practical experience of designing and implementing a child labour elimination strategy in the football industry in Sialkot, Pakistan. The analysis is supported by the extensive qualitative data collected by Save the Children UK, International Labour Organisation/International Programme on the Elimination of Child labour (ILO/IPEC) and the authors since 1997.[1]

This chapter is divided into five sections. The first section describes the social and industrial features of the football industry. The second section summarises the socioeconomic impacts of the home-based production structure of the football industry. The third section details the CSR approach that was adopted by the Atlanta Partnership to eliminate child labour from the production of hand-stitched footballs. The fourth section describes and examines the socioeconomic impacts of the child-labour-free production structure on football stitchers and their families. The final section discusses the empirical findings in the context of CSR theory and suggests an approach for further improving the implementation of CSR policies.

1 The sources that have been particularly relied on are Cummins 2000; Saeed 1998; Sialkot Education Programme 1998; the social monitoring reports published by Save the Children UK from 1998 to 2000; Marcus and Husselbee 1997; and The Atlanta Partners Report 1999.

14.1 Sialkot football industry

14.1.1 Pre-1997: the home-based production structure

The Sialkot district contributes significantly to the foreign reserves of Pakistan. Hosting three export-oriented industries (sporting goods, leather products and surgical instruments), the district is home to thousands of entrepreneurs and highly skilled labourers. To meet the recreational demands of the British Colonial Army, the people of Sialkot started developing a sporting goods industry in the 19th century. The industry has gradually developed excellence in producing labour-intensive sporting goods and ultimately, in the late 20th century, entered the international football market by exporting a football named 'TANGO' that was officially used in the World Cup. Over a period of 30 years, the Sialkot football industry has become the source of more than 75% of the world's billion-dollar football retailing market. All the major brands including Nike, Adidas, Puma, Reebok and Mitre source hand-stitched footballs from Sialkot.

Until the 1970s football production was based mainly in the city of Sialkot. During that time, football stitching was physically demanding as pure leather was used to make the footballs. The football stitchers were organised and labour unions were active in negotiating wages, annual bonuses and promoting other benefits. However, during the 1970s, under the influence of the following factors, the Sialkot football industry changed significantly:

- The introduction of 'TANGO' in the World Cup tremendously increased demand for hand-stitched footballs. A recent estimate suggests that the total annual global demand for footballs is now around 35 million. Pakistan retains about 60% of the market in terms of volume and 75% in terms of value. The Sialkot football industry has been particularly good at manufacturing professional A grade footballs but also produces B grade footballs, which are sold as toys or promotional balls.

- The introduction of artificial leather for making hand-stitched footballs simplified the football stitching process, thereby increasing the participation of certain groups, particularly women and children, in their production.

- The government of Pakistan made it obligatory for local industries to pay social security to their employees. In response, Sialkot football manufacturers introduced extensive subcontracting and piece-rates to avoid making social security payments to many football stitchers.

These factors led to the exponential growth of a complex network of village- and city-based football manufacturers, makers, contractors, subcontractors, semi-skilled football stitchers and master stitchers. As a result, the football stitching element of the overall production structure transformed into a predominantly village- and home-based activity, attracting thousands of low-income families (children, women and men). The informal labour market and home-based production drove the Sialkot football industry until 1996. Indeed, by 1998, research found that 16.6% of households in Sialkot district were involved in football stitching.

The production structure of hand-stitched footballs was set up at three different locations. Football manufacturers established city-based factories for pre-stitching processes (e.g. cutting and printing) and post-stitching processes (e.g. quality control); the rest of the process was located with village-based contractors and home-based football stitcher families. Figure 14.1 provides an overview of the football stitching processes and their locations.

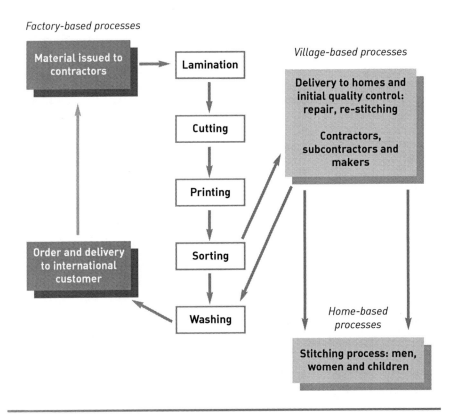

Figure 14.1 Sialkot football industry, pre-1997

14.2 Socioeconomic impacts of the home-based production structure

Football-stitcher families identified several effects of a home-based football production arrangement and informal labour market on their employment. The arrangement made football-stitching work available to all family members, including seasonal, part-time, semi-skilled workers and those who lived in remote areas of the Sialkot district. The involvement of all family members also increased the football production capacity. It gave football stitchers complete control over their work environment in terms of time and space. However, the home-based production arrangements also had specific disadvantages, including low wages, the lack of social security provision and the reduced collective bargaining power of football stitchers.

At the family level, the home-based football production arrangement led to higher income and regularity in cash flow which increased levels of food security by enabling football stitchers to consume food on a more regular basis and to participate in social activities. At the individual level, football stitchers identified several social benefits of the home-based production. For example, the involvement of children in football stitching reduced their exposure to and engagement in anti-social behaviour. In addition women football stitchers invested a greater proportion of their earnings in their children, and the earnings of young female football stitchers allowed them to contribute to the dowry, thereby facilitating their ability to get married.

Although football-stitcher families viewed the family-oriented and home-based football production arrangement as socially and economically advantageous, it proved unacceptable on ethical grounds because of the involvement of children. In 1996, the international media, trade unions and other civil-society organisations highlighted the issue of child labour in the football industry and put tremendous pressure on international football brands, local football manufacturers, the World Federation of Sporting Goods Industries (WFSGI) and FIFA to respond to the child labour problem.

In the UK, on 21 November 1996, a meeting was convened of the ILO, the United Nations Children's Fund (UNICEF), Anti-Slavery International, the Fair Trade Foundation, Oxfam, Save the Children UK, the government of Pakistan, the Sialkot Chamber of Commerce and Industries (SCCI) and other interested groups. They all showed willingness to support the Sialkot football industry in addressing the child labour issue. A mission was organised to draft a summary project document for the elimination of child labour from the football industry. ILO/IPEC, UNICEF, SCCI and Save the Children in particular led the process of analysing the child labour situation. Save the Children UK contributed significantly in proposing the social protection interventions, while ILO/IPEC proposed a child labour monitoring system based on the Garment Industry Project in Bangladesh.

14.3 The Atlanta Partnership

On 14 February 1997, at the Atlanta Super Show in the United States, the World Federation of Sporting Goods Industry (WFSGI) and the US-based Sporting Goods Manufacturers' Association (SGMA) proposed a strategy to eliminate child labour from the production of hand-stitched footballs. A partnership between business organisations and not-for-profit organisations was created to implement the strategy. The SCCI, the ILO/IPEC and UNICEF signed the partnership agreement, while Save the Children UK became a non-signatory partner. In March 1997, in collaboration with local NGOs, the Atlanta Partners began the implementation of the child labour elimination programme.

The Atlanta Partnership was primarily based on the ILO's Minimum Age Convention (No. 138) 1973 which states that no one under the age of 15 years shall be admitted to employment or work in any occupation. The Convention does permit a ratifying Member State whose economy and educational facilities are insufficiently developed, after consultation with employers and workers concerned, to initially specify a minimum age of 14 years. The United Nations Convention on the Rights of the Child was used to design the social protection programme for football-stitcher children and their families (see further below). Articles 3 (that all actions taken involving or affecting children must be in their best interests), 12 (that children must be consulted on all action likely to affect them), 27 (children have a right to an adequate standard of living) and 32 (children should be protected from economic exploitation and from performing any work that is hazardous or likely to interfere with their education or harm their health or development) were seen as of particular importance in designing the social protection programme.

14.3.1 Objectives of the Atlanta Partnership

The partner organisations formally agreed on the following primary objectives:

- To assist manufacturers who seek to prevent child labour in the manufacture or assembly of footballs in the Sialkot district and its environs

- To identify and remove children from conditions of child labour in the manufacture or assembly of footballs and provide them with educational and other opportunities

- To facilitate changes in community and family attitudes towards child labour

- To encourage other local industries and the government of Pakistan to explore how they might do more to contribute to ending child labour in other local industries

14.3.2 CSR approach to eliminating child labour

The Atlanta Partners designed an approach to achieve the aforementioned objectives, which primarily addressed the demand factors (home-based production and informal labour market) considered to be the main source of the child labour problem. A social disaster mitigation programme was also added to minimise the anticipated negative impacts of the restructuring of the production structure and the formalisation of the labour market on football-stitcher children and their families. The strategy devised to address the demand factors was called the Prevention and Monitoring Programme. It aimed to recruit local football manufacturers who would voluntarily and publicly commit to implementing the following interventions:

- Formal registration of all contractors responsible for overseeing football stitching, all football-stitching facilities (clearly identifiable and open to unannounced inspection) and all football stitchers, including documentation verifying that they were over 14 years of age

- Establishment of an internal monitoring department with a responsibility to develop and monitor the formal registration system. The department was also supposed to provide training to employees in verifying the ages of football stitchers and in writing periodic reports on its monitoring effort.

- Agreement to be verified by an independent third party

The social disaster mitigation programme was called the Social Protection and Rehabilitation Programme and included the following interventions:

- Rehabilitation of children removed from the football industry by placing them into the appropriate education system

- Prevention of child labour by discouraging new entrants in the child labour market through education

- Provision of in-kind support to facilitate the participation of children in education programmes

- Raising awareness of the community about the serious health and developmental consequences of sending children to work instead of school

- Opportunities for generating income to replace income loss

14.3.3 Operational framework

The Atlanta Partnership formally defined the roles and responsibilities of each partner organisation and an agreed framework of operation to obtain the desired results within an 18-month period. The ILO and SCCI were given responsibility for assisting local football manufacturers in developing an internal child labour monitoring system. The ILO also became the external verification body. Save the Children UK, UNICEF and ILO/IPEC led the Social Protection and Rehabilitation Programme. The framework allowed the partners to take independent decisions about location, strategy, method and outputs of their interventions as long as they showed compatibility with the objectives of the Atlanta Agreement. It also elaborated the formally agreed process of decision-making. The Programme Co-ordinating Committee (PCC) was established to take policy decisions. The Sialkot Implementation Team (SIT) was set up to decide operational issues at field level. The Sialkot Programme Forum (SPF) was formalised to channel the political support of the district administration and other important local stakeholders. Figure 14.2 explains the partners, their programme interventions and the joint operational framework, while Box 14.1 provides the chronology for the formation, development and conclusion of the Atlanta Partnership.

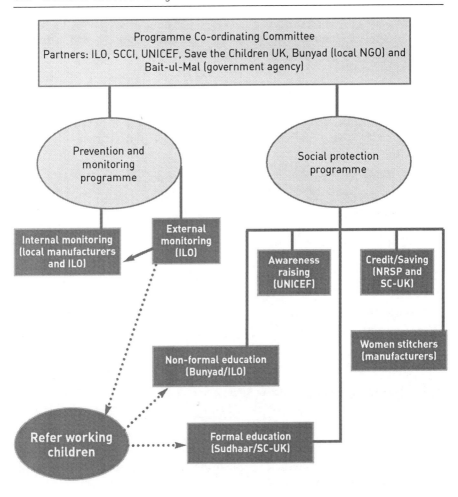

Figure 14.2 Partners, programme and operational framework of the Atlanta Partnership

14.3.4 Responses to the challenges of implementing the CSR approach

The implementation of the two-pronged strategy of the CSR approach was faced with a number of challenges to which the Atlanta Partners had to respond. These key challenges and responses are discussed below.

Voluntary participation of football manufacturers. The partner organisations and wider community of primary stakeholders asked local football manufacturers to

Early 1996	The Foul Ball Campaign, part of the International Labour Rights Fund in Washington, highlighted the involvement of children in football stitching.
June 1996	*Life* magazine reported the involvement of children in the Sialkot football industry.
21 November 1996	WFSGI, the ILO, UNICEF, Save the Children UK, Anti-Slavery International, football suppliers, global brands and representatives of the government of Pakistan met in London to work out a child labour elimination approach. WFSGI, in collaboration with the Pentland Group of Industries, facilitated and hosted the meeting.
14 February 1997	ILO, UNICEF, SCCI and Save the Children UK formed the Atlanta Partnership.
March 1997	The Atlanta Partners jointly visited Sialkot to discuss and develop an operational framework.
April 1997	The Atlanta Partners finalised the operational framework and US Labor Department, local football manufacturers, DFID, FIFA and SICA agreed to provide financial support to the partnership's child labour programme interventions.
May 1997	Save the Children published *Voices of Children* (Marcus and Husselbee 1997) which highlighted the social causes of child labour in the football industry and recommended a social protection programme for football-stitcher children and their families.
June–September 1997	The Atlanta Partners established their offices in Sialkot and finalised the details of their projects.
November 1997–March 1998	The Atlanta Partners formed several partnerships with local NGOs, which were given a task of implementing different components of the social protection programme. ILO/IPEC implemented the child labour monitoring programme.
April–June 1998	The implementation of the different components of the project became the exclusive focus of the Atlanta Partnership.
June 1998	The Partners reported on the progress of the project to international media, global brands, FIFA, WFSGI and other interest groups in France on the first day of the World Cup.
July 1998–December 2000	The Atlanta Partners achieved their targets (elimination of child labour from the production of hand-stitched footballs) and shifted ownership of the project to local NGOs and SCCI.
2001	The Atlanta Partnership officially ended.

Box 14.1 Chronology of the Atlanta Partnership

join the partnership on a voluntary basis. This was a critical decision because the successful elimination of child labour depended on the voluntary participation of all local manufacturers. The Atlanta Partnership could not eliminate child labour from the production of hand-stitched footballs if a large number of local manufacturers chose not to participate in the child labour monitoring and prevention programme. Unrealistic though this decision might appear, it was strategic since it minimised the resistance of those local football manufacturers who were against the partnership for various social, political and commercial reasons.

Abolition of family-oriented football production process. Football stitching was a family occupation, with different family members performing different tasks to complete a football. Figure 14.3 shows the five stages of football stitching and the differential involvement of family members at different production stages. Since one of the main causes of child labour was the family-orientation of football stitching, the Atlanta Partnership decided to introduce a formal registration system that only sanctioned the participation of those football stitchers who could stitch a complete ball.

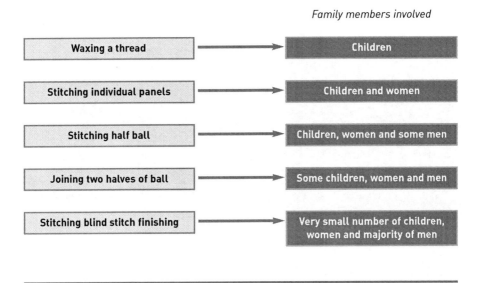

Figure 14.3 Stages of football-stitching process

Creating socially monitorable football-stitching facilities. The formal registration of workers could not guarantee the elimination of child labour if football stitching continued to be a home-based activity. The Atlanta Partnership, therefore, proposed the creation of football-stitching centres and made the registration of the centres and their associated facilities mandatory. The creation of socially monitorable football-stitching centres was also necessary from the perspective of external child labour monitoring. It was realised that, even if local football manufacturers found a way to declare houses of football-stitcher families as stitching centres free of child labour, it would be impossible to conduct surprise inspections of thousands of households. A technically appropriate solution to this problem was to construct independent, large and socially monitorable football-stitching centres and facilities. As a consequence a large number of football-stitching centres were established in the rural and semi-urban areas of the Sialkot district.

Verifying the production of footballs by registered stitchers. Even though the organisation of socially monitorable stitching centres was, technically, an effective solution, it did not guarantee the complete elimination of child labour. Football manufacturers could still provide football-stitching work to home-based workers. In order to be able to verify that football stitching would only be done by formally registered football stitchers at the registered football-stitching centres, the partners agreed to a mathematical formula offered by ILO/IPEC. This formula specified that the total number of football stitchers at a football-stitching centre needed to be equivalent to the total number of footballs stitched in a specified time. The formula was based on the assumption that a skilled adult could stitch three complete footballs a day. If a manufacturer did not have the required number of football stitchers to produce their output, the likelihood was that they were engaging home-based and, probably, child football stitchers.

Parallel implementation of the child labour monitoring and social protection and rehabilitation programmes. The partners anticipated that there would be some negative impacts from the implementation of the child labour monitoring and prevention programme on football-stitcher children and their families (e.g. the exposure of children to more hazardous alternative work, the financial loss to football-stitcher families). To mitigate these socioeconomic impacts the partner organisations decided to implement the social protection programme simultaneously.

Combining short-, medium- and long-term interventions. Even though the Atlanta Partnership was supposed to achieve its target within 18 months, the partner organisations agreed to continue implementation of the social protection programme for a longer period of time. This was largely based on the recognition that the social interventions would take a longer period of time to establish sustainable social and economic safety nets for the affected working children and their families.

Organising flexible and women-only village-based football stitching centres. In 1997, Save the Children published a research report which highlighted the negative impact of transforming home-based football stitching into factory-based stitching on the employment opportunities of women football stitchers. The report declared that many football-stitcher women would be unable to work in football-stitching centres owing to social and domestic factors. As a result, the Atlanta Partners decided to establish smaller and flexible, women-only, village-based football-stitching centres that could accommodate such women.

14.4 The Sialkot football industry post-1997

14.4.1 Child-labour-free production structure

The combined effect of these strategic decisions has been to create a child-labour-free production arrangement of manufacturing hand-stitched footballs. The majority of football manufacturers have set up an internal labour monitoring system. Over 1,000 stitching centres have been organised by local football manufacturers in both urban and rural Sialkot. These centres accommodate over 20,000 football stitchers. Figure 14.4 outlines the current structure of the Sialkot football-stitching industry.

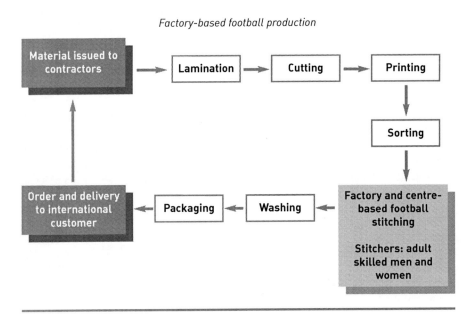

Figure 14.4 Child-labour-free production arrangements in Sialkot

The process of the elimination of child labour from the production of hand-stitched footballs has brought three important changes in the production arrangement. First, instead of family, it has placed skilled adult football stitchers (largely male) at the centre of the new production arrangement. Second, it has defined the timing and place of football-stitching work by introducing formal football-stitching centres. Third, it has firmly made football manufacturers and makers responsible for managing labour relations. Contrary to the family-oriented, home-based and subcontractor managed production arrangement, the new production arrangement is oriented around the individual (skilled male), factory-based and managed by football manufacturers.

14.4.2 Socioeconomic impacts of the CSR approach

The CSR approach resulted in the new, child-labour-free production arrangement. This has a range of effects on employment opportunities, which, in turn, have an impact on football-stitcher families. These effects and impacts are described below, summarised in Table 14.1 and illustrated in a story (Box 14.2) (The story is based on the three case studies and discussions with a few football stitchers.)

Razia, the mother of a child football stitcher, asserted that 'in these hard times, all household members need to contribute to meeting the family's basic needs'. However, when in 1997 the Sialkot football industry decided to eliminate child labour, she quickly recognised that it was not her but the industry that had the power to determine family work. A subcontractor informed her that he could no longer provide home-based employment. If she wanted to continue to work she must do so in the factory. Because of her domestic responsibilities and her distance from the factory this was impossible. She realised that not only her children but also she had lost a vital source of family income.

Her husband, Rahim, a daily wage labourer for a local builder, was also a skilled part-time football stitcher. He often worked at home with his family, combining stitching and building work in order to meet the economic needs of his family. The home-based nature of football stitching made this situation possible and its abolition had made him redundant. He decided to try to work as a part-time football stitcher in a factory but management informed him that they only recruited full-time workers. He had now lost a portion of his income and the family only had his building work for financial support.

In less than a week the family had lost a significant portion of their monthly income. Worried and not knowing what to do they decided to talk to a neighbour who had decided to become a football stitcher in a factory because she earned more money per football. Her neighbour told her that a football manufacturer was planning to establish a village-based football-stitching centre for those women who could not work in factories for social or domestic reasons. Razia felt relieved, thinking she might be able to join this village-based centre if her daughter, who was only 13 years old, could take responsibility for caring for her younger brothers and sisters. Nevertheless, she concluded that it was ultimately the company not the family that decided who should work and under what conditions.

Box 14.2 **The story of a football-stitcher family**

Stitcher families identified several effects of the new production arrangement on their employment. Many football stitchers stated that it has concentrated the provision of football-stitching work to skilled adult football stitchers and those who live closer to football-stitching centres. Since only one or two members of a family can work as full-time stitchers, the new production arrangement has decreased the overall production capacity of football stitchers at the family level. Football stitchers also mentioned that they have lost complete control over their work environment in terms of time and space. In contrast, the new production arrangements also provide specific benefits, such as higher wages, some provision of food and social security (cheap food and medical facilities are available at the centres) and the opportunity to form football-stitcher unions.

Football production structure	Perceived effects on employment	Socioeconomic impacts	
1. Individual, skilled and adult orientation 2. Centre- and factory-based 3. Managed by football manufacturers 4. Socially monitored by external social auditor	1. Less availability of football stitching work 2. Lower production capacity at family level 3. Higher wages 4. Higher collective bargaining power 5. No control of football stitchers over work environment in terms of timing and place of stitching footballs 6. Some provision of social services to those who stitch footballs at centres 7. No child labour	**Football-stitcher family** 1. Lower aggregated family income 2. Lower food security 3. Lower social participation	**Individual members** 1. Higher individual income 2. Lower social benefits for women, young girls and children 3. Higher social benefits for skilled male football stitchers 4. Fewer income-generating opportunities for seasonal, part-time and semi-skilled football stitchers

Table 14.1 Socioeconomic impacts of the child-labour-free football production structure

From the perspective of football stitchers the changes in their employment have had both negative and positive socioeconomic impacts. At the family level, it has been suggested that the combined effects of these factors led to a reduction in family income, since the number of earning members of the family has been reduced, despite a significant increase in wage rates. As a consequence, at the family level, regularity in the consumption of food and social participation has declined. Many football stitchers are also of the view that the new structure has marginalised semi-skilled, seasonal and part-time football stitchers, and those who live in the remote areas of the Sialkot district. At the individual level, football stitchers have identified several social benefits of the new production arrangement. Crucially, it offers better wages and working conditions to skilled football stitchers, particularly men.

14.5 Discussion and conclusion

The CSR approach implemented by the Atlanta Partnership, primarily addressed, in conjunction with the social disaster mitigation programme, the demand factors that cause child labour in supply chains. At the theoretical level, this CSR approach can be viewed as a derivative of the CSR theory offered by Bowen (1953), which advocated that business should comply with larger societal values. In the context of the child labour issue, the official acceptance of the Convention on the Rights of the Child (CRC) and the ILO Labour Conventions provide a global framework of societal values with which CSR activities should be aligned. In principle, therefore, it was an obligation for the football industry to eliminate child labour from the production of hand-stitched footballs. However, in addition to the design of a CSR approach reflecting social values, Davis and Bloomstrom (1966) proposed that CSR activities should be designed to respond to the specific interests and needs of those within society who are affected by business actions.

The latter approach entails the identification of interests and needs before designing a CSR approach. In the context of the football industry's CSR approach to eliminate child labour, the Atlanta Partners made significant efforts to incorporate the needs and interests of football-stitcher children and their families. ILO/IPEC and Save the Children conducted two separate research studies prior to designing the project. The former was aimed at estimating the total number of football-stitcher children and the latter focused on the causes of child labour in the football industry (as viewed by football-stitcher children and their families) proposing interventions to address the identified causes. In addition, Save the Children's research report, *Voices of Children* (Marcus and Husselbee 1997), highlighted the negative impacts of the restructuring of the hand-stitched production structure on women football stitchers.

Even though the football industry's CSR approach was firmly based on globally agreed values, and did, to an extent, incorporate the interests and needs of football-stitcher children and their families, it generated impacts and outcomes that were both positive and negative in nature. On the positive side, the CSR approach largely eliminated child labour from the production of A grade, hand-stitched footballs. It has created better working conditions for skilled male football stitchers. Many football-stitcher children and their families have also benefited from a new and improved education system and income-generation programmes. By adjusting the strategy in its implementation stage, the Atlanta Partnership has provided flexible employment opportunities for those women football stitchers who could not work (for social or domestic reasons) in the large football-stitching centres. These outcomes are all significant, but, aside from the elimination of child labour, largely arbitrary and not particularly equitable.

In contrast, the research exposes two different yet clearly interrelated patterns of negative socioeconomic outcomes. First, the CSR approach made football stitchers worse off at the family level and, second, it widened the gap between already better-off football stitchers and the marginalised football stitchers. Individual skilled football stitchers benefited from the intervention but at the cost of lower earning capacity at the family level. Likewise, semi-skilled, part-time and seasonal football stitchers, and those who live in remote areas of the Sialkot district, lost their income-generating opportunities, while individual skilled football stitchers gained better working conditions and higher wages.

Since the Atlanta Partnership's CSR approach had notable negative socio-economic impacts and outcomes at community level, it cannot be considered entirely socially responsible. If such negative impacts are to be avoided in future CSR approaches, it is essential to question why these negative impacts and outcomes occurred. In the context of the Atlanta Partnership, we can discern certain contributory factors. For example, the child labour programme had a very short time-line and the partner organisations were unable to plan collectively. However, the most significant factor was that the programme failed to take account of the needs and interests of all stakeholders. Although ILO/IPEC and Save the Children's research focused attention on football-stitcher children and their families, the research neglected to account for impacts on individual family members.

It is evident that the implementation of CSR policies based on human rights, in this case ILO Convention (138) and the Children's Rights Conventions, does not necessarily generate only positive social outcomes at community level. In fact, such policies may bring about notable negative social outcomes. In theory, therefore, the implementation process of CSR policies in a given context should be considered as important as human rights conventions themselves in terms of the final social outcomes. The current thinking on CSR, which is much more focused on defining the ethical principles and policies, needs to integrate socially responsible methods and tools of designing and planning CSR practices to ensure positive and equitable social outcomes.

Had the CSR approach incorporated a full socioeconomic impact assessment that identified and mapped all programme stakeholders at the community level and anticipated outcomes and impacts prior to implementation of the Atlanta Agreement, many of the aforementioned negative issues, outcomes and impacts could have been mitigated or avoided. At a more general level, the use of this designing and planning tool could have highlighted the need for a more balanced dualistic intervention strategy that placed as much emphasis on traditional, social development, supply-side or causation factors as demand-side symptomatic factors. Social impact assessment (SIA) will work most effectively when it involves the participation of programme stakeholders and therefore accounts for the specific strategic social development perspectives in which it is being conducted. Participatory SIA is already widely used in the social development sector, in businesses within the natural resource sector, and is a project precondition for a wide range of bilateral and multilateral agencies including the World Bank, the International Financial Corporation and the World Health Organisation (Macfarlane 1999). If CSR interventions, human rights related or otherwise, are to maintain their credibility and truly be considered 'socially responsible' in the long run, participatory SIA will need to be a much more widely adopted precondition for beneficiary project and programme planning among the general business community. It is only in this way that the introduction of positive socioeconomic impacts, which convincingly outweigh the negative impacts, can be planned for in the project and programme design and demonstrably reported.

15

SA 8000

Human rights in the workplace

Deborah Leipziger
Consultant, The Netherlands

Eileen Kaufman
Social Accountability International, USA

Social Accountability 8000 (SA 8000) is a verifiable standard designed to make workplaces more humane. By early 2003, over 200 workplaces in 35 countries in 32 sectors had been certified to be in compliance with SA 8000, and thousands more had been audited to define needed improvements to come into compliance. Over 138,000 employees work in SA 8000-certified facilities.

This chapter describes SA 8000 and the multi-stakeholder partnership by which it was developed. The aim is to analyse the role that voluntary standards can play in enhancing human rights in the workplace, in particular in the supply chains of multinational enterprises.

15.1 SA 8000

15.1.1 About Social Accountability International

Social Accountability International (SAI) is a human rights NGO dedicated to improving workplaces and communities around the world by developing and implementing voluntary standards on social responsibility. SAI convenes key stakeholders to develop consensus-based standards, accredits qualified independent organisations to verify compliance, and promotes understanding and implementation of such standards worldwide. As of the beginning of 2003, there were nine organisations accredited to perform SA 8000 audits.

SAI follows an international, consensus-based approach that actively engages in consultation, training and learning with business, workers and trade unions, government, socially responsible investors, and non-governmental organisations. The approach is multi-industry, multinational and multi-sectoral, covering sectors as diverse as toys, apparel, food and mail order.[1]

15.1.2 Development of SA 8000

> Multi-stakeholder initiatives are efforts that bring diverse stakeholders together around a set of agreed principles in the area of labour, human rights or the environment. These initiatives vary in their mission, some focussing on shared learning around best practice and others with more focussed monitoring or certification programmes (World Bank 2003b: 12).

In the mid-1990s, SAI convened a diverse group of stakeholders who developed a workplace code of conduct based on international norms and a verification system based on widely used systems. This resulted in the publication of Social Accountability 8000 (SA 8000) in 1997.

The multi-stakeholder nature of SA 8000 added legitimacy and credibility to the standard, demonstrating that it is part of a consensus and not a unilaterally declared statement by a company or an industry body. The existence of a multi-stakeholder dialogue provides a context and process for evolution of the standard as well as a built-in system for checks and balances.

15.1.3 Overview of SA 8000

The SA 8000 standard is a tool for workers, managers, customers and investors. The standard provides a systematic way of defining and verifying compliance with key human rights norms. While it is not a panacea, SA 8000 has been demonstrated and reported as a useful mechanism for specifying the responsibility for workplace rights within the supply chain (Kolk and van Tulder 2002). The standard is not intended as a substitute for governmental enforcement of regulations, but rather provides an incentive and a tool for compliance with regulations.

SA 8000[2] is based on conventions of the International Labour Organisation (ILO) and related international human rights instruments, including the Universal Declaration of Human Rights and the UN Declaration on the Rights of the Child. SA 8000 facilitates adherence to the ILO conventions in the workplace, by developing management systems to address human rights issues listed in Box 15.1, and by meeting the performance requirements detailed.

SA 8000's management systems differentiate it from most codes of conduct and statements of intent, by specifying the development of management and documentation procedures that support the performance requirements in Box 15.1. Social issues need to be integrated into all aspects of company policy and day-to-day operations. The documentation and procedures required under SA 8000 are intended to provide evidence of ongoing compliance, both before and after the

---

1 For further details, see the SAI website at www.sa-intl.org.
2 The full text of SA 8000 can be found at www.sa-intl.org.

Child labour

Child labour is forbidden under SA 8000. Certified companies must guarantee the education of children who might lose their jobs as a result of the standard.

Forced labour

Forced labour is forbidden under SA 8000. Workers cannot be required to surrender their identity papers or pay 'deposits' as a condition of employment.

Health and safety

Companies must meet basic standards for a safe and healthy working environment, including safe drinking water, clean rest-room facilities, applicable safety equipment, decent housing (if provided by the company) and necessary training in health and safety.

Freedom of association and the right to collective bargaining

Employers must respect the rights of workers to form and join trade unions and to bargain collectively without fear of reprisals.

Discrimination

SA 8000 bans discrimination on the basis of race, caste, national origin, religion, disability, gender, sexual orientation, age, union membership or political affiliation.

Disciplinary practices

SA 8000 prohibits corporal punishment, mental or physical coercion and verbal abuse of workers.

Working hours

The working week cannot exceed 48 hours, with at least one day off per week, and a cap of 12 hours of voluntary overtime per week, remunerated at a premium rate.

Compensation

Wages paid, for a standard work week, must meet all minimum legal standards and must provide sufficient income for basic needs, with at least some discretionary income.

Box 15.1 SA 8000 performance requirements

auditor is at the facility, and also to ensure that there will be continuous improvement in the social conditions of the workplace. SA 8000 requires the following management systems elements to be in place:[3]

3 There are many tools available to companies seeking help in developing management systems for SA 8000. SA 8000 training courses, offered around the world, provide many resources and contacts for managers as well as auditors. *The SA 8000 Guidance Document* (see the SAI website, www.sa-intl.org) is an excellent resource for companies. The book *SA 8000: The Definitive Guide to the New Social Standard* (Leipziger 2001) contains many practical examples of how companies can implement SA 8000, including model forms and procedures.

- Training programmes

- Communications

- Elected SA 8000 worker representatives

- Management representatives with adequate budgets

- Clear lines of authority

- Management reviews

- Control of suppliers

- Planning and policies

SA 8000 requires companies to comply with national and other applicable laws in addition to SA 8000. When there is a conflict between a national law and SA 8000 on the same issue, the more stringent standard applies.

The developers of SA 8000 drafted it to be verifiable. Third-party certification of compliance is a key element in the system, providing a public statement of compliance, a tool for workers, a system for complaints and a built-in locus for corrective actions. Like any standard, SA 8000 can also be used for lower levels of assurance. Essentially, there are three levels of assurance (first-, second- and third-party). First-party assessments (or internal audits) are internal assessments of a company's activities comparing them with the requirements of SA 8000. Such assessments might be conducted in anticipation of an audit by a certification company and can help to identify areas that need improvement. Second-party assessments (or supply chain monitoring) are supplier audits carried out by a customer company, a retailer or a brand, which arranges for audits of its suppliers. Such monitoring does not provide an external assurance that the workplace complies with SA 8000 and does not necessarily carry a corrective action component. However, such assessments may be a key step in preparing for certification. In third-party assessments (certification audits) a company is audited by an independent and external body, accredited by SAI. If the company demonstrates that it complies with SA 8000, then the certification firm grants it a certificate. If a facility does not comply, then it is required to take corrective actions to remedy the non-compliance before certification can be granted. Certification indicates compliance with the requirements of SA 8000 and requires periodic re-visits to verify continuing compliance and often further corrective actions. Certified companies are listed on SAI's website.

15.2 SA 8000 as a global voluntary standard

The experience with the development and application of SA 8000 provides many important lessons both for voluntary corporate responsibility standards generally, and for addressing human rights and labour issues in supply chains.

15.2.1 Strengths of the SA 8000 system

SA 8000 is global and cross-sectoral

The past decade has seen the rise of many national and sectoral standards. While such standards are useful for galvanising an industry, they can lead to duplication and multiple audits of the same facilities. SA 8000 applies to companies around the world and across industries, serving as a common benchmark to ensure that supply chains respect basic rights. For example, the AVE programme developed by a consortium of German retailers provides a listing of SA 8000-audited and -certified facilities for its members. The global nature of SA 8000 allows companies selecting suppliers to use a common system across their operations.

SA 8000 is building capacity

SA 8000 has developed extensive training programmes to promote worker rights. Training is very important in helping to promote the awareness necessary for sustainable improvements. There are many types of training being offered and developed: for workers on how to use SA 8000 as a tool; for managers on how to follow the requirements; for supply chain managers on how to communicate the requirements and partner with suppliers to enable compliance; and for auditors. Joint worker–manager training is under development. SAI and the International Garment, Textile and Leather Workers' Federation (IGTLWF) are conducting training in 12 countries to make codes of conduct more useful to workers.

SA 8000 includes both positive and negative rights

The human rights expectations of companies include both positive and negative obligations. These expectations are reflected in SA 8000, which prohibits child labour, forced labour and discrimination, while promoting wages that support basic needs. According to research conducted by Shareen Hertel of the Human Rights Program at Columbia University, grass-roots leaders in Mexico and Bangladesh favour a greater inclusion of positive rights in codes of conduct, rather than just prohibitions.[4]

SA 8000 has developed a strong system for complaints and appeals

One of the key elements of a certification standard is that companies can be certified, but, if they subsequently fail to meet the standard, they can lose that certification. Similarly under SA 8000, any individual or organisation has standing to complain that a certification is improper and trigger an investigation (see, for example, the case study presented in Box 15.2). Certified facilities can lose their certification and accredited bodies can lose their standing to conduct SA 8000 audits.

---

4   Correspondence between Deborah Leipziger and Shareen Hertel, 25 November 2002.

COOP Italia, with over 15% of Italian grocery sales and 4.5 million members, aims to 'respect man and working conditions'. Thus, in 1998 it undertook implementation of SA 8000 in its own operations and subsequently started to work with suppliers of the over 300 different food products bearing the COOP label.

The Centro Nuovo Modelo di Sviluppo (CNMS) is an Italian NGO working to improve working conditions in the South. In 1999, CNMS filed a complaint with COOP Italia regarding working conditions at a Kenyan supplier of pineapples to COOP Italia. The complaint was based on documented reports from its African NGO associates and allies regarding the terrible working and living conditions at the pineapple supplier's plantation in Thika, Kenya. CNMS also launched a consumer boycott in Italy.

An informal coalition emerged in support of the campaign. Through the processes of auditing labour standards at the plantations and working together on the campaign, the coalition transformed itself into a new institution—an international Solidarity Committee comprising CNMS, the Kenya Human Rights Commission (KHRC) and the Kenya Union of Commercial Food and Allied Workers (KUCFAW), along with Nairobi shantytown NGOs and with other Italian NGOs working in Africa. The Minister of Labour eventually co-operated with the human rights commission and the union. The Solidarity Committee, jointly with Del Monte and COOP, developed and committed to an improvement plan based on the SA 8000 standards, and codified the plan in a contract signed in March 2001. The contract was signed by KHRC, ChemiChemi Ya Ukweli, Kituo Cha Sheria, the Kenya Women Workers' Organisation, trade union delegates, CNMS, COOP and Del Monte.

The involvement of many stakeholders led to a consensus for a corrective action plan, to improvements in health and safety and in housing, to the opening of a school for workers' children, and to the establishment of a trade union office inside the company, the first in the history of Kenya. The Solidarity Committee and CNMS are permanently and actively monitoring the plantation and the progress of the improvements. The multi-sector coalition, comprising human rights advocates, business representatives and trade unions, continues to meet and monitor implementation of the improvement plan.

Box 15.2 Case study: working conditions in Kenyan pineapple plantations

Source: adapted from Mutunga *et al.* 2002

SA 8000 promotes corrective action

During an SA 8000 audit, the auditor alerts the facility management that it needs to take corrective action in one or more areas before gaining the SA 8000 certificate. This process is critical for guaranteeing continuous improvement.

SA 8000 leads to business benefits

Improvements to working conditions are enhanced and reinforced by the business benefits resulting from their implementation. For improvements to be sustainable they need not only supportive management and reporting systems but also incentives in the form of perceived benefits. The proponents of good practices believe that there are substantial benefits to be realised from such improvements, and there is empirical evidence from SA 8000-certified facilities to support these beliefs (see, for example, the case study presented in Box 15.3). SAI has sent

In India, a long-term partnership between apparel manufacturer Prem Durai and its customer, the Swiss company Switcher, has resulted in positive change for workers, management, the community and customers. Major investments were undertaken in equipment, technology upgrading and new management practices, and social accountability procedures were implemented.

As a result of coming into compliance with SA 8000, the following benefits were realised: overtime was halved; quality improved (product rejection levels were halved and rework fell from 20% to 8%); absenteeism was halved; and staff turnover fell from 8.5% to 4.7%. An SA 8000 Corrective Action Committee now brings management and trade union representatives together to address problems in a co-operative mode.

The company has been widely praised for its 'accomplishments with respect to wages, working hours, health and safety' (Cestre 2001). According to Neil Kearney, the General Secretary of the International Garment and Leather Workers' Trade Union, Prem Durai was able to reduce rates of overtime by dropping steps in the assembly line. The process of adopting SA 8000's management systems gave them the insight and the motivation to redesign their production line.

Box 15.3 Case study: apparel manufacture in India

Source: correspondence between Deborah Leipziger and Neil Kearney, 9 July 2001

questionnaires to all certified facilities, to test whether benefits are being realised. The results are positive; over half of the responders reported benefits in each of these categories: new sales, fewer days lost to injury, higher quality, productivity increases and better worker retention.[5]

15.2.2 Criticisms of the SA 8000 system

While SA 8000 is one of the most widely used and highly regarded labour standards, it has also been criticised. Some of these criticisms are more to do with the perspective of the specific critic: for example, some have criticised SA 8000 for being overly rigorous, whereas others have criticised it for being too lenient. For some, it is a strength that SA 8000 requires investments, while others see SA 8000 as 'expensive'.

While the authors do not necessarily agree with all of the criticisms below, the criticisms are important as they apply not just to SA 8000 but also to other voluntary initiatives aimed at addressing supply chain issues. That is, by seeing the criticisms as questions that need to be answered, the contribution of SA 8000 and other standards to addressing labour and human rights issues can be more clearly defined.

---

5   Researchers have written about the use of SA 8000 certification in action, in India, South Africa, the Philippines, Thailand, the US and Kenya. See, for example, Larson and Cox 1998; Cestre 2001; Leipziger 2001; Kaufman 2002; Mutunga *et al.* 2002. These reports/ studies provide examples of problems and solutions that have so far been experienced in the use of the SA 8000 standard as a tool for workplace improvement. Below, we summarise two of those studies.

It is easier for large companies to implement SA 8000 than smaller ones

All management standards have a bias in favour of companies that have established management systems and are certified to other management standards, such as International Organisation for Standardisation's Specification for Environmental Management Systems (ISO 14001). More research needs to be done on how small and medium-sized enterprises can overcome these barriers, perhaps with technical assistance from governments and NGOs.

SA 8000 does not address environmental issues[6]

A number of companies, such as WE Europe, are adopting SA 8000 in addition to environmental standards. However, the consensus at the time of developing SA 8000 was that environmental standards were well established and understood, whereas labour standards were not. That is, SA 8000 was deliberately designed to focus on one particular aspect of the corporate responsibility debate.

SA 8000 does not require multinational companies buying from certified suppliers to cover the costs of the audit and improvements

As with other voluntary standards (e.g. ISO 14001, ISO 9001), the facility being audited bears the costs of the audit under SA 8000. However, a significant number of multinational companies, including Toys 'R' Us and Otto Versand, provide assistance such as training and advice to suppliers. In many cases, SA 8000-certified companies are given priority over non-certified companies. That is, while there are costs associated with obtaining SA 8000 certification, there are also frequently direct financial benefits with such certification.

15.3 Code landscape

Where does SA 8000 fit in the spectrum of code and standards initiatives? There are thousands of codes of conduct: company, regional, industry-based, national, international. In the specific context of workers' rights, there are various initiatives that address different aspects of the problem, from the supply and the demand side. The multiplicity of codes raises the question of duplication or even of inconsistent requirements. There are ongoing efforts to align and, where feasible, integrate these various initiatives. The most important workers' rights initiatives (and their relationship with SA 8000) are listed below:

- The Ethical Trading Initiative (ETI)[7] is a multi-stakeholder learning initiative, convened by the UK's Department for International Development (DFID), which seeks to address public concerns about workplaces in developing countries. ETI's Base Code is congruent with SA 8000 and that of

6 Smith 2002: 36
7 www.ethicaltrade.org (last accessed 25 March 2003)

the Clean Clothes Campaign; it has substantially the same requirements and is also based on ILO and international human rights conventions.

- The Clean Clothes Campaign's[8] independent national chapters throughout Western Europe co-operate with other NGOs in the North and South and with trade unions to 'investigate ways in which a good code of conduct could be implemented, monitored and verified'. The Code, published in 1997, is congruent with SA 8000 and the ETI Base Code.

- The fair trade movement seeks to increase the living standard of workers by removing some of the risk inherent in commodities such as cacao, coffee, fruit and, most recently, clothing. FairWear is a fair trade initiative in clothing manufacture. The fair trade movement and SA 8000 are learning from each other through the ISEAL (see below) initiative.

- Worldwide Responsible Apparel Production (WRAP)[9] is the certification initiative of an industry association (the American Apparel Manufacturers' Association). It has not received endorsement from trade unions or NGOs. The WRAP code is less stringent than those of the multi-stakeholder initiatives and includes provisions of special concern to apparel importers, dealing with import quota compliance and drug smuggling prevention.

- The Fair Labor Association (FLA)[10] was convened to address public concerns about conditions of work at factories that manufacture sport shoes and apparel. The FLA plans to manage monitoring by organisations it has accredited and plans to report on these suppliers. Current participants include companies, a large number of universities with licensing agreements, and NGOs. The FLA has no trade union representation. It is brand-based rather than facility-based, and the code does not require payment of a wage adequate to meet basic needs.

- Framework agreements are increasingly being signed between companies and employers' organisations with trade unions, stating their commitment to promoting better working conditions. These framework agreements commit the partners to respect workers' rights and to agree to consultations and processes to enhance communication between the trade union and management. Based on ILO conventions, framework agreements require technical expertise to promote implementation. The management systems of SA 8000 can constitute a useful mechanism for implementing framework agreements. Likewise, the provisions for conflict resolution found in framework agreements could be useful for those working with SA 8000.

8 www.cleanclothes.org (last accessed 25 March 2003)
9 www.wrapapparel.org (last accessed 25 March 2003)
10 www.fairlabor.org (last accessed 25 March 2003)

The International Social and Environmental Accreditation and Labelling Alliance (ISEAL)[11] is seeking to increase co-ordination among accreditation and labelling organisations in the social and environmental fields by developing common systems and protocols. The members of ISEAL are: Fair Trade Labelling Organisations (FLO), Forest Stewardship Council (FSC), International Federation of Organic Agriculture Movements (IFOAM), International Organic Accreditation Service (IOAS), Marine Aquarium Council (MAC), Marine Stewardship Council (MSC), Social Accountability International (SAI) and Sustainable Agriculture Network (SAN). There are also two associate members: Global Ecolabelling Network (GEN) and Chemonics. ISEAL is researching the overlap of standards and developing a framework for increasing compatibility. Rather than create a single standard, the goal is to learn and share experiences and develop common procedures and protocols that will make each of the participating initiatives stronger.

15.4 Conclusion

SA 8000 is making a significant contribution to improving working conditions and developing management systems to allow companies to monitor working conditions. However, voluntary workers' rights standards, such as SA 8000, are still evolving, and many lessons remain to be learned. Initiatives such as ISEAL, with a range of stakeholders with experience in the development and implementation of workplace codes, should help in capturing the strengths of the different initiatives, ensuring their ongoing effectiveness and relevance, and should provide a roadmap for further improvements in labour conditions around the world.

11 www.isealalliance.org (last accessed 25 March 2003)

Corporate responsibility and social capital
The nexus dilemma in Mexican maquiladoras*

Luis Reygadas
Universidad Autónoma Metropolitana Iztapalapa, Mexico

This chapter discusses the question of corporate responsibilities in the third world's new industries, through an analysis of the different kinds of nexus between maquiladora companies and other actors in the Mexico–United States border, on issues related to human, economic and social rights. The main focus of the chapter is on the community and social policies developed, in the last 35 years, by maquiladora plants. The specific issues covered include: the construction of social capital (i.e. networks, trust, communication mechanisms); the scope of corporate social responsibility initiatives; relationships with local and federal governments, NGOs, unions and other agents; and the institutionalisation, accountability and governance of corporate responsibility. This chapter also presents some recommendations for social policies that could be adopted by companies, governments and NGOs.

An important thesis of this chapter is that corporate responsibility and human rights are not, fundamentally, questions of intentions. On the contrary, they should be seen as part of a broader process that involves: constructing social capital;[1] generating laws that encourage economic activity to adjust to the Universal

---

* The assistance of Alejandra Vasallo who translated this chapter from Spanish is gratefully acknowledged.

1 The notion of social capital has been widely discussed by authors such as Pierre Bourdieu (1983), James Coleman (1990) and Robert Putnam (1993). Anthony Giddens states that: 'social capital refers to the trust networks that individuals may access for social support, the same as people can resort to finance capital for investment' (Giddens 2001: 87). Nan Lin gives the following definition: 'social capital may be defined operationally as the *resources embedded in social networks that are accessed and used by actors to carry out actions*' (Lin 2002: 24-25).

Declaration of Human Rights; creating institutions to deal with the urban and environmental problems related to the new economy; and establishing accountability mechanisms for the companies that operate in a global context. The ethical debate on corporate responsibility must, therefore, take account of the social processes that support or hinder companies' commitment to social development.

16.1 Overview of the maquiladoras

Maquiladoras are export-oriented and work-intensive factories which take advantage of low wages in developing countries. In Mexico, the first maquiladoras were established in the mid-1960s along the US border. By the end of 2002 there were 3,244 maquiladora plants in Mexico, with 1,098,331 employees. Women occupy 55% of maquiladoras' blue-collar jobs. Most maquiladoras in Mexico belong to American companies, but Japanese, Korean, European and Mexican companies are also present. The main industrial sectors in the maquiladoras are garments/clothing, electronics and automotive.[2] In Mexico, and in other countries, maquiladoras have been criticised because of violations of human rights and their low commitment to local development.

The maquiladora export industry in Latin America is an important link in the world production chains of the electronic, automotive, garment and other industrial sectors, and, as such, cannot escape the challenge of corporate responsibility. There have been several campaigns that have put maquiladoras at the centre of public opinion. Many of these have focused on the garment industry in Central America. A famous example was the series of protests in 1991 against the maltreatment of Guatemalan workers by Korean maquiladoras: the workers were subject to beatings, confinements and forced overtime. This resulted in a national controversy, in which the National Congress, the Ministry of Labour, the Attorney General for Human Rights, and the Korean Embassy all intervened. Soon afterwards, the debate transcended the Guatemalan borders and was discussed in the US Congress and by NGOs in Canada, the USA and Mexico.[3] In other cases, corporations have accepted the presence of independent auditors. For example, a maquiladora in El Salvador has allowed civil-society organisations to carry out independent certifications of working conditions, which have resulted in some improvements for workers.

On 15 December 1995, the US garment store, Gap, agreed to have its corporate code of conduct monitored at the maquiladora 'Mandarín Internacional' in El Salvador, by an independent monitoring group, formed by the Central American University Institute of Human Rights, the Office of Legal Tutorship of the Archbishop of El Salvador, and the Labour Studies Centre (*El Boletín de la Red de Solidaridad en la Maquila* 1998: 1). Another example of companies accepting demands for responsible corporate behaviour followed the approval, on 1 February 1998, by the

2 See further www.inegi.gob.mx (last accessed 24 February 2003).
3 For more information on the Guatemalan conflicts, see CITGUA 1991: 33-34, 63-64; AVANCSO 1994: 113-15; Pinto and Carías 1994: 48-49; Reygadas 2002: 164-69.

Nicaraguan Labour Minister of a resolution for the duty-free zones, based on the Ethics Code developed by the Central American Network of Women in Solidarity with Maquiladora Workers. On the following day, the owners of the 23 maquiladoras of the industrial duty-free zone 'Las Mercedes' signed an agreement adhering to the terms of the resolution. The Ethics Code fosters women workers' rights on issues related to discrimination, salaries, social security, physical, psychological and sexual abuse, health, overtime and pregnancy (*El Boletín de la Red de Solidaridad en la Maquila* 1998: 4). More recently, in August 2001, the AFL–CIO, the American trade union of the garment industry (UNITE), religious leaders, and union and NGO representatives from Central America, the Caribbean, Mexico and Asia launched an international campaign to advocate sweatshop workers' rights. Under the slogan 'Globalisation of Justice for Garment Workers', the campaign will put pressure on big department stores such as Eddie Bauer, Banana Republic, Gap and Ann Taylor through rallies and advertisements against clothes that are manufactured in violation of labour regulations (Cason and Brooks 2001).[4]

In Mexico, there are also groups and support centres for maquiladora workers. There have been campaigns in favour of wage increases and against the use of toxic substances and compulsory pregnancy tests in the maquiladora industry.[5] However, the broader question of corporate responsibility in the maquiladora industry has been little discussed. In general, maquiladoras are assessed in terms of employment, salary, work organisation systems and the existence or absence of trade unions. Although these aspects are part of corporate responsibility, they do not include the relationship between the maquiladora industry and either their social context or human rights. Issues such as the bonds that are established between maquiladoras and the social context of the regions in which they settle and the status of maquiladoras regarding human rights have not been the object of systematic analysis among scholars of the maquiladora industry in Mexico.[6]

---

4   Many of these campaigns could be considered as part of what Antonio Negri and Michael Hardt call the rebellion of 'the crowd against the empire' (Hardt and Negri 2002: 360-65).

5   The organisations that have actively advocated the rights of maquiladora workers in Mexico include: the Orientation Centre for Female Workers (Centro de Orientación de la Mujer Obrera, COMO) in Ciudad Juárez; the Female Workers Border Committee (Comité Fronterizo de Obreras) in many cities, especially in Tamaulipas; the CITAC, in Tijuana; the Attention Centre for the Female Worker (Centro de Atención a la Mujer Trabajadora, CAMT) in Chihuahua; SEDEPAC (in many cities, especially Coahuila and Tamaulipas); and the Binational Pro-Justice Coalition in Maquiladoras (Coalición Binacional Pro Justicia en las Maquiladoras).

6   An important exception is Alfredo Hualde's study on the relationship between maquiladoras and the educational system on the northern Mexican border (Hualde 1999). Carlos Alba and Hélène Rivière d'Arc have also reflected on the interaction between the maquiladora industry and local actors in the State of Chihuahua (Alba and Rivière d'Arc 2000).

16.2 Does industrial upgrading promote social upgrading?

The maquiladora industry in Mexico has a history that goes back more than three decades. The concept of industrial upgrading has become relevant as a tool to understand the companies' economic and productive trajectories, spanning from the first assembly plants established in the second half of the 1960s to the corporate networks and the complex productive systems that characterise maquiladora companies at the beginning of the 21st century.[7] Rather than discussing industrial upgrading, my purpose here is to suggest a typology of social upgrading, which aims at assessing corporate responsibility and the contribution of companies to social development in host regions.

The typology proposed describes the social contribution of companies in terms of the following four models: (a) enclave; (b) sporadic social interventions; (c) corporate philanthropy; and (d) institutionalised social commitment. These models can be described using the following indicators: (a) the degree of maquiladoras' corporate responsibility towards local development and human rights; (b) the social welfare spheres under the influence of the maquiladora industry; (c) the kinds of interlocutor that intervene in the process; (d) the characteristics of the social capital involved; and (e) the accountability mechanisms. These indicators are considered in an increasing scale, meaning that the first model corresponds to situations in which the companies have almost no responsibility, they influence very few spheres of social life, they have a small number of interlocutors, the social capital mobilised is low, and there are no monitoring mechanisms nor any kind of accountability for its actions on the social environment (or the lack of it). In contrast, the last type (the institutionalised social commitment model) corresponds to situations in which the companies show high social commitment, a vast action range, several interlocutors, relevant social capital and institutionalised accountability. Figure 16.1 shows the relationship between the four models.

Although each model represents a higher degree of social interaction, this does not mean that every company progresses through each of the four types in a linear manner. On the contrary, there are companies that always remain in enclave conditions, while others present features corresponding to the other models from the start.

In the case of Mexican maquiladoras, there are examples of the first three types, although there is no empirical evidence of existence of the fourth type (institutionalised social commitment). It is, rather, a model built on the basis of other industries' experience. As discussed later in this chapter, this last scenario requires institutional maturing, a reconstruction of social capital and relevant governmental interventions, which means that its consolidation implies a qualitative transformation *vis-à-vis* the other three models. Therefore, between the third and fourth scenarios there is a break point. There is also a break point between the first two situations because the beginning of the upgrading process involves moving

---

7 For a discussion on the industrial upgrading process in Mexican maquiladoras, see Wilson 1992; Gereffi and Korzeniewicz 1994; Carrillo and Hualde 1996; Gereffi 1999.

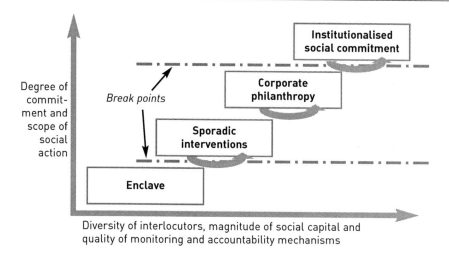

Figure 16.1 **Four models of corporate responsibility in the maquiladoras**

out of the enclave model. The characteristics of the four models of social interaction are summarised in Table 16.1.

16.2.1 The enclave model

The notion of enclave has been used in Latin America to explain the lack of integration of a foreign company into the domestic economy or national society (Zapata 1977; Sariego 1986). Many of the enclaves studied are companies located far away from important cities, and generally involve foreign companies building human settlements, or at least the urban equipment, infrastructure and means of communication necessary for the exploitation and export of some natural resource (e.g. minerals, oil, agricultural products). Maquiladoras follow a different principle: they settle in already established communities, in many cases industrial parks with all the necessary services. The main local resource that they use is the labour force. From the economic point of view, they have been classified as enclaves because many maquiladoras import most of their equipment and raw materials and later export their products without creating productive chains with other companies of the countries in which they settle. Maquiladoras could also be called enclaves in a social sense because of the weakness of their connection with other actors, and their consequent limited contribution to regional development. While the old mining, oil, port, or agricultural enclaves created infrastructure and social capital to add value to their investment, the new maquiladora enclaves obtain utilities without investing in equipment or creating new social capital. We could also speak of enclaves in terms of human and labour rights because maquiladoras, generally, do not apply the same standards regarding respect for rights as in

Corporate responsibility model	Degree of commitment to local development and fields of influence	Types of interlocutor	Characteristics of social capital	Monitoring and accountability
Enclave	● Zero responsibility for local development ● Fields of influence are exclusively jobs and wages.	● Virtually absent ● Spurious interlocutors (ghost unions, industrial developers, real estate owners) ● Government institutions intervene only in case of crisis and/or conflict.	● No social capital is created around the companies. ● Mutual suspicion between maquiladoras and interlocutors	● Virtually zero
Sporadic social interventions	● Minimum commitment, only regarding those aspects that may benefit the company ● There is training, education, transport, and benefits for employees.	● Government agencies, official unions, educational institutions, and other companies	● First networks inside and outside the plant ● Limited trust for specific projects	● Very low, highly discretionary decisions
Philanthropy	● Medium responsibility, some corporate contributions to social benefit ● The company provides some services such as day-care centres, family programmes, singles housing, environment, support to philanthropic institutions and some human rights promotion.	● Private foundations and welfare institutions, religious groups, environmental organisations, workers and families. ● NGOs and human rights groups sporadically interact with the company.	● Networks managed by companies ● Trust grows between workers, companies and other institutions, but does not include sectors that are critical of maquiladoras.	● Sporadic monitoring ● Accountability only vis-à-vis governmental authorities ● Ad hoc or non-independent monitoring
Institutionalised social commitment	● High commitment level, agreements with local institutions ● Provide long-term careers, pay taxes, sponsor foundations, create schools, social joint ventures, and promote a wide spectrum of human rights	● NGOs and human rights groups (wide spectrum) ● Representative unions ● Binational coalitions ● Monitoring bodies ● Academics	● Consolidated and institutionalised networks ● Pluralistic management networks ● Mutual trust and tolerance, including sectors that are critical of maquiladoras	● Permanent monitoring based on institutionalised agreements ● Permanent accountability vis-à-vis diverse agencies, including autonomous authorities

Table 16.1 Social upgrading in the maquiladora industry

the rest of the country or in the country of origin. An example of this is mandatory pre-employment pregnancy tests that are common in many maquiladoras.

The enclave model is typical of the initial stages of the maquiladora industry in any country. In many cases, they settle in areas with special legal regulations. Host countries usually grant legal or de facto benefits to attract companies, and they even compete to guarantee better conditions for maquiladoras. Unfortunately, the lax application of the law on human and labour rights has been one of the advantages that under-developed regions offer to attract foreign investment. Therefore, in the enclave model corporate social responsibility is virtually non-existent and the contribution of these companies to development is limited to the generation of jobs and wage payment.

In the case of Mexico, the first maquiladoras were created in the frontier cities between Mexico and the United States. This encouraged the formation of enclaves because, in many cases, the US managers continued to live on the US side of the border, while the plants were on Mexican soil. If we consider that the United States provided machinery and raw materials, we can understand how in many cases maquiladora plants were an extension of the US economy and society: they were effectively American islands floating in a Mexican sea, but they did not incorporate American standards regarding working conditions and respect for human rights.

The enclave model implies a parasitic relationship of the company with its environment, since there is no accountability framework regarding the negative consequences its operations may have on the environment, urban infrastructure, workers' health or the social development of the host region. In these contexts, monitoring of the companies is very rare, because government authorities only intervene in the case of flagrant and systematic violations of the law.

In the enclave system, maquiladoras have very few interlocutors. In general, these are limited to governmental authorities related to commercial, customs and infrastructure issues. It is rare to have interlocutors on social development issues. In fact, one of the most common features of this model is the presence of spurious interlocutors such as (corrupt) ghost unions, real estate owners or irresponsible industrial developers, who obtain profits for helping the companies to reduce their social and labour responsibilities. There tends to be no dialogue with academic sectors or with civil-society representatives, frequently resulting in a polarisation of views between the supporters and the critics of the maquiladora industry.

16.2.2 The sporadic social intervention model

It is difficult to maintain an enclave model in the maquiladora industry for a number of reasons. First of all, companies require some services that they cannot obtain adequately if they do not establish communication mechanisms with different regional and/or national authorities. Second, many companies seek to stay for a longer period in the host region, in particular when they have made large investments in equipment and machinery. Third, local actors do tend to contact maquiladoras to demand their support for certain social intervention programmes. Fourth, the lack of dialogue can result in conflicts that can affect the image and operation of maquiladoras. All of these factors contribute to the fact that many maquiladoras tend to rule out isolation and start to intervene in other spheres of local society.

The sporadic intervention model is characterised by corporate involvement in aspects of social development that directly concern the company. These interventions tend to be limited in time and fields of influence. For instance, companies may establish relationships with universities, technological institutes and technical schools to promote the training of professionals and technicians required by maquiladoras. In general, these are short-term actions, although in certain cities, especially in Ciudad Juárez and Tijuana, they have led to the creation of committees between the educational sector and the maquiladora industry to influence the curriculum and seek mechanisms to facilitate corporate donations to schools (Hualde 1999). Other areas where there may be sporadic interventions of the companies include transport and urban services linked to the operation of maquiladoras. For example, some regional associations of maquiladoras have formed an ad hoc committee to carry out different tasks with several government agencies in charge of these areas.

In spite of being sporadic, maquiladoras' social interventions widen the circle of interlocutors to include, potentially, different agencies from the local, state and national governments, educational institutions, other companies and official trade unions. This model of social interaction represents an upgrading from the enclave model, but the isolation from the surrounding environment persists. A key reason for this isolation is the suspicion that remains between maquiladoras and other agents; there is only a limited trust for very specific, short-term projects, but not enough to implement long-standing projects with lower transaction costs.[8]

The emergence of social networks inside and outside maquiladora plants is an important upgrading platform towards more ambitious social projects. However, there are still no consolidated networks. Moreover, accountability continues to be low, which allows the companies to limit their social responsibility to the aspects that may bring them an immediate and direct benefit. It is also important to emphasise that neither the issue of human rights nor their advocacy organisations are included in this model.

16.2.3 The corporate philanthropy model

Very few maquiladora companies in Mexico distinguish themselves by seeking a relationship that implies a greater collaboration with different local actors or by having a responsible attitude towards the community. Those companies that do have these relationships and responsible attitudes implement what can be described as a corporate philanthropy model. Companies that follow this model do not restrict themselves to social actions that generate direct profits; they also seek to contribute to initiatives that may bring social benefits for the community (e.g. programmes for the elderly and for children, road works, cultural activities,

---

8 On trust as a central element of the networks, see Williamson 1985; Powell and Smith-Doerr 1994. To avoid the dualism of opportunism/trust and to explore the intermediate modalities, Coutrot has introduced the notion of **forced co-operation** (Coutrot 2000).

donations to philanthropic associations, strengthening of the educational system, environmental programmes). Occasionally, human rights are included, albeit in a limited way. Frequently, companies carry out actions directed towards the workers' families: in particular, scholarship programmes, support for day-care, sport and recreational centres, health programmes and adult education (see further Reygadas 2002). Some companies join with public and social agencies to develop long-term projects: for example, to extend the number of participatory day-care centres supported by the Mexican Social Security Institute.

Corporate philanthropy strategies allow maquiladoras to extend their range of interlocutors. For instance, other actors may intervene, such as private welfare institutions and foundations, religious sectors, environmental groups and, sporadically, non-governmental organisations (some of whom may be linked to the promotion of human rights and women's rights). However, it is rare to find trade unions considered as interlocutors for the development of social programmes. This is due, in part, to the fact that there are no trade unions in many maquiladora plants, and the few that do exist have low levels of representation. It is also due to the suspicion that the majority of the companies show towards workers' labour organisations. In many cases, this hostility results in a violation of employees' right to associate freely. In general, maquiladoras do not accept as valid interlocutors those sectors that are critical of them.

The biggest limitation of the corporate philanthropy model lies in the unilateral character of corporate actions. This means that companies do not have legal responsibilities, nor are they subject to any kind of independent monitoring. Accountability takes place only *vis-à-vis* ad hoc authorities that are close to the companies. The result is that programmes are very fragile because their characteristics, scope and resources depend on the will of the corporate directors. It is common to find that these programmes are eliminated when companies have economic difficulties. Even more critical is the fact that very few companies develop these kinds of activity; the great majority do not want to get involved with the community's social problems.

16.2.4 The institutionalised social commitment model

Even 35 years after their creation, the interaction between the Mexican maquiladoras and the surrounding social environment is still very limited. Except for a small number of companies, the majority continue to be very isolated from the community and show a very low degree of responsibility towards sustainable social development and human rights in the regions where they have settled. A significant social upgrading would require shifting towards a very different model of relationship between maquiladoras and the community, characterised by companies that are strongly committed to social responsibility, regulated by legal provisions, and mediated by explicit agreements with local, regional and national institutions. In other words, it would require that maquiladoras' social actions were not reduced to those that only benefit them or they want to carry out but were extended according to social needs that are collectively diagnosed. A critical element of this would be to develop permanent programmes carried out by solid institutions that are qualified for that purpose.

An institutionalised social commitment model for maquiladoras presumes an important reorientation of government policies in the sense of demanding shared responsibility for the reconstruction of the social networks of the communities in which the companies operate. However, not everything consists of approving laws and taxes. Institutions that allow the gap between maquiladoras and society to be closed must be created as well. These institutions may require interlocutors other than government (e.g. NGOs, women's rights and human rights associations, truly representative trade unions, religious groups and academic sectors critical of the status quo). One example is the emergence of binational associations that have combined the efforts of Mexican and US pressure groups to improve the working and living conditions of maquiladora workers.

Institutionalised social commitment cannot be left to the will of a few corporate executive officers. It must become a reality through agreements that are subject to accountability, before both government authorities and society as a whole. In this context, the experience of having monitoring and supervising authorities that encourage maquiladoras to comply with minimum labour, social and human rights standards is quite interesting. A corporate responsibility model requires a substantial advancement in the construction of social capital, in particular the creation of institutionalised networks that include different agencies, even those that are critical of maquiladoras. One of the ways to achieve this is to independently monitor corporate performance on environmental, labour and human rights issues. There are many other mechanisms that may be considered to engage other actors with the companies in social and human rights programmes (e.g. as the planners or implementers of such programmes). In such cases, the management of the networks should not lie exclusively with the companies, but would require a shared and plural management.

16.3 Conclusions

The institutionalised social commitment model is clearly an ideal (or even idealised) solution for the countries where the maquiladoras operate. The question is whether the model is also more favourable for the companies. At first glance, the answer is no, because the model implies, at least in the short term, greater costs and demands attention to issues traditionally not included in the business agenda. Nevertheless, in the long run it has a great advantage over the other three models: it allows the construction of social networks and a trust environment that could be decisive for innovation, quality improvement and economic performance. The best example in favour of this model is to look at the experience of the developed countries. Their companies are successful because they are embedded in a thick institutional network that integrates them with universities, research centres, suppliers, clients, public agencies and all kind of civil-society organisations. The creation and consolidation of these links require time, money and hard work, but the rewards are numerous: a social environment suitable for business, the abundance of qualified human resources, scientific and technological innovation flows, healthy markets and political stability.

Until today, some transnational corporations (TNCs) have assumed corporate responsibility for human rights and social development in their home countries, but they have not extended this commitment towards the developing countries. In fact, maquiladoras in Mexico and other third-world countries were created as a corporate strategy to avoid environment, labour and social responsibilities common in Europe, the United States or Japan. This avoidance provides TNCs with gigantic profits, but is also a source of criticism and conflicts, and could be self-defeating for the corporations' future.

Mexican maquiladoras have gone through the social upgrading break points only when they have been confronted with conflicts or crisis, when the poor relationship or lack of integration with local society provoked union resistance or public criticisms. These companies have a preventative approach: they promote social welfare or respect human rights only in order to forestall conflict. They do not have a proactive approach (i.e. to foster human and social rights as a strategy for long-term improvement). Such activities are seen as a cost and not as an investment in social capital.

In order to cross the boundary towards an institutionalised social commitment model, companies, government and civil-society organisations could consider the following strategies:

1. Promote human rights in corporations. In Latin America, the idea that businesses have no relationship with human rights still persists. Strategic alliances between corporations, ombudsmen and NGOs could provide the platform to demonstrate the financial and reputational advantages associated with corporate commitment to human rights.

2. Diversify the companies' interlocutors. Companies have to surround themselves with a 'constellation' of diverse partners that help them to build the social capital required to meet their challenges on social rights, environmental issues, technological innovation, human rights and welfare programmes. Companies should open their doors and initiate dialogue with a wide range of interlocutors (NGOs, community leaders, academics, etc.).

3. Change the way in which trade unions are treated. Maquiladoras are conspicuous because of their hostile treatment of unions. Trade unions are seen as enemies or, at best, as organisations that have to be tolerated. However, it is also relevant to note that many unions have avoided making commitments to improved productivity (e.g. in return for improved work conditions), thereby reinforcing mutual distrust. Both sides have to change strategies if they want to break this vicious circle.

4. Stop gender discrimination. Compulsory pre-employment pregnancy tests and sexual harassment are common human rights violations in maquiladoras. It is urgent to suppress those tests and to favour recruitment and promotion mechanisms that do not discriminate against women.

5. Foster human rights and working standards certification. The companies that voluntarily undergo verification of their human rights performance and achieve certain standards of working conditions could gain competitive advantages (e.g. better corporate image, better employee relationships). The independence of certification agencies is, however, critical to ensure credibility. It is also critical that interlocutors such as NGOs and academics recognise and promote those companies that improve their labour and human rights performance. That is, there should be external recognition and credit for these companies.

In Mexican and Latin American maquiladoras, human rights have tended to be neglected. Many foreign companies have poor links with local society and there is a lot of work required to ensure that companies do behave in a responsible manner. This chapter has presented, first, a model that describes the reasons why companies are not fully integrated with local communities and, second, practical recommendations for actions that can maximise the social contribution of the maquiladoras.

Part 4
Community and government

17

From fuelling conflict to oiling the peace
Harnessing the peace-building potential of extractive-sector companies operating in conflict zones

Jessica Banfield

International Alert, UK

The emergence of transnational corporations (TNCs) as major actors in the global political economy has been accompanied by notable flashpoint cases where corporations have been caught up in violent conflict in one way or another, for instance in Angola, Burma, Colombia, Indonesia and Nigeria. The past few years have seen an increasing international focus on the financial dimensions of conflict, including both licit and illicit resource extraction, as well as illicit arms and drugs trafficking, organised crime, money laundering and diversion of humanitarian aid (Berdal and Malone 2000; Collier and Hoeffler 2001; Le Billon *et al.* 2002). The search for mechanisms to limit direct conflict-feeding private-sector activities is under way, including measures to influence extractive TNCs' operations in conflict risk zones. While such mechanisms, and the curtailment of negative corporate impacts on conflict, are of crucial significance to any broader effort to promote a more just globalised market, companies have a further role to play in actively contributing to peace-building. This positive potential has received less international attention, though it is now beginning to be addressed by some intergovernmental organisations (IGOs), governments, companies and NGOs (Nelson 2000; Haufler 2001; Bennett 2002).[1] This chapter will discuss the role that

---

1 The 'bottom-line' business case for engaging in conflict prevention was first mapped out in Nelson 2000. The conflict-transformation NGO International Alert has a programme on 'Business and Conflict' that works in-country and at the research and policy levels to generate understanding and develop tools that will enable TNCs specifically in the oil,

extractive-sector TNCs operating in conflict-prone zones can play in both perpetuating and preventing conflict, and will offer an overview of current policy and corporate responses and options.

17.1 Understanding corporate–conflict impacts

The nature of violent conflict has shifted dramatically in the post-Cold War era. Whereas war used to occur as an expression of inter-state foreign policy, it now more commonly takes place within states.[2] High levels of civilian casualties, human rights abuses and refugee flows mean that civil wars generate humanitarian crises, posing serious challenges to the international system. Civil conflict is caused by factors that often appear intractable in their complexity (Rupesinghe 1998: 58). Conflict resolution or transformation is the process of addressing these causes, and working with those concerned to redefine relationships and bring about a change in the conflict context. To this end, relationship-building across sectoral and social divides is key. Conflict transformation practitioners advocate the use of 'multi-track diplomacy': actors at different levels of society engaging in peace-building work (Lederach 1995). However, the role of the private sector as one such actor has only recently begun to receive attention within the field (Nelson 2000: 55; Champain 2002).

Conflict transformation theory views conflict as a natural feature of human existence, an inevitable accompaniment to change. The kind of significant shift in the economic base of a country that a major foreign investment represents is 'change' and thus, in a general sense, can be expected to lead to conflict. Where conflict leads to violence, however, a profound breakdown in human relationships has occurred (Rupesinghe 1998: 28). Through increased conflict-sensitivity, companies can anticipate ways in which they might reinforce sources of violent conflict, such as social dividers or poor governance, and develop and implement mitigating strategies to counter these.

Unfamiliar risk and management challenges derived from weak legal frameworks and governance structures confront foreign investing companies in many developing-country contexts. These challenges have become increasingly taxing in an era of increased Western shareholder and media expectation of performance on 'corporate social responsibility' (CSR), and are compounded in conflict-prone

mining and gas sectors to fulfil their potential in both respects. When considering the links between business and conflict, it is important to emphasise that the private sector is both vast and heterogeneous. In order to give some focus, International Alert's work looks at TNCs in the extractive sector (chosen because of the frequency with which they operate in conflict countries) and at local businesses (legitimate small, medium and leading companies nationally based in conflict countries). This chapter presents some of the key findings of International Alert's work with TNCs. For more information, see www.international-alert.org.

2 Between 1989 and 2000 more than 90% of armed conflicts took place within rather than between states (Wallensteen and Sollenberg 2001).

zones, where the probability of significant and dramatic human rights abuses also becomes much higher.

Understanding of the interface between business and conflict is nevertheless limited. Conflicts arising between or within TNCs themselves, and how to resolve these, have received detailed analysis within the corporate sector, with theories often drawing on conflict transformation techniques.[3] Political conflict in host societies, however—and the role that business plays in this—has not benefited from such in-depth thinking.[4] In conventional extractive sector analyses, violent conflict is reduced to a risk factor which is then computed into financial risk ratings in relation to investment decisions. The primary issue at stake in this approach is the impact that conflict (existing or potential) might have on the company, through imposing increased transaction, security, reputation and other costs (Nelson 2000: 20; Bowden *et al.* 2001). The reverse dynamic—the impact of the company on conflict—has been under-researched and largely ignored in management decision-making. Some progress has been made in understanding corporate impact on the local physical and social environment: environmental and social impact assessments (ESIAs) are becoming increasingly sophisticated in approach and in some cases legally required. However, ESIA methodologies typically tend to be limited to an analysis of corporate impact at the local operational level, are inadequately formulated when it comes to involving community and other perspectives, and do not specifically seek to understand the spectrum of corporate impacts on conflict.

Corporate–conflict impacts can be both direct and indirect. Corporate activity at the micro level—in the immediate physical vicinity of a foreign investment (e.g. a mine, pipeline or factory)—will have direct impacts on existing or potential conflict there. These impacts are determined by corporate and host-government choices on factors such as the physical location of an investment, employment of local staff and security arrangements, and the intersection of these decisions with community perceptions and agendas. Conflict at the micro level may occur directly between the company and local communities; indigenous communities are increasingly challenging mining companies on a range of issues (Kapelus 2002). Alternatively, or in addition, the company may emerge as an unwilling actor in already existing conflict between groups.[5]

3   See, for instance, books published for the Pfeiffer imprint of John Wiley and Sons.
4   Different models have been proposed by organisations working on conflict transformation to help to define and categorise civil conflict, however. The Swedish International Peace Research Institute, for instance, has introduced battlefield-related deaths as an indicator with which to measure the intensity of conflict. The Dutch human rights research institute PIOOM has developed this idea to try to encompass all victims of conflict, including those not directly engaged in fighting. Nobel prize-winner Johan Galtung distinguishes between direct, structural and cultural violence in order to capture the effects of endemic violence that can exist in unequal societal structures. Christian Scherrer has developed a useful typology of civil conflict, including seven categories ranging from anti-regime/ideological conflicts to genocide, and the Carnegie Commission has developed a 'three stages of conflict' model (see, further, Schmid 2000).
5   Both Shell in the Niger Delta and BP in Colombia have, in different ways, been caught up in one or both of these micro conflict dynamics.

At the national or macro level, an extractive TNC will have a range of indirect impacts on conflict. At root, these relate to the fact that its investment often represents the major source of revenue in a context where institutions are weak and decision-making about use of such revenues constrained. This dynamic will affect issues such as human rights, corruption and wealth distribution, and can often lead to or fuel conflict.[6] Even in cases where conflict pre-dates the company's engagement, and is geographically far from its own site, a company becomes involved, through the very process of contributing to state coffers.

In addition to these negative impacts, by their possession of a vast array of skills, resources, expertise and capacity, TNCs can exert a range of potentially positive impacts on conflict dynamics, though they do not yet have the strategic commitment or practical tools in place to fulfil this potential. There is real creative potential invested within TNCs as key actors in conflict-prone countries to contribute to the resolution or transformation of conflict, however apparently remote it may be from their immediate operating sphere.

17.2 Policy and corporate responses

The range of possible strategies for managing corporate–conflict dynamics is depicted in Figure 17.1. 'Compliance' with an emerging legal framework and risk minimisation (or 'do no harm') both relate to minimising negative impacts, whereas 'peace-building' relates to the resolution or transformation of conflict.[7] Corporate and policy responses are emerging to the spectrum of corporate–conflict impacts, although to date these have tended to focus on negative directly or indirectly conflict-feeding dynamics (the bottom two strata). The positive potential of extractive TNCs to contribute to peace-building has, so far, received the least attention. Given the gravity of conflict-feeding impacts in terms of TNC complicity in possible loss of life and human rights abuses, this prioritisation is understandable. However, the balance of attention needs to be redressed in order also to unlock peace-building potential.

17.2.1 Measures to promote compliance

International norms and codifications of standards are emerging. Key among these are the US/UK Voluntary Principles on Security and Human Rights (see Chapter 19 by Bennett Freeman and Genoveva Hernández Uriz) and the UN Sub-Commission on Human Rights Norms and Responsibilities of TNCs and other Business Enterprises with regard to Human Rights, currently in draft form (see Chapter 3 by Peter Muchlinski and Chapter 2 by Geoffrey Chandler). Both of these

6 This is an extension of Terry Lynn Karl's thesis on the 'curse' of oil (Karl 1997).
7 The 'do no harm' concept is borrowed from recent research into minimising negative impacts of humanitarian aid and other development assistance, and lends itself well to understanding corporate–conflict dynamics (Andersen 1999).

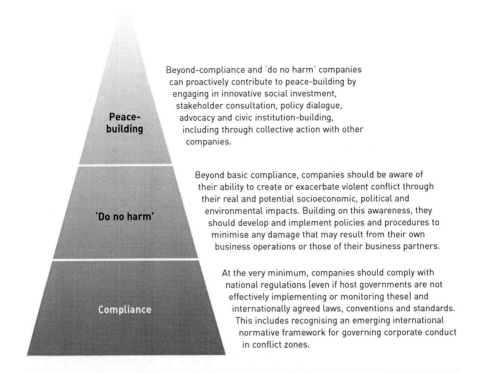

Figure 17.1 **Strategies for managing corporate–conflict dynamics**

Source: adapted from Nelson 2000

initiatives are geared towards promoting corporate compliance with international humanitarian law. Two years on from agreeing the Voluntary Principles, while companies inside the process (and some outside it) have publicly embraced them and are committed to integrating them into their policy statements and corporate strategies, questions remain over the extent to which they have been applied. Equally, there is a lack of clarity on the role of participating NGOs and governments in supporting and contributing to the process of implementation and subsequent evaluation. With regard to implementation of the Draft Norms, it is envisaged that TNCs will adopt internal rules for compliance, and be subject to periodic external monitoring, including by NGOs. The Norms were due to be discussed again at the Working Group Sub-Commission meeting in July 2003.

Over the last decade, the use of UN sanctions has increased dramatically. Examples of UN Security Council resolutions relevant to businesses operating in zones of conflict and geared to promoting corporate compliance with the international system include: the import of fuel to and export of diamonds from UNITA rebels in Angola; the import of fuel to and export of timber and gems from the Khmer Rouge in Cambodia; the import of Sierra Leone Revolutionary United Front (RUF) diamonds to and export of rough diamonds from Liberia. A lack of adequate national legislation and enforcement by some governments has, however, undermined these efforts. The design of sanctions has also come under increasing scrutiny because of the disproportionate impact they can have on the populations of targeted countries. In response to this, the search is under way for more refined, targeted or 'smart' sanctions; an international community of experts is working on this under the Stockholm Process.[8] The creation of UN expert panels tasked with investigating violations of UN sanctions has also been a welcome step. Their work has been hampered when experts have not had full access to information, and the panels' more radical recommendations have not been implemented. However, through a policy of 'naming and shaming', they have at least raised awareness about who is evading sanctions (Lilly and Le Billon 2002).

17.2.2 Measures to promote 'do no harm'

In July 2000, the biennial World Diamond Council in Antwerp agreed to take concerted action to stamp out the trade in conflict diamonds. In September of the same year the diamond industry's efforts received government backing when a ministerial meeting held in Kimberley, South Africa, resulted in the Kimberley Process. The initiative brings together 38 governments, representatives from the diamond industry and NGOs. In December 2001 it reached agreement to set up a global certification scheme on conflict diamonds by 2002. This control system aims to stop 'blood diamonds' from entering the legitimate diamond market. In February 2002 the UN Security Council adopted a resolution supporting the scheme.[9] The European Union (EU) is committed to the process, although its initial requirement that member states' legislation should follow from February 2003 was postponed following delays from important diamond-producing companies in putting the system in place. Again, implementation is the test. While the Kimberley Process may provide a useful model for other conflict commodities (such as timber and coltan[10]—although in many ways certifying other commodities raises many additional specific problems), NGOs remain disappointed with the pace of change.

To address growing concern about the distorting impacts of extractive-sector investments on some developing-country governance structures meanwhile, and in response to pressure mounted by the 'Publish What You Pay' campaign, UK Prime Minister Tony Blair launched the Extractive Industry Transparency Initiative (EI-TI) at the 2002 World Summit on Sustainable Development in Johannesburg. This initiative aims to increase transparency over payments by companies to governments and government-linked entities, and in this sense can be seen as a measure to promote a 'do no harm' approach at the macro level. Italy, Norway, Indonesia, the Central African Republic, France and South Africa as well as the UK

8 www.smartsanctions.se/reports/The%20Stockholm%20Process.htm
9 UNGA Resolution 56/263, www.globalpolicy.org/security/issues/diamond/2002/0206gares. htm
10 Coltan is columbite-tantalite ore from the Democratic Republic of Congo.

are all involved at this stage, as are a range of NGOs, the World Bank and UNDP. The initiative was discussed further at a June 2003 meeting in London.

The UN Global Compact, launched by UN Secretary-General Kofi Annan in 1999 in order to promote good corporate citizenship globally, calls on business leaders, trade unions and NGOs to join forces behind a set of nine core values (or principles) in the areas of human rights, labour standards and the environment. In order to sign the Global Compact, companies must express support for the nine principles in their mission statements and annual reports, and a concrete example of progress or lessons learned in implementing them must be made annually. The Global Compact also facilitates thematic cross-sectoral dialogues on relevant issues and focused during 2001–2002 on the role of companies in conflict zones. High-level representatives from leading companies and NGOs, as well as from the development policy world, were brought together in a series of meetings, in order to identify key issues and challenges, as well as to develop practical recommendations for companies operating in conflict zones (subsequent dialogues have focused on sustainable development, HIV/AIDS, supply chains and labour practice). Most of the issues discussed at the conflict dialogue related to a 'do no harm' approach to operating in conflict zones (e.g. transparency, revenue sharing and conflict impact assessment). While a valuable network was created through this process, concrete policy initiatives did not emerge, though research is ongoing by some participants.

17.2.3 Measures to promote peace-building

The peace-building potential invested in extractive TNCs has received the least attention in international policy debates around the role of the private sector in conflict transformation. The UN Sub-Commission on Human Rights Norms and Responsibilities notes in its preamble TNCs' 'capacity to foster economic well-being, development, technological improvement and wealth' (see Amnesty International *et al.* 2002). One of the UN Global Compact Dialogue on Companies in Conflict Zones focus working groups has explored the contributions that companies can make through multi-stakeholder dialogue processes. Meanwhile, key donor governments have now expressed an interest in developing further policy understanding of the range of positive and negative impacts of business in conflict zones. During 2002 both the German and the Belgian Ministries for Foreign Affairs organised high-level conferences on this theme, and both Sweden and the UK organised smaller seminars. Canada, the UK, Norway and Sweden are among several governments currently funding research and other work into this area. The OECD Development Assistance Committee Network on Conflict Peace and Development Co-operation has identified business and conflict as one area of work for 2002–2004.

17.2.4 Conflict and the CSR debate

Corporate actors—particularly those extractives wishing to position themselves at the forefront of CSR—have taken a place at the table at many of these initiatives. This is testimony to two trends: first, a discovery within the CSR community at both corporate and policy levels that the private sector has a role to play in contributing to sustainable development (Fox *et al.* 2002; Holliday *et al.* 2002); second, an awareness that conflict as currently understood by business is not being effectively managed. With regard to the challenges of operating in conflict zones, corporate actors have begun to speak openly of a need for more sophisticated risk assessment and social impact processes, and to discuss conflict prevention more specifically (BP 2003).

CSR events are now including a focus on conflict; the largest CSR event of 2002, Business for Social Responsibility's annual conference in Miami, featured a panel session on this. By attempting to fulfil its potential in conflict transformation, business can at one and the same time contribute to the stabilisation and health of future markets, and lower the various costs associated with operating in conflict zones. Active private-sector engagement in conflict prevention thus complements the growing profit-motivated interest in CSR among leading companies. From the NGO perspective, the CSR agenda represents an opportunity to influence corporates in this regard. However, CSR strategy often amounts to what one expert has called 'a method for minimising costs' (Kapelus 2002). There are, therefore, significant tensions between the entry points and goals of CSR and those of conflict transformation. TNCs' CSR activities are frequently informed by priorities that are far removed from real sociopolitical needs or from the priorities of conflict transformation.

The recent interest of both corporate and policy actors in addressing the links between TNC activity and conflict is important. However, it must be emphasised that the search for practical solutions with regard to measures to promote compliance and 'do no harm' is still at a very early stage, and there are serious questions over the practical effects of most of these given the difficulties faced in implementation. While advocates of a position that companies should not only be guided by international humanitarian law but also be held legally accountable to it are growing in number, the means for enforcing these standards remain weak (International Council on Human Rights Policy 2002). Meanwhile, little thought has yet gone to mechanisms for promoting a more proactive peace-building role for TNCs. Countries with a significant extractive-sector presence continue to be plagued by suffering and under-development. This demands that international attention turns towards the important task of clarifying what are fast becoming international norms regarding operating in conflict zones, and searching for both penalties and sanctions when companies transgress these (International Council on Human Rights Policy 2002).[11] Deepened understanding of the constructive and creative potential located in the private sector to contribute to peace-building must also be developed.

---

11 The International Peace Academy, together with FAFO, the Norwegian Institute for Applied Social Sciences, and others, have also been leading the way in investigating what this framework might look like. See Lilly and Le Billon 2002 for an overview of existing legal and voluntary mechanisms geared towards addressing the negative links between business and conflict. More work on policy options for promoting a peace-building role for business is required (Banfield *et al.* 2003).

17.3 Principles for corporate engagement in conflict zones

TNCs can contribute to conflict prevention and peace-building by adopting a conflict sensitive compliance, 'do no harm' and peace-building approach in their three key areas of activity: core business, social investment and policy dialogue (Nelson 2000: 64).[12] Core business relates to the impacts that business can have through its core business operations (in the workplace, the marketplace and along supply chains). Social investment relates to social investment, community development and philanthropy programmes. Policy dialogue is a term used to describe business engagement in dialogue with governments and other stakeholders, advocacy and institution building, and can relate to the difficult structural issues that often underpin conflict. It also relates to companies supporting initiatives and developments such as those discussed above at the global and regional levels.

Five sets of management policies and processes that companies need to establish in order to minimise negative impacts and maximise positive ones, and to guide their interventions in the above areas have been identified (Nelson 2000: 7):

1. Strategic commitment: CEO and board-level leadership on CSR issues, supported by internal management systems, compliance, incentive and training structures to embed policies into the company's daily activities

2. Risk and impact analysis: assessment of the conflict-related risks and impacts of the company's core business and social investment activities on a systematic and comprehensive basis. As discussed, corporate impacts on conflict have not been properly understood to date. In order to develop more effective analysis procedures, corporate–conflict impacts need to be made central to analysis. Stakeholder engagement, as a key component of effective conflict analysis, needs to be significantly improved. Engagement in this way will facilitate the construction of balanced and accurate micro- and macro-level conflict analyses, which should alert an investing company to the ways in which its operations might make situations worse at all levels, and how to avoid these.[13]

12 Much strategic thinking on social issues is done at the HQ level of leading companies, and in fact these categorisations, though useful, can tend to reinforce a conventional division between levels of activities. It is therefore important that interventions in all three areas be conducted strategically and in a co-ordinated fashion. While there is recognition that issues and activities that were previously seen as a 'bolt-on' to business strategies are no longer optional, mainstreaming and putting cutting-edge ideas into practice at all levels of TNC activities is still very much a work in progress and social investment all too often reverts to traditional philanthropy.

13 The question of whether to enter or continue operating in a region where TNC operations are aggravating conflict is a difficult one. Many of the companies leading in CSR that have been confronted with this dilemma have used the argument that if they pull out other less scrupulous companies will simply take their place. In fact, the increasing amount of offshore oil deposits and the technological requirements of the sector generally mean that this argument does not always hold.

3. Dialogue and consultation: identification of and engagement with key stakeholder groups on a regular and consultative basis. The idea of corporate engagement with stakeholders is far from new. It is firmly on the curricula of business schools, and can be found in most leading extractive TNCs' project planning and public statements (McPhail and Davy 1998). Even though TNC approaches to stakeholder engagement are becoming increasingly systematic and sophisticated, they remain at odds with a conflict-transformation approach. This stems from the convention of affording the company and not the country analytical priority, and a failure to factor in the special circumstances of conflict zones. Acknowledgement of the impact of business on the country more widely is, therefore, often missed, along with opportunities to contribute in a more positive way. Meanwhile, TNCs tend to position themselves as the agent engaging stakeholders, rather than a stakeholder and protagonist in a broader political (or conflict) economy itself. Thus their own impacts are again not properly framed. Related to this problem, there is commonly a perceived need to take responsibility and ownership—in fact to 'control' stakeholder engagement on the part of the company. As conflict-transformation practitioners have shown, this is not appropriate in dialogue processes. The lack of engagement of company personnel, except from 'external relations' or equivalent departments, and the ways in which output of the consultations is utilised, are also problematic areas. For example, community members' comments are typically solicited merely to respond to predetermined mitigation measures on a predetermined project, thereby reinforcing a powerful–powerless relationship between the company and community. In conflict-prone situations, such power relations can foster anger and trigger outbreaks of violence. Operating in conflict zones requires a shift in mind-set and a more nuanced approach. Relationship-building with other actors is, in and of itself, a contribution to peace-building.[14]

4. Partnership and collective action: development of mutually beneficial and transparent partnerships with other companies, civil-society organisations and government bodies to address sensitive political and public policy issues and to invest in practical projects. In understanding the optimum role for TNCs in conflict prevention and peace-building, as with the broader debate on business and sustainable development, controversy essentially revolves around the boundaries and limits of various roles and responsibilities for different actors. Figure 17.2 gives a few ideas for appropriate roles for different issues, with companies taking a lead role in some areas, and a support role in others.

14 International Alert has engaged the international oil industry in Azerbaijan, facilitating a multi-stakeholder dialogue process with local business and civil-society actors. Through dialogue, priority conflict prevention issues where oil companies could play a role have been identified, and cross-sectoral partnership and projects to address these initiated (Killick 2002).

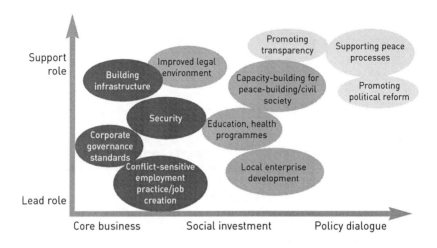

Figure 17.2 Company interventions in conflict transformation: roles and
responsibilities

5. Evaluation and accountability: identification of key performance indicators for measuring and monitoring the company's impacts and reporting on these to internal and external stakeholders

Contrary to conventional views, interventions made in partnership with others and in a supportive capacity are just as important as those where TNCs take a lead role, particularly because they will tend to relate to addressing and influencing the crucial governance and development issues that are so important in conflict-prone zones. Issues should be identified and appropriate roles determined through stakeholder analysis and dialogue. In addition, by working together, meanwhile, the impact of individual companies on promoting optimum business standards, on making meaningful contributions to social development through social investment initiatives, and on conducting dialogue for governance change will all be enhanced.[15] Companies should also inform themselves of other national-level development frameworks—either government or IGO—and find ways of inserting themselves into these where their competences are most suited. Social investments should be made through competent and carefully chosen local partners, and relationships must be informed by a long-term commitment (a full-time presence building these relationships and overseeing engagement is necessary, although the creation of a 'company-NGO' must be avoided). Companies must be willing to abandon 'branding' of projects; and following through on social investment or

15   While some might argue that TNCs co-operate extensively at the global level to further their shared interest in an international operating environment/regime that favours their activities (Cutler *et al.* 1999), at the in-country level they are driven by competitive concerns—to the detriment of their potential impact on conflict transformation or broader sustainable development processes.

community development projects is important, through staying on the boards or steering committees of projects, and making multi-year commitments.

17.4 Conclusions

This chapter has sought to provide a synthesis of the current debate on the role of extractive TNCs operating in zones of conflict. Conflict straddles other issues put on the CSR agenda (including human rights, corruption and the environment). It is, however, limiting to see conflict as the 'fourth pillar' of CSR, given the current limitations of CSR approaches themselves, which privilege corporate reputation over other concerns. While many of the structural causes of conflict are addressed obliquely in the growing move to try to harness the private sector as a resource for promoting sustainable development, the role for business in conflict transformation warrants its own special attention. Until a more nuanced and less company-centred perspective on conflict is achieved, the risk of feeding into or creating conflict dynamics in a given country remains high, and with it the risk of TNCs becoming caught up in human rights abuses and other issues of concern. The peace-building potential located in foreign investing TNCs continues to go untapped. Extractive companies must be open to change, by attaching greater significance to community engagement and the outputs of this, and using their influence with host governments in a way that is constructively critical, and at all times in partnership with others. Transparency about their own operations, the money they are investing in developing countries, as well as their decision-making and priorities when it comes to social investment, are all of key importance. More effective conflict analysis, including of the impacts of their own operations at all levels, is also essential. By pursuing a goal of conflict-sensitivity, TNCs in the extractive sector can increasingly allow themselves to shift away from 'fuelling the conflict' to 'oiling the peace', thereby contributing to a more stable environment at both local and global levels.

Extracting conflict

Gary MacDonald
Monkey Forest Consulting Ltd, Canada

Timothy McLaughlin
Independent Consultant, USA

Allegations of human rights violations most often stem from the actions of national governments. However, oil, gas, mining and other extractive resource companies by their nature are prone to generating a type of conflict with host communities that can lead to a wide range of human rights violations. In the worst but, thankfully, rare cases, community activists such as Ken Saro Wiwa in Nigeria have lost their lives as a result of direct or indirect conflict with large multinational resource companies. In other cases, community leaders living near large resource projects have suffered harassment and imprisonment at the hands of their governments. In many of these situations, national governments have been accused of acting in self-interest or, worse, on behalf of foreign companies rather than in the interests of the people they represent.

Physical abuse, arbitrary detention, displacement, denial of land rights: these and more are the all-too-common abuses most people would recognise and characterise as forms of human rights violations. But human rights encompasses much more than just freedom from abuse at the hands of unrepresentative governments or corrupt political administrations. The Universal Declaration of Human Rights details a great many more rights in its 30 articles than just the typical abuses reported by the media and human rights watchdog groups. Among others, these include the freedom of thought, conscience and religion, movement, opinion and expression, assembly and association, education and cultural life. These broader and more subtle notions of respect, dignity, community and self-determination constitute fundamental human rights that are at the same time harder to identify (and, therefore, rarely reported on by the media) and easier to violate, especially unintentionally. Moreover, these rights are especially subject to abuse during conflicts involving actors with divergent cultures and problem-solving habits, and when communication is poor and signals easily misunderstood—as is often the case with extractive company–host community dynamics. Because they tend to see the world as closed, mechanical systems and are driven by the need to extract oil, ore or timber as efficiently as possible, resource extraction companies inadvertently put in place the very dynamics that lead to conflict with the communities that host their projects. Human communities, in contrast, are not mechanical but open, dynamic, self-organising systems. However, because they can be ill equipped to manage complex relationships with technically driven companies, they often find their interests and their fundamental right to self-determination and aspiration taking second place to the needs of the companies. The common result is a company–community relationship characterised by diverging perceptions and goals and very often outright conflict. This chapter attempts to show how companies co-create that reality through inadequate management systems and through their tendency to externalise problems and solutions.

18.1 Developing dependence

Unlike industries that depend on cheap labour, such as apparel or light manufacturing, extractive resource companies have limited control over where they can operate. Geology and geography are the major determinants. Many of the largest undeveloped ore bodies, oil and gas fields, and productive forests are found in the least developed areas. Such resources present companies with a host of challenges that cannot necessarily be resolved through engineering solutions or using the experience gained in more developed regions. Because of their proximity to the resource, communities in developing areas become host to modern, technologically driven industries whose main interest is extracting resources at the least possible cost. Such communities are nearly always ill equipped to manage complex relationships with highly technical companies. All too often, fundamental cultural differences complicate relationships between corporations and local peoples, particularly when the communities include indigenous peoples who have traditional values that differ from those of their new neighbours. Such communities often lack the capacity to represent or oversee their development in ways that are understandable to Western corporate organisations. Also, traditional communities are often pressured by central governments and by transient workers from other areas of their own countries that may have different visions of local development needs. These host communities often attract the interest and support of activist non-governmental organisations (NGOs), many based in already developed economies, whose goals can include challenging extractive companies wherever they operate.

Meanwhile, company staff often feel that local communities rarely skilfully or clearly identify what grieves them. Companies often believe they are forced to deal with pent-up economic development demands from communities that say they are ignored by their political leadership or do not share in the benefits that come from company operations. Communities rightly complain they must bear an unfair amount of the burden of hosting a resource project. This is particularly the case for companies developing greenfield projects in remote areas far from developed centres. Host communities can quickly become dependent on a company's economic presence, leading to situations where one of the most fundamental of human rights—to have a say over one's destiny—is inadvertently subordinated to corporate needs to have efficient, cost-effective operations that satisfy shareholder demands for profitability.

This is not to say that corporations are inherently evil or even exclusively cost- and profit-oriented. Without a doubt, some companies pay little more than lip service to corporate social responsibility (CSR) and define new responsibilities through the narrow lenses of shareholder value and a quantifiable bottom line. Still, in a post-Enron era, many large companies are taking stock of their core corporate values and guiding principles while they re-evaluate their broader societal roles and re-examine their responsibilities as managers, employers and members of communities. For transnational companies, particularly those that extract resources in developing economies, the challenges are even greater and require a fundamental redefinition of social responsibility as a function of their business models.

In most cases, companies operating in economically depressed regions do so with an abundance of good intentions. In the past decade, extractive companies have realised that they need to develop a 'social licence to operate', along with the conventional regulatory and business licences granted by host governments. However, true to their nature, many corporations have focused on quantifiable efforts such as conventional philanthropy or 'giving' programmes. Others have identified and funded construction of much-needed infrastructure for local communities by building schools, clinics, roads and fulfilling other community needs. Once set on either (or both) of these two paths, most companies find themselves inadvertently assuming the role of local governments as key service providers and face open-ended demands from communities grown dependent on company largesse.

Host national and local governments often contribute to this dynamic by diverting development funding away from the area directly affected by company operations in the belief that the company will assume even more of the financial and development burden. This turns into a sort of self-fulfilling prophecy as communities demand assistance from corporations simply because they appear to listen while governments turn a deaf ear to community pleas. In the end, companies find themselves in a role where it becomes increasingly easier to externalise their problems by looking outside their gates for the causes of conflicts, rather than looking at the fundamental nature of the relationships they have created with their host communities.

18.2 The truth is not out there

Once they have placed the sources of company–community conflict outside the company and its operations, companies naturally look for external solutions rather than contemplate changes in their management style or changes in internal systems or processes. For example, even peaceful demonstrations by communities tend to result in companies deploying more guards to safeguard their people, property and assets. Companies may also make formal or informal requests for additional support from police or other local security authorities. This typifies the 'silo' mentality prevalent in many extractive companies which react to situations by applying security solutions to non-security problems. That is, an increase in guards with even a semi-official police presence alongside them often undermines the dignity of local communities and highlights the economic disparities between the two sides.

Most communities intend to protest peacefully and, true or not, feel they can control their own fringe elements who may espouse harsher methods of expressing grievance (e.g. through more violent confrontation). As well, communities know that they lack the clout that companies enjoy when they demand services from local authorities who may place emphasis on extractive projects as 'national assets'. More aggressive community members will see the presence of additional guards or more police as justifying their harsher approach. In this way, the company's security solution to what was a social challenge creates a new security problem that then justifies the original security solution. The company and the community become locked into a repeating and sometimes escalating pattern of conflict.

Whether operating in North America or in developing regions of the world, executives often see social or 'soft' issues as a kind of black box that consumes company resources with little predictable result. Indeed, community relations departments at many companies are literally referred to as 'cost centres vice revenue' generators. In this sense, cost centres are those parts of the business that increase the costs of extracting resources but are not regarded by management as adding a concomitant value to the company's bottom line as do, for example, operations, labour or exploration. Other cost centres might include public affairs, advertising, human resources, training and general administration. Community relations and community development activities are costs that corporations are willing to bear in times of plenty (such as when commodity or oil prices are high) but these costs are often the first to be constrained when prices decline. Deciding to engage in philanthropic projects is easy when shareholders are receiving high returns on their investments. It is just as easy to decide to cut funding when those returns are leaner. While there has been progress in redefining business models to include the value of a company's reputation to the bottom line, calculating the value of an effective social licence remains one of the largest gaps in the 21st-century business model.

Because social and system-based solutions that emphasise process over outcome are difficult to quantify and measure (and quantitative measurement has an almost unshakeable grip as the tool used by corporate managers to demonstrate progress), extractive companies often see these types of solution as difficult to manage. Often, the best that can be said is that such solutions reduce risk—which is only evident by examining the qualities of the relationship in their cultural and community context as contrasted with a community system's response to a company's plans or actions. It is much easier and seemingly less time-consuming to opt for an 'easy' solution based on measurable factors (such as how many guards there are in a security system or how much money is being spent on community development programmes) rather than to engage people about the nature of the system that both company and community find themselves in. In essence, companies seek quantifiable 'products' or outcomes in preference to open-ended processes such as sustained company–community engagement. Company management tends to be more comfortable when calculating the costs of producing an ounce of gold, barrel of oil or board foot of lumber than valuing the effect of respecting local culture or the rights of self-determination.

Organisational theorist Karl Weick (1979) postulated in his 'theory of enactment' that the environment an organisation worries about is, in fact, put there by that organisation. As noted above, companies sometimes create security problems when they begin noticing and dealing with community grievances or other social challenges to their operations. In seeking to break the cycle of conflict, progressive company managers often find they can do so only by changing the fundamental ways they interact with communities and by looking internally, rather than only externally, for solutions.

Over the last several years, for example, many companies operating in British Columbia on Canada's west coast have struggled to engage with their host communities, among them many indigenous groups—or First Nations as they are referred to in Canada—in ways that break down barriers between company and community. This has meant companies have had to rethink how they manage their role as the leading economic driver, particularly in communities that have been long dependent on forestry or hydroelectric power generation as the primary industries. One such company, BC Hydro, the main electric power supply company to the city of Vancouver, faced seemingly never-ending grievances from First Nations communities that felt their tribal cultures were being undermined by the company's need for access to land and water. However, in the 1980s, BC Hydro began to fundamentally redefine how it dealt with indigenous communities, giving them more say over the location of new power lines, access roads and dams, and tied the communities' access to development assistance more closely to the company's business performance. As a result of their new access to the company, communities came to more fully understand the economic pros and cons of how BC Hydro made business decisions, and were better able to make decisions that protected their cultural values within the context of economic development. The result has been a stronger social licence to operate, enabling BC Hydro to ensure continued access to lands, resources and developments, while trying to minimise the loss of traditional culture or community aspirations.

Still, it is hard for companies to break old habits and retreat from paternalistic and dependency-driven relationships with communities. In another example from British Columbia, a Canadian forestry company recently decided, for bottom-line financial reasons, to sell a parcel of land in a suburb close to the city of Vancouver. At the same time, the community that surrounds the land had been going through an aspirational change, wanting to grow from being just a bedroom community to a more robust, stand-alone community with a clearer sense of self-identity. The company had bought the facilities and land from another forestry company less than 20 years ago and did not fully appreciate the property's historic value to the community. The community sees this land and the industry on it as the historical foundation for its economic and, just as important, social growth over the last century. But changes in the forest industry have put the company in a position where it must sell the land.

Early in the process, the mayor of the municipality spoke about his vision for developing the land in a way that would reflect and give substance to the community's sense of history. Acting alone, the company sold off equipment no longer in use, unintentionally disrespecting the community's sense of history and alerting it to a potential loss of historically important artefacts. In typical fashion, the company only responded to the community's complaints by donating photographs and the occasional old saw blade, rather than by responding to people's underlying interests, their view of their history. Neither the company nor the community believes the best use of the land is to have it lie vacant. It is in both of their interests to see it developed in a way that will enhance its economic value. But the company's desire to protect its ability to act unilaterally could nullify its ability to gain community approval for a changed use. In the end, the company could effectively lose control over the eventual disposal of the land by refusing to cede more aspirational control to the host community.

18.3 Developing problems

Where companies operate in the world appears to have only secondary impact on this dynamic. Companies operating both in the developed North and in the developing South have faced similar situations. A recent ground-breaking study by the US-based Business for Social Responsibility (BSR) and Newmont Mining Corporation (2003) examined ten mining projects from around the world that failed as a result of non-financial factors: namely, company–community conflicts. In a few cases, conflict was expressed in violent upheaval, such as the events surrounding Vista Gold's Amayapampa and Capasirca gold mines in Bolivia (see, further, Chapter 10 by Simon Handelsman) or Aurora Gold's mine in Indonesia's Sulawesi Province. In other cases, conflict was expressed in peaceful protest that resulted in regulatory action, such as Geddes Resources' Windy Craggy copper mining project in the Tatshenshini Wilderness of British Columbia. The joint BSR–Newmont study, which forms part of a forthcoming guide to help companies understand how to better develop a social licence to operate, looked for common elements that led to the projects failing. Researchers spoke with representatives from companies, local and international NGOs, representatives from community-based organisations, and with secondary sources.

Jim Rader, who leads the BSR team that works with companies in the extractive sector, said that what was striking throughout all of the interviews were the differences in *perception* between the company and NGO representatives about the nature of the issues that drove the conflicts. Rarely, he said, did the perceptions of the two sides coincide about what the key issues were in the dispute that led to a conflict. That is, neither side was able to go beyond perceiving the 'positions' of the other and grasp their underlying interests. Rader noted that such situations improve dramatically when companies and communities are able to better align their interests into a shared vision for the development of the project.

18.4 Developing dissent

What companies most often have difficulty accepting is their role in co-creating reality. Just like the fate of the mythical animal in Austrian physicist Erwin Schrödinger's cat-in-the-box brain teaser, the environment a company experiences does not exist separately from the company itself.[1] Even though it is hard to perceive, the environment a company experiences is co-created through its acts of observation and interaction. What it chooses to notice and worry about influences the environment it experiences. When communities complain, whether through dialogue with the company or in open defiance, companies tend to take steps quickly to respond to those stated positions. These responses usually involve economic incentives or, in the case of demonstrations, increased security. Rarely do companies work through those positions in a process of sustained engagement with stakeholders to identify communities' underlying and more important interests and values. In this dynamic, what often become violated, again unintentionally, are the communities' right of self-determination and aspiration.

The huge Yanacocha gold mine in northern Peru partly owned by Newmont Mining is an instructive example. The mine started less than a decade ago when the country was emerging from multiple national security crises, in part driven by the violent home-grown extremist group Sendero Luminoso (Shining Path) that was terrorising Andean communities. The mining project was originally thought to have a short life-span of only a few years. The mine's developers (joint venture partners Newmont, Peru's Buenaventura Mining and the International Financial Corporation of the World Bank Group) originally analysed local social issues, informed by a belief that they would be developing a short-term, low-impact operation. However, as Newmont carried out further exploration, it became clear the reserve might take as long as 25 years to exploit and would have a more significant and lasting social and environmental impact than originally envisaged.

As Minera Yanacocha and its Peruvian management team moved into exploiting this vast resource high in the Andes, they believed that the major challenges to the operation from outside its gates would stem from the rural communities close to

---

1   In that famous paradox, Schrödinger hypothesised that a researcher must necessarily affect the outcome of any experiment simply through the act of observing the results of the experiment. By way of example, Schrödinger said that, if a researcher placed a cat in a box with only the ability to feed or poison itself, the researcher could not know the well-being of the cat without opening the box, and thereby affecting the outcome of the experiment. Schrödinger's thinking paved the way for later developments in quantum theory and eventually complexity theory. Schrödinger first presented this thinking in 'Die gegenwärtige Situation in der Quantenmechanik' ('The Present Situation In Quantum Mechanics'), in *Die Naturwissenschaften* (*The Natural Sciences*) 23 (1935).

its operations. To manage these, Minera Yanacocha created an effective series of expanding programmes, aimed at supporting the economic development of people in the rural communities. Over time, community members, the company and the government became used to a relationship driven by the company's need to both generate assent through development aid and avoid dissent from communities which were profiting from the mine. Indeed, the Andean peoples have been long accustomed to being on the receiving end of paternalistic relationships with oppressive outsiders; by their own reckoning, first from the Spanish *conquistadores*, later from the political elite in Lima and now from the mine's management. The company naturally viewed any and all dissent as a sign of trouble and usually dealt with it by creating new economic or social programmes, such as supporting the development of rural schools.

While that cycle continued higher up the mountain, in more recent years people in Cajamarca, the city nearest the mine, began to feel left out of the economic benefits from the mine while bearing a share of its burden. Cajamarquinos complained about the rising cost of living and about negative impacts on the quality of the drinking water supply, among other grievances. As a result, dissent from urban dwellers began to vex the company more frequently. Company efforts to respond to the complaints by introducing mine-funded development programmes in the city, in the same way it did for rural communities, seemed to have little effect. In fact, the more the company concerned itself solely with responding to Cajamarquinos' dissent, the more effective dissent became as a tool for the community. Soon, a variety of groups were organising large-scale protests that resulted in frequent road blocks in the countryside just outside the city. These roadblocks and demonstrations threatened to halt the mine's operation and (naturally) led the company to impose enhanced security and to a greater reliance on co-operation with the national police.

18.5 The threat–reward machine

In the extractive sector, the threat–reward dynamic is driven by a mentality informed by a view of the world as a closed, mechanical system. For years, successful extractive companies have earned rewards for finding technical solutions for exploiting resources that are in geographically or geologically challenging places. Extractive companies have traditionally grown by finding and exploiting new oil fields or ore bodies (i.e. a business model depending on growth through increasing inputs to expand outputs). As in other sectors, progress in the extractive industries has been marked by companies' ability to master technical challenges. As a result, it becomes 'easy' and natural to take an approach informed by a view that systems break down because of some defective piece that can be identified, removed, repaired and replaced, enabling the system to work as before.

Experience drawn from dealing with simpler mechanical processes, where all inputs can be identified and tracked, may lead to a belief that similar principles apply in other systems as well. In fact, the theoretical underpinnings of engineering are similar to many of the ideas we take for granted from our school days (e.g. the idea that every action has an equal and opposite reaction), and that influence our perception of how the world works. Until recently, engineers were educated by learning to solve problems only in the 'real world' of structures and processes, relying on rigorous quantitative analysis. However, knowledge of how mechanical systems operate does not lend itself to understanding or analysing how human systems work. In human systems, it is difficult if not impossible to observe all the inputs to the system, much less analyse them or fully comprehend their innumerable interactions and relations. Even at an experiential level, the view that the world operates as a closed system does not really hold true. Yet nearly every extractive company assigns engineers and operations managers to oversee community affairs.

If we look at communities from a perspective informed by entropy and other Newtonian-style principles, we come to think of them as closed systems not unlike machines. This is convenient for company managers because it takes relationship-building, community engagement and management out of the 'black box', making it easier for traditional engineers to fit how communities act and react into a world-view that maintains it is possible to analyse and fix elements that are 'not working' (e.g. community dissent). In doing so, managers create a situation that perpetuates the dynamics that initially led to the conflict. Recall Schrödinger's ill-fated cat. Managers effectively create the environment of dissent they must deal with. The dynamic results in outcomes such as: (a) the creation of security situations where originally there were social challenges and peaceful disagreements; and (b) rewarding dissent with development aid.

. In the case of Minera Yanacocha cited above, company managers fed the cycle of dissent, rewarding the road blocks that virtually choked the company's ability to operate by simultaneously employing both carrot and stick approaches. Company security officers were deployed to protect corporate assets, while the local government supported the company by sending Peruvian police to disperse crowds. Later, company managers approved new economic aid, thinking they were responding to community interests while they were in fact rewarding dissent. Prior to the demonstrations, the company missed opportunities to engage more effectively with community stakeholders, better understand their interests and involve them in decision-making over how the company spent its development assistance. For example, early on a local Catholic priest and a local academic joined forces to create an organisation to monitor and act on impacts from the mine. Because of the dissent they represented and harnessed, the pair was seen to be opposed to the company rather than simply actors representing a specific moment in the system's life—a moment that gave vital information about the relationship, the company's role in it and the values underlying the actors' interests.

Even internally, companies often provide incentives that reinforce this closed-system approach. For example, with few exceptions, extractive companies link rewards for personal performance to measurable outputs such as barrels of oil produced or tonnes of ore mined but not to the quality of the relationship a company has earned with its host communities. Unless or until performance is based on broader criteria, including minimising the direct and indirect costs communities must pay when playing host to an extractive industry, companies are bound to continue creating the very contentious environments in which they operate.

Communities are open, dynamic, self-organising systems that defy comprehensive understanding when looking only at their individual elements. Communities are vastly more than the sum of their parts. Instead, we have to find some way to work with the whole system—the community as a whole, as a dynamic system—as well as with the individual or identifiable parts (e.g. ethnic or religious groups, farmers, informal or formal community leadership). As organisational theorist and complexity thinker Margaret Wheatley says: 'From a systems consciousness, we understand that no problem of behaviour can be understood in isolation. We must account for dynamics operating in the whole system that are displaying themselves in these individual moments' (Wheatley 2003).

Treating a community as a closed system increases the likelihood of conflict generated from well-meaning attempts to identify and repair elements that are not functioning. When it comes to dealing with communities, we may actually be trying to 'fix' things that are just fine and, in doing so, create misunderstandings and eventually conflict where, originally, there was none.

Relationships with the communities at the Minera Yanacocha mine continued to deteriorate until the company started to address the system that was the Cajamarquino community as a whole. Over the past three years, the company has been successfully working to change the conflict-based dynamic in its relationships with local communities by becoming involved in two processes designed to increase its engagement as part of the community. First of all, instead of adopting the older model of attempting to identify a particular economic or social problem that it could respond to programmatically (i.e. 'fix'), the company embarked on a process of working with community leaders to help them to identify their aspirations and the ways in which those aspirations could be developed. For example, the company has worked closely with community members to design and develop a foundation whose purpose will be to identify just how Cajamarquinos want to pursue development. Second, the company has engaged outside non-profit groups to build capacity in surrounding communities to better identify and express their grievances, in essence, teaching communities how to protest peacefully.

Similarly, a separate but parallel engagement process facilitated by the Compliance, Advisor and Ombudsman office of the International Finance Corporation seeks to involve the company in a co-operative process of participation in regular roundtable discussions with community leaders on relationship issues. One of the first essential steps to progress in this area is creating the ability to respond to challenges in a way that decreases stress for both the community and company managers. As Wheatley (2003) says:

> People who are stressed lose the ability to recognize patterns, to see the bigger picture. And as people become overloaded and over-whelmed with their tasks, they have no time or interest to look beyond the demands of the moment. Therefore, it is essential that the organization sponsor processes that bring people together so that they can learn of one another's perspectives and challenges. If the organization doesn't make these processes happen, people will continue to spiral inward. This inward spiralling has a devastating

impact on performance. People become overwhelmed by the volume of tasks, they lose all sense of meaning for their work, and they feel increasingly isolated and alone. Everybody is busier and more frantic, but the major thing they are producing is more stress. The other serious consequence is that both individual and organizational intelligence decline dramatically as people lose the larger context for their work.

Managing risk and building trust
The challenge of implementing the Voluntary Principles on Security and Human Rights

Bennett Freeman
Former Deputy Assistant Secretary of State
for Democracy, Human Rights and Labor, USA

Genoveva Hernández Uriz
European University Institute, Italy

Since the Voluntary Principles on Security and Human Rights were announced by the US Department of State and the UK Foreign and Commonwealth Office in December 2000, they have gained recognition as the successful outcome of an unprecedented dialogue between companies and NGOs convened by governments. The only major human rights standard forged with the direct participation of extractive-sector companies, they are also the most concrete and specific standard developed thus far in any sector to address the roles and responsibilities of business in zones of conflict. Yet, while the Voluntary Principles offer a model of engaging business on human rights, they also embody the dilemmas of making such engagement produce tangible results over time.

The implementation challenges facing the Voluntary Principles can only be met by a co-ordinated and sustained commitment on the part of governments and the companies themselves, along with efforts on the part of NGOs and the local communities where the companies operate. Meeting those challenges will test the creativity and flexibility of all the parties, no less than the initial dialogue that produced the Voluntary Principles in 2000. The visibility and sensitivity of the process will ensure that whatever progress is achieved or setbacks incurred will set precedents for further engagement with business on human rights, even beyond the extractive sectors. Moreover, as a model set of non-binding principles, the success or failure of the Voluntary Principles on Security and Human Rights will shed light on the broader debate over the credibility of voluntary approaches to corporate social responsibility.

This chapter addresses the challenges that the Voluntary Principles face nearly three years after their adoption, and assesses some of the wider implications of

244 Business and Human Rights

meeting these challenges. The chapter reviews the substantive content of the Voluntary Principles and the continuing process of dialogue among diverse stakeholders, which has made the initiative distinctive and has the potential to make it even more dynamic. A series of steps are then proposed which companies, NGOs and the convening governments can and should take to ensure the effective implementation of the Principles on a country-specific basis. Finally, the Voluntary Principles are examined in terms of the emerging debate over voluntary standards with respect to the advantages and disadvantages of non-binding approaches, their competitive implications, and possibilities for incorporation into other legal instruments even in the absence of direct regulation.

19.1 The Voluntary Principles: substance and process

The year-long dialogue convened by the State Department and the Foreign Office in March 2000 did not attempt to address all the issues that have put extractive-sector companies under the harsh spotlight of international NGOs and the local communities where they operate. Instead, the dialogue focused exclusively on the clash between security and human rights: how to balance the companies' legitimate need to meet real security threats in certain countries with NGOs' and local communities' insistence that company security arrangements respect human rights.[1] The success of the dialogue in reaching consensus was due, in part, to its focus on company relationships with security forces and host-country governments.

The Voluntary Principles are framed around three concrete sets of issues: (a) the criteria that companies should consider as they assess the risk of complicity in human rights abuses in their security arrangements, including their relations with local communities and diverse stakeholders; (b) company relationships with state security forces, both military and police; and (c) company relationships with private security forces. The Principles provide practical guidance to companies, particularly to country and security managers, on how to incorporate international human rights standards and emerging best practices into policies and decisions that sometimes have life and death consequences. For example, the Risk Assessment section of the Voluntary Principles offers a roadmap of key human rights 'factors' to be taken into account as companies plan or update their security arrangements. These include identifying not only conventional security risks (as most companies do as a matter of course) but also broader conflict impact assessments such as the human rights records of public and private security forces operating or available in the region, the strength of the rule of law and judicial processes, and equipment transfers between companies and security forces. Most

---

1 For the key NGO and press reports on extractive-company interactions with security forces that focused the attention of the US and UK governments on the issues and led to the Voluntary Principles, see HRW 1998, 1999b; Shari 1998.

significantly, companies are called on to 'consider the available human rights records' of potential security providers, both public and private, so that 'awareness of past abuses and allegations can help companies to avoid recurrence as well as to promote accountability'. The Public Security section urges that 'the type and number' of forces should be 'competent, appropriate and proportionate to the threat'. The most far-reaching provision in this section calls on companies to 'record and report any credible allegations of human rights abuses by public security in their areas of operation to appropriate host government authorities' and 'where appropriate . . . urge investigation and that action be taken to prevent any recurrence'. This provision breaks new ground by effectively encouraging companies both to report potential abuses and to urge accountability for such abuses, an important step in countries where impunity has prevailed.

The Voluntary Principles explicitly refer to international law standards in relation to the use of force by regular and private armies, stating that security forces should respect the UN Code of Conduct for Law Enforcement Officials and the UN Basic Principles on the Use of Force and Firearms. The UN Code of Conduct for Law Enforcement Officials requires security forces to respect human rights and imposes a number of concrete obligations in this regard: to use force only when strictly necessary and to the extent necessary for the performance of their duty; to ensure the protection of the health of persons in their custody; and to report any violation of the Code to their superior authorities. The Code prohibits officials from invoking superior orders or exceptional circumstances to justify an act of torture or other cruel, inhuman or degrading treatment or punishment, or to commit acts of corruption. The UN Basic Principles on the Use of Force and Firearms contain more detailed provisions, including the circumstances and way in which firearms can be used, the policing of persons in custody or detention, and training and reporting obligations. The Voluntary Principles both complement and extend these two UN codes by urging companies to consult with governments and civil society on the full range of issues affecting the conduct and accountability of security forces with respect to human rights.

The Voluntary Principles use different benchmarks for the application of the two UN standards to companies' operations. In their interaction with governmental forces, companies 'should take all appropriate measures to promote observance' of these two codes. With respect to their interaction with private security forces, the Voluntary Principles break new ground by urging companies to use their leverage to include the UN Code of Conduct for Law Enforcement Officials and the UN Basic Principles on the Use of Force and Firearms in contracts 'where appropriate'. If observed and if effectively implemented, the Voluntary Principles can alter the dynamics between companies, security forces and local communities by lowering risks of human rights abuses and identifying companies with the rule of law while, at the same time, maintaining necessary security for company facilities and personnel. Yet the Principles also raise difficult operational issues on the ground with military commanders and, ultimately, political and diplomatic issues with the host-country governments that cannot necessarily be resolved by the companies alone.

Seven US- and UK-based companies (Chevron and Texaco separately prior to their merger, Conoco, BP, Shell, Rio Tinto and Freeport McMoRan) and nine major

NGOs (including Human Rights Watch, Amnesty International, International Alert, the Lawyers Committee for Human Rights, along with the Prince of Wales International Business Leaders Forum, Business for Social Responsibility and the International Federation of Chemical, Mining and General Workers) agreed to 'support the process and welcome the principles' in December 2000 because they saw an opportunity to serve their own core interests.[2] The companies wanted the benefit of such rules of the road developed jointly with the NGOs, several of which had published detailed reports alleging company complicity in human rights abuses in the 1990s. While the NGOs would probably have preferred a legally binding approach that was subject to independent monitoring, they decided that engaging was better than missing a chance to develop a standard that (albeit voluntary) the companies would be expected to implement and which in turn could be used as the basis for further scrutiny.

The motivations of the US and UK governments in convening and driving the process were just as clear. They shared a concern over the implications of such serious allegations made against a number of their flagship companies. They shared a commitment to work together with companies and NGOs to promote corporate social responsibility, partly in response to the growing backlash against globalisation. At least as important, they also shared an economic and strategic interest in ensuring that their companies could continue to operate in Colombia amid that country's armed insurgency. They shared the same interest in Nigeria and Indonesia, two key countries facing fragile political transitions to democracy against a backdrop of low-intensity but violent regional conflicts threatening their unity and stability. For example, Texaco was forced to halt operations in the Niger Delta in August 1999 due to large-scale community protests, while in the strife-torn Indonesian province of Aceh, ExxonMobil shut production at its Arun LNG facility for several months in early 2001 after the facility came under attack from armed separatists.

The process would probably never have been convened nor the Voluntary Principles negotiated, agreed and announced without the key convening and drafting role of the US and UK governments. Both the companies and the NGOs looked to the two governments to announce the Voluntary Principles while shielding them, respectively, from perceptions that the companies were imposing a new standard on sensitive host-country governments, or that the NGOs were implying that the issues at stake were not only addressed but resolved without further scrutiny required on their part. Moreover, both the companies and the NGOs continue to look to the governments to lead and support the process of implementation especially by engaging the host governments of the countries where the issues matter most.

The Bush Administration has carried the initiative forward together with the UK government: convening four full plenary sessions of the participants from early 2001 to early 2003; briefing other key governments; and encouraging country-

2   For detailed accounts of the dialogue and negotiating process that produced the Voluntary Principles, see Freeman *et al.* 2001; Freeman 2001a, 2001b, 2002. For press coverage of the launch of the Voluntary Principles on 20 December 2000, see Alden and Buchan 2000; Behr 2000; Dreazan 2000; Stout 2000.

specific implementation steps on the part of the companies. The process was expanded in May 2002 when an additional US-based company, Newmont Mining, joined the process and was followed by Occidental Petroleum and ExxonMobil. The Netherlands joined in May 2002 in light of its joint home country relationship with Shell (shared with the UK), followed by Norway, which, together with Statoil and Norsk Hydro, subscribed to the Principles at the Washington plenary session held in January 2003. These new participants bring the number of companies to eleven and convening governments to four. More importantly, they reflect and reinforce the emergence of the Voluntary Principles as the global standard on security and human rights issues for extractive companies.

The government of Canada and several Canadian companies have also indicated an interest, along with other US- and UK-based companies which have been following developments closely. When the process can be further expanded without diluting progress made so far, it would be useful to add the governments of Australia, South Africa and Chile (together with the international mining companies based in those countries), along with the governments of Mexico and Brazil (together with their state-owned oil companies which also operate abroad). Adding governments from the South will be critical to adding balance to a process thus far convened by home-country governments of the North, which have focused, for the most part, on interactions of their companies with host-country governments and security forces of the South.

19.2 Implementation challenges and opportunities

At the present time, the consolidation and implementation of the Principles on the ground is even more important than the further expansion of the number of signatories. Nearly three years after their launch, the credibility of the Voluntary Principles is on trial, and the ability of the process to demonstrate concrete progress is being tested. The NGOs inside the process and others outside it cannot be expected to accept such progress on trust alone. Progress must be demonstrated in specific contexts and countries, and trust can be developed through further dialogue and new patterns of co-operation.

Moreover, the process cannot operate in a vacuum as the clash between large-scale extractive operations and remote, impoverished communities in zones of conflict remains acute. Although the Voluntary Principles offer a global standard, the combination of past incidents and recent tensions continue to make them most relevant in Nigeria, Indonesia and Colombia. In 2002 and early 2003, the salience of the Voluntary Principles was highlighted in all three countries:

- In early July 2002, hundreds of unarmed women from surrounding communities occupied ChevronTexaco's oil terminal at Escravos in the Niger Delta, while others took over several nearby flow stations. Shell faced similar protests the next month. A violent pre-election uprising by ethnic Ijaw militants in March 2003 resulted in fatalities, intervention by the Nigerian military, and production shutdowns by both Chevron-Texaco and Shell.

● At the end of August 2002, two American citizens and an Indonesian were killed near Freeport McMoRan's giant Grassberg mine in the highlands of Papua, Indonesia. While the Indonesian military blamed the separatist OPM for the killings, speculation has intensified that elements connected to Kopassus, the special forces arm of the army, were responsible. The incident may have been intended as a signal to Freeport to maintain funding levels for its security arrangements with the military, and to curtail its contacts with pro-independence elements in Papua.

● In September 2002, US military advisers began arriving in Saravena in east-central Colombia to begin training two Colombian army brigades to protect the 500-mile Caño Limon-Covenas pipeline operated by Occidental Petroleum that has been a frequent target of guerrilla attacks. Some 100 special forces personnel reinforced the effort in early 2003.

These developments pose challenges for the companies, and for their host- and home-country governments alike. Their response will test the Voluntary Principles as a framework for balancing security and human rights. At stake is not only the companies' 'social licence to operate' in zones of conflict and in close proximity to indigenous communities, but also the companies' ability and willingness to continue operating in difficult circumstances—even with such large fixed investments on the ground. If the Voluntary Principles are to become a fully operational framework, the convening governments and participating companies and NGOs must together sharpen the focus of the process around the twin objectives of managing risk and building trust. While it is essential to continue the dialogue in the conference rooms of the foreign ministries of convening governments, it is now just as important to extend the dialogue and take actions on the ground in the countries where the threats remain most acute.

Tangible steps can be taken on three interlocking levels to give the Voluntary Principles more operational texture: one set of steps by the companies on their own; a second by the companies and NGOs working together; and a third by the convening home-country governments, working directly with host-country governments and security forces.

19.2.1 Implementation: companies

Companies should intensify the integration of the Voluntary Principles into their statements of company policy, training and community engagement programmes on a global basis, through the following actions:

● Revising operating guidelines and procedures for their facilities and personnel in relevant countries to reflect provisions of the Voluntary Principles. Many managers in the field have little experience on these issues and would benefit from guidance materials and other support to help them implement the Voluntary Principles in specific situations and in specific countries.

● Integrating the content of the Voluntary Principles into training programmes. Personnel, from project site managers to company security
guards, could benefit from training that addresses not only key provisions
such as the use of force and equipment transfers but also basic human
rights issues. Case studies and role-playing scenarios would be useful,
especially if tailored to country conditions.

● Adding clauses to security contracts with public and private security
forces detailing expectations on key issues such as use of force and
company equipment, and prior human rights records of individual units
and commanders. Since much of the content of the Voluntary Principles
calls on companies to reach certain understandings with security forces,
it would be helpful to codify such understandings to the extent possible
(even if these contractual arrangements are not made public).

● Integrating relevant provisions of the Voluntary Principles into community engagement programmes so that security and community relations
staffs co-ordinate their activities more fully. These programmes require a
willingness to expand communication and consultation on security
issues with the local communities near company operations. Community-based security can be strengthened by hiring and training local
community residents as security guards where conditions warrant. This
approach depends not only on informing local communities about their
rights but also on their responsibilities for ensuring security. It depends
even more fundamentally on developing trust and co-operation with
local government authorities and security forces over time.

● Building understanding of the Voluntary Principles through direct dialogues with host-country governments and militaries at the national and
regional levels. It is especially important to engage with national oil
companies such as the Nigerian National Petroleum Company (NNPC) in
Nigeria, ECOPETROL in Colombia and Pertamina in Indonesia, which
have a stake in working with their foreign partners to address security
issues in ways that minimise risks to reputation as well as to production.

BP Indonesia is trying to develop such a community-based approach for its
planned Tangguh LNG project in Papua. Moreover, it has taken the unprecedented
step of annexing the full text of the Voluntary Principles to its contract with
Pertamina, and has also developed a set of security guidelines for private security
contractors based explicitly on them. Other companies may want to consider
similar steps as they plan new projects, or revise their policies and procedures in
connection with existing ones.

19.2.2 Implementation: companies working with NGOs

Far more interaction should take place between the companies and NGOs outside
the now annual plenary sessions convened by the governments. In addition to
communicating the progress they have made and the problems they have encoun-

tered in their implementation of the Voluntary Principles, companies should work with NGOs in four areas:

- Consulting on risk and conflict assessment criteria and planning with respect to global policy and specific countries. The companies and NGOs should strengthen mutual understanding and trust by sharing information, methods and analysis, especially as new issues emerge or incidents occur.

- Developing the human rights content of training programmes undertaken with both public and private security forces. The International Committee of the Red Cross has joined the Voluntary Principles process as an observer. Its impartiality and expertise make it ideally suited to facilitate and contribute directly to this kind of co-operation. Likewise, other NGOs may be willing to work with private companies in specific countries.

- Reporting on their implementation of the Voluntary Principles at the annual plenary sessions convened by the governments, as well as through other company communications channels. Such reports would strengthen the credibility of company implementation efforts, and encourage greater confidence on the part of the NGOs.

- Considering the Human Rights Watch proposal that companies begin 'incident reporting' in the absence of viable or acceptable third-party monitoring. Companies could offer oral or written briefings on their response to specific incidents and issues addressed by the Voluntary Principles, while respecting the voluntary and non-binding character of the overall process.

Such direct consultation and co-operation must be handled sensitively to remain consistent with the core interests and appropriate roles of the companies and NGOs alike. NGOs would have to be willing to engage on this basis without diminishing their ability to scrutinise and criticise company security policies and practices. Companies, no doubt, would have to find and test the appropriate limits of information they would be willing to share. Finding these reasonable balances on the part of companies and NGOs will build confidence in the process, and develop further the Voluntary Principles as a model of constructive engagement that builds trust and produces results.

19.2.3 Implementation: home-country governments

The convening governments should be prepared to take a more active role in working with host-country governments to institutionalise the Voluntary Principles with military and police forces. The home-country governments of companies operating in Nigeria, Indonesia and Colombia, among others, can use the Voluntary Principles as a framework for helping their companies navigate some of the toughest threats to their investments, while remaining on the ground in such important countries. The Voluntary Principles can also be used as a framework for working with host governments and military forces to strengthen respect for human rights and accountability for abuses. These are sensitive issues which ultimately reflect on all parties and shape the climate of bilateral relations and co-operation on other interests.

The US, UK, Dutch and Norwegian governments can contribute to the implementation process in Nigeria in light of the recent incidents in the Niger Delta, and against the backdrop of local community clashes with security forces throughout the 1990s. These governments should extend the briefing process, which so far has focused on senior federal government officials, to encompass the national oil company, military and police as well as state government and civil-society leaders in the Niger Delta. Accelerating this process is urgent in Nigeria; further unrest in the Delta remains likely as the revenue allocation process channelling funds back to the states and local communities remains incomplete and expectations for tangible improvements remain unmet.

The US government, in particular, has raised the bar for testing the credibility of the Voluntary Principles in Colombia through its direct support for pipeline security. It will have a high political price to pay if such protection, however inadvertently, becomes connected to new allegations of human rights abuses by US-funded and -trained forces operating around an American company's operations. With the US military being increasingly called on to extend security protection to large-scale, foreign-owned oil, gas and pipeline facilities in Colombia and elsewhere (such as Georgia), the line between the national interest of those countries and the corporate interests of the companies involved also becomes blurred. This development not only opens up new opportunities for expanded human rights training but also exposes companies to new and different risks. In the event that US-trained forces exceed their mandates and are found complicit in human rights abuses, companies will be exposed to potentially significant new liabilities as well as risks to their operations and ultimately to their reputations. For these reasons, the US advisers now on the ground training and equipping the Colombian army brigades to protect the Caño Limon–Covenas pipeline should also reinforce human rights training for their Colombian counterparts. They should also work with Occidental Petroleum to take appropriate steps to implement the Voluntary Principles.

The US and UK governments, together with the governments of Australia, The Netherlands and other countries, face the most sensitive situation alongside the companies in Indonesia. In the wake of the Bali bombing in October 2002 and threats to oil company facilities in Aceh and elsewhere in Sumatra, American pressure on the Indonesian government to crack down on terrorism has become the overriding priority of US–Indonesian bilateral relations. Stronger security co-operation is surely in the interests of both the Indonesian and the US governments, as well as of the foreign extractive companies operating across the archipelago. Yet, as military and intelligence co-operation are strengthened to counter further terrorist attacks, the NGO and media spotlight will remain trained on the Indonesian government and military's record on human rights. The US government has pushed for accountability for past abuses by the military, in East Timor in particular. No doubt it recognises that, while the bilateral relationship and foreign investment environment both depend on a full Indonesian commitment to counter terrorism, congressional and public support for the relationship could be undermined by further abuses. It has already been put on notice by Senator Leahy, who has urged that US training assistance to the Indonesian military be halted if the military is found to have planned the killings near the Freeport mine in Papua. Those killings also threaten the long-term security and viability of extractive-company operations in Papua if accountability is not achieved.

The Voluntary Principles will not provide security, the most critical priority. However, they can contribute to accountability, on the part of both the companies and the security forces. Long-term security will not occur in Indonesia without greater accountability, together with renewed efforts to achieve reconciliation in regions of unrest. While the companies will continue to share the main responsibility for implementing the Voluntary Principles, the US government should help engage the host government and military in the process constructively. Such a signal from the US can also help overcome any doubts to its commitment to the Voluntary Principles in Indonesia stemming from its August 2002 intervention in the lawsuit against ExxonMobil,[3] when it asked a federal court to drop the case due to the complications it could cause in US–Indonesian bilateral relations.

While most attention has focused on the risks facing extractive operations in Nigeria, Colombia and Indonesia, the Voluntary Principles may also be useful in other countries, even those without current armed conflict or unrest but with records of human rights abuses or tensions with local communities. These countries range from Peru and Ecuador in South America to Papua New Guinea in the South Pacific (where oil and mining companies have had tense relations with indigenous peoples), to several countries in Africa (including Chad and Cameroon, where the major pipeline project supported by the World Bank passes through regions previously torn by strife, and Equatorial Guinea, where major oil companies have established a presence in a country long governed repressively). The Caspian is another region where the Voluntary Principles are relevant, especially as a security corridor is established alongside the Baku–Ceyhan pipeline from Azerbaijan through Georgia to Turkey.

Finally, much attention has been paid recently to the activities of private security companies, especially those based in the US, which are playing a growing role in advising and training military and police forces around the world. Whether or not these firms are unofficial extensions of US foreign policy, the US government has an opportunity through its official licensing process to encourage them to integrate human rights training into their activities. Such training could include issues addressed by the Voluntary Principles, such as use of force and community engagement, while co-ordinating with similar training undertaken by the companies themselves.

Implementing the Voluntary Principles on Security and Human Rights is challenging enough since they already address the most pervasive human rights risks facing the operations and reputations of extractive companies around the

---

3 The suit alleged that ExxonMobil had been complicit in human rights abuses in Aceh, including the charge that it had provided land-moving equipment used by the Indonesian military to dig mass graves (*John Doe et al. v. Exxon Mobil Corporation et al.*, 2001 US Dist. Ct, D.C., C.A. No. 01-CV-1357).

world. Yet their implementation is further complicated by the fact that they connect not only to the collision of extractive companies and remote communities on the frontlines of globalisation but also to sensitive diplomatic relationships and even geopolitical challenges at the same time. They raise difficult questions about the blurred, overlapping roles and responsibilities of companies, NGOs and governments. They address directly, even if only in certain countries, the turbulent but necessary balance that must be struck between security and human rights in an era of local conflicts and global terrorism. The imperative of finding that balance will only increase in what has also become an era of accountability.

19.3 The voluntary principles and the debate over voluntary approaches

Implementation of the Voluntary Principles on Security and Human Rights may have significant implications for the broader debate on voluntary versus mandatory approaches to corporate social responsibility. That debate has been given new impetus by the pressures for accountability mounting on both the corporate social responsibility and corporate governance agendas. Not surprisingly, the Voluntary Principles have been criticised explicitly on the grounds that 'they are not accompanied by a monitoring mechanism and require no follow-up by states such as incorporation in national laws' (International Council on Human Rights Policy 2002: 148). More generally, commentators have emphasised the weaknesses of voluntary initiatives, criticisms that are directly relevant to the Voluntary Principles even if they are not directed explicitly at it. These critiques of voluntary approaches are largely based on the dual grounds of their perceived lack of efficacy and legitimacy.

First, voluntary approaches are deemed by some to be insufficient to ensure compliance because they ultimately depend on a corporation's professed commitment; that commitment is often seen to be motivated by a desire not only to meet high standards but also to withstand and overcome criticism from media and NGOs (Mock 2000: 15; Sullivan and Frankental 2002: 84). Moreover, voluntary standards by definition apply only to those corporations that accept them. Even among companies committed to corporate responsibility, implementation of voluntary standards inevitably varies among companies according to their different management structures and cultures, their internal compliance and reporting systems, and their different attitudes towards engaging with external stakeholders. To the critics of voluntary approaches, such arguments amount to a compelling case for the adoption of binding norms. Such norms would level the playing field for all corporations and contribute not only to substantive justice but also to greater certainty and clarity in the application of human rights to non-state actors.

Second, critics of self-regulation argue that voluntary codes are also undermined because they are produced through dialogues with unaccountable constituencies outside the legislative process. This criticism may be directed at the Voluntary

Principles as the outcome of a dialogue among Western home-country governments, companies and NGOs, conducted outside a legislative or other regulatory process and without the participation of host-country governments, companies and NGOs from the developing world where the issues are most salient. For their part, the US and UK governments recognised that legislation or another form of regulation would almost certainly have been opposed by the companies, and that a non-binding approach could best gain positive company participation in the development and implementation of guidelines intended to be adapted flexibly to different operating environments around the world. The conveners also decided at the outset that a broader global dialogue would take years to complete, and that achieving a more narrowly based agreement could be the basis for further progress towards a more inclusive global process and standard.

The Voluntary Principles notwithstanding, there is not always necessarily a wide gap between self-regulation and the development of legally binding norms. In many sectors of business regulation, self-regulation through industry practices has preceded the adoption of laws (Braithwaite and Drahos 2000: 481).[4] Yet the lack of democratic accountability in an area such as security raises acute legitimacy concerns for any voluntary approach, especially since issues at the heart of fundamental rights such as proportionality in the use of violence, arbitrary arrests and humanitarian law issues, and the treatment of the wounded are at stake. These human rights concerns would weigh heavily against leaving implementation of such voluntary initiatives subject to the will of a few actors.

Yet, at the present time, the adoption of legally binding norms by national parliaments and international treaties in this sector seems unrealistic. States do not have the political will to sanction their companies or even to let other bodies hold them accountable (as the intervention by the US State Department to oppose the lawsuit against ExxonMobil demonstrates). While the Voluntary Principles are unlikely to be legislated in the foreseeable future, the challenge of balancing security with human rights safeguards will remain an implacable problem for companies and an inescapable test of corporate responsibility.

Moreover, meeting this challenge will continue to involve national security interests on the part of host-country governments and foreign policy interests on the part of the companies' home-country governments. In instances such as those already highlighted in Indonesia and Colombia, the burden of implementation of the Voluntary Principles rests not only with the companies but also depends on the diplomatic efforts on the part of their home-country governments in engaging with the host-country governments on sensitive issues such as the vetting, training and deployment of forces.

Paradoxically, the blunt instrument of a legislated or regulated approach originating with the home-country governments of the companies may be less effective in allowing the kind of sensitive and flexible diplomatic engagement of those governments necessary for the successful implementation of the Voluntary Principles. However, once the key host-country governments and their security

---

4   It has been argued that corporations increasingly do establish institutions that 'govern' in the absence of or in co-ordination with governance arrangements involving states at the international level (Claire Cutler *et al.* 1999: 370).

forces indicate a willingness to use the Voluntary Principles as a policy framework for guiding interactions with extractive companies, such mandatory legislated or regulated approaches might then become both possible and desirable on a reciprocal basis on the part of the companies' home- and host-country governments.

Demonstrating the Principles' effectiveness in their current format as a forum for dialogue and exchange of best practices is a particularly challenging exercise in an area such as security and human rights, where there remains uncertainty about how to internalise human rights protections in companies' operations. As the number of companies joining the Voluntary Principles process grows, it is possible that those setting the highest standards can exert a gravitational pull on other companies by drawing them into the process, by obliging them to compete on the same basis and by encouraging them to interact with the same NGOs. Even as a non-binding standard, the Principles can effectively set the standard for the entire extractive sector, since those outside the process risk being perceived by interested stakeholders as indifferent to the challenge of balancing human rights and security. Interestingly, several oil and mining companies that are not participants in the official process have nonetheless made public statements of their adherence to the Voluntary Principles.

Initiatives such as the Voluntary Principles may alter competitive conditions as they may oblige companies to raise their standards of corporate responsibility. In fact, the Voluntary Principles essentially provide companies with policy guidelines and operational tools to facilitate compliance by armed forces with basic principles of what is already positive international law. In this sense, barriers to entry are low for companies that embrace the Voluntary Principles in so far as they explicitly pledge only to 'support the process and welcome the principles', and implicitly commit to implement a standard that only breaks new ground in the specific areas emphasised above. There is no further predetermined set of obligations mandated by what remains in letter and spirit a voluntary process. Yet there are barriers to entry in so far as the Voluntary Principles are not an entirely inclusive process open to any additional companies willing to make these explicit and implicit commitments. The convening governments, in consultation with the established participants, have agreed thus far on the inclusion of additional companies as well as governments and NGOs, and have been disinclined to include companies currently operating in Burma or Sudan. Moreover, as already argued, there is a growing expectation on the part of NGOs in the process that the commitment of the companies in the process must be demonstrated by performance. The new companies that have entered the process have acknowledged that a relatively low barrier to entry is offset by a high expectation of performance backed by NGO scrutiny.

Yet the lack of a formal reporting or monitoring mechanism makes it difficult to assess what implementation really means to the different actors engaged in the dialogue. The kinds of action proposed earlier that the companies can take on their own (in areas such as contractual clauses with security providers) and those that the companies and NGOs can undertake together (such as consultation on risk assessment and human rights training, as well as incident reporting) can serve as an interim template to define and guide what implementation means.

The Voluntary Principles, though a substantive standard, rely on a process approach which will remain viable and credible (particularly to NGOs) only in so far as the process transcends its dialogue format and demonstrates tangible outcomes. The recommendations made earlier that the companies accept some degree of semi-formal but flexible reporting, if not informal monitoring, are intended to establish such concrete credibility. Such reporting, for example, can focus on the implementation of specific measures such as the incorporation of the Principles in contracts with security forces, the provision of training to employees and the mainstreaming of the Principles in community engagement programmes. Other aspects of implementation can be highlighted more effectively through a process-oriented approach, especially regarding factors that may vary substantially from community to community. Such an approach could rely, for example, on reporting the consultations held with host governments and local communities about the impact of security arrangements on those communities or on the implementation of risk assessments. These kinds of steps, and others that should evolve as the process gains further texture and participants, can help to reconcile the strengths and weaknesses of binding and non-binding norms. The central challenge is to bridge the gap between two poles: (a) a substantive standard linked to a continuing multi-stakeholder dialogue increasingly focused on implementation issues, though without formal reporting or enforcement mechanisms; and (b) a set of legislated or regulated binding obligations with the force of law but without regular dialogue and interaction among companies and stakeholders.

The extent to which the Voluntary Principles remain a living document and an evolving process will also help to bridge this gap between binding and non-binding norms. The conveners and participants in the process should be flexible enough to demonstrate the continuing relevance and efficacy of the principles in response to incidents and issues on the ground, as well as to legal and policy developments in the international community. They should also recognise the need, acknowledged in the Preamble to the Voluntary Principles, to revise and adapt specific provisions over time. A clear example of this need for revising and strengthening the Voluntary Principles' content is provided by the provisions on the use and transfer of company equipment. According to the Principles,

> Companies should, to the extent reasonable, monitor the use of equipment provided by the Company and to investigate properly situations in which such equipment is used in an inappropriate manner [and] equipment imports and exports should comply with all applicable laws and regulations. Companies that provide equipment to public security should take all appropriate and lawful measures to mitigate any foreseeable negative consequences, including human rights abuses and violations of international humanitarian law.

It should be noted here that most of the lawsuits brought in the US under the Alien Tort Claims Act (ATCA) against extractive companies have dealt with the provision of material or logistical support to security forces (for example, *Doe et al. v. ExxonMobil et al.* alleges ExxonMobil's provision of land-moving equipment to the Indonesian military). Greater precision in monitoring obligations and in terms such as 'all appropriate measures' would be useful to determine the degree of due diligence that companies would have to apply to avoid legal responsibilities *vis-à-vis* third parties.

The fact that a company has endorsed the Voluntary Principles and is implementing them may, at some point, be a factor to be taken into account by the court when examining a company's complicity in an alleged human rights abuse. The complicity analysis in ATCA lawsuits has, so far, dealt with the companies' actual logistical support for, or acquiescence to, alleged human rights abuses (*John Doe I v. Unocal Corp.*; *Wiwa v. Royal Dutch Petroleum Co.*):[5] a company implementing the Voluntary Principles may be able to demonstrate that it has applied a high standard of due diligence to avoid the commission of human rights abuses in its operations. However, the possibility of factoring such due diligence into a judicial decision may depend on credible company reporting of Voluntary Principles implementation efforts, together with informal NGO monitoring or possibly even formal third-party verification.

It can be expected that the Voluntary Principles will produce some collateral effects in the realm of soft law, since explicit adherence to them will create expectations about companies' behaviour. Over time, soft law norms can evolve and lead to the creation of customary norms, if a sufficient number of companies abide by the same standard of conduct with the sense that 'they are doing the right thing'. The Voluntary Principles' inclusion in referential soft law is desirable because it would accelerate their transformation into *lex mercatoria* over time. Since the Voluntary Principles urge companies to insert them as contractual clauses in their arrangements with private security forces, they have the potential of gaining legally binding status *vis-à-vis* third parties. The more the Principles are perceived as the legitimate standard, the more they will be incorporated in contractual instruments, in which case a violation of the Voluntary Principles will trigger the contractual responsibility of the non-complying party.

As practice is starting to show, insertion in contractual clauses does not need to be restricted to private law agreements with security forces. The Voluntary Principles may also become part of international investment law through their incorporation in international natural resource agreements. In fact, their incorporation into the AMDAL (social and environmental impact assessment required by Indonesia law for the BP Tannguh LNG project) has in effect transformed the Voluntary Principles into the 'Mandatory Principles' for that joint venture, since they are now annexed with the force of law to the project contract. Of course, this is still an isolated example, and many corporations remain reluctant to assume any binding commitments. Yet, in the next few years, companies can expect an intensification of international campaigns for transparency and disclosure in the extractive sector. This will affect both the disclosure and the content of international oil concessions.

Even in the likely event that the Voluntary Principles are not enshrined into legislation or treaties soon, they can be included in other soft law instruments that provide authoritative reference to companies' ethical conduct. For example, the Voluntary Principles should be included in the upcoming revision of the OECD

---

5   *John Doe I v. Unocal Corp.*, 2002 WL 31063976 (9th Cir. Cal.); *Wiwa v. Royal Dutch Petroleum Co.*, 2002 WL 319887 (S.D.N.Y.).

Guidelines for Multinational Enterprises (OECD 2000), which so far barely touch on the human rights responsibilities of companies beyond the employment arena. Other soft law instruments that would benefit substantially from inclusion of the Voluntary Principles would be the operational policies of international development banks. For example, the World Bank's Operational Policies, Procedures and Practices (2003) address environmental and social impacts of projects but not security issues. The World Bank Group could adopt minimum security standards as part of its Extractive Industries Review of its role in the oil, gas and mining sectors. If the Voluntary Principles are endorsed by the World Bank and other international development banks, they may exert substantial leverage over parties to the project (since their breach would permit the bank to call back loans) and would also act as trend-setters in international project finance (Kingsbury 1999: 323).

The Draft Norms on Responsibilities of Transnational Corporations and Other Business Enterprises with Regard to Human Rights presented by the UN Sub-Commission on the Promotion and Protection of Human Rights (see further Chapter 3 by Peter Muchlinski) state that security arrangements for transnational corporations and other business enterprises shall observe international human rights norms and the laws and professional standards of the country or countries in which they operate. The Draft Norms still have hurdles to surmount, and the legal status they will acquire if adopted is uncertain. However, if the Draft Norms become a code of conduct for companies, this reference to professional standards may pave the way for the application of the Voluntary Principles as the authoritative standard in the area of security.

19.4 Conclusion

The resistance of companies to new regulation and preference for voluntary standards should, at a minimum, challenge them to demonstrate their concrete commitment to the standards they adopt. Implementing the Voluntary Principles on Security and Human Rights gives companies the chance to set an important example of how a voluntary initiative ultimately can be implemented by a diverse group of actors operating largely outside a regulatory framework, yet in ways consistent with both international human rights norms and national laws while being incorporated into specific projects and contracts at the same time.

The Voluntary Principles will bear a special burden in the corporate responsibility and human rights communities over the next few years. They will be judged as a leading test case of whether a non-binding standard, linked to a continuing multi-stakeholder dialogue, can influence not only company policies and actions but also those of host-country governments and security forces on the ground. The Voluntary Principles can become a true hybrid standard and process: one that remains voluntary in letter and spirit, but gains a kind of mandatory dynamism which blurs the distinctions and transcends the debate between voluntary and mandatory approaches.

More significantly, the Voluntary Principles address grave situations and difficult dilemmas which sometimes have fatal consequences; they were not designed
to demonstrate the efficacy of voluntary initiatives but to prevent human rights
abuses and to save lives. If the Voluntary Principles can succeed on those grounds,
then they will have earned further standing as a model as the business and human
rights communities continue to debate voluntary versus mandatory approaches
and to define appropriate roles and responsibilities.

20
Taking responsibility for bribery
The multinational corporation's role in combating corruption

David Hess
University of Michigan Business School, USA

Thomas Dunfee
University of Pennsylvania, USA

Corruption is an under-appreciated impediment to the realisation of human rights in developing countries. While government officials profit from bribes taken from multinational corporations and others, many citizens' rights are compromised. Like any economic transaction, corruption has both a demand side and a supply side. Public officials demand bribes, and private citizens or organisations, such as businesses, supply the bribes. Any system to control corruption by attacking only one side of the transaction will surely fail. An effective anti-corruption system requires a variety of measures attacking corruption from all sides (Dunfee and Hess 2001). In this chapter, we focus on the attempts made to control the supply side.

The chapter proceeds by reviewing the impact of corruption on human rights. In the following section, we evaluate the international efforts to outlaw corruption and their effectiveness to date. Next, we discuss a corporate principles approach to controlling bribery in international business transactions and review current corporate practices. The final section looks specifically at Royal Dutch/Shell's efforts at combating corruption.

20.1 Corruption as an impediment to the realisation of human rights

A common understanding of international human rights laws and obligations is established in international treaties and declarations. The most well known of these are the Universal Declaration of Human Rights (UDHR), the International Covenant on Economic, Social and Cultural Rights (ICESCR), and the International Covenant on Civil and Political Rights (ICCPR) (Green 2001). In addition to establishing the content of substantive human rights, such agreements also place obligations on states to allow the realisation of these rights. For example, the ICESCR proclaims:

> Each State Party to the present Covenant undertakes to take steps, individually and through international assistance and co-operation, especially economic and technical, to the maximum of its available resources, with a view to achieving progressively the full realization of the rights recognized in the present Covenant by all appropriate means.

One of the greatest impediments to the realisation of rights recognised under such international agreements is corruption. Corruption's pernicious impact takes many forms. Most directly, corruption diverts critical resources in ways that personally enrich public officials, instead of being used to promote human rights. The scope of diversion can be mind-boggling. As just one example, in the 1990s, two South Korean presidents were convicted for corruptly amassing a fund of over US$900 million (Hess and Dunfee 2000). International assistance may be diverted to private hands in a gross distortion of its humanitarian purposes. Foreign aid sent to Zaire (now known as the Democratic Republic of Congo) in the 1980s and 1990s was allegedly sent to the offshore accounts of President Mobutu Sese Seko. While Seko accumulated one of the world's largest fortunes, ever-increasing numbers of his country's citizens were reduced to abject poverty (World Bank 1998; Dunfee and Hess 2001). Locally, funds intended for domestic development may be skewed towards projects where bribes can be extracted, such as construction, and away from public projects that would allow the realisation of the rights to education and health (Tanzi 1998). In addition, these construction projects can be so heavily influenced by corruption that they fail to provide the citizens with any benefit. For example, the corrupted 'bean curd' bridges of China were collapsing on completion, causing numerous deaths and injuries (Hess and Dunfee 2000).

Corruption also prevents a country from developing its economy. In addition to rights recognised under the ICCPR and the ICESCR, the United Nations adopted the Declaration on the Right to Development in 1986 (Sengupta 2002). While the right to development has been controversial in the past—the United States voted against the 1986 declaration—the Vienna Declaration at the 1993 UN World Conference on Human Rights, and similar actions at subsequent intergovernmental conferences, have established this right as an 'undeniable fact' (Sengupta 2002: 842). Included in this right is a process of development whereby the underprivileged can have their 'living standard raised and capacity to improve their position strengthened' (Sengupta 2002: 848). Although the obligations and duties of governments are not necessarily to provide the realisation of development, they must establish the conditions for individuals to realise that right (Sengupta 2002).

By engaging in corruption, governments are not creating the conditions necessary to allow its citizens to realise their right to development. In addition to the factors discussed above, corruption significantly hinders a country's economic development. A recent study found that corruption acts as a significant 'tax' on foreign direct investment and reduces such investment (Wei 2000). Due to its secrecy, corruption acts more as a distortion to the economy rather than as a simple tax. For example, allocative efficiency is likely to be distorted when country leaders accept payments to limit entry by certain firms or to grant monopolies (Shliefer and Vishny 1993). The reduction of corruption makes it more likely that economic development will not simply lead to greater income inequalities and a continued reduction of the income-earning potential of underprivileged citizens (Tanzi 1998). Instead, the benefits of economic development are more likely to be fairly distributed.

20.2 International efforts to combat corruption

The worldwide focus on combating corruption has increased tremendously in the past ten years. Most significantly, the members of the Organisation for Economic Co-operation and Development (OECD) signed the Convention on Combating Bribery of Foreign Public Officials in International Business Transactions in 1997, which entered into force in February 1999. This convention requires the signatory countries to criminalise the payment of bribes to foreign officials and to prohibit practices that allow the concealment of bribe payments (e.g. off-the-books accounts). As of October 2002, 34 countries have passed legislation ratifying the convention.[1]

The OECD Convention, apparently, has not had a major impact on multi-national firms. In 2002, Transparency International conducted a survey of executives of foreign and domestic corporations operating in 15 emerging market economies.[2] Only 19% of the respondents to this survey stated that they were either familiar with the Convention or at least knew something about it.[3] In addition, only 27% of respondents stated that the level of corruption by foreign companies of senior public officials had decreased in the past five years. The private sector's (and general public's) limited awareness of the international efforts to outlaw bribery restricts the effectiveness of these attempts.

Ending the entrenched practice of bribery will require aggressive enforcement of the new anti-bribery legal regime. Although it is too soon to know whether there

1   The 34 countries are: Argentina, Australia, Austria, Belgium, Brazil, Bulgaria, Canada, Chile, Denmark, Finland, France, Germany, Greece, Hungary, Iceland, Italy, Japan, Korea, Luxembourg, Mexico, the Netherlands, New Zealand, Norway, Poland, Portugal, the Slovak Republic, Slovenia, Spain, Sweden, Switzerland, the Czech Republic, Turkey, the United Kingdom, the United States. Source: OECD website for Fighting Bribery and Corruption, www.oecd.org/EN/home/0,,EN-home-86-3-no-no-no-,00.html (last visited 10 December 2002).

2   Those 15 countries were: Argentina, Brazil, Colombia, Hungary, India, Indonesia, Mexico, Morocco, Nigeria, the Philippines, Poland, Russia, South Africa, South Korea and Thailand.

3   Transparency International Bribe Payers Index 2002, available online at www.transparency.org (last visited 10 December 2002).

will be adequate prosecutorial effort, there is some heartening evidence of a willingness to prosecute bribe-paying companies. In Lesotho in 2002, the government prosecuted a Canadian company, Acres International Ltd, and imposed a US$3.5 million fine (Yew 2002). Acres was charged with paying US$320,000 to the engineer overseeing the Lesotho Highlands Water Project. The case has gained notoriety because it is one of the few times local authorities have attempted to prosecute the corporation paying the bribe, as they typically focus only on the official receiving the bribe. In this case, the official receiving the bribe from Acres was sentenced to 18 years in jail (Yew 2002). It is important to note that, at the time of writing, Acres was appealing its conviction.

While the Acres case is encouraging, enforcement of anti-corruption laws will require a significant amount of resources by various countries. It is yet to be seen how many countries are willing and able to expend these resources. In addition, many think that corrupt practices will simply adapt around these laws and continue to thrive (Berenbeim 2000). For example, in Transparency International's index of countries whose corporations are perceived as most likely to pay bribes, the United States (where the Foreign Corrupt Practices Act has been in place since 1977) ranked 13th out of 21 countries in a ranking from least likely to pay bribes to the most likely. This placed the US behind such countries as Canada, the UK and Australia.

To eradicate corruption, a criminal law approach by itself is not likely to work. Instead, the government must work with the private sector and civil society. Only with various initiatives attacking corruption from different angles will it be possible to reach a 'tipping point', after which we will see a continuous and increasing decline in corruption (Dunfee and Hess 2001). The remainder of this chapter focuses on the initiatives of the private sector.

20.3 A corporate principles approach to combating corruption

Corporations know where they are paying their bribes, or, at a minimum, know where they are at the greatest risk of their agents paying bribes. By this fact alone, the private sector is a crucial element in ending corruption. Corporations must be able to stand up to demands for bribes and must also reward employees for doing so. To do this, corporations need assurances that their competitors are behaving in the same manner.

Two recent initiatives to achieve this goal are the C² Principles (Combating Corruption) adopted by the Caux Round Table (see Box 20.1) and the Business Principles for Countering Bribery published jointly by Social Accountability International and Transparency International. The Business Principles consists of two simple principles: namely, 'The enterprise shall prohibit bribery in any form whether direct or indirect' and 'The enterprise shall commit to implementation of a Programme to counter bribery'. These principles are accompanied by a list of areas a company's anti-corruption programme should cover and the requirements

C² Principles

1. To disclose publicly and make widely known its endorsement of the C² Principles

2. To establish a clearly articulated written policy prohibiting any of the firm's employees from paying or receiving bribes or 'kickbacks'

3. To implement the policy with due care and take appropriate disciplinary action against any employee discovered to have made payments in violation of the policy

4. To provide training for employees to carry out the policy, and to provide continuing support, such as help-lines, to assist employees to act in compliance with the firm's policy

5. To record all transactions fully and fairly, in accordance with clearly stated record-keeping procedures and accounting controls, and conduct internal audits to assure no improper payments are made

6. To report annually on the firm's bribery and corruption policy, along with a description of the firm's experiences implementing and enforcing the policy

7. To have the annual report in Principle 6 audited either by an independent financial auditor or an independent social auditor, or both

8. To require all agents of the firm to affirm that they have neither made nor will make any improper payments in any business venture or contract to which the firm is a party

9. To require all suppliers of the firm to affirm that they have neither made nor will make any improper payments in any business venture or contract to which the firm is a party

10. To establish a monitoring and auditing system to detect any improper payments made by the firm's employees and agents

11. To report publicly any solicitations for payments, or report privately to a monitoring organisation or a social auditor

12. To establish a system to allow any employee or agent of the firm to report any improper payment without fear of retribution for their disclosures

Box 20.1 C² Principles

for implementing the programme. While the C² Principles require a company to publicly adopt the principles, the Business Principles do not, as they are meant only for purposes of creating a 'starting point' for companies and establishing benchmarks for best practices.

To simplify matters, we have classified the C² Principles into the basic themes of policies, procedures and publication (Hess and Dunfee 2000). Principles 1–4 establish required policies, Principles 5, 8, 9, 10 and 12 set forth necessary procedures, while Principles 1, 6, 7 and 11 set forth required disclosures that the organisation should publish or otherwise make known. In general, these themes also apply to the anti-corruption programme recommendations of the Business Principles.

The theme of policies refers to the establishment of an anti-bribery policy for the company. This includes establishing a code of conduct that clearly articulates a prohibition on bribery. Currently, many companies address the issue of bribery in their codes of conduct, but the depth of treatment the topic receives can vary greatly from company to company. One reason for this disparity in treatment is the lack of a universal agreement on what constitutes corruption (Gordon and Miyake 2001) owing to the absence of a dialogue on the topic. For example, in the year of Transparency International's founding (1993), few governments would even openly discuss the issues of bribery and corruption (Boswell 1999). Now, with the recent OECD convention and other inter-governmental initiatives, a consensus is developing to provide companies with guidance.

Two recent studies on the treatment of bribery in multinational corporations' codes of conduct provide insight into extant practices. Gordon and Miyake (2001) considered 118 codes issued by individual firms and 128 codes issued by industry associations and NGOs, while Berenbeim (2000) surveyed companies on their anti-corruption practices and received 151 responses from corporations headquartered all over the world. In these studies, while corporations appear to find it easy to provide a general definition of corruption, they find it significantly more difficult to define a workable standard to guide employees (Gordon and Miyake 2001). Among the difficulties in providing a working definition of bribery are: how to deal with such matters as gifts and entertainment; facilitation payments (small payments to lower-level public officials to encourage them to perform their duties more quickly, such as providing a licence to conduct business); and how to operate in different cultural environments. For example, for gifts, Gordon and Miyake (2001) find that some companies establish specific monetary limits, others direct their employees to follow local law, and others simply leave discretion to the employee (e.g. 'not excessive'). In response to these difficulties, many codes provide only a general prohibition on bribery, without further defining it or providing guidance to the company's employees. A 1995 study of 109 US companies found that, while 36% of the companies had anti-bribery provisions, only 14% defined 'grease' payments (Spalding and Reinstein 1995).

The legal environment of a company also affects its choice of definitions. Berenbeim (2000) found that, owing to the Foreign Corrupt Practices Act (FCPA), US companies are more likely to provide a detailed definition of bribery based on the statute. Non-US companies, on the other hand, are more likely to use only general terms. Presumably, as the OECD Convention gains more recognition, it will influence non-US corporations' definitions of bribery for their employees.

To ensure that employees comply with these policies, the next theme—procedures—is required. The necessary procedures include appropriate accounting and auditing processes, as well as procedures to ensure that all agents employed by the firm are aware of the firm's anti-bribery policies and that management uses due diligence when selecting these agents (e.g. avoid the hiring of agents with a reputation for paying bribes). Finally, procedures must be in place to allow employees to report any violations of the company's policy.

Corporations seeking to reduce corruption recognise the importance of these procedures. Gordon and Miyake (2001) found that company codes mentioning bribery are twice as likely to discuss issues of record-keeping, whistle-blowing and internal monitoring than company codes that do not mention bribery. These basic compliance measures were found to be similar to other financial control practices, thus allowing managers to use existing knowledge to implement anti-bribery procedures (Gordon and Miyake 2001). Such firms were also commonly seen to require local managers to certify that they have complied with the corporation's policies. In addition, Berenbeim's (2000) study found that companies with more effective anti-corruption programmes often require joint-venture partners and agents to explicitly accept compliance with their corporate anti-bribery policies. These companies recognised a duty to prevent corruption and not to pass that obligation on to another actor in the channel of distribution.

Unfortunately, many of these practices are not currently widespread. For example, Spalding and Reinstein's (1995) study of US corporations found that, while 93% of the companies had codes of ethics, only 20% monitored compliance with the code and only 35% had compliance with the code certified annually by management. With respect to the FCPA, only 26% of companies had their compliance efforts independently audited and only 11% reported FCPA compliance to the board's audit committee. Many view these controls as necessary because it is common in FCPA violations for management to override internal accounting controls (Spalding and Reinstein 1995).

One of the most valued procedures in the fight against corruption is a whistle-blowing programme. These programmes encourage employees to report violations of the company's policies and to ask questions about anti-bribery rules without fear of punishment. To achieve these goals, company programmes typically allow the anonymous reporting of violations. While whistle-blowing has been a valuable tool for US companies, it faces significant challenges in other parts of the world. Berenbeim (2000) reports a resistance to whistle-blowing in Western Europe. Some suggest that this is due to concern about returning to an 'informer society'. Likewise, Husted (2002) argues that whistle-blowing works well in countries with cultures like the US, but will not work as well in Latin American cultures. The specific cultural factors that Husted considers are individualism/collectivism and power–distance relationships. In Latin America, Husted argues, the cultures are more collectivist and leaders are accorded more power compared with the US. These factors work against whistle-blowing, as trust in leadership will only be undermined by extreme cases of abuse of power and members of society will work to protect the in-group, rather than follow an obligation to society in general.

On the other hand, others argue that an appreciation and acceptance of whistle-blowing can become an effective tool against corruption throughout the world if implemented appropriately (Berenbeim 2000). The key is for management to understand the potential cultural barriers to effective implementation and to develop sound policies to address those concerns. Creating an organisational culture accepting of whistle-blowing is one of the challenges facing global business in establishing an effective anti-corruption culture.

The final theme is publication, which is a requirement of disclosure. Included in this theme are a public commitment to upholding the principles and the disclosure of company efforts in implementing an anti-corruption programme. This theme works to control both the supply of corruption and the demand. To reduce the demand side of bribery, Principle 11 of the C^2 Principles requires the disclosure of bribe solicitations. This is consistent with the recent Publish What You Pay initiative, which has gained the support of numerous NGOs and UK Prime Minister,

Tony Blair.[4] Under this initiative, oil, gas and mining companies are encouraged to disclose all payments made to developing-country governments (including taxes, fees and royalties). Through this disclosure, citizens and other interested parties can better determine where these payments are going and work to increase government accountability. For example, in Angola, some estimate that US$1 billion of oil payments to the government goes missing every year. At the same time, the country receives US$200 million annually in foreign aid to help reduce hunger (Harden 2002).

On the supply side, publication works to establish best practices for combating corruption. By publishing a detailed code of conduct for operations in a certain country, a company provides assistance to its employees in resisting bribery. With disclosure, however, such codes can also assist other companies in combating corruption. For example, managers attempting to promote non-discrimination in apartheid South Africa in the 1980s stated that the disclosure of company practices under the Sullivan Principles allowed them to better implement their own policies (Hess and Dunfee 2000). In other words, these managers were not forced to reinvent the wheel, but could build on the experiences of others. In addition, disclosure provides information to the public, which encourages a dialogue to develop on appropriate norms of behaviour (Dunfee and Hess 2001).

Overall, the adoption of anti-corruption principles works to push all corporations to develop anti-corruption cultures. Through a principles approach, corporations do not have to worry that they will be acting alone in the fight against corruption. Those corporations that are serious in their attempts to reduce bribe payments should start with industry-wide initiatives to adopt the principles. An industry-based strategy will ensure that a corporation's competitors are playing by the same rules, as any firms attempting to free-ride on the 'no bribes' policies of others should be easily identifiable (Hess and Dunfee 2000). Industry-based initiatives are also of value because the publication aspect furthers the transfer of knowledge on fighting corruption. This sharing of experiences allows best practices to emerge, which is to the benefit of all in the industry. In addition to pressure from industry associations, NGOs and other parties can also play a significant role. For example, some argue that the World Bank could have considerable influence by requiring all firms bidding on World Bank-financed contracts to have an appropriate code of conduct (Dunfee and Hess 2001).

The C^2 Principles and the Business Principles both push companies to go beyond simply having a compliance culture with respect to corruption and towards a culture of integrity. Key to establishing such a culture is the active involvement of senior management, coupled with an emphasis on communicating the importance of the programme to all employees (Paine 1994; Berenbeim 2000). For example, management must acknowledge and actively reassure employees that lost business may be the consequence of following an anti-bribery policy, but employees will only be punished for not following the policy. That is, any incentives must reward resisting corruption and not obtaining a contract at any cost.

There are of course barriers to the adoption and effective implementation of anti-corruption principles. Corruption and bribery may exist at any point in the channel of distribution of a good. Corporations must not pass their anti-corrup-

4   See www.publishwhatyoupay.org (last visited 2 December 2002).

tion obligations on to another actor, but instead ensure that their suppliers, agents and partners are all adhering to a 'no bribes' policy (see Principle 9 of the C² Principles). These responsibilities will be difficult to implement for complex global enterprises, but they are not unlike the challenges facing SA 8000-certified companies to ensure that their suppliers and subcontractors are meeting appropriate labour standards. Other barriers include the short-term costs of refusing contracts that require a bribe payment. While the long-term benefits of operating in a corruption-free environment will outweigh these costs, the short-term costs may be significant when less scrupulous companies continue to supply bribes. To lessen these free-rider problems, we encourage industry associations to push all their members to adopt anti-corruption principles and to monitor each other. In addition to the strong interests of corporations in ensuring that their competitors are operating in a bribe-free manner, other stakeholders also have a strong interest in achieving this goal. These pressures are discussed in the following section.

20.4 Stakeholder pressures and anti-corruption principles

Key corporate stakeholder groups should be in support of the adoption of anti-corruption principles. Investors will be behind anti-corruption initiatives because bribe payments reduce profits and skew competition (making it more difficult for shareholders to value their investments). In addition to grand corruption,[5] which the World Bank estimates at 5% of all foreign direct investments into corrupt countries (Walsh 1998), even facilitation payments can significantly reduce efficiency and lower profits. While facilitation payments are often referred to as 'grease' or 'speed' payments, they actually encourage government officials to reduce the speed of bureaucracy in order to extract more bribes (Tanzi 1998). The most recent empirical evidence finds that these payments force managers to spend more time with government officials, not less (Kaufman and Wei 2001).

Other aspects of paying bribes that hurt investors include civil and criminal fines. While the risk of punishment has not been high in the past, a greater push from countries adopting the OECD Convention may encourage home-country enforcement. Furthermore, the recent case of Acres International in Angola suggests that developing countries may also start prosecuting multinational firms.

In addition to investors, consumers may also push for corporations to adopt anti-corruption principles. Similar to the consumer backlash against companies employing sweatshop labour, consumers may place pressure on companies that continue to engage in corrupt practices. With a greater public awareness of the connection between corruption and human rights problems, a company that is prosecuted for bribery, or fails to demonstrate that it has an effective anti-

---

5 Grand corruption involves significant bribes to high-ranking public officials to encourage them to take actions that they were not likely to have done without the bribe payment.

corruption programme, may suffer significant damage to its reputation in the marketplace. In addition to the efforts of NGOs such as Transparency International, a corporate principles approach can greatly assist in raising that public awareness. While we cannot accurately forecast the negative impact of a reputation for being a bribe payer on a firm's performance in the market, we are optimistic that the impact of such a reputation will only increase as the public's understanding of corruption and its harmful effects continues to improve.

Recent changes in the social reporting guidelines issued by the Global Reporting Initiative (GRI) provide evidence of the growing importance of the issue of corruption among interested stakeholders. Established in 1997, the GRI has become one of the most influential initiatives in terms of establishing standards for organisations to measure and publicly report their economic, environmental and social performance.[6] As part of its mission, the GRI promulgates a set of guidelines on social reporting that is updated to reflect the latest experience of corporations and the comments of interested parties. In the most recent set of guidelines (issued in 2002), the GRI added a social performance indicator for bribery and corruption. Based on the input of its stakeholders, the GRI recognised the importance of this issue and listed it alongside performance indicators for such issues as child labour, discrimination, and customer health and safety (GRI 2002).

20.5 The anti-corruption efforts of Shell

The Royal Dutch/Shell corporation is often praised for its 'no bribes' policy. Shell is an oil, gas and chemical company operating in over 100 countries. In response to various public relations crises in the mid-1990s (including the controversy surrounding the disposal of the Brent Spar and the execution of Ken Saro-Wiwa in Nigeria), Shell recommitted itself to operating under a set of business principles of appropriate behaviour and to greater transparency in its actions. Through this recommitment, Shell established its 'no bribes' policy. This policy clearly states that bribery will not be tolerated and that employees engaging in corruption will have their employment terminated and will, if possible, be prosecuted. To implement this policy, Shell developed a programme based in part on its study of best practices at 15 multinational corporations. Overall, Shell's anti-corruption programme (see Box 20.2) is based on a set of practices similar to the C^2 Principles.

As part of this effort, Shell published its policies on bribery in a booklet entitled *Dealing with Bribery and Corruption: A Management Primer.*[7] This document provides its employees with an understanding of what constitutes bribery and distinguishes bribery from facilitation payments and gifts. For example, to help employees distinguish between a bribe and a gift, the *Management Primer* notes that gifts can be given directly and openly, while bribes must be given in secret and often

6 For further information about the Global Reporting Initiative, see www.globalreporting.org (last visited 24 January 2003).
7 Available online at www.shell.com (last visited 9 December 2002).

Shell's Policies and Procedures

1.	Senior management commitment	● Set the ethical tone 'at the top'
2.	Written policies	● Company-wide policies should be supplemented by codes for local conditions
3.	Internal controls and record-keeping	● Including an 'ethics ledger' of requested facilitation payments
4.	Auditing	● Ensure that employees and third parties are complying with the 'no bribes' objectives
5.	Communication channels	● Hotlines to report corruption problems and assurances that employees will not suffer for reporting problems or losing business due to adherence to integrity principles
6.	Accountability	● Require managers to certify compliance with the principles
7.	Training	● Include extra training for employees in positions of high risk for corruption
8.	Third-party checks	● Due diligence processes for selecting and continuing relationships with suppliers and contractors
9.	Investigations	● Investigate allegations of bribery

Box 20.2 Shell's Policies and Procedures

Source: Royal Dutch/Shell 1999

through intermediaries. With respect to facilitation payments, Shell does not condone them, but also does not place an absolute prohibition on them. Instead, it instructs the individual Shell companies to address these matters in their local business guidelines for employees ('with the aim of eliminating it') and at all times to obey local law. In recognition of the difficulty of establishing bright line rules in such areas of bribery, Shell provides short case studies of actual situations from the company's experience to assist employees in their training.

Company compliance with the policies is monitored by the Audit Committee and Social Responsibility Committee, which oversees the implementation of Shell's business principles and control mechanisms. One such control procedure is the letter of representation. A letter of representation is a formal document signed by the chief executive officer and chief financial officer of that country's company and sent to the Shell Group's comptroller. In the document, these officers state that all transactions have been recorded properly and that no bribes have been paid. In situations where facilitation payments have been made or bribes discovered, these payments are included in the document and the officers are required to provide follow-up reports on how they have attempted to deal with the problem.

Shell also publishes its efforts. Each year, Shell distributes a report entitled *People, Planet and Profits*, which details its performance on environmental and social matters. KPMG and PricewaterhouseCoopers verify components of this report. Included in *People, Planet and Profits* reports are details of the bribery solicitations received or offered by the company's employees for the year. In 2001, Shell reported that its employees either solicited bribers or were offered bribes in 13 situations (with a total estimated financial value of US$26,000), up from only four cases in 2000 (total estimated financial value of US$89,000). Shell also reported that employees had refused bribes in nine cases, employees were dismissed in three cases, and one case was not yet settled. In addition, Shell reported two cases where non-employee agents offered or solicited bribes. The accuracy of these numbers can be challenged, however, as they do not reflect allegations of corruption that the company could not prove, and, of course, instances that were not detected or reported. Overall, though, Shell has demonstrated a willingness to combat corruption and to begin the process of obtaining the experience necessary to remove all forms of bribery in its business transactions throughout the world.

20.6 Conclusion

Reducing corruption is a win–win situation in that it is simultaneously pro-business and pro-human rights. The reduction of corruption reduces barriers to investment in foreign countries, allows a more efficient use of capital and promotes economic growth. This provides a more conducive environment for business while, at the same time, improving the human rights conditions in developing countries, including the right to development. To attain these benefits, corporations must play a vital role in ending corruption. As indicated in our review of corporate codes of conduct, many corporations are demonstrating a willingness to get out of a cycle of corruption. These companies are experimenting with policies and procedures to ensure that corruption does not exist at any point along the chain of distribution of their goods or services. While many companies' efforts may be seen as potentially ineffective, best practices are emerging. In addition to developing successful anti-corruption programmes, a key challenge facing these companies is reining in those competitors that persist in supplying bribes. To achieve all these goals, adopting anti-corruption principles is an important first step.

Taking the business and human rights agenda to the limit?
The Body Shop and Amnesty International 'Make Your Mark' campaign

Heike Fabig*
University of Sussex, UK

Richard Boele*
Australian Institute of Corporate Citizenship, Australia

21.1 NGO pressure and business change

As many of the case studies discussed in this book testify, business activities can result in a range of human rights problems and challenges. There is considerable pressure by civil society, notably through non-governmental organisations (NGOs), on transnational corporations (TNCs) to improve their human rights track record (Fabig and Boele 1999; Starr 2000). The emergence of TNCs as a direct target of NGO pressure is an important new reality (Vander Stichele and Pennartz 1996; Bray 1997). Reacting to both the opportunities and the threats of globalisation, the world of NGOs has undergone some significant institutional changes. New NGOs with interdisciplinary mission statements (such as Global Witness and Project Underground) have been created which integrate environmental and human rights perspectives to sustainable development, and which explicitly focus on the role of TNCs at that intersection. Some of these new NGOs specifically target the corporate world—as a whole, on a specific sector or industry basis, or individual businesses. Existing NGOs have diversified and formed new alliances, thus transcending old boundaries set by issues and geography. Examples of diversification and new alliances include Friends of the Earth and Greenpeace, which have actively campaigned against businesses, especially resource-extraction companies.

---

* Much of the information used in this chapter stems from the authors' personal knowledge gained via participatory observation and active immersion in The Body Shop and the Make Your Mark campaign.

Human Rights Watch (HRW) took the early lead in this area by issuing the first report on the human rights record of a transnational company—interestingly, Enron (see HRW 1999a, 1999b). Amnesty International UK established a Business Group,[1] which issued *Human Rights Guidelines for Companies* (Amnesty International UK 1998) and a number of corporate social responsibility-related reports (Avery 2000; Frankental and House 2000). UK development NGOs such as Oxfam and Christian Aid have also directly tackled the behaviour of corporations in areas at the intersection of development, environment and human rights (Christian Aid 1996; O'Reilly and Tickell 1999).

As civil society organisations have identified the increasing importance of business as political actors and targets, corporations are coming to terms with the increasing power of NGOs (Johnston 1997; *Financial Times* 1999). This has prompted a variety of reactions by companies ranging from dismissive (such as De Beers's initial reaction to the issue of 'conflict diamonds') to proactive (such as Shell's change in business principles to include specifically a reference to the Universal Declaration of Human Rights after the Ogoni crisis [Shell International 1998]).

There has always been an element of the business world that has endeavoured to 'use the masters' tools' to bring down the campaigners' house. The sophisticated techniques used by the conservative business world to reshape public opinion—revoking gains made by the environmental movement, and turning politicians and the public against increased environmental regulation—have received much attention (see, for example, Chatterjee and Finger 1994; Burton 1995; Rowell 1996; Greer and Kenny 1996; Welford 1997; Beder 1997). Despite these corporate attempts to counter the NGO pressure for more environmentally and socially responsible business practice, some companies have read the writing on the wall and reacted in a more positive, receptive and proactive manner. They responded by making public statements in support of human rights and taking internal steps to train and sensitise employees to the issue—for example, the various voluntary codes of the textile industry addressing child labour (for an overview, see Schoenberger 2000). The Body Shop, the company that is the focus of this chapter, has made corporate responsibility and human rights core to its corporate identity. In its mission statement, the company defines its reason for being as: '[t]o dedicate our business to the pursuit of social and environmental change' (BSI 1995).

Possibly the two more prominent new management tools of our times, which have had a weighty influence in the corporate responsibility debate so far, have been stakeholder management (see Freeman 1984; Wheeler and Sillanpää 1997; Harrison and St John 1998) and the concept of triple-bottom-line auditing and reporting (see Elkington 1997). As part of demonstrating their transparency to stakeholders, companies have opened up dialogue with their traditional enemies and engaged NGOs in a debate to address these new social and environmental challenges. Until relatively recently in corporate history,[2] business was not pre-

---

1 The Amnesty International UK Business Group was initially chaired by a former Shell director (Sir Geoffrey Chandler, who has also contributed to this book) and, more recently, a former BP executive (Christopher Marsden).
2 See Vogel's study of corporate accountability movements in the United States from the 1950s to the late 1970s, particularly the black civil rights movement and the anti-Vietnam War movement.

pared to 'give in' to NGO demands, fearing loss of power and legitimacy (Vogel 1978: 30-35, 71-89). This attitude has changed significantly. In a radical shift, many scholars and business leaders now reason that it can be in companies' long-term economic interests to cede some power and legitimacy to NGOs that can confer legitimacy on their operations (Murphy and Bendell 1997; Elkington 1997; Bendell 2000).

Some dialogues between business and civil society have progressed beyond the level of basic communications to forge partnerships (Fabig and Boele 1999). NGOs entering such partnerships aim to reward good business practice with an endorsement or active co-operation. They encourage the idea of the consumer's 'market vote' that influences the corporate world to be more socially and environmentally responsible. In some instances, NGOs and companies may get together on product collaboration or to establish informal codes of conduct or stewardship regimes. This has been most visible on the environmental front where companies have worked with non-commercial organisations to help solve a business problem, often after a period of prolonged action from pressure groups (see Murphy and Bendell 1997; Bendell 2000). This increasing dialogue between civil society and the corporate world is a particularly interesting phenomenon of the current corporate responsibility debate (Murphy and Bendell 1997; Heap 1998, 2000; Bendell 2000). If planned and implemented carefully, such relationships can offer both actors useful tools to discuss and promote global corporate responsibility and sustainable development. There are a small number of outstanding cases of corporate community engagement, with partnerships focused on capacity-building and power-sharing at the core of their success (for some examples, see Murphy and Bendell 1997; Fabig and Boele 2003). In this chapter, we take a closer look at one such radical partnership approach, that of corporate lobbying for social change. We will illustrate this process by examining the 1998 joint human rights campaign between The Body Shop and Amnesty International.

21.2 Background to Amnesty International, The Body Shop and corporate campaigning

Founded in the UK in 1961, Amnesty International (AI) is the world's largest membership-based human rights organisation with over a million members in over a hundred countries. AI has a governance structure elected by its members and a number of paid professional staff implementing the organisation's democratically decided policy. These staff work at the London-based International Secretariat (known as the IS), or in country-based sections. Each of these sections holds a certain level of independence within the boundaries of the AI mandate and the organisation's policies.

The Body Shop, a worldwide retail chain of skin and hair care products, reflects a similar power relationship between the corporate headquarters (on the English south coast) and its national and international companies. BSI owns operations in the UK, the US, France, Germany and Singapore; the remaining outlets are independently owned and operated as franchises. They, too, manage a careful balance between their independence and policies set by the company's head office, known as The Body Shop International or BSI. The company was established in the 1970s with the opening of one small shop in the UK. By 1998 the company had over 1,400 shops in 47 markets (as The Body Shop calls the countries in which it retails) (BSI 2001) and an estimated 86 million-plus customers visiting its stores worldwide (BSI 1999b).

The Body Shop sees its approach to ethical business on three levels: first, through compliance to wider corporate responsibility (CR) issues such as fair trade, community involvement, and reducing and recycling packaging; second, through public disclosure via dialogue and discussion with the company's stakeholders, via social and environmental audits; and, third, through corporate campaigning (BSI 2001: 5). The company sees its third goal in terms of 'play[ing] an active part in campaigning for positive change in the way business operates, with the ultimate aim of making a positive social and environmental impact on the world at large' (BSI 2001: 5).

Corporate campaigning is, unlike corporate giving or corporate community relations and investment, still a relatively rare phenomenon in the CR discourse and practice. The Body Shop has campaigned with NGOs via its stores since the 1980s, first on environmental and animal rights issues and later on human rights (Roddick 1991). The Co-operative Bank in the UK teamed up with NGOs and placed a number of advertisements in UK newspapers as part of its campaign against the production and use of land mines (Williams 1999). In Australia, the wine-maker Southcorp campaigned with the Australian Conservation Foundation on salinity (Southcorp 2003). In North America, Liz Claiborne campaigned on the issue of domestic violence in the US (Liz Claiborne 2002), while Avon and the fashion industry have been involved in raising awareness around breast cancer (Avon 2000).[3]

Many, including those NGOs that need to decide whether to engage with a commercial enterprise in a campaign, question the motivation and performance of corporate campaigns such as those undertaken by The Body Shop. Why indeed does a company producing shampoo and body lotion engage in NGO-style politics through its customers? The Body Shop has made its corporate responsibility policies and practices a fundamental part of its identity and customer appeal. The company designed many of its products and based its image on socially and environmentally responsible business concepts: ideals of sustainable business, green consumerism and market-based environmentalism that began to emerge forcefully at the time of the company's conception (Fabig 2002). While there have been a number of criticisms made of the company's motivation and performance (Survival International 1992, 1993; Entine 1994, 1995)—and indeed the company has acknowledged difficulties and mistakes and addressed some criticisms (BSI 1996b, 1996c, 1997c)—the company is generally seen as a 'good' corporate citizen and features in a number of socially responsible investment portfolios. Although The Body Shop's brand is based around values, the company's 1995 audit found from UK focus groups that most people *did* '*not* shop in The Body Shop because of

3 See also 'Fashion Targets Breast Cancer', http://fashiontargetsbreastcancer.com, last accessed 17 September 2002.

the company's values and beliefs . . . Nevertheless, the company's values are respected and seen as largely genuine' (BSI 1996a: 69 [our emphasis]).

While this chapter does not allow us to delve too deeply into the question of the motivation for corporations to engage in corporate campaigns, the decision to campaign, and indeed The Body Shop's 'ethical business' philosophy as such, must be seen in the context of the personality of the company founders, Anita and Gordon Roddick, and what they consider good business sense (see Roddick 1991, 1997, 2000). Emphasising personal and corporate 'differentness' is a point of pride for both Anita Roddick and her company, especially in the corporate offices. The company particularly prides itself on its almost NGO-style company culture and wants to be seen not so much as a different type of business but a 'business–NGO hybrid' (Roddick 2000). As such, The Body Shop may well be the only company that could conceive to work in such close partnership with Amnesty International. Furthermore, The Body Shop was possibly the only transnational company that Amnesty International could imagine collaborating with to the extent that it did.

The Body Shop is probably also unique because, from 1995 onwards, the company had a full-time human rights campaigner as a permanent member of staff. The position was created in global public affairs, the department from which the company's campaigns were run. In 1998, this small department included a general manager, two other campaigners (one on animal rights and the other on women's issues), a researcher and some support staff. In essence, it operated as a small NGO within BSI, functioning both as a resource for the company in the core issue areas and as an internal advocate for each area.

21.3 The 'Make Your Mark' campaign

21.3.1 Campaign history

'Make Your Mark' was The Body Shop's third campaign with Amnesty International in ten years. In 1988 a joint campaign marked the 40th anniversary of the Universal Declaration of Human Rights (UDHR) and in 1991 it was the 30th anniversary of Amnesty's founding. Make Your Mark is of particular interest because of its scale: it became The Body Shop's largest human rights campaign with a presence in 34 countries (BSI 1999a). Indeed, it may well be the largest corporate–NGO collaborative campaign in support of human rights ever conducted. Over three million of The Body Shop's customers were engaged in support of human rights defenders. Probably its most significant achievement was raising awareness of human rights and the work of human rights defenders in the minds of people who may not have otherwise encountered human rights issues.

During 1995 and 1996, a large part of The Body Shop's campaigning resources were committed to campaigning in support of the Ogoni people's environmental and human rights (Fabig 1999, 2002).[4] In mid-1996, the idea for a major human

4   The Ogoni people are a small ethnic group living in the oil rich Niger Delta. Their

rights campaign was mooted. It was informally introduced to the company at the international franchisee meeting in September 1996 (BSI 1996d). Indeed, the entire approval process for the campaign was informal. It started with the campaigns manager for human rights seeking approval for the campaign from his general manager. All influential members of senior management and the board were consulted to ensure that they were behind the direction of the campaign and in order to identify how the campaign could support their aspect of the business. It was generally understood within the company that it would run a major campaign each year, and the UDHR's 50th anniversary became the campaign for 1998. No formal decision was ever taken by the board or the executive to run the Make Your Mark campaign.

While no formal process existed for campaign approvals, no campaign could succeed without the personal approval and enthusiasm of Anita Roddick. There were no initial problems in gaining her approval owing to her strong personal commitment to human rights as had been demonstrated by her support for Human Rights Watch, the previous Amnesty campaigns and the Ogoni campaign (Fabig 1999, 2002).

The next step was to secure Amnesty's commitment. A meeting was arranged in April 1997 with the then Secretary-General of Amnesty International, Pierre Sané, as an essential step to forge a personal connection, vital for Anita to 'get excited' and firmly commit the company to the campaign. Considerable discussions were held before this meeting between The Body Shop's human rights campaigns manager (Richard Boele) and the campaigns programme director at the Amnesty IS (Robbie Marsland). They were, in practice, the providers of direction to the partnership, agreeing how they would brief their respective organisational heads so that the meeting went as smoothly as possible. The meeting was a success with an in-principle agreement that the two organisations would work with each other on a joint campaign. Marsland and Boele were now the core of the partnership between two global organisations. Nearly all communications at the international level went through them. While there was some exchange of letters between Anita Roddick and Pierre Sané, it was left to the two campaigners from their respective organisations to guide, negotiate and drive the partnership.

Having thus decided to hold a UDHR campaign in partnership with Amnesty International, The Body Shop initiated its Make Your Mark campaign and had to find a way to plug it into Amnesty's planned campaign. The initial challenge was that Amnesty's plans for 1998 were already well advanced. The focus for Amnesty was to be collecting signatures in support of the UDHR (the campaign was later called 'Get Up Sign Up'). Its secondary focus was to highlight the work of those human rights activists who embody the rights contained in the UDHR. This aspect

struggle for environmental and social justice illustrates well the formation of new NGO alliances mentioned. As the Nigerian government and Northern-based transnational oil companies enriched themselves on the abundant natural resources and oil reserves, the Ogoni people faced poverty, pollution and environmental degradation as well as repression by the then military dictatorship in Nigeria. When they took their struggle against the oil companies to the international community in 1993, it not only outlined the interconnections between development, environment and human rights, but also demonstrated the responsibilities of TNCs in these three areas (Boele *et al.* 2001a, 2001b).

of the campaign was called 'Defend the Defenders'. Ideally for Amnesty, The Body Shop would join in the central part of the campaign and put its resources into also collecting signatures. However, within The Body Shop this was seen as too traditional a campaign action that would not work for the company as it would fail to intrigue or excite customers, who were used to the company offering engaging ways of connecting with an issue through in-store actions. Thus, the company decided that the second aim, Defend the Defenders, was a more appropriate aspect it could support with a joint campaign.

The Body Shop felt a campaign around individual human rights defenders—real people with personal stories—allowed customers to connect with human rights in a way a petition could never achieve. It was also an opportunity to draw a link with the individual-based campaigning that was the focus of The Body Shop's previous Ogoni campaign (Fabig 1999, 2002). To further individualise people's commitment to human rights, the company preferred to collect customer's thumbprints rather than signatures. This was the first dilemma for Amnesty. Its major campaign partner chose not to support its primary campaign; rather, it had chosen to focus on the secondary campaign. A compromise was found: in small print above where customers thought they were leaving their thumbprints in support of a particular human rights defender it said they were also expressing their support for the UDHR. As such, each thumbprint collected by The Body Shop served two purposes: to support a defender and to 'sign up' to the UDHR (BSI 1997a, 1997b).

The Body Shop made a selection from the large list of human rights defenders that Amnesty aimed to profile during 1998. The selection had a deliberate bias towards young women defenders to reflect The Body Shop's customer profile. At the company's 1997 international head franchisee meeting, a Human Rights Defenders Case Book prepared by global public affairs in conjunction with Amnesty researchers was handed out and The Body Shops in the various markets were invited to pick a defender to support in their country that offered them the best opportunity to campaign in their context. Amnesty expressed concern that this could result in one or a small group of defenders receiving more attention than others—as indeed it did. Yet for The Body Shop it was critical that the markets had ownership of the campaign. The majority of the 32 participating markets chose Ngawang Sangdrol, a young Tibetan nun who had spent most of her life in prison. Preparations for the campaign continued from the end of 1997 until its launch in May 1998. Two head office briefings were provided by BSI to the markets (BSI 1997a, 1997b). These provided the rationale and strategy of the campaign and offered the products and services available from head office to support the campaign. They included a range of materials such as action stations, postcards, T-shirts and a list of all the Amnesty sections in The Body Shop markets and their key contacts.

Thus, while an agreement had been made between The Body Shop International and the International Secretariat of Amnesty International, both parties' local constituents were free to choose to participate in the joint campaign. Just as each market of The Body Shop chose to participate and chose a defender, each Amnesty International Section still had to agree to campaign with The Body Shop in its country. Putting the agreement into practice raised a number of challenges in particular countries (discussed further below). Some of these experiences provide interesting illustrations of the difficulties of campaigning in partnership globally, especially the acceptability and practicalities of a worldwide partnership between a corporate actor and an NGO.

The Make Your Mark campaign was launched by His Holiness The Dalai Lama and Amnesty International Head of Campaigns, Samuel Zan Akologo, in May 1998 in Atlanta, and ended with a series of events in Paris on 10 December 1998 including The Body Shop-sponsored Amnesty International Human Rights Concert (BSI 1999a). It is of interest to note that securing the presence of the Dalai Lama at the launch was a difficult task as his office was nervous about appearing to endorse a corporation. There had been considerable debate about His Holiness appearing to endorse any company after his picture had appeared in 'Think Different' Apple computer advertisements in 1997. There were perhaps four factors influencing the Dalai Lama's agreement to launch a campaign with a company. First, The Body Shop had Amnesty International as a partner, a human rights organisation with an impeccable reputation. Second, Ngawang Sangdrol received enormous support from the campaign. Third, the Dalai Lama was being asked to endorse a human rights campaign and not a product. Finally, The Body Shop's human rights campaigner's own personal relationship with the Tibetan cause may have contributed to overcoming any reservations.

Equally, there were defenders who did not want to participate in The Body Shop's campaign. Amnesty made an effort to contact the chosen human rights defenders to ensure they agreed to being profiled by the company. One of those chosen (from Latin America) responded that she did not want a corporation campaigning on her behalf.

21.3.2 'Challenging' markets and sections

To the surprise of some Amnesty campaigners, The Body Shop had a retail presence in countries regarded as having a poor or dubious human rights record, such as a number of Middle East countries where The Body Shop brand was considered a luxury 'English' product, and where the core values that characterised it in the UK, Canada and elsewhere were secondary. These countries became known in The Body Shop as the 'challenging markets'. The company had to respond to its commitment to a global campaign by attempting to ensure that some campaign was undertaken in these countries. One example of a 'challenging market' was Saudi Arabia. The Amnesty International Middle East campaigners and researchers were especially keen to see a campaigning presence in Saudi Arabia during the UDHR year, and saw The Body Shop presence and campaign commitment as an opportunity to engage in awareness-raising around human rights. Amnesty people met with the Saudi franchisees in 1997 and discussed ways in which The Body Shop could run a campaign that would be acceptable to the Saudi government. A solution was found in which the Saudi franchisees would seek permission from their government to campaign on Bosnian Muslims missing because of the war in former Yugoslavia. The franchisees and the Amnesty researchers were hopeful but, unfortunately, the Saudi government neither approved nor declined the application to run the campaign. Other 'challenging markets' chose not to participate. Malaysia was one of these, basing its decision on the then significant economic downturn in Asia. Other Gulf State markets also opted out. In total, 13 out of a total of 47 Body Shop markets chose not to participate in the campaign.

The German Amnesty section refused to campaign with The Body Shop on principle. They simply believed that it would be wrong for the organisation to be seen to be aligning itself with a business. The Body Shop's human rights campaigner flew to Germany in an attempt to answer their concerns but, as it was an issue of principle for the section, the trip was not successful. The Body Shop and Amnesty International in Germany each conducted its own separate campaigns in support of human rights during 1998.

Switzerland presented another challenge. Only months before the campaign launch in May 1998 the Swiss AI section came across the writings of US journalist Jon Entine. Entine was known in The Body Shop as a 'corporate stalker' (Roddick 2000: 225), having written considerable amounts of critical material on the company's values approach and corporate responsibility performance (Entine 1994, 1995; Cowe and Entine 1996; Roddick 2000). The Swiss section of Amnesty International asked for the International Secretariat to respond to the accusations made in the Entine material. The IS, in turn, asked The Body Shop to provide responses. The IS appeared not to have conducted any formal due diligence process on The Body Shop before agreeing to the partnership and so was unprepared to respond itself.

21.3.3 Dilemmas

There were many discussions between The Body Shop's human rights campaigner, people within The Body Shop and those working for Amnesty about who gained the greatest reputational benefit from the partnership. Perhaps an indication to the answer is contained in The Body Shop's own internal materials. An internal company document from 1997 explained that the company chose Amnesty because of its 'immense credibility in the human rights movements' (BSI 1997b). For The Body Shop it was this 'immense credibility' that was a defining aspect of the campaign. The company absolutely recognised the value that Amnesty as a partner conferred on the company's brand, a brand partially built on this type of NGO campaigning.

At the same time, the partnership enhanced the campaign, both in terms of the number of commitments collected and in terms of raising the profile of human rights defenders. The resources The Body Shop put into the campaign were significant. Of the 13 million signatures and thumbprints collected in support of the UDHR, over 3 million were from The Body Shop and most of these were collected within a 4–6 week campaigning window (BSI 1999a).

The International Secretariat of Amnesty International committed to The Body Shop based on past experience and trust. While these are commendable aspects on which to base a commitment to a joint campaign, it was not enough to respond to the Swiss section when they came across Jon Entine's criticisms of the company. Perhaps the lesson is that, however much you trust your campaign partner, it is important to know as many of their 'skeletons in the closet' before engaging with them.

While Amnesty International's apparent lack of due diligence may have been an issue for the organisation, there was an even greater lack of preparation by The Body Shop. The company relied on existing processes and commitments to address human rights and took no additional steps to assess its own human rights risks that may have increased because of involvement in the campaign. There was a sense in the company that its human rights house was in order (Laframboise 1998). This was a risky assumption. For example, apart from general issues (including some of those referred to by Jon Entine, especially in the context of the company's fair trade programme and its global sourcing practices), one of the defenders could have presented a dilemma for The Body Shop. Dita Indah Sari, a jailed Indonesian labour activist, was fighting for better workers' rights especially in factories producing mass goods for Western markets. Not only did The Body Shop have a non-engaged approach to unions at its factories, but Sari's general anti-corporate stand and campaigns on sweatshop labour could have presented the company with potential embarrassment, given that it sources from high-risk geographic areas. What would have happened if she had decided to challenge The Body Shop on its policy to source from low-income countries and the company's systems and processes for managing working conditions in its supply chain?

Beyond the opportunity that challenging markets presented to Amnesty, the organisation made no attempt to influence the company's internal structures and policies relating to human rights. A joint campaign such as this was certainly an opportunity in which the company could have been influenced to further its internal approach to human rights in the form of a stronger policy or a strengthened sourcing screening process. This poses the question of how effective NGOs are when working in partnership with companies in using the partnership as an opportunity to drive and advance their agenda in the company. Further research into such opportunities would be valuable for NGOs contemplating corporate partnerships.

21.4 Conclusion

Business–NGO campaigning partnerships and solo corporate campaigns have not received much analytical attention, by NGOs, the corporate world or within academia. A review of the Amnesty UK Business Group's newsletters in the years since Make Your Mark sees no mention of the campaign or of its possible use as a lesson or an example to other businesses. This is probably the first examination of Make Your Mark and its relevance to the human rights corporate agenda. This may suggest that corporate campaigning is not seen as an important aspect of the discourse. Yet, with companies wanting to take more proactive steps on human rights, the human rights and corporate responsibility movement must articulate more clearly what it seeks to gain from corporations promoting human rights. The movement must consider the desirability and viability of the campaigning company, and raise questions regarding the political accountability of such corporate campaigns.

On a practical level, the Make Your Mark experience shows that both actors engaging in this unusual form of corporate campaigning need to be prepared to consider thoroughly their own and their partner's human rights exposures and position. For example, if the partnership were formed today, would Amnesty check The Body Shop's corporate social and environmental reputation? Would Amnesty spend the time to consider how human rights were integrated in the company's structure and systems? Would the partnership be based on more than the agency of one key individual or department within the company?

An important issue in corporate–NGO partnerships is that of power balance and relationship between fundamentally different partners. As Murphy and Coleman have argued, '[a]lthough power differentials between participants often remain, the partners need some degree of countervailing power in order for partnership to happen' (Murphy and Coleman 2000: 213). To some extent, both the corporation and the NGO must be dependent on each other for the partnership to work (Gray 1989; Gray and Wood 1991; Wood and Gray 1991). While corporations generally hold material (e.g. economic and financial) power, civil-society organisations hold moral power, in terms of offering both negative threats and positive endorsements. The Amnesty International and The Body Shop Make Your Mark campaign could be considered a good example of such power-sharing. Despite the potential and real problems, the two organisations established an intriguing type of partnership: (a) the corporate community actively working for social change via a far-reaching type of corporate–community partnership; and (b) corporate lobbying and campaigning for social change.

A crucial and as yet unexamined issue that corporate campaigns throw up is that of corporate political accountability. Throughout history, various corporate accountability movements have been concerned with obtaining information from companies and enhancing their public accountability and transparency. Political accountability refers to the least elaborated and least discussed accountability field: that dealing with the economic power and political influence of corporations. While we generally think about business in terms of economic contributions and power, companies equally exert political power. The business world has always used economic arguments (such as development, growth, jobs, investment climate) to influence the political debate and specific government policies (Cheit 1964; Vogel 1989). Furthermore, corporations engage in pressure-group-style politics. They have adopted traditional civil-society processes and strategies to further their political and economic aims (Cheit 1964; Vogel 1991; Carey 1997; Beder 1997). Indeed, there is a long history of corporations acting as political actors (see, for example, Nader and Green 1973; Unseem 1984; Tool and Samuels 1989; Greider 1992; Trento 1993; Grefe and Linsky 1995; Boggs 2000).

Corporations have not always used their political power solely for their own well-being. Throughout history, enlightened entrepreneurs have used their political clout to appeal for improved business standards and government regulation. Some, as we have shown here, such as The Body Shop, have gone a step further and have engaged in NGO-style corporate campaigns, either in partnership with NGOs or on their own. While at times using the same techniques as 'conservative' corporate lobbying, this corporate 'constructive' campaigning for social and environmental change starts from fundamentally different motivations and aims.

Nevertheless, questions remain over the political accountability of such corporate campaigns, especially with regard to issues such as the power balance, motivation and fundamental desirability of corporate campaigns.

Larger questions need to be posed regarding corporations as political actors, and particularly corporate campaigning. What would the world be like if all the major corporations did their own NGO-style campaign, each of them 'owning' its cause? Can we imagine companies lining up to market their 'pet' causes while fundamental social change issues such as poverty, income inequality and human rights are left unaddressed? This introduces the danger of moving the debate about social change into the corporate arena where corporations (often partly responsible for the power issues underlining social inequality and under-development), through their choice of campaigns and issues, begin to set the social change agenda. Will civil-society movements, such as the human rights movement, be able to compete with corporations on the definition of problems, issues that need addressing and the agenda-setting process? Questions also remain about the choice of campaigning partners. For example, what if corporations move beyond the Amnesty Internationals and begin to create their own human rights 'NGOs' or, through their choice of NGO partners, give legitimacy to human rights organisations that may be of questionable credibility. The potential impact on the human rights movement could be hugely significant. The campaign also illustrates the contested nature of what a corporation's responsibilities are in relation to human rights. Is corporate campaigning for human rights what the human rights movement really wants as the logical conclusion of their demands of business? Perhaps a line has already been crossed; is it only a question of time until Nike launches a major campaign with international trade unions to stamp out the use of sweatshop labour in the sportswear industry?

Further research into these corporate campaigns may provide more solid indications about corporate motivations to campaign, and the place of corporate campaigns in the corporate social responsibility debate. The extent to which The Body Shop's corporate campaigning has set some kind of precedent and will change the business world remains to be seen. The Body Shop's decision to campaign is strongly linked to the personality and personal views of its founder, both of which have heavily influenced the genetic make-up of the company. In that sense, corporate campaigning as BSI undertook it may not be a strategy easily adopted by other companies, and may remain unique in the corporate world.

Nevertheless, the NGO and business communities alike need to address the question of whether there is a role for campaigning in partnership with corporations and, if so, over which issues and with which NGO partners. What is the motivation of the business world to engage in corporate campaigns for social change? Is campaigning a legitimate and appropriate role for companies to perform? Should corporations cross the line into the realm of civil society and engage in social and environmental campaigns? Or is it an extensive, and possibly dangerous, public relations exercise? These are serious questions that need to be addressed urgently by all sectors of society.

22
Moving forwards

Rory Sullivan
Insight Investment, UK

Perhaps the defining feature of the material presented in this book is the sheer breadth of the issues covered:

- Case studies and examples are presented from over 20 different countries.

- The law and policy approaches considered range from the international to the local, and from regulation to self-regulation.

- The human rights issues discussed include the right to life, labour standards, child labour, conflict, the right to development, freedom of association, bribery and corruption, access to justice, the right to property, and the right to health.

- The actors involved include companies, national and local government, international institutions, domestic courts, regulatory bodies, bilateral and multilateral organisations, shareholders, trade unions, local communities, non-governmental organisations, community-based organisations, religious groups, industry associations and not-for-profit organisations.

The analysis of the relationship between business and human rights is further complicated by the rate of change in many of the factors that influence this relationship. As just one example, the international political landscape has altered dramatically since this book was first proposed (in mid-2002). At that time, the business and human rights debate was starting to explore the international institutions and approaches that could be used to regulate companies. Despite the lack of political interest in regulating transnational corporations (TNCs), there was an increasing confidence that a corporate accountability convention would emerge (perhaps as part of the negotiations around further trade liberalisation). In these discussions, the United Nations was seen as a key interlocutor. However, at the time of writing (mid-2003), the situation has changed completely. The insistence of the United States and the United Kingdom on going to war with Iraq, without the support of the United Nations and in the face of strong opposition from most European countries, has undermined these assumptions about the future. The UN appears to have been fatally undermined and corporate accountability, at least in the short term, has been removed from the political agenda. Yet these changes may, ultimately, strengthen the support for strong international institutions that ensure that all international actors, including TNCs, are held to account for their actions.

Rather than trying to predict the future, this chapter draws together some of the key themes and lessons from the book. The specific issues considered are: (a) the human rights responsibilities of companies; (b) the law and policy options for ensuring the human rights performance of corporations; and (c) corporate responses to human rights issues.

22.1 Human rights responsibilities of companies

This book has focused on the responsibility of TNCs and the private sector more generally for the protection and promotion of human rights. There is a growing consensus that the responsibilities of companies should not be confined to their workforce but should also extend to situations where they can exert influence (e.g. in their supply chains) or contribute to the creation of an enabling environment for the realisation of human rights. There is also a growing understanding of what the specific expectations of companies are, with the work of the UN Sub-Commission on Human Rights (in its 'Draft Norms on Responsibilities of Transnational Corporations and other Business Enterprises with Regard to Human Rights') representing a particularly important step forwards.

While some companies have accepted responsibility, many others are trying to avoid taking responsibility. Woolfson and Beck, Handelsman, and MacDonald and McLaughlin present case studies of companies' failure to accept their responsibility for the protection and promotion of human rights, leading to human rights violations occurring or being exacerbated. In contrast, the case studies from Leipziger and Kaufman, Hess and Dunfee, and Freeman and Hernández Uriz illustrate the positive outcomes that can be achieved when companies accept responsibility and engage constructively with specific human rights issues. It is interesting that the approaches taken by companies range from compliance with local standards, through to compliance with norms based on international standards, and even to acting as human rights advocates. The case studies in which companies have 'pushed the envelope' (Fabig and Boele's discussion of The Body Shop's partnership with Amnesty International; Freeman and Hernández Uriz's discussion of the positive contribution of companies to an international initiative on security; Lim and Cameron's discussion of multinationals contributing to rural development; Reygadas's analysis of the different models of societal interaction in the Mexican maquiladoras) are of particular importance in this regard. They show that companies can effectively contribute to human rights issues beyond their areas of direct operations. More importantly, they show that it is possible for companies to work with government, NGOs and other stakeholders on human rights issues, and that taking a leadership position can provide commercial interests while also enhancing the protection and promotion of human rights.

22.2 Law and policy

Concerns about the impacts of companies on human rights have been exacerbated by the apparent limitations in the international legal framework for ensuring the performance of companies. Under international human rights law, nation-states are still considered as the primary if not exclusive holder of duties. The idealised conception of international law cascading into domestic legislation and thereby creating binding obligations on companies is less than reassuring in practice. In some countries, in particular those that want to attract foreign direct investment, low (or no) human rights standards may actually be a source of commercial advantage. In others, the relationship between host governments and TNCs may have the effect of exacerbating human rights violations. For example, energy and mining projects are typically organised through leases from or joint ventures with local governments. These governments can be highly repressive, even military dictatorships, and can in some cases (e.g. Indonesia, Colombia, Nigeria) be engaged in what amounts to a civil war with ethnic, tribal, political or other groups. The issues around doing business with repressive regimes have been canvassed in a number of the case studies presented here (see, for example, the chapters by Handelsman, van der Putten *et al.*, and Banfield).

It may be that, by looking to international or domestic law for solutions, we are looking in the wrong places. While self-regulation is not popular with NGOs (who tend to prefer hard law approaches), it may be the only viable approach to corporate responsibility and accountability. Governments have convened dialogues between companies, NGOs, trade unions and national governments (examples include the Voluntary Principles on Security and Human Rights, the UN Global Compact, and the Extractive Industries Transparency Initiative). These initiatives have been supported by companies as they offer the advantages of creating a level playing field, helping build trust between companies and other stakeholders, avoiding regulation and providing a means for companies to share experience and information in a non-competitive way.

While such initiatives have proved useful in defining the normative expectations of companies, they also raise important questions. Some of these questions relate to the dependability of voluntary approaches. The history of self-regulation has been less than auspicious: many self-regulatory regimes have failed to deliver on their promises, while others have been criticised for setting extremely low standards. Furthermore, virtually all self-regulatory regimes suffer from a lack of demonstrable performance improvements. The self-regulatory initiatives that are emerging at the international level (e.g. the Voluntary Principles) also face important questions about their legitimacy. For example, is it reasonable that developing countries are either not involved or are unable to participate? Is it reasonable for participating companies to interfere in the legitimate internal affairs of a state? Do these initiatives represent the capture of public policy by TNCs? Are the rights and aspirations of local communities excluded from consideration? Are these regimes simply a new form of colonialism? Does self-regulation have the effect of undermining the central role of states in protecting and promoting human rights?

22.3 Management responses

There is a growing consensus on what companies should do at the corporate level to manage their human rights issues. Measures include adopting a corporate human rights policy, assigning responsibilities throughout the organisation, implementing management systems and processes, and monitoring and reporting on performance (see further the chapter by Sullivan and Seppala). To date, however, few companies have adopted such systems. The reasons include: the lack of a strong business case (at least in the short term); the lack of acknowledgement of corporate responsibility for human rights (many companies only consider the implementation of such systems in response to NGO pressure); the absence of certain tools (e.g. the lack of agreed human rights performance indicators has meant that companies have been less willing to report); and the tendency for human rights management to be dispersed through different parts of the organisation (e.g. health and safety, personnel, environment). There is also a specific problem of the gaps between 'head office policy' and 'operational performance'. While companies have started to accept responsibility for human rights issues, on-the-ground performance remains problematic. In part, this reflects the complexity of human rights issues which means that corporate policy documents cannot cover every eventuality or provide guidance on every situation that may occur. It also reflects the fact that the regional business units of TNCs tend to have a high degree of autonomy where corporate policies are seen as 'guides to action' rather than prescriptive obligations.

Despite these limitations in corporate human rights management processes, one of the key lessons from the case studies is that many of the controversies that companies find themselves embroiled in may be avoided. That is, lack of preparation, lack of foresight and lack of understanding of the social, political, environmental, cultural, economic context can heighten the likelihood that something will go wrong or that the responses adopted will exacerbate rather than mitigate the issues. The role of human rights management systems is not simply to protect the company but also to ensure that the company's impact on human rights accentuates the positives and minimises the negatives. Even with the best management systems and the best implementation, things can still go wrong. The chapter by Kazmi and Macfarlane highlights this dilemma. While the programme to eliminate child labour from the football-stitching industry in Sialkot was well designed, built on international conventions and was based on dialogue with stakeholders, it still resulted in negative consequences on family units and children. The chapter highlights the importance of not only being prepared but also being prepared to adapt and respond as situations develop and evolve. It also highlights the importance of listening to and taking on board the views and expectations of stakeholders (or, as argued by MacDonald and McLaughlin, companies need to beware of creating a reality that is at odds with the real needs of communities).

Lim and Cameron's chapter highlights this issue from a different context. The efforts of the Thai government and NGOs to encourage TNCs to establish facilities in rural areas is seen as an important part of the country's efforts to combat HIV/AIDS (on the basis that providing rural employment will minimise the movement of people from rural areas and thereby provide the social stability that is seen as a necessary part of the fight against HIV/AIDS). While the programme has been effective in terms of the number of companies setting up in rural areas and the economic (wages) and social (e.g. employee training) development benefits, the impact on the incidence of HIV/AIDS remains the subject of debate. That is, even though the programme has been successful by its measurable outcomes, it is less clear that it has made a contribution to the key health issue. Indeed, it may be that seeing TNCs as a contributor to the fight against HIV/AIDS is inappropriate and that the primary contribution should be seen and recognised as their contribution to rural development and poverty alleviation.

22.4 Epilogue

Describing the social responsibilities of companies in the language of human rights presents a fundamental challenge to the common conception of corporate social responsibility as something of an add-on to or outside companies' core business. The language of human rights means that expectations are expressed in moral terms and that these expectations cannot be traded off on the grounds of cost–benefit assessments. The language of human rights also allows local, national and international issues to be brought within the same frame of reference. Furthermore, in the context of globalisation, the protection and promotion of human rights may enable the positive benefits of globalisation to be enhanced while ensuring that the adverse impacts, in particular on the poor, the weak and the disenfranchised, are minimised.

However, expressing corporate responsibilities in the language of human rights may actually have the effect of perpetuating many of the problems with globalisation. The reason is that a human rights approach may not address the relationship with political economy that underlies so many human rights violations. That is, the underpinning causes of human right problems (e.g. poverty, over-consumption, inequality, conflict) will not be addressed merely by addressing their symptoms. As just one example, Handelsman, in his chapter, discusses the issues around the Freeport mine. The company's responses are a good illustration of how companies can effectively respond to and engage with concerns around human rights and security in an extremely complex and difficult situation. Yet, in this interpretation, the more fundamental questions around the nature and scale of the Freeport operations remain unanswered. An alternative perspective is that:

> Freeport's history in Indonesia exemplifies the dynamics of multi-national corporate investment in the extractive industries and the relationship of these corporate investments with governments . . . If a mine can be personified, then Grasberg is the Incredible Hulk on cocaine, driven mad by the demands of its owners on the other side of the planet, and set to destroy all in its path . . . The Amungme's cosmology depicts this mountain as the sacred head of their mother and its rivers are her milk. To the Amungme, Freeport is digging out her heart (Kennedy and Abrash 2001).

Bibliography

ACFOA (Australian Council for Overseas Aid) (1995) *Troubles at Freeport: Eyewitness Accounts of West Papuan Resistance to the Freeport-McMoRan Mine in Irian Jaya, Indonesia and Indonesian Military Repression, June 1994– February 1995* (Canberra: ACFOA).

ADB (Asian Development Bank) (2000) *Special Evaluation Study on the Policy Impact of Involuntary Resettlement* (Manila, Philippines: ADB).

Addo, M. (1999) 'Human Rights and Transnational Corporations: An Introduction', in M. Addo (ed.), *Human Rights Standards and the Responsibility of Transnational Corporations* (London: Kluwer Law International): 5-37.

Alba, C., and H. Rivière d'Arc (2000) 'Empresarios Locales: ¿Actores del Cambio Político?', in C. Alba and A. Aziz (eds.), *Desarrollo y Política en la Frontera Norte de México* (Mexico City: CIESAS-IRD-UACJ): 21-37.

Alden, E., and D. Buchan (2000) 'Oil Groups Back Rules to Guard Human Rights', *Financial Times*, 21 December 2000: 12.

Alston, P. (2002) 'Resisting the Merger and Acquisition of Human Rights by Trade Law: A Reply to Petersmann', *European Journal of International Law* 13: 815-44.

Amnesty International (1997) 'Bolivia: Attack on president of the permanent human rights assembly provokes international condemnation' (press release; London: Amnesty International, 27 January 1997).

—— (1998) *Human Rights Guidelines for Companies* (London: Amnesty International [UK] Business Group [1st edn 1997]).

—— and International Business Leaders Forum (2002) *Business and Human Rights: A Geography of Corporate Risk* (London: Amnesty International UK and International Business Leaders Forum).

Amnesty International (The Netherlands) and Pax Christi International (2000) *Multinational Enterprises and Human Rights* (Utrecht, Netherlands: Amnesty International [The Netherlands] and Pax Christi International).

Amnesty International, Pax Christi, Fatal Transactions, NIZA (2002) 'Rules of Engagement: How Business Can be a Force for Peace', *Conference Reader*, November 2002.

Andersen, M. (1999) *Do No Harm: How Aid Can Support Peace—or War* (Boulder, CO: Lynne Rienner).

—— (2002) 'Transnational Corporations and Environmental Damage: Is Tort Law the Answer?', *Washburn Law Journal* 41: 399-425.

Andriof, J., and M. McIntosh (eds.) (2001) *Perspectives on Corporate Citizenship* (Sheffield, UK: Greenleaf Publishing).

Annan, K. (2001) 'Laying the Foundations of a Fair and Free World Trade System', in G. Sampson (ed.), *The Role of the World Trade Organization in Global Governance* (Tokyo: United Nations University Press): 19-27.

Anti-Slavery Society (1990) *West Papua, Plunder in Paradise* (Indigenous Peoples and Development Series, Report No. 6; London: Anti-Slavery Society).

Arnold, D., and N. Bowie (2003) 'Sweatshops and Respect for Persons', *Business Ethics Quarterly* 13: 221-42.

Atlanta Partners (1999) *The Atlanta Partners Report 1999. The Sialkot Child Labour Project: Milestone Reached* (Atlanta, GA: The Atlanta Partners).

AVANCSO (Asociación para el Avance de las Ciencias Sociales en Guatemala) (1994) *El Significado de la Maquila en Guatemala: Elementos para su Comprensión* (Guatemala City: AVANCSO).

Avery, C. (1999) *Business and Human Rights in a Time of Change* (London: Amnesty International).

Avon (2000) 'Kiss Goodbye to Breast Cancer', http://avon.avon.com, last accessed 17 September 2002.

Banfield, J., D. Lilly and V. Haufler (2003) *TNCs in Conflict Prone Zones: Public Responses and a Framework for Action* (London: International Alert).

Basic Principles on the Use of Force and Firearms by Law Enforcement Officials, Eighth United Nations Congress on the Prevention of Crime and the Treatment of Offenders, Havana, 27 August–7 September 1990, UN Doc. A/CONF.144/28/Rev.1 at 112 (1990).

Baxi, U. (1998) 'Voices of Suffering and the Future of Human Rights', *Transnational Law and Contemporary Problems* 8: 125-75.

Beck, M., and C. Woolfson (2000) 'The Regulation of Health and Safety in Britain: From Old Labour to New Labour', *Industrial Relations Journal* 31.1: 35-50.

Beder, S. (1997) *Global Spin: The Corporate Assault on Environmentalism* (Melbourne: Scribe Publications).

Behr, P. (2000) 'Companies Sign Pact on Human Rights', *Washington Post*, 21 December 2000: E10.

Bendell, J. (ed.) (2000) *Terms for Endearment: Business, NGOs and Sustainable Development* (Sheffield, UK: Greenleaf Publishing).

Bennett, J. (2002) 'Multinational Corporations, Social Responsibility and Conflict', *Journal of International Affairs* 55.2 (Spring 2002): 393-410.

Berdal, M., and D. Malone (2000) *Greed and Grievance: Economic Agendas in Civil Wars* (Boulder, CO: Lynne Rienner).

Berenbeim, R.E. (2000) *Company Programs for Resisting Corrupt Practices: A Global Study* (Conference Board Report No. 1279-00-RR; New York: The Conference Board).

Beyleveld, D. (1991) *The Dialectical Necessity of Morality* (Chicago: University of Chicago Press).

Blumberg, P. (2002) 'Asserting Human Rights against Multinational Corporations under United States Law: Conceptual and Procedural Problems', *American Journal of Comparative Law* 50: 493-529.

Boele, R., H. Fabig and D. Wheeler (2001a) 'Shell, Nigeria and the Ogoni: A Study in Unsustainable Development. *I.* The Story of Shell, Nigeria and the Ogoni People. Environment, Economy, Relationships: Conflict and Prospects for Resolution', *Sustainable Development* 9.2: 74-86.

——, —— and —— (2001b) 'Shell Nigeria and the Ogoni: A Study in Unsustainable Development. *II.* Corporate Social Responsibility and "Stakeholder Management" versus a Rights-Based Approach to Sustainable Development', *Sustainable Development* 9.3: 121-35.

Boggs, C. (2000) *The End of Politics: Corporate Power and the Decline of the Public Sphere* (New York: Guilford Press).

Bond, K., D. Celentano, S. Phonsophakul and C. Vaddhanaphuti (1997) 'Mobility and Migration: Female Commercial Sex Work and the HIV Epidemic in Northern Thailand', in G. Herdt (ed.), *Sexual Cultures and Migration in the Era of AIDS: Anthropological and Demographic Perspectives* (Oxford, UK: Clarendon Press).

Boochalaksi, W., and P. Guest (1998) 'Prostitution in Thailand', in L. Lim (ed.), *The Sex Sector: The Economic and Social Bases of Prostitution in Southeast Asia* (Geneva: International Labour Office).

Boswell, N. (1999) 'The Law, Expectation, and Reality in the Marketplace: The Problems of and Responses to Corruption', *Law and Policy in International Business* 30: 139-46.

Bourdieu, P. (1983) 'The Forms of Capital', in J. Richardson (ed.), *Handbook of Theory and Research for the Sociology of Education* (Westport, CT: Greenwood Press): 241-58.

Bowden, A., M. Lane and J. Martin (2001) *Triple Bottom Line Risk Management: Enhancing Profit, Environmental Performance and Community Benefit* (New York: John Wiley).

Bowen, H. (1953) *Social Responsibility of the Businessman* (Boston, MA: Little, Brown).

Bowie, N. (1999) *Business Ethics: A Kantian Perspective* (Malden, MA: Blackwell Publishers).

—— (ed.) (2002) *The Blackwell Guide to Business Ethics* (Malden, MA: Blackwell Publishers).

BP (2003) 'National and Regional Review: Southern Caucasus', www.caspiandevelopmentandexport.com.

Braithwaite, J., and P. Drahos (2000) *Global Business Regulation* (Cambridge, UK: Cambridge University Press).

Branigin, W. (2000) 'Claim against Unocal rejected: Judge cites evidence of abuses in Burma but no jurisdiction', *Washington Post*, 8 September 2000: E10.

Bray, J. (ed.) (1997) *No Hiding Place: Business and the Politics of Pressure* (London: Control Risks Group).

Brickley, J., C. Smith and J. Zimmerman (2000) *Managerial Economics and Organizational Architecture* (New York: McGraw–Hill, 2nd edn).

Brock, D. (1993) *Life and Death: Philosophical Essays in Biomedical Ethics* (New York: Cambridge University Press).

Browne, J. (1997) 'Corporate Responsibility in an International Context', presentation to the Council on Foreign Relations, New York, 13 November 1997.

—— (2002) 'BP Exerting Positive Influence' (London: BPAmoco; for similar more recent statements from Lord Browne, see BP's Environmental and Social website at www.bp.com/environ_social/index.asp).

Brundtland, G.H. (2000) 'Outstanding Issues in the International Response to HIV/AIDS: The WHO Perspective', presented at the *XIII International AIDS Conference*, Durban, South Africa, 9-14 July 2000.

BSI (The Body Shop International) (1995) *Our Agenda* (includes Mission Statement, Trading Charter, Human Rights Statement, etc.; Littlehampton, UK: BSI).

—— (1996a) *Measuring Up: A Summary of The Body Shop Values Report 1995* (Littlehampton, UK: BSI)

—— (1996b) *Values Report 1995: The Body Shop Approach to Ethical Auditing* (Littlehampton, UK: BSI).

—— (1996c) *Values Report 1995: The Social Statement* (Littlehampton, UK: BSI).

—— (1996d) 'Body in Motion Follow up Pack, SEA/Campaigns in Motion: Campaigns as Participation', internal BSI document produced for the International Head Franchisee Meeting, September 1996.

——(1997a) 'Defend the Defenders, History and Commitment to Human Rights', internal BSI head office briefing document for Make Your Mark campaign, December 1997.

—— (1997b) 'Defend the Defenders', internal presentation materials for Make Your Mark campaign, December 1997.

—— (1997c) *Values Report 1997* (Littlehampton, UK: BSI).

—— (1999a) *Celebrating Defenders of Human Rights, Make Your Mark* (Littlehampton, UK: BSI).

—— (1999b) 'The Body Shop—About Us: Company Profile', www.thebodyshop.co.uk/aboutus/body-profile.htm, last accessed 24 January 2000.

—— (2001) 'The Body Shop', www.the-body-shop.com/global/who_we_are/Index.asp, last accessed 28 August 2002.

BSR (Business for Social Responsibility) and Newmont Mining (2003) *Social Licence to Operate* (San Francisco: BSR and Newmont Mining Company).

Burton, B. (1995) 'Sabotaging Environmentalism with Bombs, Spikes and Other Dirty Tricks', paper presented at *Environmentalism, Public Opinion and the Media Conference*, University of Tasmania, Hobart, Australia, 1–2 December 1995.

Carey, A. (1997) *Taking the Risk out of Democracy: Corporate Propaganda versus Freedom and Liberty* (Chicago: University of Illinois Press).

Carrillo, J., and A. Hualde (1996) 'Maquiladoras de Tercera Generación: El Caso de Delphi-General Motors', *Espacios: Revista Venezolana de Gestión Tecnológica* 17.3 (July/September 1996): 111-34.

Carson, W. (1982) *The Other Price of Britain's Oil* (Oxford, UK: Martin Robertson).

Cason, J., and D. Brooks (2001) 'Lanzan campaña internacional contra talleres de sudor en EU y el Tercer Mundo', *La Jornada*, Mexico City, 8 August 2001.

Cernea, M. (1993) 'Disaster-related Refugee Flows and Development Cause Population Displacement', in M. Cernea and S. Guggenheim (eds.), *Anthropological Approaches to Resettlement: Policy, Practice and Theory* (Boulder, CO: Westview Press).

—— (1996) 'Bridging the Research Divide: Studying Refugees and Development Oustees', in T. Allen (ed.), *In Search of Cool Ground: War, Flight and Homecoming in Northeast Africa* (London: James Currey).

—— and C. McDowell (eds.) (2000) *Risks and Reconstruction: Experiences of Resettlers and Refugees* (Washington, DC: World Bank).

Cestre, G. (2001) *Social Accountability and Performance: The Switcher/Prem Group Experience in India* (Lausanne, Switzerland: University of Lausanne).

Champain, P. (2002) 'Assessing the Corporate Sector in Mainstreaming Conflict Prevention', in L. van de Goor and M. Huber (eds.), *Mainstreaming Conflict Prevention: Concept and Practice. Conflict Prevention Network Yearbook 2000-01* (Baden-Baden, Germany: Nomos Verlagsgesellschaft).

Chandler, A. (1977) *The Visible Hand: The Managerial Revolution in American Business* (Cambridge, MA: Harvard University Press).

Chantavanich, S. (2000) *Mobility and HIV/AIDS in the Greater Mekong Subregion* (Manila, Philippines: Asian Development Bank).

Chatterjee, P., and M. Finger (1994) *The Earth Brokers: Power, Politics and World Development* (London: Routledge).

Cheit, E. (ed.) (1964) *The Business Establishment* (Hoboken, NJ: John Wiley).

Christian Aid (1996) *The Global Supermarket* (London: Christian Aid).

Churchill, G. (1995) *The Status of Traditional Land Rights in Irian Jaya under Indonesian Law* (private publication).

CITGUA (Ciencia y Tecnología para Guatemala, AC) (1991) *La Maquila en Guatemala* (Guatemala City: CITGUA).

Claire Cutler, A., V. Haufler and T. Porter (1999) 'Private Authority and International Affairs', in A. Claire Cutler, V. Haufler and T. Porter (eds.), *Private Authority and International Affairs* (Albany, NY: SUNY Press).

Clapham, A. (1993) *Human Rights in the Private Sphere* (Oxford, UK: Clarendon Press).

—— (2000) 'The Question of Jurisdiction under International Criminal Law over Legal Persons', in M. Kamminga and S. Zia-Zarifi (eds.), *Liability of Multinational Corporations under International Law* (The Hague: Kluwer Law International): 139-95.

Clark, I. (1999) *Globalisation and International Relations Theory* (Oxford, UK: Oxford University Press).

Clarkson, M. (1995) 'A Stakeholder Framework for Analyzing and Evaluating Corporate Social Performance', *Academy of Management Review* 20.1: 92-117.

Code of Conduct for Law Enforcement Officials G.A. Res. 34/169, annex, 34 UN GAOR Supp. (No. 46) at 186, UN Doc. A/34/46 (1979).

Coleman, J. (1990) *Foundations of Social Theory* (Cambridge, MA: Harvard University Press).

Coles, D., and D. Green (2002) *Do UK Pension Funds Invest Responsibly? A Survey of Current Practice on Socially Responsible Investment* (London: Just Pensions).

Collier, P., and A. Hoeffler (2001) *Greed and Grievance in Civil War* (Washington, DC: World Bank).

Coutrot, T. (2000) *L'Entreprise Néo-liberal Nouvelle Utopie Capitaliste?* (Paris: Editions la Decouverte).

Cowe, R., and J. Entine (1996) 'Fair Enough?', *Guardian Weekend*, 14 December 1996: 30-35.

Cullen, Rt Hon. Lord (1990) *The Public Inquiry into the Piper Alpha Disaster* (Vols. 1 and 2; London: HMSO).

Cummins, E. (2000) 'The Pakistan Football Stitching Industry', unpublished internal report, DFID and Save the Children UK.

Cutler, A., V. Haufler and T. Porter (eds.) (1999) *Private Authority and International Affairs* (New York: State University of New York Press).

Davis, K., and R. Bloomstrom (1966) *Business and its Environment* (New York: McGraw–Hill).

DeGeorge, R. (1993) *Competing with Integrity in International Business* (New York: Oxford University Press).

De Geus, A. (1997) *The Living Company: Habits for Survival in a Turbulent Business Environment* (Boston, MA: Harvard Business School Press).

Department for International Development (2002) 'Extractive Industries Transparency Initiative', www.dfid.gov.uk.

DesJardins, J. (2003) *An Introduction to Business Ethics* (New York: McGraw–Hill).

Diary of Online Papua Mouthpiece (2002) 'Cultural/Environmental Impact and Development', www.westpapua.net/docs/papers/paper5/culture_enviro.htm.

Donaldson, T. (1989) *The Ethics of International Business* (New York: Oxford University Press).

—— and L. Preston (1995) 'The Stakeholder Theory of the Corporation: Concepts, Evidence and Implications', *Academy of Management Review* 20.1: 65-91.

Donnely, J. (1999) 'Human Rights and Asian Values: A Defence of "Western" Universalism', in J. Bauer and D. Bell (eds.), *The East Asian Challenge for Human Rights* (Cambridge, UK: Cambridge University Press): 60-87.

Downing, T. (1996) 'Mitigating Social Impoverishment when People are Involuntarily Displaced', in C. McDowell (ed.), *Understanding Impoverishment: The Consequences of Development-Induced Displacement* (Oxford, UK: Berghahn Books).

—— (2002) *Avoiding New Poverty: Mining-Induced Displacement and Resettlement* (London: International Institute for Environment and Development and World Business Council for Sustainable Development).

Dreazan, Y. (2000) 'Global Standards of Human Rights Are Released', *Wall Street Journal*, 21 December 2000: A6.

Drzemczewski, A. (1983) *European Human Rights Convention in Domestic Law* (Oxford, UK: Oxford University Press).

Dunfee, T., and D. Hess (2000) 'The Legitimacy of Direct Corporate Humanitarian Investment', *Business Ethics Quarterly* 10.1: 95-109.

—— and —— (2001) 'Getting From Salbu to the "Tipping Point": The Role of Corporate Action within a Portfolio of Anti-Corruption Strategies', *Northwestern Journal of International Law and Business* 21.2: 471-90.

Dunning, J. (1993) 'Introduction: The Nature of Transnational Corporations and their Activities', in J. Dunning (ed.), *The Theory of Transnational Corporations* (London: Routledge): 1-22.

Dworkin, G. (1988) *The Theory and Practice of Autonomy* (Cambridge, UK: Cambridge University Press).

Eide, A., H. Bergsen and P. Goyer (eds.) (2000) *Human Rights and the Oil Industry* (Groningen, Netherlands: Intersentia).

Eisinger, A. (1998) 'China's Trade in Human Organs', *Lancet* 351.9112: 1,365.

El Boletín de la Red de Solidaridad en la Maquila (1998) 'Monitoreos independientes en maquiladoras de Centroamérica', *El Boletín de la Red de Solidaridad en la Maquila* 3.1 (January–March 1998).

Elias, O., and C. Lim (1998) *The Paradox of Consensualism in International Law* (The Hague: Kluwer Law International).

Elkington, J. (1997) *Cannibals with Forks: The Triple Bottom Line of 21st Century Business* (Oxford, UK: Capstone Publishing).

Engler, R. (1967) *The Politics of Oil: A Study of Private Power and Democratic Directions* (Chicago: University of Chicago Press).

Entine, J. (1994) 'Shattered Image', *Business Ethics* 8.5: 23-28.

—— (1995) 'Exploiting Idealism: Jon Entine on how The Body Shop Betrayed its Customers', *Utne Reader* 76 (January/February 1995): 100.

Evans, T. (2002) 'A Human Right to Health?', *Third World Quarterly* 23.2 (April 2002): 197-215.

Fabig, H. (1999) 'The Body Shop and the Ogoni', in M. Addo (ed.), *Human Rights Standards and the Responsibility of Transnational Corporations* (London: Kluwer Law International): 309-22.

—— (2002) 'Implementing Corporate Responsibility: The Case of The Body Shop International and its Corporate Campaign with the Ogoni People', doctoral thesis submitted to the University of Sussex, UK.

—— and R. Boele (1999) 'The Changing Nature of NGO Activity in a Globalising World: Pushing the Corporate Responsibility Agenda', *IDS Bulletin* 30.3: 58-87.

—— and —— (2003) 'Timber Logging in Clayoquot Sound/Canada: Community–Corporate Partnerships and Community Rights', in J. Frynas and S. Pegg (eds.), *Transnational Corporations and Human Rights* (London: Palgrave).

Fernandes, W. (2000) 'From Marginalisation to Sharing the Project Benefits', in M. Cernea and C. McDowell (eds.), *Risks and Reconstruction: Experiences of Resettlers and Refugees* (Washington, DC: World Bank).

Figueres Olsen, J., J. Salazar-Xirinachs and M. Araya (2001) 'Trade and Environment at the World Trade Organization: The Need for a Constructive Dialogue', in G. Sampson (ed.), *The Role of the World Trade Organization in Global Governance* (Tokyo: United Nations University Press): 155-81.

Financial Times (1999) 'World's Most Respected Companies', *Financial Times*, 7 December 1999.

Fitzmaurice, M. (1996) 'The Contribution of Environmental Law to the Development of Modern International Law', in J. Makarczyk (ed.), *The Theory of International Law at the Threshold of the 21st Century* (The Hague: Kluwer Law International): 909-25.

Forsythe, S. (2002) 'How Does HIV/AIDS Affect African Business?', in S. Forsythe (ed.), *State of the Art: AIDS and Economics* (International AIDS Economics Network [IAEN]).

Forum for the Future (2002) *Sustainability Pays* (Manchester, UK: CIS).

Fox, T., H. Ward and B. Howard (2002) *Public Sector Roles in Strengthening Corporate Social Responsibility: A Baseline Study* (Washington, DC: World Bank).

Frankental, P. (2002) 'The UN Universal Declaration of Human Rights as a Corporate Code of Conduct', *Business Ethics* 11.2: 129-33.

—— and F. House (2000) *Human Rights: Is It Any of Your Business?* (London: Amnesty International [UK] and Prince of Wales International Business Leaders Forum).

Frankfurt, H. (1988) *The Importance of What We Care About* (Cambridge, UK: Cambridge University Press).

Frederick, R. (ed.) (1999) *A Companion to Business Ethics* (Malden, MO: Blackwell Publishers).

Freeman, B. (2001a) 'New Drill for Oil Companies', *Amnesty International (UK) Business Group Newsletter* 5: 1, 7.

—— (2001b) 'Drilling for Common Ground', *Foreign Policy Magazine*, July/August 2001.

—— (2002) 'A Model for Dialogue: The Voluntary Principles on Security and Human Rights', in M. McIntosh (ed.), *Visions of Ethical Business 4* (London: FT Prentice Hall): 18-21.

——, M. Pica and C. Camponovo (2001) 'A New Approach to Corporate Responsibility: The Voluntary Principles on Security and Human Rights', *Hastings International and Comparative Law Review*, Spring 2001: 423-49.

Freeman, R. (1984) *Strategic Management: A Stakeholder Approach* (New York: Basic Books).

Freeport-McMoRan Copper & Gold Inc. (2001a) *Social, Employment and Human Rights Policy* (New Orleans: Freeport-McMoRan).

—— (2001b) *Working toward Sustainable Development: 2000 Economic, Social and Environmental Report* (New Orleans: Freeport-McMoRan).

French, P. (1979) 'The Corporation as a Moral Person', *American Philosophical Quarterly* 16: 207-17.

—— (1995) *Corporate Ethics* (Fort Worth, TX: Harcourt Brace).

Frentrop, P. (2002) *Corporate Governance, 1602–2002: Ondernemingen en Hun Aandeelhouders sinds de VOC (Corporate Governance, 1602–2002: Enterprises and their Shareholders since the Dutch East India Company)* (Amsterdam: Prometheus).

Friedman, M. (1970) 'The Social Responsibility of Business is to Increase its Profits', *New York Times Magazine*, 13 September 1970.

Frynas, J. (2001) 'Corporate and State Responses to Anti-Oil Protests in the Niger Delta', *African Affairs* 100.398 (January 2001): 27-54.

Galbraith, J. (1967) *The New Industrial State* (Boston, MA: Houghton Mifflin).

Gereffi, G. (1999) 'Mexico's Industrial Development in the Past 25 Years: Climbing Ahead or Falling Behind in the World Economy?', paper presented at the seminar *Mexico in the Integration*, US–Mexico Centre, University of California, San Diego, June 1999.

—— and M. Korzeniewicz (eds.) (1994) *Commodity Chains and Global Capitalism* (Westport, CT: Greenwood Press).

Gewirth, A. (1978) *Reason and Morality* (Chicago: University of Chicago Press).

—— (1982) *Human Rights: Essays on Justification and Applications* (Chicago: University of Chicago Press).

Giddens, A. (2001) *The Third Way: The Renewal of Social Democracy* (Cambridge, UK: Polity Press [1998]).

Goldfield, N. (1999) 'Trust, Obligations and Power', in N. Goldfield (ed.), *Physician Profiling and Risk Adjustment* (Gaithersburg, MD: Aspen Publications): 3-19.

—— (2001) *National Health Reform: American Style* (Tampa, FL: American College of Physician Executives).

—— and D. Nash (1989) *Physician Leaders: Past and Future Challenges* (Tampa, FL: American College of Physician Executives).

Gordon, K., and M. Miyake (2001) 'Business Approaches to Combating Bribery: A Study of Codes of Conduct', *Journal of Business Ethics* 34.3-4: 161-73.

Government of Canada (1998) *Voluntary Codes: A Guide for their Development and Use* (Ottawa: Government of Canada).

Granges Inc. (1996) Granges Inc. 1996 Form 14A (Proxy Solicitation Material). Filed September 1996 with the US Securities and Exchange Commission.

Gray, B. (1989) *Collaborating: Finding Common Ground for Multiparty Problems* (San Francisco: Jossey-Bass).

—— and D. Wood (1991) 'Collaborative Alliances: Moving from Practice to Theory', *Journal of Applied Behavioural Science* 27.1: 3-22.

Green, M. (2001) 'What We Talk About When We Talk About Indicators: Current Approaches to Human Rights Measurement', *Human Rights Quarterly* 23.4: 1,062-97.

Greener, R. (2000) 'Impact of HIV/AIDS on Poverty and Income Inequality in Botswana', *South African Journal of Economics* 68.5 (December 2000): 888-916.

Greer, J., and B. Kenny (1996) *Greenwash: The Reality behind Corporate Environmentalism* (New York: Apex Press).

Grefe, E., and M. Linsky (1995) *The New Corporate Activism: Harnessing the Power of Grassroots Tactics for Your Organisation* (New York: McGraw–Hill).

Greider, W. (1992) *Who Will Tell the People? The Betrayal of American Democracy* (New York: Simon & Schuster).

GRI (Global Reporting Initiative) (2002) *2002 Sustainability Reporting Guidelines* (Washington, DC: GRI).

Gribben, C., and L. Olsen (2003) *Will UK Pension Funds Become More Responsible?* (London: Just Pensions).

Grootaert, C., and H. Patrinos (eds.) (1999) *The Policy Analysis of Child Labour: A Comparative Study* (London: Macmillan).

Group of 77 (2001) Statement by Dr Kamal Kharrazi, Minister for Foreign Affairs of the Islamic Republic of Iran, at the 25th Annual Ministerial Meeting of the Group of 77, New York, 16 November 2001.

Halal, W. (2001) 'The Collaborative Enterprise: A Stakeholder Model Uniting Profitability and Responsibility', *Journal of Corporate Citizenship* 2 (Summer 2001): 27-42.

Hambun, J., and E. Reid (1994) 'Women, the HIV Epidemic and Human Rights', *Women's International Network News* 20.2 (Spring 1994): 31.

Handelsman, S. (2002) *Report on Human Rights and the Minerals Industry* (London: Mining, Minerals and Sustainable Development Project, International Institute for Environment and Development).

Harden, B. (2002) 'The Year in Ideas: Forced Transparency', *New York Times*, 15 December 2002: 92.

Hardt, M., and A. Negri (2002) *Imperio* (Buenos Aires: Paidós).

Harrison, J., and C. St John (1998) *Foundations in Strategic Management* (Cincinnati, OH: Thomson/South-Western College Publishing).

Hartman, L., D. Arnold and R. Wokutch (2004) *Rising above Sweatshops: Innovative Management Approaches to Global Labor Challenges* (Westport, CT: Praeger).

Harvard Law School Human Rights Program (1999) *Business and Human Rights* (Cambridge, MA: Harvard Law School Human Rights Program).

Haufler, V. (2001) 'Is There a Role for Business in Conflict Management?', in C. Croker, F. Hampson and P. Aall (eds.), *Turbulent Peace* (Washington, DC: United States Institute for Peace).

Heap, S. (1998) *NGOs and the Private Sector: Potential for Partnerships?* (INTRAC Occasional Paper Series, No. 27; Oxford, UK: INTRAC).

—— (2000) *NGOs Engaging with Business: A World of Difference and a Difference to the World* (Oxford, UK: INTRAC).

Henderson, D. (1999) *The MAI Affair: A Story and its Lessons* (London: Royal Institute of International Affairs).

—— (2001) *Misguided Virtue: False Notions of Corporate Social Responsibility* (London: Institute for Economic Affairs).

Henry, C., and P. Farmer (2001) 'Risk Analysis: Infections and Inequalities in a Globalizing Era', *Development* 42.4: 31-34.

Herkströter, C. (1996) 'Multinationals willen debat met samenleving aan' ('Multinationals Want to Start Debate with Society'), *NRC/Handelsblad*, 14 October 1996.

—— (1997) 'Multinationale bedrijven zijn niet de plaatsvervanger van de politiek' ('Multinational Companies are not a Substitute for Politics'), *Internationale Spectator* 51.10 (October 1997): 550-54.

Hermes Pensions Management Ltd (2002) *The Hermes Principles: What Shareholders Expect of Public Companies—and What Companies Should Expect of their Investors* (London: Hermes Pension Management Limited).

Hess, D., and T. Dunfee (2000) 'Fighting Corruption: A Principled Approach', *Cornell International Law Journal* 33.3: 593-626.

Hjelle, L., and D. Ziegler (1981) *Personality Theories: Basic Assumptions, Research, and Applications* (New York: McGraw–Hill).

Holliday, C., S. Schmidheiny and P. Watts (2002) *Walking the Talk: The Business Case for Sustainable Development* (Sheffield, UK: Greenleaf Publishing).

HRW (Human Rights Watch) (1998) *Colombia: Concerns Raided by the Security Arrangements of Transnational Oil Companies* (New York: Human Rights Watch).

—— (1999a) *The Enron Corporation: Corporate Complicity in Human Rights Violations* (New York: HRW).

—— (1999b) *The Price of Oil: Corporate Responsibility and Human Rights Violations in Nigeria's Oil Producing Communities* (New York: HRW).

Hualde, A. (1999) *Aprendizaje Industrial en la Frontera Norte de México: La Articulación entre el Sistema Educativo y el Sistema Productivo Maquilador* (Mexico City: Secretaría del Trabajo y Previsión Social).

Human Rights Quarterly (1998) 'The Maastricht Guidelines on Violations of Economic, Social and Cultural Rights 1997', *Human Rights Quarterly* 20: 691-705.

Hummels, G., S. Boleij and K. van Steensel (2001) *Duurzaam beleggen: Meerwaarde of meer waarde* (The Hague: SMO).

Husain, I., and P. Badcock-Walters (2002) 'Economics of HIV/AIDS Impact Mitigation: Responding to Problems of Systematic Dysfunction and Sectoral Capacity', in S. Forsythe (ed.), *State of the Art: AIDS and Economics* (International AIDS Economics Network [IAEN]).

Husted, B. (2002) 'Culture and International Anti-corruption Agreements in Latin America', *Journal of Business Ethics* 37.1: 413-22.

Institute of Chartered Accountants in England and Wales (1999) *Internal Control: Guidance for Directors on the Combined Code* ('The Turnbull Report'; London: Accountancy Books).

International Council on Human Rights Policy (2002) *Beyond Voluntarism: Human Rights and the Developing International Legal Obligations of Companies* (Versoix, Switzerland: International Council on Human Rights Policy).

Jackson, J. (2000) *The Jurisprudence of GATT and the WTO* (Cambridge, UK: Cambridge University Press).

Jägers, N. (2002) *Corporate Human Rights Obligations: In Search of Accountability* (Antwerp: Intersentia).

Johnston, B. (ed.) (1997) *Life and Death Matters: Human Rights and the Environment at the End of the Millennium* (Walnut Creek, CA: AltaMira Press).

Jones, G. (1996) *The Evolution of International Business: An Introduction* (London: Routledge).

Jonson, A., and S. Toulmin (1988) *The Abuse of Casuistry* (Berkeley, CA: University of California Press).

Joseph, S. (1999) 'Taming the Leviathans: Multinational Enterprises and Human Rights', *Netherlands International Law Review* 46: 171-203.

—— (2000) 'An Overview of the Human Rights Accountability of Multinational Enterprises', in M. Kamminga and S. Zia-Zarifi (eds.), *Liability of Multinational Corporations under International Law* (The Hague: Kluwer Law International): 75-93.

Just Pensions (2001) *Socially Responsible Investment and International Development* (London: Just Pensions).

Kamminga, M. (1999) 'Holding Multinational Corporations Accountable for Human Rights Abuses: A Challenge for the EC', in P. Alston (ed.), *The EU and Human Rights* (Oxford, UK: Oxford University Press): 553-69.

Kapelus, P. (2002) 'Mining, Corporate Social Responsibility and the "Community": The Case of Rio Tinto, Richards Bay Minerals and the Mbonambi', *Journal of Business Ethics* 39: 275-96.

Karl, T. (1997) *The Paradox of Plenty: Oil Booms and Petro-States* (Los Angeles, CA: University of California Press).

Kaufman, D., and S. Wei (2001) *Does 'Grease Money' Speed Up the Wheels of Commerce?* (Washington, DC: World Bank).

Kaufman, E. (2002) 'SAI Reports Benefits for Employers and Workers from SA 8000 Workplace Standard', *ISO Management Systems*, March/April 2002.

Keller-Herzog, A., and S. Szabo (1997) 'Globalization and Development', *Development Express* 8: 1-2.

Kennedy, D., and A. Abrash (2001) 'Repressive Mining in West Papua', in G. Evans, J. Goodman and N. Lansbury (eds.), *Moving Mountains: Communities Confront Mining and Globalisation* (London: Zed Books): 59-74.

Kerin, J., T. Harris and M. Schubert (2002) 'Cheaper Drugs for World's Poorest', *The Australian*, 16 November 2002: 1.

Killick, N. (2002) *Case Study No. 4: Oil and Gas Development in Azerbaijan* (London: Natural Resources Cluster, Business Partners for Development).

Kingsbury, B. (1999) 'Operational Policies of International Institutions as Part of the Law-Making Process: The World Bank and Indigenous Peoples', in G. Goodwin-Gill and S. Talmon (eds.), *The Reality of International Law: Essays in Honour of Ian Brownlie* (Oxford, UK: Oxford University Press): 323-42.

Kinley, D. (2002) 'Human Rights as Legally Binding or Merely Relevant?', in S. Bottomley and D. Kinley (eds.), *Commercial Law and Human Rights* (Aldershot, UK: Ashgate Dartmouth): 25-45.

Klein, N. (2000) *No Logo: Taking Aim at the Brand Bullies* (London: Flamingo).

Kolk, A., and R. van Tulder (2002) 'The Effectiveness of Self-Regulation: Corporate Codes of Conduct and Child Labour', *European Management Journal* 20.3: 260-71.

Kongsin, S. (1997) 'Economic Impacts of HIV/AIDS Mortality on Households in Rural Thailand', in G. Linge and D. Porter (eds.), *No Place for Borders: The HIV/AIDS Epidemic and Development in Asia and the Pacific* (Sydney: Allen & Unwin).

—— and C. Watts (2000) 'Conducting a Household Survey on Economic Impact of Chronic HIV/AIDS Morbidity in Rural Thailand: Methodological Issues', presented at the *AIDS and Economics Symposium*, Durban, South Africa, 7-8 July 2000.

Kornhauser, W. (1959) *The Conflict between the Scientific Mind and the Management Mind* (Princeton, NJ: Opinion Research Corporation).

—— (1962) *Scientists in Industry: Conflict and Accommodation* (Berkeley, CA: University of California Press).

Kram, D. (2001) 'Illegal Human Organ Trade from Executed Prisoners in China', Case Study 632, www.american.edu/TED/prisonorgans.htm, last accessed 22 March 2003.

Laframboise, D. (1998) 'Human Rights and a Corporate Sellout. Impolite Trade/The Body Shop prides itself on its ethical business practices. So why all the trade with China?', *Globe and Mail*, January 1998.

Larson, E., and B. Cox (1998) 'Social Accountability 8000: Measuring Workplace Conditions Worldwide', *Quality Digest*, February 1998.

Lawrence, A. (2002) 'The Drivers of Stakeholder Engagement: Reflections on the Case of Royal Dutch/Shell', *Journal of Corporate Citizenship* 6 (Summer 2002): 71-84.

Le Billon, P., J. Sherman and M. Hartwell (2002) 'Controlling Resource Flows to Civil Wars: A Review and Analysis of Current Policies and Legal Instruments', background paper for the International Peace Academy *Economic Agendas in Civil Wars* Conference, Bellaggio, Italy, 20-24 May 2002.

Lederach, J. (1995) *Preparing for Peace: Conflict Transformation across Cultures* (Syracuse, NY: Syracuse University Press).

Leipziger, D. (2001) *SA 8000: The Definitive Guide to the New Social Standard* (London: FT Prentice Hall).

Lilly, D., and P. Le Billon (2002) *Regulating Private Sector Activities in Conflict Zones: A Synthesis of Strategies* (London: Overseas Development Institute).

Lim, H. (2001) *Trade and Human Rights: What's at Issue?* (working paper submitted to the Committee on Economic, Social and Cultural Rights; UN Document No. E/C.12/2001/WP.2, 10 April 2001).

Lim, S. (2001) 'Poverty, Rural Women and HIV: Implications for Project Appraisal', *Monthly Bulletin of the Institute of Humanities* 198 (December 2001): 1-17.

—— (2002) 'Dynamic Comparative Advantage and Primary Product Export Opportunities', *Primary Industry Management* 5.3 (September 2002): 19-22.

——, K. Taweekul and J. Askwith (2002) *Harnessing the Private Sector for Social Development* (Hamilton, New Zealand: Economics Department, University of Waikato).

Lin, N. (2002) *Social Capital: A Theory of Social Structure and Action* (New York: Cambridge University Press).

Liz Claiborne (2002) 'Love is not Abuse', www.lizclaiborne.com/loveisnotabuse/default.asp, last accessed 17 September 2002.

Loewenson, R., and A. Whiteside (2001) *HIV/AIDS: Implications for Poverty Reduction* (UNDP Policy Paper; New York: UNDP).

Macfarlane, M. (1999) 'An Evaluation of Social Impact Assessment Methodologies in the Mining Industry', unpublished PhD thesis submitted to the University of Bath, UK.

MacIntyre, A. (1984) *After Virtue* (Notre Dame, IL: University of Notre Dame Press, 2nd edn).

Maitland, I. (2001) 'The Great Non-debate Over International Sweatshops', in T. Beauchamp and N. Bowie (eds.), *Ethical Theory and Business* (Englewood Cliffs, NJ: Prentice Hall, 6th edn).

Malkki, L. (1995) *Purity and Exile: Historical Memory and National Identity among Hutu Refugees in Tanzania* (Chicago: University of Chicago Press).

Mapes, T., and S. Dhume (2002) 'Indonesian police link ambush of two Americans to military unit', *Wall Street Journal*, 29 October 2002.

Marcus, R., and D. Husselbee (1997) *Stitching Footballs: Voices of Children in Sialkot* (London: Save the Children UK).

Martin, S. (2003) 'Forced Migration Emergencies: Options for the Reform of the Humanitarian Regime', presented at the International Association for the Study of Forced Migration Conference, *Forced Migration and Global Processes*, Chiang Mai, Thailand, 5–9 January 2003.

Marx, G. (2002) 'Imperiled pipeline gets US troops in Colombia', *Chicago Tribune*, 12 November 2002: 1, 20.

McCulloch, N., L. Winters and X. Cirera (2001) *Trade Liberalization and Poverty: A Handbook* (London: Centre for Economic Policy Research).

McDowell, C. (ed.) (1996) *Understanding Impoverishment: The Consequences of Development-Induced Displacement* (Oxford, UK: Berghahn Books).

—— (2002) 'Involuntary Resettlement, Impoverishment Risks and Sustainable Livelihoods', *Australasian Journal of Disaster and Trauma Studies* 2.

—— and A. de Haan (1997) *Migration and Sustainable Livelihoods: A Critical Review of the Literature* (Working Paper No. 65; Brighton, UK: Institute of Development Studies).

McGee, J. (1998) 'Commentary on "Corporate Strategies and Environmental Regulation: An Organizing Framework" by A.M. Rugman and A. Verbeke', *Strategic Management Journal* 19: 377-87.

McKinlay, J., and J. Marceau (2002) 'The End of the Golden Age of Doctoring', *International Journal of Health Services* 32.2: 379-416.

McPhail, K., and A. Davy (1998) *Integrating Social Concerns into Private Sector Decisionmaking: A Review of Corporate Practices in the Mining, Oil and Gas Sectors* (World Bank Discussion Paper No. 384; Washington, DC: World Bank).

Mehta, P., and S. Singh (2001) 'Current Issues in Human Rights, Development and International Trade in the WTO', *Interights Bulletin* 13: 143-45.

Melden, A. (1977) *Rights and Persons* (Berkeley, CA: University of California Press).

Ministry for Foreign Affairs, Sweden (2001) *Transboundary Water Management as an International Public Good* (Stockholm, Sweden: ODI and ARCADIS).

Minzberg, H., B. Ahlstrand and J. Lampel (1999) *Op strategie-safari: Een rondleiding door de wildernis van strategisch management* (Dutch translation of *Strategy Safari: A Guided Tour through the Wilds of Strategic Management*; Schiedam, Netherlands: Scriptum).

Mistry, P., and N. Olesen (2002) *Increasing Foreign Direct Investment in LDCs: The Role of Public Private Interaction in Mitigating Risks* (Stockholm: Ministry of Foreign Affairs).

Mock, W. (2000) 'Corporate Transparency and Human Rights', *Tulsa Journal of Comparative and International Law* 8: 15-26.

Muchlinski, P. (1999) *Multinational Enterprises and the Law* (Oxford, UK: Blackwell Publishers, rev. pbk edn).

—— (2000a) 'The Social Dimension of International Investment Agreements', in J. Faundez, M. Footer and J. Norton (eds.), *Governance Development and Globalization* (London: Blackstone Press): 373-96.

—— (2000b) 'The Rise and Fall of the Multilateral Agreement on Investment: Where Now', *International Lawyer* 34: 1,033-53.

—— (2001a) 'Human Rights and Multinationals: Is There a Problem?', *International Affairs* 77.1: 31-49.

—— (2001b) 'Corporations in International Litigation: Problems of Jurisdiction and the United Kingdom Asbestos Case', *International and Comparative Law Quarterly* 50: 1-25.

—— (2002) 'Holding Multinationals to Account: Recent Developments in English Litigation and the Company Law Review', *Company Lawyer* 23.6: 168-79.

Munninghoff, H. (1995) *A Report on the Human Rights Violations against the Local People in the Area around Timika, Region of FakFak, Irian Jaya, Year 1994–1995* (Jayapura, Indonesia: Catholic Church of Jayapura, 3 August 1995).

Murphy, D., and J. Bendell (1997) *In the Company of Partners: Business, Environmental Groups and Sustainable Development Post-Rio* (Bristol, UK: The Policy Press).

—— and G. Coleman (2000) 'Thinking Partners: Business, NGOs and the Partnership Concept', in J. Bendell (ed.), *Terms for Endearment: Business, NGOs and Sustainable Development* (Sheffield, UK: Greenleaf Publishing): 207-15.

Mutunga, W., F. Gesualdi and S. Ouma (2002) *Exposing the Soft Belly of the Multinational Beast: The Struggle for Workers Rights at Del Monte Kenya* (Nairobi: Kenya Human Rights Commission).

Myners, P. (2001) *Institutional Investment in the United Kingdom: A Review* (London: HM Treasury).

Nader, R., and M. Green (eds.) (1973) *Corporate Power in America: Ralph Nader's Conference on Corporate Accountability* (New York: Grossman Publishers).

Nakashima, E., and A. Sipress (2002) 'Indonesia military allegedly talked of targeting mine', *Washington Post*, 3 November 2002: A18.

Nelson, J. (2000) *The Business of Peace: The Private Sector as a Partner in Conflict Prevention and Resolution* (London: International Alert, Council on Economic Priorities and International Business Leaders Forum).

Newcomer, L. (1997) 'Measures of Trust in Health Care', *Health Affairs* 16.1: 50-51.

Nobel, P. (1999) 'Social Responsibility of Corporations', *Cornell Law Review* 84: 1,255-65.

Nussbaum, M. (2001) *Women and Human Development* (New York: Cambridge University Press).

O'Reilly, P., and S. Tickell (1999) 'TNCs and Social Issues in the Developing World', in M. Addo (ed.), *Human Rights Standards and the Responsibility of Transnational Corporations* (London: Kluwer Law International): 273-88.

OAS (Organisation of American States) (1997) *Report on the Events at Amayapampa, Llallagua, and Capasirca: Northern Part of the Department of Potosí, Bolivia, December 1996* (Washington, DC: OAS, Inter-American Commission on Human Rights).

OECD (Organisation for Economic Co-operation and Development) (1999) *Codes of Corporate Conduct: An Inventory* (Paris: OECD).

—— (2000) *OECD Guidelines for Multinational Enterprises* (Paris: OECD).

Oxfam and Médecins Sans Frontières (2002) 'Sydney Summit a step back for access to medicines, but it is not the end of the story' (press release, 15 November 2002; www.msf.org, last accessed 19 November 2002).

Oxley, A. (2002) 'Protesters ignore the benefits of breaking down trade barriers', *The Australian*, 14 November 2002: 11.

Paine, L. (1994) 'Managing for Organizational Integrity', *Harvard Business Review* 72.2 (March/April 1994): 106-17.

Pax Christi (1998) *Multinational Enterprises and Human Rights: A Documentation of the Dialogue between Amnesty International/Pax Christi and Shell* (Utrecht, Netherlands: Pax Christi Netherlands).

Petersmann, E. (2002) 'Time for a United Nations "Global Compact" for Integrating Human Rights into the Law of the Worldwide Organizations: Lessons from European Integration', *European Journal of International Law* 13: 621-50.

Pettersson, B. (2002) 'Development-Induced Displacement: Internal Affair or International Human Rights Issue?', *Forced Migration Review* 12 (January 2002): 16-19.

Physician's Weekly (1998) 'Wrestling HMOs: Physicians are Beneficiaries of State-Patient Protection laws', *Physician's Weekly* 15.43 (16 November 1998; www.physweekly.com/archive/98/11_16_98/twf.html, last accessed 22 March 2003).

Picciotto, S. (1998) 'Linkages in International Investment Regulation: The Antinomies of the Draft Multilateral Agreement on Investment', *University of Philadelphia Journal of International Economic Law* 19: 731-68.

Pieterse, J. (1997) 'Globalisation and Emancipation: From Local Empowerment to Global Reform', *New Political Economy* 2.1 (March 1997): 79-92.

Pinto, D., and H. Carías (1994) *Cultura y Modernización en Guatemala: Caso de la Maquila* (Guatemala City: USAC).

Pitayanon, S., S. Kongsin and W. Janjareon (1997) 'The Economic Impact of HIV/AIDS Mortality on Households in Thailand', in D. Bloom and P. Godwin (eds.), *The Economics of HIV and AIDS: The Case of South and South East Asia* (New Delhi: Oxford University Press).

Pitts, M. (2001) 'Crime and Corruption: Does Papua New Guinea have the capacity to control it?', *Pacific Economic Bulletin* 16.2: 128-34.

Pogge, T. (2002) *World Poverty and Human Rights* (Cambridge, UK: Polity Press).

Post, J., L. Preston and S. Sachs (2002) 'Managing the Extended Enterprise: The New Stakeholder View', *California Management Review* 45.1: 6-28.

——, W. Frederick, A. Lawrence and J. Weber (1996) *Business and Society: Corporate Strategy, Public Policy, Ethics* (New York: McGraw–Hill, 8th edn).

Powell, W., and L. Smith-Doerr (1994) 'Networks and Economic Life', in N. Smelser and J. Swedberg (eds.), *Handbook of Economic Sociology* (New York: Princeton University Press/ Russell-Sage): 368-402.

Presencia (1996) 'News/Noticias Presencia, Bolivia', *Presencia*, 26-30 December 1996.

PT Freeport Indonesia (1996) General Chronology of Recent Events at PT Freeport Indonesia, Irian Jaya (internal document).

Punchard, E. (1989) *Piper Alpha: A Survivor's Story* (London: W.H. Allen).

Putnam, R. (1993) *Making Democracy Work: Civic Traditions in Modern Italy* (Princeton, NJ: Princeton University Press).

Rajagopal, B. (2001) 'The Violence of Development', *Washington Post*, 8 August 2001.

—— (2002) 'Out—Damned Spot! Hydropower, Forced Resettlement, and Blood on the Hands', *The World Paper* 2 (January 2002).

Reygadas, L. (2002) *Ensamblando Culturas: Diversidad y Conflicto en la Globalización de la Industria* (Barcelona: Gedisa).

Rice, D. (2002) 'Human Rights Strategies for Corporations', *Business Ethics* 11.2: 134-36.

Roddick, A. (1991) *Body and Soul* (London: Ebury Press).

—— (1997) 'The Bottom Line of a Thriving Business: A Social Agenda', *Independent on Sunday*, 23 March 1997.

—— (2000) *Business as Unusual* (London: Thorsons HarperCollins).

Rowell, A. (1996) *Green Backlash: Global Subversion of the Environmental Movement* (London: Routledge).

Royal Dutch/Shell (1995) Corporate letter to Ms S. Archer, Isle of Arran, in response to concerns over Shell's role in Nigeria, 22 November 1995.

—— (1997) Revised *Statement of General Business Principles. March 1997* (The Hague: Royal Dutch/Shell).

—— (1998) *Profits and Principles: Does There Have to Be a Choice?* (The Hague: Royal Dutch/ Shell).

—— (1999) *Dealing with Bribery and Corruption: A Management Primer* (The Hague: Royal Dutch/Shell).

Rupesinghe, K. (1998) *Civil Wars, Civil Peace: An Introduction to Conflict Resolution* (London: Pluto).

Saeed, A. (1998) *Women's Stitching Centres: Exploring Avenues* (London: Save the Children UK [Pakistan programme] on behalf of the Sialkot Implementation Team).

Saltford, J. (2000) *United Nations Involvement with the Act of Self-determination in West Irian (Indonesian West New Guinea) 1968 to 1969* (private publication).

Sampson, G. (2001) 'Overview', in G. Sampson (ed.), *The Role of the World Trade Organization in Global Governance* (Tokyo: United Nations University Press): 1-18.

Sariego, J. (1986) *Enclaves y Minerales en el Norte de México: Historia Social de los Mineros de Cananea y Nueva Rosita* (Mexico City: Universidad Iberoamericana).

Save the Children UK (1998-2000) *Social Monitoring Reports, Child Labour Project, Sialkot* (Islamabad, Pakistan: Save the Children UK).

Schmid, A. (2000) *Thesaurus and Glossary of Early Warning and Conflict Prevention Terms* (London: PIOOM/FEWER).

Schoenberger, K. (2000) *Levi's Children: Coming to Terms with Human Rights in the Global Marketplace* (New York: Atlantic Monthly Press).

Schulkink, U. (2002) 'Affordable Access to Essential Medication in Developing Countries: Conflicts between Ethical and Economic Imperatives', *Journal of Medical Philosophy* 27.2: 179-95.

Scudder, T. (1993) 'Development-Induced Relocation and Refugee Studies: 37 Years of Change and Continuity among Zambia's Gwebme Tonga', *Journal of Refugee Studies* 6.3: 123-52.

Sen, A. (1985) 'Well-being, Agency and Freedom: The Dewey Lectures 1984', *Journal of Philosophy* 82: 169-203.

—— (1987) *On Ethics and Economics* (Oxford, UK: Blackwell Publishers).

—— (1999a) 'Human Rights and Asian Values', in T. Machan (ed.), *Business Ethics in the Global Marketplace* (Stanford, CA: Hoover Institution Press): 37-62.

—— (1999b) *Development as Freedom* (New York: Alfred A. Knopf).

—— (2000) 'East and West: The Reach of Reason', *The New York Review of Books*, 20 July 2000: 33-38.

Sengupta, A. (2002) 'On the Theory and Practice of the Right to Development', *Human Rights Quarterly* 24.4: 837-89.

Shari, M. (1998) 'What did Mobil know? Mass graves suggest a brutal war on local Indonesian guerrillas—in the oil giant's backyard', *Business Week*, 28 December 1998: 68-74.

—— and S. Prasso (2000) 'Freeport–McMoRan: A Pit of Trouble', *Business Week*, 31 July 2000.

Shell International (1998) *General Business Principles* (London: Shell International Petroleum Corporation).

Shleifer, A., and R. Vishny (1993) 'Corruption', *The Quarterly Journal of Economics* 108.3: 599-617.

Sialkot Education Programme (1998) *Annual Report 1998: Preventing Child Labour in Sialkot* (Sialkot, Pakistan: Sialkot Education Programme).

Sillitoe, P. (2000) *Social Change in Melanesia: Development and History* (Cambridge, UK: Cambridge University Press).

Singhanetra-Renard, A. (1997) 'Population Movement and the AIDS Epidemic in Thailand', in G. Herdt (ed.), *Sexual Cultures and Migration in the Era of AIDS: Anthropological and Demographic Perspectives* (Oxford, UK: Clarendon Press).

Smith, D. (2002) *Demonstrating Corporate Values: Which Standard for Your Company?* (London: Institute of Business Ethics).

Southcorp (2003) 'Environment and Community', www.southcorp.com.au/company/environment.htm, last accessed 24 March 2003.

Spalding, A., and A. Reinstein (1995) 'The Audit Committee's Role Regarding the Provisions of the Foreign Corrupt Practices Act', *Journal of Business Strategies* 12.1: 23-35.

Spar, D. (1998) 'The Spotlight and the Bottom Line: How Multinationals Export Human Rights', *Foreign Affairs* 77: 7-12.

Starr, A. (2000) *Naming the Enemy: Anti-Corporate Movements Confront Globalization* (Sydney: Pluto Press).

Stout, D. (2000) 'Oil companies agree to protect rights in remote areas', *New York Times*, 21 December 2000: A6.

Sullivan, R. (2002) 'Enron: One Step Forward or Two Steps Back for Effective Self-Regulation?', *Journal of Corporate Citizenship* 8 (Winter 2002): 91-104.

—— and D. Hogan (2002) 'The Business Case for Human Rights: The Amnesty International Perspective', in S. Bottomley and D. Kinley (eds.), *Commercial Law and Human Rights* (Aldershot, UK: Ashgate Publishing): 69-87.

—— and P. Frankental (2002) 'Corporate Citizenship and the Mining Industry: Defining and Implementing Human Rights Norms', *Journal of Corporate Citizenship* 7 (Autumn 2002): 79-91.

—— and H. Wyndham (2001) *Effective Environmental Management: Principles and Case Studies* (Sydney: Allen & Unwin).

Survival International (1992) 'Rainforest harvest projects harm, not help, Indian communities: Survival International voices misgivings about Body Shop and Cultural Survival', press release, 15 June 1992.

—— (1993) 'Harvest Moonshine Taking you for a Ride: A Critique of the Rainforest Harvest, its Theory and Practice' (London: Survival International); a shortened version of this article appeared in *The Ecologist* 23.4 (July/August 1993).

Sydney Morning Herald (2002) 'Australian spy agency dobs in Indonesian military', *Sydney Morning Herald*, 5 November 2002.

Tabaksblat, M. (1997) 'Dialogue with Society', speech by Unilever NV Chairman Morris Tabaksblat at the Veerstichting Symposium, Leiden, Netherlands, 17 October 1997, www.unilever.com/news/speeches/englishspeeches_886.asp, accessed 18 December 2002.

Tanzi, V. (1998) 'Corruption around the World: Causes, Consequences, Scope, and Cures', *IMF Staff Papers* 45.1: 559-94.

Tatsuo, I. (1999) 'Liberal Democracy and Asian Orientalism', in J. Bauer and D. Bell (eds.), *The East Asian Challenge for Human Rights* (Cambridge, UK: Cambridge University Press): 27-59.

Teokul, W. (1999) 'Social Development in Thailand: Past, Present and Future Roles of the Public Sector', *ASEAN Economic Bulletin* 16.3 (December 1999): 360-72.

Tool, M., and W. Samuels (eds.) (1989) *State, Society and Corporate Power* (New York: Transaction Publications).

Trebilcock, M., and R. Howse (1999) *The Regulation of International Trade* (London: Routledge, 2nd edn).

Trento, S. (1993) *The Powerhouse: Robert Keith Gray and the Selling of Access and Influence in Washington* (New York: St Martin's Press).

Turton, D. (1996) 'Migrants and Refugees', in T. Allen (ed.), *In Search of Cool Ground: War, Flight and Homecoming in Northeast Africa* (London: James Currey).

UKOOA (United Kingdom Offshore Operators' Association) (2002) 'UK Oil and Gas Industry Publishes First Report on Progress towards Sustainability' (News Release, 23 July 2002; London: UKOOA).

UNAIDS (Joint United Nations Programme on HIV/AIDS) and WHO (World Health Organisation (2001) *AIDS Epidemic Update—December 2001* (Geneva: UNAIDS).

—— and —— (2002) *AIDS Epidemic Update—December 2002* (Geneva: UNAIDS).

UNCTAD (UN Conference on Trade and Development) (1994) *World Investment Report 1994* (Geneva: UNCTAD).

—— (1996) *International Investment Agreements: A Compendium* (vol. I; Geneva: UNCTAD).

—— (1998) *Bilateral Investment Treaties in the Mid-1990s* (Geneva: UNCTAD).

—— (1999a) *The Social Responsibility of Transnational Corporations* (Geneva: UNCTAD).

—— (1999b) *World Investment Report 1999* (Geneva: UNCTAD).

—— (2000a) *International Investment Agreements: A Compendium* (Geneva: UNCTAD).

—— (2000b) *Employment* (Issues in International Investment Agreements; Geneva: UNCTAD).

—— (2001a) *Social Responsibility* (Issues in International Investment Agreements; Geneva: UNCTAD).

—— (2001b) *Statistical Profiles of the Least Developed Countries* (Geneva: UNCTAD).

UNDP (United Nations Development Programme) (2000a) *HIV Impact Assessment Tool: The Concept and its Application* (New York: UNDP).

—— (2000b) *Human Development Report 2000* (New York: Oxford University Press).

—— (2002) *Human Development Report 2002: Deepening Democracy in a Fragmented World* (New York: UNDP).

UN CESCR (United Nations Committee on Economic, Social and Cultural Rights) (2000) 'General Comment 14: The Right to the Highest Attainable Standard of Health' (UN Document No. E/C.12/2000/4; New York: United Nations, 11 August 2000).

UN High Commissioner for Human Rights (2002) 'Liberalization of Trade in Services and Human Rights' (UN Document No. E/CN.4/Sub.2/2002/9; New York: United Nations, 25 June 2002).

UN Human Rights Committee (1982) 'General Comment 6: The Right to Life' (New York: United Nations, 30 April 1982).

UN OCHA (United Nations Office for the Co-ordination of Humanitarian Assistance) (1992) *Guiding Principles on Internal Displacement* (New York: UN).

UN Sub-Commission on Human Rights (Working Group on the Working Methods and Activities of Transnational Corporations) (2002a) *Human Rights Principles and Responsibilities for Transnational Corporations and Other Business Enterprises: Introduction* (UN Doc.E/CN.4/Sub.2/2002/WG.2/WP.1/Add.1).

—— (2002b) 'Draft Norms on Responsibilities of Transnational Corporations and Other Business Enterprises with regard to Human Rights' (UN Doc.E/CN.4/Sub.2/2002/13, www1.umn.edu/humanrts/links/tncreport-2002.html, 15 August 2002), accessed 17 March 2003.

Unseem, M. (1984) *The Inner Circle: Large Corporations and the Rise of Business Political Activity in the US and UK* (Oxford, UK: Oxford University Press).

US Department of State (1996) *Indonesia Human Rights Practices, 1995* (Washington, DC: US Department of State).

—— (2001) *Bolivia Human Rights Practices, Country Report, 2000* (Washington, DC: US Department of State).

—— (2002a) *Bolivia Country Commercial Guide, FY2002* (Washington, DC: US Commercial Service, US Department of State).

—— (2002b) *Indonesia Country Commercial Guide FY2002* (Washington, DC: US Commercial Service, US Department of State).

Van der Putten, F. (2001) *Corporate Behaviour and Political Risk: Dutch Companies in China, 1903-1941* (Leiden, Netherlands: CNWS Publications).

—— (2003) 'De definitie van Corporate governance en de invloed van aandeelhouders' ('The Definition of Corporate Governance and the Influence of Shareholders'), *Filosofie in Bedrijf* 15.1: 59-62.

Vander Stichele, M., and P. Pennartz (1996) *Making it our Business: European NGO Campaigns on Transnational Corporations* (London: Catholic Institute for International Relations).

Vanlandingham, M., and N. Grandjean (1997) 'Some Cultural Underpinnings of Male Sexual Behaviour Patterns in Thailand', in G. Herdt (ed.), *Sexual Cultures and Migration in the Era of AIDS: Anthropological and Demographic Perspectives* (Oxford, UK: Clarendon Press).

Varghese, B. (2002) 'The Economics of Social and Structural Interventions for HIV Prevention in Developing Countries', in S. Forsythe (ed.), *State of the Art: AIDS and Economics* (International AIDS Economics Network [IAEN]).

Veatch, R. (1981) *Theory of Medical Ethics* (New York: Basic Books).

Vernon, R. (1999) Intervention in discussion in Harvard Law School *Business and Human Rights* (Cambridge, MA: Harvard Law School Human Rights Program): 49.

Vincent, R. (1986) *Human Rights and International Relations* (Cambridge, UK: Cambridge University Press).

Vista Gold (1996a) 'Capacirca/Amayapampa Bolivia Projects: Update' (press release; Vista Gold Corp., 20 December 1996).

—— (1996b) 'Bolivia conflict resolved' (press release; Vista Gold Corp., 23 December 1996).

—— (1997a) *1996 Annual Report* (Denver, CO: Vista Gold Corp.).

—— (1997b) Vista Gold Corp. 1996 Form 20F (Foreign Issuer Annual Report). Filed May 1997 with the US Securities and Exchange Commission.

—— (1997c) 'Vista Gold secures land surface rights in Bolivia' (press release; Vista Gold Corp., 2 April 1997).

—— (1998) Vista Gold Corp. 1997 Form 20F (Foreign Issuer Annual Report). Filed April 1998 with the US Securities and Exchange Commission.

—— (1999) 'Vista update on Bolivia' (press release; Vista Gold Corp., 16 September 1999).

—— (2000) 'Vista Gold announces agreements in Bolivia' (press release; Vista Gold Corp., 7 February 2000).

—— (2001) Vista Gold Corp. 2000 Form 10K (Reporting Company Annual Report). Filed March 2001 with the US Securities and Exchange Commission.

—— (2002) Vista Gold Corp. 2001 Form 10KSB (Small Business Issuer Annual Report). Filed September 2002 with the US Securities and Exchange Commission.

Vogel, D. (1978) *Lobbying the Corporation: Citizen Challenges to Business Authority* (New York: Basic Books).

—— (1989) *Fluctuating Fortunes: The Political Power of Business in America* (New York: Basic Books).

—— (1991) 'Business Ethics: New Perspectives on Old Problems', *California Management Review* 33.4: 101-17.

Voon, T. (1999) 'Multinational Enterprises and State Sovereignty under International Law', *Adelaide Law Review* 21: 219-52.

Waelde, T. (1998) 'Sustainable Development and the 1994 Energy Charter Treaty: Between Pseudo-Action and the Management of Environmental Investment Risk', in F. Weiss, E. Denters and P. de Waart (eds.), *International Economic Law with a Human Face* (The Hague: Kluwer Law International): 223-70.

—— (1999) 'Non-conventional Views on "Effectiveness": The Holy Grail of Modern International Lawyers: The New Paradigm? A Chimera? Or a Brave New World in the Global Economy?', *Austrian Review of International and European Law* 4: 164-203.

Wallensteen, P., and M. Sollenberg (2001) 'Armed Conflict, 1989–2000', *Journal of Peace Research* 38.5: 629-44.

Walsh, D. (1987) *Corporate Physicians: Between Medicine and Management* (New Haven, CT: Yale University Press).

Walsh, J. (1998) 'A World War on Bribery', *Time*, 22 June 1998: 16.

Ward, H. (2001) *Governing Multinationals: The Role of Foreign Direct Liability* (London: Royal Institute of International Affairs).

Wartick, S., and D. Wood (1998) *International Business and Society* (Oxford, UK: Blackwell).

WCD (World Commission on Dams) (2000) *Dams and Development: A New Framework for Decision-Making* (London: Earthscan Publications).

Webb, K. (1999) 'Voluntary Initiatives and the Law', in R. Gibson (ed.), *Voluntary Initiatives: The New Politics of Corporate Greening* (Peterborough, Canada: Broadview Press): 32-50.

Wei, S. (2000) 'How Taxing is Corruption on International Investors?', *Review of Economics and Statistics* 82.1: 1-11.

Weick, K. (1979) *The Social Psychology of Organizing* (Reading, MA: Addison-Wesley).

Weissbrodt, D. (2000) 'The Beginning of a Sessional Working Group on Transnational Corporations within the UN Sub-Commission on Prevention of Discrimination and Protection of Minorities', in M. Kamminga and S. Zia-Zarifi (eds.), *Liability of Multinational Corporations under International Law* (The Hague: Kluwer Law International): 119-38.

Weissman, R. (1996) 'A Long Strange TRIPs: The Pharmaceutical Industry Drive to Harmonize Global Intellectual Property Rules, and the Remaining WTO Legal Alternatives Available to Third World Countries', *University of Pennsylvania Journal of International Economic Law* 17: 1,069-1,125.

Welford, R. (1997) *Hijacking Environmentalism: Corporate Responses to Sustainable Development* (London: Earthscan Publications).

Wheatley, M. (2003) 'When Change is Out of Our Control', in M. Effron, R. Gandossy and M. Goldsmith (eds.), *Human Resources for the 21st Century* (Toronto: John Wiley & Sons Canada).

Wheeler, D., and M. Sillanpää (1997) *The Stakeholder Corporation: A Blueprint for Maximizing Stakeholder Value* (London: Pitman Publishing).

——, H. Fabig and R. Boele (2002) 'Paradoxes and Dilemmas for Stakeholder Responsive Firms in the Extractive Sector: Lessons from the Case of Shell and the Ogoni', *Journal of Business Ethics* 39.3 (September 2002): 297-318.

Whiteside, A. (1998) 'How the Transport Sector Drives HIV/AIDS—and How HIV/AIDS Drives Transport', *AIDS Analysis Africa* 8.2 (April 1998): 5-15.

Willets, P. (1997) 'Political Globalization and the Impact of NGOs upon Transnational Companies', in J. Mitchell (ed.), *Companies in a World of Conflict* (London: Earthscan Publications): 195-226.

Williams, S. (1999) 'How Principles Benefit the Bottom Line: The Experience of The Co-operative Bank', in M. Addo (ed.), *Human Rights Standards and the Responsibility of Transnational Corporations* (The Hague/London: Kluwer Law International): 63-68.

Williamson, O. (1985) *Las Instituciones Económicas del Capitalismo* (Mexico City: Fondo de Cultura Económica).

Wilson, J. (2003) 'US Goes Deeper into Colombian Conflict', *Financial Times*, 30 January 2003: 5.

Wilson, P. (1992) *Exports and Local Development: Mexico's New Maquiladoras* (Austin, TX: University of Texas Press).

Winstanley D., J. Clark and H. Leeson (2002) 'Approaches to Child Labour in the Supply Chain', *Business Ethics: A European Review* 11.3 (July 2002): 210-23.

Wolde-Selassie, A. (2002) 'Gumz and Highland Resettlers: Differing Strategies of Livelihood and Ethnic Relations in Metekel, Northwestern Ethiopia', PhD thesis, Faculty of Social Sciences, University of Göttingen, Germany.

Wolf, M. (2001) 'What the World Needs from the Multilateral Trading System', in G. Sampson (ed.), *The Role of the World Trade Organization in Global Governance* (Tokyo: United Nations University Press): 183-208.

Wood, D., and B. Gray (1991) 'Toward a Comprehensive Theory of Collaboration', *Journal of Applied Behavioural Science* 27.2: 139-62.

Woolfson, C., J. Foster and M. Beck (1996) *Paying for the Piper: Capital and Labour in Britain's Offshore Oil Industry* (London: Mansell).

World Bank (1996) *Resettlement and Development: The Bankwide Review of Projects Involving Involuntary Resettlement, 1986–1993* (Washington, DC: World Bank Environment Department).

—— (1997) *Confronting AIDS: Public Priorities in a Global Epidemic* (Oxford, UK: Oxford University Press).

—— (1998) *Assessing Aid* (New York: Oxford University Press).

—— (2003a) 'Policies, Procedures and Practices: The World Bank Group Operational Manual', http://wbln0018.worldbank.org/institutional/manuals/opmanual.nsf, last accessed 17 March 2003.

—— (2003b) *Terms of Reference: Study of Options for Strengthening CSR Implementation among Suppliers in Global Supply Chains* (Washington, DC: World Bank Group, March 2003).

World Health Organisation (1991) 'Guiding Principles on Human Organ Transplantation', *Lancet* 337: 1470-71.

WTO (World Trade Organisation) (1996) 'Ministerial Declaration, Singapore, 16 December 1996' (commonly referred to as the 'Singapore Declaration').

—— (2001a) 'Ministerial Declaration, Doha, 14 November 2001' (commonly referred to as the 'Doha Declaration'; WTO Document No. WT/MIN[01]/DEC/1).

—— (2001b) 'Declaration on the TRIPS Agreement and Public Health' (WTO Document No. WT/MIN[01]/DEC/2, 14 November 2001).

Yew, M. (2002) 'Lesotho court fines Acres', *Toronto Star*, 29 October 2002: C1.

Zadek, S., and M. Forstater (1999) 'Making Civil Regulation Work', in M. Addo (ed.), *Human Rights Standards and the Responsibility of Transnational Corporations* (London: Kluwer Law International): 69-76.

Zapata, F. (1977) 'Enclaves y Sistemas de Relaciones Industriales en América Latina', *Revista Mexicana de Sociología* 39.2 (April/June 1977): 451-73.

Zarsky, L. (2002) 'Global Reach: Human Rights and Environment in the Framework of Corporate Accountability', in L. Zarsky (ed.), *Human Rights and the Environment: Conflicts and Norms in a Globalizing World* (London: Earthscan Publications): 31-54.

Abbreviations

ACFOA	Australian Council for Overseas Aid
ADB	Asian Development Bank
AFL–CIO	American Federation of Labor–Congress of Industrial Organizations
AI	Amnesty International
AIDS	acquired immuno-deficiency syndrome
AIUK	Amnesty International UK
ATCA	Alien Tort Claims Act
AVANCSO	Asociación para el Avance de las Ciencias Sociales en Guatemala (Association for the Advancement of the Social Sciences in Guatemala)
AVE	Außenhandelsvereinigung des Deutschen Einzelhandels eV (foreign trade association of the German retail trade)
BCE	before the Common Era
BIT	bilateral investment treaty
BSI	The Body Shop International
BSR	Business for Social Responsibility
C²	Combating Corruption
CAMT	Centro de Atención a la Mujer Trabajadora (Attention Centre for the Female Worker, Mexico)
CAP	Consolidated Inter-Agency Appeal Process
CEO	chief executive officer
CESCR	Committee on Economic, Social and Cultural Rights
CIS	Co-operative Insurance Society
CITAC	Centro de Información para Trabajadores y Trabajadoras (Information Centre for Male and Female Workers, Mexico)
CITGUA	Ciencia y Tecnología para Guatemala, AC (Science and Technology for Guatemala)
CNMS	Centro Nuovo Modelo di Sviluppo, Italy
COMIBOL	Corporación Minera de Bolivia
COMO	Centro de Orientación de la Mujer Obrera (Orientation Centre for Female Workers, Mexico)

COW	contract of work
CPR	common property resource
CR	corporate responsibility
CRC	Convention on the Rights of the Child
CSR	corporate social responsibility
DFID	Department for International Development (UK)
DoE	Department of Energy (UK)
DSD	Defence Signals Directorate (Australia)
DSU	Dispute Settlement Understanding
ECHR	European Convention on Human Rights
EI-TI	Extractive Industry Transparency Initiative
ESIA	environmental and social impact assessment
ETI	Ethical Trading Initiative
EU	European Union
FAFO	Institute for Applied Social Sciences, Norway
FCPA	Foreign Corrupt Practices Act (USA)
FDI	foreign direct investment
FFIJD	Freeport Fund for Irian Jaya Development
FIFA	Fédération Internationale de Football Association
FLA	Fair Labor Association
FLO	Fair Trade Labelling Organisations International
FSC	Forest Stewardship Council
GATS	General Agreement on Trade in Services
GATT	General Agreement on Tariffs and Trade
GDP	gross domestic product
GEN	Global Ecolabelling Network
GRI	Global Reporting Initiative
HIV	human immunodeficiency virus
HQ	headquarters
HRW	Human Rights Watch
HSE	Health and Safety Executive (UK)
IACHR	Inter-American Commission on Human Rights
IAEN	International AIDS Economics Network
ICCPR	International Covenant on Civil and Political Rights
ICESCR	International Covenant on Economic, Social and Cultural Rights
ICRC	International Committee of the Red Cross
IDP	internally displaced people
IFOAM	International Federation of Organic Agriculture Movements
IGO	intergovernmental organisation
IGTLWF	International Garment, Textile, and Leather Workers' Federation
ILO	International Labour Organisation
IMF	International Monetary Fund
IOAS	International Organic Accreditation Service

IPEC	International Programme on the Elimination of Child labour
IS	International Secretariat (Amnesty International)
ISEAL	International Social and Environmental Accreditation and Labelling Alliance
ISO	International Organisation for Standardisation
ITO	International Trade Organisation
KHRC	Kenya Human Rights Commission
KUCFAW	Kenya Union of Commercial Food and Allied Workers
LDC	least developed country
LNG	liquefied natural gas
MAC	Marine Aquarium Council
MAI	Multilateral Agreement on Investment
MDB	multilateral development bank
MNC	multinational corporation
MNE	multinational enterprise
MSC	Marine Stewardship Council
NAFTA	North American Free Trade Agreement
NGO	non-governmental organisation
NNPC	Nigerian National Petroleum Company
OAS	Organisation of American States
OCHA	Office for the Co-ordination of Humanitarian Assistance (UN)
ODA	official development assistance
OECD	Organisation for Economic Co-operation and Development
OPM	Organisasi Papua Merdeka (Free Papua Movement)
PCC	Programme Co-ordinating Committee
PDA	Population and Community Development Association (Thailand)
PIOOM	Project Interdisciplinair Onderzoek naar Oorzaken van Mensenrechtenschendingen (Interdisciplinary Research Programme on Root Causes of Human Rights Violations, Netherlands)
plc	public limited company (UK)
RUF	Revolutionary United Front (Sierra Leone)
SA 8000	Social Accountability 8000
SAI	Social Accountability International
SAN	Sustainable Agriculture Network
SCCI	Sialkot Chamber of Commerce and Industries
SEC	Securities and Exchange Commission (USA)
SEDEPAC	Servicio, Desarrollo y Paz, Asociación Civil (Service, Development and Peace, Civil Association, Mexico)
SEE	social, environmental and ethical
SGMA	Sporting Goods Manufacturers' Association (USA)
SIA	social impact assessment
SIP	statement of investment principles
SIT	Sialkot Implementation Team
SME	small or medium-sized enterprise
SPF	Sialkot Programme Forum

SRI	socially responsible investment
TBIRD	Thai Business Initiative in Rural Development
TNC	transnational corporation
TRIPs	Agreement on Trade-Related Aspects of Intellectual Property Rights
UDHR	Universal Declaration of Human Rights
UKOOA	United Kingdom Offshore Operators' Association
UN	United Nations
UNAIDS	Joint United Nations Programme on HIV/AIDS
UNCTAD	United Nations Conference on Trade and Development
UNDP	United Nations Development Programme
UNGA	United Nations General Assembly
UNICEF	United Nations Children's Fund
UNITA	União Nacional para a Independência Total de Angola (National Union for the Total Independence of Angola)
UNITE	Union of Needletrades, Industrial and Textile Employees (USA)
USAID	United States Agency for International Development
USCA	United States Court of Appeal
WCD	World Commission on Dams
WFSGI	World Federation of Sporting Goods Industries
WHO	World Health Organisation
WIPO	World Intellectual Property Organisation
WRAP	Worldwide Responsible Apparel Production
WTO	World Trade Organisation
WWF	World Wide Fund for Nature

Biographies

Dr **Denis G. Arnold** is Assistant Professor of Philosophy at the University of Tennessee, Knoxville, USA. He received his PhD in philosophy from the University of Minnesota. He is a past fellow of the National Endowment for the Humanities. His publications have appeared in numerous journals, including *American Philosophical Quarterly* and *Business Ethics Quarterly*. He is co-editor of *Rising above Sweatshops: Innovative Management Approaches to Global Labor Challenges* (Praeger, 2004). His current research focuses on the ethical dimensions of global capitalism.
darnold1@utk.edu

Jessica Banfield is project officer on the policy strand of International Alert's Business and Conflict programme. The programme seeks to promote a peace-building role for business, focusing both on TNCs in the extractive sector and on local private-sector actors. Her previous experience includes working at the international secretariat of Transparency International (TI), as assistant project manager on the first issues of TI's *Global Corruption Report*, and three years as a journalist and editor, based first in London at *African Business* magazine and subsequently in Johannesburg. Jessica has an MA in international studies and diplomacy from London University's School of Oriental and African Studies.
jbanfield@international-alert.org

Professor **Matthias Beck** is Professor in Risk Management at Glasgow Caledonian University. He gave evidence at Lord Cullen's public inquiry into safety in the rail industry, following the Ladbroke Grove disaster. He has written extensively on issues of risk, business and financial regulation. He has authored/co-authored articles on corporate responsibility and co-authored the book *Paying for the Piper* with Charles Woolfson and John Foster (Mansell, 1996). He is currently examining UK regulatory responses to the Enron scandal.
mpb@gcal.ac.uk

Richard Boele is a founding director of the Australian Institute of Corporate Citizenship. He works as a corporate social responsibility consultant and social auditor, and his clients have included Westpac, Sydney Water, Newmont, BP, the Novo Group, BHP Billiton, the UK government and Amnesty International. He collaborated with The Body Shop while working in The Hague at the Unrepresented Nations and People's Organisation (UNPO) and later took a full-time permanent position of human rights campaigner at The Body Shop's head office in the UK. He devised the 'Make Your Mark' campaign for The Body Shop and was responsible for the communication and collaboration with Amnesty International. He previously held key positions with human rights organisations in Australia and Europe. His civil-society experience ranges from work with local communities around the world to transnational organisations such as the United Nations. Richard is a Visiting Fellow at Macquarie University's Graduate Centre for the Environment in Sydney, Australia. He also holds an Industrial Fellowship with the Centre for Stakeholding and Sustainable Enterprise at the Kingston University Business School in London, UK.

richard@aiccglobal.com

Michael Cameron graduated from the University of Waikato with a BMS (Bachelor of Management Studies) with First Class Honours in 2003. He is currently involved in research towards his PhD thesis in economics, 'The Relationship between Poverty and HIV/AIDS Prevalence in Northern Thailand'.

mpc9@waikato.ac.nz

Sir Geoffrey Chandler was Founder-Chair of the Amnesty International (UK) Business Group from 1991 to 2001. He began his career as a journalist on the BBC and *Financial Times*, subsequently spending 22 years with the Royal Dutch/Shell Group in a number of posts in the UK and overseas. He was a Director of Shell Petroleum, Shell Petroleum NV and Shell International and was the initiator of Shell's first Statement of General Business Principles in 1976. He was Director General of the UK National Economic Development Office 1978–83, Director of Industry Year 1986, and chaired the National Council for Voluntary Organisations 1989–96. He has honorary degrees from a number of universities and is the author of books on Greece and Trinidad and of numerous articles on corporate responsibility and human rights.

geoffchand@aol.com

David Coles retired from being a partner in KPMG in September 2001. In 1998, he founded KPMG's Sustainability Advisory Services group in the UK and, over a period of three years, built the group up to a total of 30 sustainability professionals in the UK. Since retiring from KPMG he has been active on the Just Pensions project, co-authoring the report *Do UK Pension Funds Invest Responsibly?* with Duncan Green (Just Pensions, 2002). He has also become the chairman of EIRIS.

david-joan.coles@ntlworld.com

Gemma Crijns MA has been Managing Director of the EIBE/Institute for Responsible Business at Nyenrode University, the Netherlands, since May 2001. Before this, she worked for 20 years in the Dutch section of Amnesty International in various capacities, including Co-ordinator External Relations and Co-ordinator Economic Relations. At Amnesty International she developed a business and human rights programme and established intensive counselling and stakeholder relations with Dutch multinational enterprises. She has broad experience of working with Dutch and international business, governmental and non-governmental organisations on topics related to human rights and corporate social responsibility.

g.crijns@nyenrode.nl

Professor **Thomas W. Dunfee** is a professor at the Wharton School of the University of Pennsylvania, where he holds the Kolodny Chair of Social Responsibility in Business. Tom was president of the Academy of Legal Studies in Business (1989–90), served as editor-in-chief of the *American Business Law Journal* (1975–77) and served as president of the Society for Business Ethics (1995–96). His current research interests focus on the role of morality in markets, how social contract theory can be applied to business and professional ethics and global business ethics. He is the author of many books, including *Ties That Bind: A Social Contracts Approach to Business Ethics* (with Thomas Donaldson; Harvard Business School Press, 1999), *Ethics for Business and Economics* (editor with Thomas Donaldson; Dartmouth, 1997) and *Business Ethics: Japan and the Global Economy* (editor with Yukimasa Nagayasu; Kluwer, 1993). Tom is on the editorial board of several journals including the *Academy of Management Review, Business Ethics Quarterly, Journal of Business Ethics* and *The Business and Society Review*. dunfeet@wharton.upenn.edu

Heike Fabig is a PhD student in corporate responsibility at the Graduate Research Centre for the Comparative Study of Culture, Development and Environment at the University of Sussex, UK. Her research (Fabig 2002) examines the engagement of The Body Shop with the campaign for social and environmental justice of the Ogoni people in Nigeria. She previously worked as a human rights campaigner for a Flemish non-governmental organisation (focusing on the collective human rights of indigenous peoples), as a researcher, for the Fair Trade Department, and consultant for The Body Shop International (1997–98) , and as a tutor at the University of Sussex's School of African and Asian Studies (1998–2000). She currently lives in Australia. heikefabig@hotmail.com

Bennett Freeman is Managing Director, Corporate Responsibility, Burson-Marsteller, based in Washington, DC. In 2002, as Principal of Sustainable Investment Strategies, a Washington, DC-based consultancy, he co-authored a human rights impact assessment of the issues facing the BP Tangguh project in Papua, Indonesia, the first such assessment undertaken of a major energy project anywhere in the world. As US Deputy Assistant Secretary of State for Democracy, Human Rights and Labor, Freeman led the dialogue and negotiations up to the launch of the Voluntary Principles in December 2000. He serves on the Board of Directors of Oxfam America and on the Business and Economic Relations Group of Amnesty International USA. bennettfreeman@hotmail.com

Dr **Norbert Goldfield** is Medical Director for 3M Health Information Systems. In this capacity, he develops tools for payment and quality measurement of health services. He is editor of *The Journal of Ambulatory Care Management* and his most recent book is *National Health Reform, American Style* (American College of Physician Executives, 2001). He is a practising internist. He has helped to form several volunteer organisations, including Hampshire Health Access (providing access to care for the uninsured in the author's county) and the Palestinian Medical Access Partnership (providing surgeries to Palestinian children). nigoldfield@msn.com

Simon Handelsman is an international minerals development engineer and adviser. He previously worked for the UN Minerals Resources Group and during his ten-year career there he visited over 40 developing countries, on over 100 advisory missions. More recently, he has conducted a detailed review of the human rights issues and challenges facing the minerals industry, as a part of the Mining Minerals and Sustainable Development project. He is presently conducting graduate research on this subject at the University of British Columbia. He has also been a guest lecturer at both New York and Columbia Universities. Simon was born and educated in the UK, and holds a BSc in Mining Engineering from the University of Nottingham. He is a US/Canadian citizen and a long-time resident of New York City. sdh@pobox.com

Genoveva Hernández Uriz is a doctoral candidate at the European University Institute (Florence, Italy), where she is writing her dissertation on the application of human rights standards to the oil industry. She also holds degrees from Harvard Law School, The College of Europe (Bruges, Belgium) and Universidad de Zaragoza (Spain). She is the author of several articles about human rights and international economic law.
Genoveva.Hernandez@IUE.it

Professor **David Hess** is an assistant professor at the University of Michigan Business School. He has authored articles on topics such as corruption and bribery in international business, corporate community involvement programmes, the governance of public pension funds and corporate social accounting, auditing and reporting. David received a JD from the University of Iowa, and MA and PhD degrees in management from the Wharton School of the University of Pennsylvania.
dwhess@umich.edu

Dr **Harry Hummels** is Chairman of the EIBE/Institute for Responsible Business and is the ING Bank Professor of Socially Responsible Investments (SRI) at Nyenrode University, the Netherlands. His work concentrates on the study of SRI, corporate social responsibility and organisational ethics. Together with his colleague, Theo Brouwers, he is also Director of Socially Responsible Investments at ING Bank Netherlands.
h.hummels@nyenrode.nl

Eileen Kohl Kaufman is Executive Director of Social Accountability International. She is a graduate of Wellesley College, where she earned a BA in economics, and she also holds an MA in economics and an MBA in finance from Columbia University. Eileen has been with SAI since it was incorporated in May 1997. Prior to joining SAI, she worked at the NYC Departments of Environmental Protection, Design and Construction, and the NYC Water Board. At the organisation's inception, she worked at the Council on Economic Priorities, co-authoring *Paper Profits*, an analysis of paper mill pollution and its control.
eileen@sa-intl.org

Bahar Ali Kazmi is a principal researcher of the Corporate Citizenship Unit (CCU) 'Global Companies and Poverty Reduction Project', supported by DFID and the Resource Centre for the Social Dimensions of Business Practice, at Warwick Business School. He is also completing his doctorate on the subject of partnerships between business and non-business organisations. He holds an MA in philosophy from Punjab University (Pakistan) and an MA in development studies from the University of East Anglia (UK). He has worked in South Asia and has extensive research and social development programme management experience from working for Save the Children UK, with a national and regional thematic focus on child labour, CSR and partnerships. He has worked as a consultant for ILO/IPEC, the European Commission, and the government of Pakistan and Save the Children, regional offices. In recent years, he has been working extensively on short training programmes on partnerships and child labour for business managers.
bahar.ali@wbs.ac.uk

Professor **David Kinley** has been a legal academic and human rights advocate for 15 years specialising in the areas of international and domestic human rights law. Currently he is Professor of International Law and founding Director of the Castan Centre for Human Rights Law at Monash University in Melbourne, Australia. He is the author or editor of four books, including: *Human Rights in Australian Law* (The Federation Press, 1998), which is a leading text in the area of human rights law; *Human Rights Explained* (www.hreoc.gov.au/hr_

explained, 1998), a major human rights resource published on the Internet; and *Commercial Law and Human Rights* (edited with Stephen Bottomley; Ashgate, 2001). He is also the author of some 50 articles, book chapters, reports and papers published internationally on a range of legal matters, but especially on human rights law. He is currently working on a major Australian Research Council project (2002–2004) on corporations and human rights, and will take up a Fulbright Scholarship in Washington, DC, in 2004 looking at the relationship between international economic actors (such as the WTO) and human rights law.
david.kinley@law.monash.edu.au

Deborah Leipziger is a consultant in the field of corporate social responsibility. Her clients have included the UN's Global Compact, Warwick University and Social Accountability International. She is an adviser to Morley Fund Management, advising them on their approach to socially responsible investment. Deborah played a key role in the development of the Social Accountability 8000 standard and its Guidance Document. She is the author of *SA 8000: The Definitive Guide to the New Social Standard* (FT Prentice Hall, 2001), and the co-author of *Living Corporate Citizenship* (FT, 2002) and *Corporate Citizenship: Successful Strategies of Responsible Companies* (FT, 1998). Deborah resides in The Hague, with her husband and three daughters.
thehague@wanadoo.nl

Dr **Steven Lim** is a senior lecturer in Economics at the University of Waikato (New Zealand) and a Visiting Professor at Senshu University (Japan). He graduated with a PhD from the University of Adelaide, Australia, in 1996, specialising in the Chinese economic reforms. More recently he has been involved in poverty research work in Thailand, mainly investigating the links between poverty and HIV/AIDS. He is also a consultant in development economics, having worked on projects funded by the World Bank, UNDP and the Thai and New Zealand governments.
slim1@waikato.ac.nz

Dr **Magnus Macfarlane** has a PhD in business and social impact assessment. He is an accredited social accountant and assurance provider, with over ten years' experience in the field of corporate social responsibility, working both as a consultant and as a research fellow at the universities of Oxford, Bath and Warwick, UK. He is experienced in the development and implementation of a wide range of non-financial corporate performance mechanisms, including environmental and socioeconomic impact assessment, livelihood and stakeholder analysis, sustainability indicators and targets, monitoring, and strategic partnership. He has particular expertise in implementing and integrating social and environmental accounting and assurance systems, and is providing ongoing advice to three major blue-chip companies in this area. He has published widely and provided analysis, training and advice to leading companies (such as BP, Shell, Rio Tinto, BAT and Placer Dome) and institutions (such as the ILO, UNDP, World Bank, DTI and DFID).
magnusmacfarlane@aol.com

For more than a decade, **Gary MacDonald** has helped clients on four continents engage with communities undergoing complex social change. A former journalist, he was Newmont Mining Corporation's first director of social development. He has created effective programmes for companies seeking to assess their impacts on, or to engage with, host communities. He has served on the boards of a variety of non-profit organisations, such as the Tradeworks Training Society and Bolivia's Inti Raymi Foundation. He has contributed to UN-led initiatives such as the Global Compact working group on the role of business in conflict zones and participates in studies of how business can contribute to, ameliorate or help recover from, conflict situations.

gary@monkey-forest.net

Adam McBeth is a Postgraduate Research Fellow with the Castan Centre for Human Rights Law, working on the Centre's Australian Research Council project on the legal human rights responsibilities of corporations. He is also a PhD candidate in law at Monash University, Melbourne, Australia, specialising in the relationship between international human rights law and international economic law in protecting human rights in the course of commercial enterprise. Adam is a frequent contributor to Australian government consultations on human rights and has made a number of submissions to parliamentary inquiries. He previously worked as a solicitor in Melbourne.

adam.mcbeth@law.monash.edu.au

Dr **Christopher McDowell** is the Director of the Applied Anthropology Programme at Macquarie University in Sydney, and he teaches on development, refugees, humanitarianism and human rights. He has undertaken extensive research in southern and East Africa, Europe, and South and South-East Asia. His current research is in Indonesia (asylum-seekers) and Thailand (resettlement following the construction of the Pasak Jolasith Dam). His publications include a book on the war in Sri Lanka and refugee movements to Europe (*A Tamil Asylum Diaspora* [Berghahn, 1996]) and two edited volumes on development, displacement and resettlement (*Risks and Reconstruction* [World Bank, 2000], with Michael Cernea, and *Understanding Impoverishment* [Berghahn, 1996]). Dr McDowell has undertaken a number of consultancies for European governments, the UN (most recently in East Timor) and NGOs.

christopher.mcdowell@mq.edu.au

Timothy McLaughlin is an independent consultant who specialises in helping multinational oil, gas and mining companies develop and improve their strategies and practices to obtain and maintain a social licence to operate. His work has included developing new corporate policies and practices to improve risk assessment strategies, conflict resolution and human rights policies; advising on global developments in corporate social responsibility trends and their potential impact on company operations and reputations; developing community engagement, sustainable community development/gift strategies; and developing strategic partnerships with NGOs and other organisations. His work has involved operations in North and South America, South-East Asia and Central Asia. He previously worked for ten years for the United States Foreign Service and served in diplomatic positions in Indonesia and the Philippines.

tmclaughlin@igc.org

Professor **Peter Muchlinski** LLB LLM is Professor of Law and International Business at the University of Kent and is Principal Adviser to the United Nations Conference on Trade and Development (UNCTAD) on their major issues papers series concerning international investment agreements. From 1998 to 2001 he was the Drapers' Professor of Law at Queen Mary and Westfield College (University of London) and from 1997 to 1999 he was Visiting Professor at the International Development Law Institute, Rome. His research interests are in the regulation of multinational enterprises, the social dimension of international business regulation, and international and European business law. He is the author of the authoritative text *Multinational Enterprises and the Law* (Blackwell, 1999).

p.t.muchlinski@ukc.ac.uk

Professor **Luis Reygadas** is an anthropologist, a professor at the Universidad Autónoma Metropolitana Iztapalapa (Mexico) and an expert on industrial anthropology and corporate culture. He has published seven books and many articles about trade unions, production systems, social history and work cultures in the Mexican mining industry and in the maquiladora plants in Mexico and Guatemala.
lreygadas@yahoo.com.mx

Nina Seppala is a doctoral researcher at Warwick Business School, UK, where she is conducting research on business–government relations in countries where systematic human rights abuses occur. She has previously worked on democracy promotion for International IDEA and training in peace-making and preventative diplomacy for the United Nations Institute for Training and Research.
nina.seppala@phd.wbs.ac.uk

Rory Sullivan has been Director, Investor Responsibility with Insight Investment since October 2002. He is a member of the Amnesty International (UK) Business Group and, from 1998 to 2001, was the Convenor of the Amnesty International (Australia) Business Group. In Australia, he presented evidence to parliamentary inquiries on the Multilateral Agreement on Investment (1998), Australia's Relationship with the World Trade Organisation (2001) and the Corporate Code of Conduct Bill (2001). In the UK, he has been a member of the Steering Committee for the CORE (Corporate Responsibility) Coalition and he prepared the Amnesty International (UK) submissions to the European Commission's Green Paper on Corporate Social Responsibility (2001), the Global Reporting Initiative (2002) and the FTSE4Good Human Rights Consultation (2002).

Rory has worked in Australia, South-East Asia, Africa and Europe on projects such as development strategy, community-right-to-know programmes, corporate environmental management and reporting, and auditing social and environmental performance. Most recently, he worked with the Natural Resources Cluster of the World Bank's Business Partners for Development programme, where he was responsible for the evaluation of tri-sector partnerships for development (health, education, water) between governments, extractive companies and civil-society organisations. He was previously an adviser to Environment Australia and to the OECD on the development and implementation of pollution release and transfer registers.

Rory holds a first-class honours degree in electrical engineering (University College Cork, Ireland), masters' degrees in environmental science (University of Manchester, UK) and environmental law (University of Sydney, Australia) and a PhD in law and public policy at Queen Mary, University of London. He is the author (with Hugh Wyndham) of *Effective Environmental Management: Principles and Case Studies* (Allen & Unwin, 2001) and the editor (with Michael Warner) of *Putting Partnering to Work* (Greenleaf Publishing, 2004). He has written over 100 articles, book chapters and papers on human rights, environmental policy and development issues.
rory.sullivan@insightinvestment.com

Dr **Frans-Paul van der Putten** has been a researcher at the EIBE/Institute for Responsible Business of Nyenrode University, the Netherlands, since November 2001. Between 1995 and 2001 he worked at the Institute for the History of European Expansion (IGEER), part of Leiden University's Centre for Non-Western Studies (CNWS). His research focuses on foreign direct investment in China, the political and social behaviour of companies, and the activities of multinational enterprises in developing countries.
f.vdputten@nyenrode.nl

Dr **Charles Woolfson** is a Director of the Centre for Corporate Accountability, which campaigns for effective legal remedies for corporate killing. He lectures at the University of Glasgow where he is Reader in Industrial Relations. He is member of the British Committee of the International Centre for Trade Union Rights and a member of the editorial board of its journal, *International Union Rights*. He has published on industrial relations issues, regulation, and safety and health at work in the UK and in Central and Eastern Europe.

C.A.Woolfson@socsci.gla.ac.uk

Index

Health insurance   145, 149
Health professionals   143-54
  corporatisation of   146-49, 153, 154
  and organ harvesting   149-52
Henderson, David   78
Herald of Free Enterprise   117
Herkströter, C.A.J.   83-91
Hermes Pensions Management Ltd   92,
  93, 94, 95, 99
Hertel, Shareen   201
Hippocratic oath   144-45, 147-49, 154
HIV/AIDS
  medicines for   62, 149
  and poverty   171-73, 177-78, 288
  and TBIRD programme   176-78, 288
  Thailand   170-80, 288
Human rights
  and comparative advantage   66-67, 70-71
  current position   31-32, 40-43
    international trade law   56-61
  definition of   15-18
  differing views on   88-90
  management of   102-12, 287-88
    business case for   111-12
    and developing countries   109-10
    framework for   102-106
    monitoring/reporting on   105-106
    review processes   106
    and stakeholders   110-11
  philosophy of   71-75
  policies   104
    business case for   96-98, 111-12
    companies with   107-108
  see also Corporate social responsibility;
    Developing countries; Draft
    Norms; Ethics; Stakeholders;
    Transnational corporations;
    Voluntary codes
Human Rights Watch   24, 122, 246, 250,
  273, 277
Husted, B.   266

ICI   107
Ikea   107
ILO
  see International Labour Organisation
Indah Sari, Dita   281
India   157, 162, 165, 167
  SA 8000   203
Indonesia   220, 225
  lawsuits filed   129, 130
  mining in   126-32, 248, 289

and US government   251-52
and Voluntary Principles   246, 249, 250,
  257
see also Conflict zones; Extractive
  industries; Freeport; Security
  forces
Infrastructure development
  privatisation of   155-68
Intellectual property rights   56-57, 62-63
Inter-American Commission on Human
  Rights (IACHR)   136-37
International AIDS Economics Network
  (IAEN)   176
International Alert   220-21, 229, 246
International Chamber of Commerce
  30
International Committee of the Red
  Cross (ICRC)   129, 250
International Covenant on Civil and
  Political Rights 1966   16, 43
International Covenant on Economic,
  Social and Cultural Rights 1966   16,
  54, 167, 261
International Development, UK
  Department for (DFID)   94, 123, 181,
  204
International Federation of Chemical,
  Mining and General Workers   246
International Financial Corporation
  238, 241
International Garment, Textile, and
  Leather Workers' Federation   201,
  203
International Labour Organisation (ILO)
  and child labour   182-86, 187-89, 195-96
  core conventions of   16
  Declaration on Fundamental Principles
    and Rights at Work   35, 41
  Minimum Age Convention (No. 138) 1973
    186, 196
  Tripartite Declaration of Principles
    Concerning Multinational
    Enterprises and Social Policy   41
International law   16
International Programme on the
  Elimination of Child Labour (IPEC)
  182, 187-89, 195-96
International Social and Environmental
  Accreditation and Labelling Alliance
  (ISEAL)   206
International Trade Organisation (ITO)
  55

and Voluntary Principles 243, 244, 246-47, 250-53, 254
see also Amnesty International UK; Blair, Tony; Piper Alpha

United Kingdom Offshore Operators' Association (UKOOA) 118

United Nations (UN) 15-18
Act of Free Choice 1969 126
Basic Principles on the Use of Force and Firearms 25, 42, 245
Charter 67
Children's Fund (UNICEF) 185, 187-89
Code of Conduct for Law Enforcement Officials 25, 42, 245
Conference on Environment and Development 35
Conference on Trade and Development 58
Convention against Torture 42
Convention on the Rights of the Child 186, 195
Convention Relating to the Status of Refugees 166
Declaration on the Right to Development 261
Development Programme 75, 77, 226
Draft Norms on the Responsibilities of Transnational Corporations and other Business Enterprises in Regard to Human Rights 29-30, 34, 39-43
legal status of 47-51
peace-building potential 223-24, 226
and Voluntary Principles 258
Global Compact 26, 226
issue areas 35
and sale of human organs 150, 151
Guiding Principles on Internal Displacement 163, 166, 167, 168
High Commissioner for Forced Migrants 166
High Commissioner for Human Rights 60, 61-62, 66
sanctions, use of 224-25
Secretary-General 26, 226
Security Council 224, 225
Special Representative on Internal Displacement 166-67
Sub-Commission on Human Rights 16-17, 29, 38, 285
see also Draft Norms
Vienna Declaration 261
and war in Iraq 284-85

United States of America
and Colombia 123, 248, 251

corporations, and bribery 263, 265, 266
Department of State 243, 244, 254
egalitarianism in 145
Foreign Corrupt Practices Act 263, 265, 266
and Indonesia 251-52
law courts, jurisdiction of 44-46
medical systems 146
Oil Industry Information Committee 120
and Voluntary Principles 243, 244, 246-47, 250-53, 254

Universal Declaration of Human Rights 1948 (UDHR) 15, 39, 43, 232
early influence of 25
and Hippocratic oath 145
and 'Make Your Mark' campaign 276, 277-78
and right to freedom 76-77
and right to well-being 78, 80
and UN Global Compact 35

Unocal 44-45, 107, 257

Venezuela 122

Vienna Declaration 261

Vista Gold Corporation
in Bolivia 133-42
see also Da Capo Resources

Voluntary codes/declarations 38-39, 42-43, 243-44
or regulation 28-30, 51, 253-59, 286-87
and private law suits 51
'soft law' instruments 38, 47, 50, 257-58
workers' rights 204-206
see also Law; Regulation; SA8000; Voluntary Principles

Voluntary Principles on Security and Human Rights 29-30, 223-24, 243-59
challenges/opportunities of 247-53
and mining companies 132, 139-40, 141
monitoring/reporting 255-56, 257
Public Security section 245
Risk Assessment section 244-45
substance/process of 244-47
and voluntary approach, debate on 253-58, 286-87
see also Extractive industries; Security forces

Wages, SA8000 199
War on Want 94